BISHOP FABIAN BRUSKEWITZ
The Catholic Church:
Jesus Christ Present in the World

BISHOP FABIAN BRUSKEWITZ

The Catholic Church:
Jesus Christ Present in the World

Thomson-Shore

ISBN 0-615-13122-0
Copyright Bishop Fabian Bruskewitz
Printed in the United States of America

To order call: 402-488-0921
Or write: Catholic Chancery
                   P.O. Box 80328
                   Lincoln, NE 68501

Photo credits: Front cover photo of the "Good Shepherd" art-glass window at St. Gregory the Great Seminary near Seward, Neb., by Chase Becker. Back cover photo of Bishop Bruskewitz by *The Picture Man* of Lincoln, Neb.

CONTENTS

Part One: Sacraments

1. The Eucharist
   Eucharistic Encyclical I   15
   Eucharistic Encyclical II   18
   Eucharistic Encyclical III   20
   Eucharistic Encyclical IV   23
   Eucharistic Encyclical V   26
   Eucharistic Encyclical VI   29
   Eucharistic Encyclical VII   32
   Eucharistic Encyclical VIII   35

2. Anointing of the Sick   38

Part Two: Vocations

1. The Priesthood
   Eternal Priesthood   43
   A Good Priest   46

2. Religious Life
   Ripe Harvest   49
   The Religious Vocation I   51
   The Religious Vocation II   54

3. Family Life
   The Rights of Families I   57
   The Rights of Families II   59
   The Rights of Families III   62
   Fatherhood   65
   Children   67
   The Lay Vocation   69
   The Dignity of Women   72
   Older Persons   74
   Martial Fidelity   77
   Defend Marriage I   79
   Defend Marriage II   82
   Defend Marriage III   84

Part Three: Faith

1. Doctrine
    Doctrinal Development I   91
    Doctrinal Development II   93
    Doctrinal Development III   95
    Doctrinal Development IV   98
    Liberalism in Religion   100

2. Social Doctrine
    Social Doctrine I   104
    Social Doctrine II   107
    Social Doctrine III   109
    Social Doctrine IV   112
    Social Doctrine V   115
    Social Doctrine VI   118

3. Sunday
    Sunday I   121
    Sunday II   124
    Sunday III   126
    Sunday IV   128

Part Four: The Catholic Church: Christ Present in the World

1. The Church
    One and Only   135
    Aspects of the Church I   137
    Aspects of the Church II   140
    Aspects of the Church III   142
    The Church I   145
    The Church II   147
    The Church III   150
    The Church IV   152
    The Church V   155
    The Church VI   157
    The Church VII   160
    The Church VIII   163
    The Church IX   166
    The Church X   169
    The Church XI   171
    The Church XII   174
    The Church XIII   177
    The Church XIV   180

2. Scripture
New Bible Insights 183
Book of Revelation I 185
Book of Revelation II 188
Book of Revelation III 190
Book of Revelation IV 192

3. Ten Commandments
Commandments I 195
Commandments II 197
Commandments III 200
Commandments IV 202
Commandments V 204
Commandments VI 207
Commandments VII 209
Commandments VIII 212
Commandments IX 214
Commandments X 217
Commandments XI 219
Commandments XII 222
Commandments XIII 224
Commandments XIV 227
Commandments XV 229
Commandments XVI 231
Commandments XVII 234
Commandments XVIII 237
Commandments XIX 239
Commandments XX 242
Commandments XXI 244
Commandments XXII 247
Commandments XXIII 249
Commandments XXIV 252
Commandments XXV 254

Part Five: Catechetics and Catholic Schools

1. Catechetics
Sound Catechetics I 265
Sound Catechetics II 267
Sound Catechetics III 270

2. Catholic Schools
Our Schools 273

Part Six: Communion of Saints

1. Saints, Angels, and Devotions
   Sacramentals   279
   Angels   281
   Infant of Prague   283

2. Life of Blessedness
   Blessed Teresa of Calcutta I   286
   Blessed Teresa of Calcutta II   289
   Blessed Teresa of Calcutta III   292
   Jasna Gora I   295
   Jasna Gora II   297
   Mary and the Church I   300
   Mary and the Church II   302
   Mary and the Church III   305

Part Seven: Contemporary Issues

1. The Sacredness of Life
   Clever Apes   313
   Suicide   315
   Professional Killers   318

2. Abortion
   Sad Anniversary   321
   Humanae Vitae   323
   Day of Infamy   326
   Pilate's Mouthful   328

3. Stewardship of Creation
   Disciple's Response   331
   Betting, Lotteries, and Gambling   333

4. Sexuality
   Fornication   336
   Youthful Purity   338
   Cohabitation   341
   Evil Human Cloning I   343
   Evil Human Cloning II   346

FOREWORD BY THE AUTHOR

Since the publication in 1997 of my book, *A Shepherd Speaks*, consisting of an edited collection of articles which I had written during the previous five years in my diocesan weekly, the *Southern Nebraska Register*, kind friends and colleagues insistently have suggested that another collection of such articles might be welcomed by an appreciative reading public.

These same friends and colleagues mentioned that a new selection from those weekly articles, gathered from a larger group of writings and from over a longer period of time, might be of even greater use to many of those who found significant benefits from my first book. Flattered, of course, by such advice, but realistically understanding the limitations of this sort of literature, I have acceded to their suggestion, and now offer this new book to the reading public.

This is being done with profound gratitude to Cathy Blankenau Bender, the composition manager and Kim Breitfelder, the circulation manager for the *Southern Nebraska Register*, and to the priests, religious, and laity of the Diocese Lincoln, whose constant support, patience with my shortcomings, and dedication to the Catholic Faith continue to edify, uphold, and bless me.

+Fabian W. Bruskewitz
Bishop of Lincoln

Editor's Note

Every effort for accuracy has been made in *The Catholic Church: Jesus Christ Present in the World*. Editors have striven to be faithful to accepted and standard practices in literary usage while recognizing variances in editing styles and individual authors' writing styles and preferences. For example, in this book, there are several different approaches used in the capitalization of divine pronouns. According to standard editing practice, when a reference from another author's work is quoted directly, that quote is presented exactly as it appears in the original source. Sometimes when an author is quoted, he himself may be quoting another author in the same citation. In that case, divine pronouns might appear in the same reference both in upper and lower case. In addition, the Revised Standard Version, Catholic Edition, of the Bible, which is the source for Scripture quotations in this book, as well as the *Catechism of the Catholic Church*, both use lower case for divine pronouns. When quoting Scripture or the *Catechism*, referenced passages appear exactly as they do in the original. When using his own words, Bishop Bruskewitz prefers to capitalize divine pronouns and the sacraments.

Part One

SACRAMENTS

THE EUCHARIST

Eucharistic Encyclical

I

THE WAIT

With his usual sense of the appropriate, our Holy Father, Pope John Paul II, signed and issued his newest encyclical letter on last Holy Thursday, April 17, 2003. It is addressed by the Successor of Saint Peter "to Bishops, priests, deacons, men and women in the consecrated life, and all the faithful laity" on the theme "the Eucharist and its relationship to the Church." The Pope entitled his letter *On the Eucharist in Its Relationship to the Church* (*Ecclesia de Eucharistia*).

The opening sentences set the tone for the document. "The Church draws her life from the Eucharist. This truth does not simply express a daily experience of faith, but recapitulates *the heart of the mystery of the Church*" (no.1). Later on the Pope remarks, "The Church was born of the paschal mystery. For this very reason, the Eucharist, which is in an outstanding way the sacrament of the paschal mystery, *stands at the center of the Church's life*" (no. 3).

In the document, the Supreme Pontiff numerous times cites Sacred Scripture, the Councils of the Church, especially the Second Vatican Council and the Council of Trent, the *Catechism of the Catholic Church*, the writings of his predecessors in the See of Rome, and his own previous apostolic letter about the Holy Eucharist, dated February 24, 1980 (*Dominicae cenae*). The encyclical also contains many citations from liturgical and canonical texts.

ORGANIZATION

The Pope organizes the encyclical in six chapters, with an introduction and a conclusion. The chapter titles give a clear outline of the Holy Father's thinking. They are: "The Mystery of Faith", "The Eucharist Builds the Church", "The Apostolicity of the Eucharist and of the Church", "The Eucharist and Ecclesial Communion", "The Dignity of the Eucharistic

Celebration", and "At the School of Mary, 'Woman of the Eucharist'".

The Holy Father explains that, as Christ's Vicar on earth, his intention in the encyclical is to "rekindle" Eucharistic "amazement" in continuity with the recent Jubilee heritage left to the Church. He says,

> To contemplate the face of Christ, and to contemplate it with Mary, is the "program" which I have set before the Church at the dawn of the third millennium, summoning her [the Church] to put out into the deep on the sea of history with the enthusiasm of the new evangelization. To contemplate Christ involves being able to recognize him wherever he manifests himself in his many forms of presence, but above all in the living sacrament of his Body and his Blood. *The Church draws her life from Christ in the Eucharist*; by him she is fed and by him she is enlightened. The Eucharist is both a mystery of faith and a "mystery of light". (no. 6)

PURPOSES

There can be little doubt that among the Pope's purposes in writing the encyclical is the correction of some abuses and aberrations that have crept into various sectors of the Church's life regarding the Blessed Sacrament. It seems that the secular information media have focused almost exclusively on that aspect of the document. However, the main goal and purpose of the encyclical is far more profound. In a candid statement at the beginning of the letter, the Pope says, "I cannot let this Holy Thursday 2003 pass without halting before the 'Eucharistic face' of Christ and pointing out with new force to the Church the centrality of the Eucharist ... From this 'living bread' she [the Church] draws her nourishment. How could I not feel the need to urge everyone to experience it ever anew?" (no. 7).

Citing the Dogmatic Constitution on the Church of the Second Vatican Council (*Lumen gentium*, no. 23), our Holy Father notes,

> The ecclesial communion of the Eucharistic assembly is a communion with its own *Bishop* and with the *Roman Pontiff*. The Bishop, in effect, is the *visible* principle and the foundation of unity within his particular Church. It would therefore be a great contradiction if the sacrament par excellence of the Church's unity were celebrated without true communion with the Bishop. As Saint Ignatius of Antioch wrote, "That Eucharist which is celebrated under the Bishop, or under one to whom the Bishop has given this charge, may be considered certain." (no. 39)

SUNDAY MASS

One of the matters that the Pope brings up in the encyclical is something that he has previously treated extensively in some of his other works in the course of his twenty-five –year pontificate, that is, the highest importance of the Sunday Mass in each parish and for each individual Catholic. "The Eucharist's particular effectiveness in promoting communion is one of the reasons for the importance of Sunday Mass", which is "fundamental for the life of the Church and of individual believers ... . The faithful have the obligation to attend Mass, unless they are seriously impeded ... . Through sharing in the [Sunday] Eucharist, *the Lord's Day* also becomes *the Day of the Church*, when she can effectively exercise her role as the sacrament of unity" (no. 41).

The Pope repeats what the *Catechism of the Catholic Church* (CCC 1385) teaches. "Anyone conscious of a grave sin must receive the sacrament of Reconciliation before coming to communion" (no. 36). Missing Mass on Sunday without a grave reason is, of course, a grievous sin. Citing the Apostle Paul (1 Cor 11:28) and the Council of Trent, the Holy Father states, "I ... reaffirm that in the Church there remains in force, now and in the future, the rule ... 'one must first confess one's sins, when one is aware of mortal sin'. ... If a Christian's conscience is burdened by serious sin, then the path of penance though the sacrament of Reconciliation becomes necessary for full participation in the Eucharistic Sacrifice" (nos. 36-37).

Pope John Paul II also makes clear that someone whose outward conduct is "seriously, clearly, and steadfastly" contrary to the Church is to be considered, according to the Code of Canon Law, like those who "obstinately persist in manifest grave sin", and such persons "are not to be admitted to Eucharistic communion" (no. 37). The Supreme Pontiff says,

> Given the very nature of ecclesial communion and its relation to the sacrament of the Eucharist, it must be recalled that "the Eucharistic Sacrifice, while always offered in a particular community, is never a celebration of that community alone. In fact, the community, in receiving the Eucharistic presence of the Lord, receives the entire gift of salvation and shows, even in its lasting visible particular form, that it is the image and true presence of the one, holy, catholic, and apostolic Church." (no. 39)

APRIL 25, 2003

Eucharistic Encyclical
II

WHAT IS THAT?

Last Holy Thursday, April 17, 2003, our Holy Father, Pope John Paul II, issued an encyclical, the fourteenth of his pontificate, *On the Eucharist in its Relationship to the Church*. As is usual with these documents, the official title is taken from the first sentence of the Latin text, *Ecclesia de Eucharistia*. The present Pope has issued, in the course of his twenty-five years as the Bishop of Rome, many and varied documents, including apostolic constitutions, apostolic letters, apostolic and postsynodal exhortations, and so on. However, pontifical encyclicals are somewhat special and have a particular nuance of their own.

Technically speaking, encyclicals are circular letters about doctrinal, moral, and disciplinary issues addressed either to the hierarchy of the Catholic Church or, as is the case with *Ecclesia de Eucharistia*, to a wider audience. In this most recent encyclical the letter is intended, in the Pope's words, for "Bishops, priests and deacons, men and women in the consecrated life, and all the lay faithful". The modern use of the encyclical as an important means by which the Bishop of Rome exercises his primacy and his special office of teaching in his capacity as the Vicar of Christ on earth dates from the extensive use of this method by Pope Leo XIII, who was Pope from 1878 to 1903.

ASSENT

Pope Pius XII definitively set down the value and significance of encyclical letters for the Catholic world.

> Nor must it be thought that what is expounded in Encyclical Letters does not of itself demand consent, since in writing such Letters the Popes do not exercise the supreme power of their Teaching Authority. For these matters are taught with the ordinary teaching authority, of which it is true to say "He who heareth you, heareth me" (Lk 10:16); and generally what is expounded and inculcated in Encyclical Letters already for other reasons appertains to Catholic doctrine. But if the Supreme Pontiffs in their official documents purposely pass judgment on a matter up to that time under dispute, it is obvious that that matter, according to the mind and will of the Pontiffs, cannot be any longer considered a question open to discussion among theologians .... [The] deposit of faith our divine Redeemer has given for authentic

interpretation not to each of the faithful, not even to theologians, but only to the Teaching Authority of the Church. [1]

Commenting on the recent Eucharistic encyclical, one observer noted, "Pope John Paul II, who began his papal ministry with the encyclical *Redemptoris hominis* (The Redeemer of Mankind), focusing on Jesus Christ as the Center of the cosmos and of all history, now takes up the real presence of Christ in the Eucharist as one of the most important issues that concerns him in this past quarter of a century and which he considers decisive for the future of the Church."

MARY

In this year, which the Pope has declared "the year of the rosary" extending from last October to next October, and as we approach the month of May, which traditionally is given over to the veneration of the Blessed Virgin Mary and to devotion to her, it is very appropriate to ponder particularly the last chapter of *Ecclesia de Eucharistia*, which the Pope dedicates to the Blessed Virgin. He entitles that chapter "At the School of Mary, 'Woman of the Eucharist'". It is somewhat unexpected to find a chapter linking the Blessed Mother to the Holy Eucharist in a papal encyclical about the Blessed Sacrament.

Remarking about this linkage, the Pope says,

> At first glance, the Gospel is silent on this subject. The account of the institution of the Eucharist on the night of Holy Thursday makes no mention of Mary. Yet we know that she was present among the Apostles who prayed "with one accord" (cf. Acts 1:14) *in the first community which gathered after the Ascension in expectation of Pentecost.* Certainly Mary must have been present at the Eucharistic celebrations of the first generation of Christians, who were devoted to the "breaking of the bread" (Acts 2:42). (no. 53)

MAGNIFICAT

The Pope takes up the theme that other spiritual writers through the centuries have observed, namely, the Eucharistic overtones of Mary's splendid prayer (Lk 1:46-55) called the Magnificat, in which she praises God for filling the hungry with good things. He encourages us to reread "the Magnificat in a Eucharistic key", remembering that, like that Canticle of Mary, "the Eucharist ... is first and foremost praise and thanksgiving" (no. 58) to God. He notes that the well-known Eucharistic hymn "*Ave Verum*" begins with the words,

"Hail, true Body of Christ, born of the Virgin Mary."

The Supreme Pontiff observes, "At the Annunciation Mary conceived the Son of God in the physical reality of his body and blood, thus anticipating within herself what to some degree happens sacramentally in every believer who receives, under the signs of bread and wine, the Lord's body and blood: (no. 55) "In a certain sense Mary lived her *Eucharistic faith* even before the institution of the Eucharist, by the very fact that she *offered her virginal womb for the Incarnation* of God's Word" (no. 55). The Holy Father also remarks, "There is a profound analogy between the *Fiat* ['Let it be done to me'] which Mary said in reply to the angel and the Amen which every believer says when receiving the body of the Lord"(no. 55).

The Pope writes that at the Visitation (Lk 1:39–45) Mary became "the first tabernacle in history, in which the Son of God, still invisible to our human gaze, allowed himself to be adored by Elizabeth, radiating his light as it were through the eyes and voice of Mary" (no. 55). He says that we should be inspired every time we receive Holy Communion by the thought of "the unparalleled model of love" (no. 55) shown by our Blessed Mother, who cradled Jesus in her arms at His human birth on the first Christmas.

The Holy Eucharist is called "the Mystery of Faith", which, according to the Holy Father, always should bring to mind the fact that Mary, as the Mother and model of the Church, is proclaimed in God's inspired word as "Blessed is she who believed" (Lk 1:45). It should be recalled that "Mary, throughout her life at Christ's side and not only on Calvary, made her own *the sacrificial dimension of the Eucharist* ... Mary is present, with the Church and as the Mother of the Church, at each of our celebrations of the Eucharist" (nos. 56–57).

MAY 2, 2003

Eucharistic Encyclical
III

PERSONAL

In his introductory remarks to his latest encyclical letter, *Ecclesia de Eucharistia* (*On the Eucharist in Its Relationship to the Church*), Pope John Paul II illustrates how, as many observers have pointed out, this encyclical is among the most personal of the official documents he has issued during his pontificate. The Holy Father at the beginning notes, "I cannot let this Holy Thursday 2003 pass without halting before the 'Eucharistic face' of Christ and pointing out with new force to the Church the centrality of the Eucharist. From it the Church draws her life. From this 'living bread' she draws her nourishment. How could I not feel the need to urge everyone to experience it anew?" (no. 7).

The Pope remarks,

> When I think of the Eucharist and look at my life as a priest, as a Bishop, and as the Successor of Peter, I naturally recall the many times and places in which I was able to celebrate it. I remember the parish church of Niegowic, where I had my first pastoral assignment, the collegiate church of Saint Florian in Krakow, Wawel Cathedral, Saint Peter's Basilica, and so many basilicas and churches in Rome and throughout the world. I have been able to celebrate Holy Mass in chapels built along mountain paths, on lakeshores and seacoasts; I have celebrated it on altars built in stadiums and in city squares ... This varied scenario of celebrations of the Eucharist has given me a powerful experience of its universal and, so to speak, cosmic character. Yes, cosmic! Because even when it is celebrated on the humble altar of a country church, the Eucharist is always in some way celebrated *on the altar of the world*. It unites heaven and earth. It embraces and permeates all creation. (no. 8)

CONTINUITY

One of the features of this encyclical, as in so many of our Holy Father's works, is its emphasis on consistency and continuity with the great traditions that always carry the weight of Catholic truth. For example, he writes about his great admiration for "the doctrinal expositions of the Decrees on the Most Holy Eucharist and on the Holy Sacrifice of the Mass promulgated by the Council of Trent" (no. 9). He says, "For centuries those Decrees guided theology and catechesis, and they are still a dogmatic reference point for the continual growth and renewal of God's People in faith and love for the Eucharist" (no. 9). The Ecumenical Council of Trent, of course, took place in the sixteenth and early seventeenth century.

The Pope makes it clear that he intends in his Eucharistic teaching to apply and amplify what his recent predecessors taught. He cites specifically encyclical letters "in times closer to our own" by Pope Leo XIII (*Mirae caritatis* of 1902), by Pius XII (*Mediator Dei* of 1947), and by Pope Paul VI (*Mysterium fidei* of 1965). He also sees his present recent encyclical as deriving from the documents of the Second Vatican Council, especially the Dogmatic Constitution on the Church (*Lumen gentium*) and the Constitution on the Sacred Liturgy (*Sacrosanctum concilium*).

Finally, he says that his intention in writing the encyclical is to "take up anew the thread" of what he previously wrote concerning the Holy Eucharist (in the apostolic letter, *Dominicae cenae* of 1980) and to do so "with even greater emotion and gratitude" in his heart (no. 9).

SHADOWS

The Supreme Pontiff mentions in the encyclical various "positive signs of Eucharistic faith and love." He says,

> The Magisterium's commitment to proclaiming the Eucharistic mystery has been matched by interior growth with the Christian community. Certainly, *the liturgical reform inaugurated by the Council* has greatly contributed to a more conscious, active, and fruitful participation in the Holy Sacrifice of the Altar on the part of the faithful. In many places, *adoration of the Blessed Sacrament* is also an important daily practice and becomes an inexhaustible source of holiness. (no. 10)

However, the Bishop of Rome ruefully says that "unfortunately, alongside these lights *there are also shadows*", and he hopes "that the present Encyclical Letter will effectively help to banish the dark clouds of unacceptable doctrine and practice, so that the Eucharist will continue to shine forth in all its radiant mystery" (no. 10). "The Eucharist is too great a gift to tolerate ambiguity and depreciation" (no. 10).

The Supreme Pontiff also writes about his "profound grief" at some of the evils he observes:

> In some places the practice of Eucharistic adoration has been almost completely abandoned. In various parts of the Church abuses have occurred, leading to confusion with regard to sound faith and Catholic doctrine concerning this wonderful sacrament. At times one encounters an extremely reductive understanding of the Eucharistic mystery. Stripped of its sacrificial meaning, it is celebrated as if it were simply a fraternal banquet. Furthermore, the necessity of the ministerial priesthood, grounded in apostolic succession, is at times obscured and the sacramental nature of the Eucharist is reduced to its mere effectiveness as a form of proclamation. This has led here and there to ecumenical initiatives which, albeit well-intentioned, indulge in Eucharistic practices contrary to the discipline by which the Church expresses her faith. (no. 10)

GIFT

The Holy Father reiterates the Catholic Church's ancient faith and unbroken tradition, linking the Holy Eucharist to the dying and rising of Jesus (1 Cor 11:23) and, thus, to God's supreme act of self-giving, Christ's sacrifice of His human life voluntarily for our salvation (Jn 10:18). "The Church has received the Eucharist from Christ her Lord not as one gift—however precious—among so many others, but as *the gift par excellence*, for it is the gift of himself, of his person in his sacred humanity, as well as the gift of his saving work. Nor does it remain confined to the past, since 'all that Christ is—all that he did and suffered for all men—participates in the divine eternity, and so transcends all times" (no. 11).

The Holy Eucharist also involves the gift of the Holy Spirit. The Holy Father says, "Through our communion in his body and blood, Christ also grants us his Spirit. Saint Ephrem writes: 'He called the bread his living body and he filled it with himself and his Spirit.... He who eats it with faith eats Fire and Spirit....'" Thus by the gift of His body and blood, Christ increases within us the gift of his Spirit, already poured out in Baptism and bestowed as a 'seal' in the sacrament of Confirmation" (no. 17). The Pope also says, "By giving the Eucharist the prominence it deserves, and by being careful not to diminish any of its dimensions or demands, we show that we are truly conscious of the greatness of this gift" (no. 61).

MAY 9, 2003

Eucharistic Encyclical
IV

MUCH MORE

It is sometimes overlooked that the altar at Mass is not just a table, but also a "stone of sacrifice", that is to say, the twofold function of the altar demonstrates that every Holy Mass is not "merely a fraternal banquet"; rather it is first of all the paschal event, a real "making present again the dying and rising of Jesus". To be sure, the Mass also makes present the Last Supper of our Redeemer on earth. It is a sacred meal, situated in what was called in the Greek language in the early days of Christianity the "agape" or "love feast". However, it is much more. It is perfect praise, worship, and adoration given to God the Father, because it is the re-presentation of the sacrifice of the Cross, and, indeed, it is identical with that very sacrifice of Christ.

Counteracting a certain lack of balance in current thinking about these matters was one of the main purposes our Holy Father, Pope John Paul II, when he decided to write his recent encyclical letter (*Ecclesia de Eucharistia*), which he issued last Holy Thursday. The Pope says,

> [The Savior himself] in instituting it [the Eucharist] did not merely say: "This is my body", "this is my blood", but went on to add: "which is given for you", "which is poured out for you" (Lk 22:19-20). Jesus did not simply state that what he was giving them to eat and drink was his body and his blood; he also expressed *its sacrificial meaning* and made sacramentally present his sacrifice, which would soon be offered on the Cross for the salvation of all. (no. 12)

The Supreme Pontiff then quotes the *Catechism of the Catholic Church*: "The Mass is at the same time, and inseparably, the sacrificial memorial in which the sacrifice of the cross is perpetuated and the sacred banquet of communion with the Lord's body and blood" (CCC 1382). "The sacrifice of Christ and the sacrifice of the Eucharist are *one single sacrifice*" (CCC 1367).

THE SAME

The Bishop of Rome explains, "The Mass makes present the sacrifice of the Cross; it does not add to that sacrifice nor does it multiply it. What is repeated is its *memorial* celebration, its 'commemorative representation...', which makes Christ's one, definitive, redemptive sacrifice always present in time. The sacrificial nature of the Eucharistic mystery cannot therefore be understood as something separate, independent of the Cross or only indirectly referring to the sacrifice of Calvary" (no. 12). This is the main reason why liturgical laws for the Latin Rite demand that a crucifix always be on, above, or very near the altar in our churches.

The Holy Father explicitly desired in his encyclical to reaffirm and expound the doctrine explicated in the Council of Trent, which states, "in the Mass it is one and the same Victim Who now makes His offering through the ministry of priests, and it is He Who then offered Himself on the Cross, the only difference being in the manner of the offering" (Denizinger S. Inchirodum 1743).

The Pope says,

> By virtue of its close relationship to the sacrifice of Golgotha, the Eucharist is *a sacrifice in the strict sense*, and not only in a general way, as if it were simply a matter of Christ's offering himself to the faithful as their spiritual food. The gift of his love

and obedience to the point of giving his life (cf. Jn 10:17–18) is in the first place a gift to his Father. Certainly, it is a gift given for our sake and indeed for that of all humanity (cf. Mt 26:28; Mk 14:24; Lk 22:20; Jn 10:15), yet it is *first and foremost a gift to the Father*: "a sacrifice that the Father accepted, giving, in return for this total self-giving by his Son, who 'became obedient unto death' (Phil 2:8), his own paternal gift, that is to say the grant of new immortal life in the resurrection..." (no. 13)

Joining Him

The Second Vatican Council teaches, "Christ, indeed, always associates the Church with Himself in this great work [the sacred liturgy and the Mass that is the heart of the liturgy], in which God is perfectly glorified and men are sanctified. The Catholic Church is His beloved Bride who calls to her Lord and through Him offers worship to the Eternal Father."[2]

This is why the Pope says, "In giving his sacrifice to the Church, Christ has also made his own the spiritual sacrifice of the Church, which is called to offer herself in union with the sacrifice of Christ. This is the teaching of the Second Vatican Council concerning the faithful: "Taking part in the Eucharistic Sacrifice, which is the source and summit of the whole Christian life, they offer the divine victim to God, and offer themselves along with it [*Lumen gentium*, no. 11]" (no. 13).

Each Mass is perfect worship given to God the Father by the "whole Christ", Head and members, the entire Mystical Body. When attending and participating in Mass, Catholics should ever try to be conscious that they are mystically joined to Jesus and to each other in offering to the heavenly Father our absolutely necessary adoration, which is Christ's atoning and redeeming death. The human priest at Mass stands "in the Person of Christ", but still at every Mass the Priest, Jesus, and the Victim, Jesus, are really the same as on Mount Calvary.

Resurrection

The Holy Father reminds us,

> Christ's passover includes not only his passion and death, but also his resurrection... The Eucharistic Sacrifice makes present not only the mystery of the Savior's passion and death, but also the mystery of the resurrection which crowned his sacrifice. It is as the living and risen One that Christ can become in the Eucharist the "bread of life" (Jn 6:35, 48), "the living bread" (Jn 6:51). Saint Ambrose reminded the newly initiated that the Eucharist applies the event of the resurrection to their lives: "Today Christ is yours,

yet each day he rises again for you." Saint Cyril of Alexandria also makes clear that sharing in the sacred mysteries is "a true confession and a remembrance that the Lord died and returned to life for us and on our behalf." (no. 14)

Saint Thomas Aquinas, in one of his most famous Eucharistic hymns, calls the Eucharist "a pledge of future glory". Jesus offered perfect worship to God, not just on the Cross, but also in His Resurrection. This is why when we attend Holy Mass in the way in which the Second Vatican Council instructs us to do, namely, "knowingly and actively", God applies to our souls what Christ won for us on the Cross, and He plants anew within us the promise of sharing our Lord's Resurrection victory one day forever.

May 30, 2003

Eucharistic Encyclical
V

IDENTICAL

In his encyclical letter of last Holy Thursday, *Ecclesia de Eucharistia*, our Holy Father makes it clear that there must be a correct balance, that is, not "either-or", but "both-and", when viewing the Holy Eucharist, seeing it as a sacrament, including Holy Communion and Christ's abiding presence, a sacred meal making present the Last Supper, but also seeing it as a sacrifice, making present anew the paschal mystery, that is, the dying and rising of Jesus, so that down through the centuries we could experience and participate in the perfect worship given to God the Father by our Savior on the Cross and in what our Savior merited in His sufferings for us.
The Pope writes,

> In the wake of Jesus' own words and actions, and building upon the ritual heritage of Judaism, the *Christian liturgy was born*. Could there ever be an adequate means of expressing the acceptance of that self-gift which the divine Bridegroom continually makes to his Bride, the Church, by bringing the Sacrifice offered once and for all on the Cross to successive generations of believers and thus becoming the nourishment for all the faithful? Though the idea of a "banquet" naturally suggests familiarity, the Church has never yielded to the temptation to trivialize this "intimacy" with her

Spouse by forgetting that he is also her Lord and that the "banquet" always remains a sacrificial banquet marked by the blood shed on Golgotha. (no. 48)

The *Catechism of the Catholic Church* states, "The sacrifice of Christ and the sacrifice of the Eucharist are *one single sacrifice*" (CCC 1367).

DOCTRINE

The Second Vatican Council teaches, "Through the ministry of priests the spiritual sacrifice of the faithful is completed in union with the sacrifice of Christ the only Mediator, which in the Eucharist is offered through the priests' hands in the name of the whole Church in an unbloody and sacramental manner until the Lord himself comes."[3] The Council of Trent instructs us, "In Holy Mass the Victim is one and the same as on Mount Calvary, that is, the same Person now offers His sacrifice through the ministry of priests Who then offered Himself on the Cross. Only the manner of offering is different. And since in the divine sacrifice that is celebrated in the Mass the same Christ Who offered Himself once in a bloody manner on the altar of the Cross is contained and offered in an unbloody manner, the sacrifice of the Mass is truly propitiatory" (DS 1743).

The great Council goes on to say,

> Christ our Lord and God was once and for all to offer Himself to God the Father by His death on the Cross and to accomplish there an everlasting redemption. But, because His priesthood was not to end with His death, He, at the Last Supper, on the night He was betrayed, wanted to leave to His beloved Spouse, the Church, a visible sacrifice as human nature demands, by which the bloody sacrifice, which He was to carry out once and for all on the Cross, would be able to be made continually present, its memory perpetuated until the end of the world, and its salutary power be applied for the forgiveness of the sins we daily commit. (DS 1740)

MYSTERIOUS

Jesus Christ our Lord is in heaven in His human Body and Soul, seated at the right hand of the Father. He is (and always was) the second Person of the Blessed Trinity and now is in impassible and perfect happiness even in His human nature. He is not hurt, harmed, or mutilated in Mass. The Mass is not an absolute sacrifice independent of the unique sacrifice by which Jesus redeemed us. It is a relative sacrifice, making present over again the one and only sacrifice of Christ and receiving all its efficacy from Calvary, because it is identical with the sacrifice of the Cross except for being different in the manner of offering. The Mass is not a mere commemoration or only a sacrifice of praise and thanks, but it is in truth the Body and Blood of Christ, mystically separated by the different words of the twofold consecration, being offered to God the Father under the appearances of bread and wine.

Just as transubstantiation itself is part of a divine mystery that can never be fully understood by a created intellect in this world, but must be believed because revealed by God, so the sacrificial nature of the Mass can be only partly grasped now, while its full understanding must await the Christian's entry into the other and better world. Father Theophil Tschipke writes, "The saving action of God transcends all limits of space and time. In His eternity, God acts in the present. Events accomplished long ago in the human nature of Christ and the other mysteries of His human nature united to the Person of the Word are universal instruments, effective in the divine plan for the restoration of the supernatural order. The life, death, and resurrection of Christ belong to all ages and all men."

TESTIMONY

Pope Saint Gregory the Great says, "No Christian can doubt that at the time of offering during Mass, at the words of the priest, the heavens are opened, the choirs of angels are present in the mystery of Jesus Christ, the lowest things are knit with the highest, earthly things are united with those that are heavenly, and the visible is made one with the invisible."[4] Saint Bede the Venerable said, "When we celebrate the solemn ceremonies of the Mass, we immolate to God the most sacred Body and precious Blood of our Lamb, by Whom we have been redeemed from sins unto the attainment of our salvation."

Pope Leo XIII writes,

> After [Christ's] Ascension, the same Sacrifice [of the Cross] is continued by the Eucharistic Sacrifice. They greatly err, therefore, who reject this doctrine, as if it diminished the reality and efficacy of the Sacrifice which Christ offered on the Cross [Heb 9:28]. ... That atonement for the sins of men was absolutely complete: nor there any other atonement besides that of the Cross in the Eucharistic Sacrifice.... It was the Divine counsel of the Redeemer that the Sacrifice of the Cross should be perpetuated. This perpetuity is in the most Holy Eucharist, which is not an empty similitude or a mere commemoration, but the very Sacrifice flows from the death of Christ.[5]

Theologians often cite the Prophet Malachi (1:11) in connection with the daily sacrifice of the New Testament: "From the rising of the sun to its setting my name is great among the nations and in every place incense is offered to my name, and a pure offering." Saint John Fisher says, "That same true Lamb, Christ Jesus, Who suffered on the cross becomes our pasch also on the altar. There are not two paschal victims nor two sacrifices, but one pasch and one sacrifice, the one making present the other. For in both the same true Lamb, Jesus Christ, as He was immolated on the cross once in His death, so now is immolated daily when we renew the memorial of His death."

JUNE 13, 2003

Eucharistic Encyclical
VI

TRUE LOVE

Saint Peter Julian Eymard once said, "We believe in the love of God for us. To believe in love is everything. It is not enough to believe in the Truth. We must believe in Love, and Love is our Lord in the Blessed Sacrament. That is the faith that makes our Lord loved. Ask for this pure and simple faith in the Eucharist. Men will teach you, but only Jesus will give you the grace to believe in Him. You have the Eucharist. What more do you want?"

In a certain sense those words of that saint from more than one hundred years ago constitute a beautiful summary of a substantial part of the recent encyclical *Ecclesia de Eucharistia*, issued last April 17, by our Holy Father, Pope John Paul II. A holy priest once remarked that true love must have three basic foundations, sacrifice, union, and presence. It is interesting and important to note that Christ, the divine Bridegroom of His Spouse, the Catholic Church (Eph 5:25–32), constantly and perennially provides those three foundational elements to her in the most Holy Eucharist.

The Holy Eucharist is the sacrament in which Jesus Christ, whole and entire, Body, Soul, and Divinity, is offered (sacrifice), received (union), and contained (presence). Saint Alphonsus Liguori says, "This sacrament infuses into the soul great interior peace, a strong inclination to virtue, and great willingness to practice it, thus rendering it easy to walk in the path of perfection."

GRACE

The Supreme Pontiff writes in the encyclical about the need for both visible and invisible dimensions which are vital and necessary prior to Eucharistic Communion. He says,

> Invisible communion, though by its nature always growing, presupposes the life of grace, by which we become "partakers of the divine nature" (2 Pet 1:4), and the practice of the virtues of faith, hope, and love. Only in this way do we have true communion with the Father, the Son, and the Holy Spirit. Nor is faith sufficient; we must persevere in sanctifying grace and love, remaining within the Church "bodily" as well as "in our heart" [*Lumen gentium*, no. 14]; what is required, in the words of Saint Paul, is "faith working through love" (Gal 5:6). (no. 36)

The Successor of Saint Peter goes on to say,

> Keeping these invisible bonds intact is a specific moral duty incumbent upon Christians who wish to participate fully in the Eucharist by receiving the body and blood of Christ. The Apostle Paul appeals to this duty... (1 Cor 11:28). Saint John Chrysostom, with his stirring eloquence, exhorted the faithful: "I too raise my voice, I beseech, beg, and implore that no one draw near to this sacred table with a sullied and corrupt conscience. Such an act, in fact, can never be called 'communion', not even were we to touch the Lord's body a thousand times over, but 'condemnation', 'torment', and 'increase of punishment'." (no. 36)

PENANCE

The Pope cites the *Catechism of the Catholic Church*, which, he says, "stipulates that 'anyone conscious of a grave sin must first receive the sacrament of Reconciliation before coming to communion' [CCC 1385]" (no. 36). The Vicar of Christ on earth says,

> I therefore desire to reaffirm that in the Church there remains in force, now and in the future, the rule by which the Council of Trent gave concrete expression to the Apostle Paul's stern warning when it affirmed that, in order to receive the Eucharist in a worthy manner, "one must first confess one's sins, when one is aware of mortal sin"... If a Christian's conscience is burdened by serious sin, then the path of penance through the sacrament of Reconciliation becomes necessary for full participation in the Eucharistic Sacrifice. (nos. 36–37)

The Holy Father, of course, mentions the "stern warning" given by Saint Paul: "Whoever, therefore, eats the bread or drinks the cup of the Lord in an unworthy manner will be guilty of profaning the body and blood of the Lord… Anyone who eats and drinks without discerning the body eats and drinks judgment upon himself" (1 Cor 11:27–29).

Visible

Reaffirming the ancient teaching and discipline of the Church, the Pope says that "the judgment of one's state of grace obviously belongs only to the person involved." But he notes, "However, in cases of outward conduct which is seriously, clearly, and steadfastly contrary to the moral norm, the Church, in her pastoral concern for the good order of the community and out of respect for the sacrament, cannot fail to feel directly involved. The *Code of Canon Law* refers to this situation of a manifest lack of proper moral disposition when it states that those who 'obstinately persist in manifest grave sin' are not to be admitted to Eucharistic communion" (no. 35).

In the Pope's teaching, "The profound relationship between the invisible and visible elements of ecclesial communion is constitutive of the Church as the sacrament of salvation. Only in this context can there be a legitimate celebration of the Eucharist and true participation in it" (no. 35). The visible dimension "entails communion in the teaching of the Apostles and in the sacraments and in the Church's hierarchical order" (no. 35).

According to the Roman Pontiff,

> Ecclesial communion … is … visible and finds expression in the series of "bonds" listed by the [Second Vatican] Council when it teaches: "They are fully incorporated into the society of the Church who, possessing the Spirit of Christ, accept her whole structure and all the means of salvation established within her, and within her visible framework are united to Christ, who governs her through the Supreme Pontiff and the Bishops, by bonds of the profession of faith, the sacraments, ecclesiastical government, and communion" ([*Lumen gentium*, no. 14]. (no. 38)

The Pope teaches,

> The Eucharist, as the supreme sacramental manifestation of communion in the Church, demands to be celebrated in *a context where the outward bonds of communion are also intact…* The Bishop, in effect, is the *visible* principle and foundation of unity within his particular Church. It would therefore be a great

contradiction if the sacrament *par excellence* of the Church's unity were celebrated without true communion with the Bishop. As Saint Ignatius of Antioch wrote: "That Eucharist which is celebrated under the Bishop, or under one to whom the Bishop has given this charge, may be considered certain" (nos. 38–39)

"From this it follows that a truly Eucharistic community cannot be closed in upon itself, as though it were somehow self-sufficient, rather, it must persevere in harmony with every other Catholic community" (no. 39).

JUNE 27, 2003

Eucharistic Encyclical
VII

REAL PRESENCE

Cardinal John Henry Newman remarked,

> Catholics do not see that it is impossible at all, that our Lord should be in Heaven yet on the Altar; they do not indeed see *how* it can be both, but they do not see *why* it should not be; there are many things which exist, though we do not know *how*;… there are many truths which are not less truths because we cannot picture them to ourselves or conceive them; but at any rate, the Catholic doctrine concerning the Real Presence is not more mysterious than how Almighty God can exist, yet never have come into existence.[6]

In his latest encyclical, our Holy Father speaks about the "Real Presence" of Christ in the Blessed Sacrament.

> The sacramental re-presentation of Christ's sacrifice, crowned by the resurrection, in the Mass involves a most special presence which—in the words of Pope Paul VI—"is called 'real', not as a way of excluding all other types of presence as if they were 'not real', but because it is a presence in the fullest sense: a substantial presence whereby Christ, the God-Man, is wholly and entirely present". This sets forth once more the perennially valid teaching of the Council of Trent: "the consecration of the bread and wine

effects the change of the whole substance of the bread into the substance of the body of Christ our Lord, and of the whole substance of the wine into the substance of his blood. And, the holy Catholic Church has fittingly and properly called this change transubstantiation." (no. 15)

Saint Cyril

The Pope quotes Saint Cyril of Jerusalem: "Do not see in the bread and wine merely natural elements, because the Lord has expressly said that they are his body and his blood: faith assures you of this, though your senses suggest otherwise" (no. 15). Saint Cyril, who was the Catholic Bishop of Jerusalem in the fourth century, also is noted for saying, "If Jesus Who is God says that This is His Body, how dare you contradict Him! Wherefore with full assurance let us partake of the Body and Blood of Christ that we can be made of the same Body and Blood with Him. Thus we come to bear Christ within us and, according to Peter, become partakers of the divine nature (2 Pet 1:4)."[7]

The Supreme Pontiff says, "Before this mystery of love, human reason fully experiences its limitations. One understands how, down the centuries, this truth has stimulated theology to strive to understand it more deeply" (no. 15). However, he cautions, using the words of his predecessor, Pope Paul VI, "Every theological explanation which seeks some understanding of this mystery, in order to be in accord with the Catholic faith, must firmly maintain that in objective reality, independently of our mind, the bread and wine have ceased to exist after the consecration, so that the adorable body and blood of the Lord Jesus from that moment on [the consecration of the Mass] are really before us under the sacramental species of bread and wine" (no. 15).[8]

Communion

Pope Saint Pius X says, "Holy Communion is the shortest and safest way to heaven. There are others: innocence, but that is for little children; penance, but we are afraid of it; generous endurance of life's trials, but when they come we weep and ask to be spared. The surest, easiest, and shortest way is the Eucharist." Pope Saint Leo the Great says, "In Holy Communion we are changed into the Flesh of Him Who became our flesh." Saint John Vianney says, "Upon receiving Holy Communion the adorable Blood of Jesus Christ really flows in our veins and His Flesh is really blended with ours."

In his Eucharistic encyclical, *Ecclesia de Eucharistia*, Pope John Paul II writes, "The saving efficacy of the sacrifice is fully realized when the Lord's body and blood are received in communion. The Eucharistic Sacrifice is intrinsically directed to the inward union of the faithful with Christ through communion... *The Eucharist is a true banquet*, in which Christ offers himself as our nourishment [see Jn 6:53–57; Mt 26:28]" (no. 16).

Saint Augustine of Hippo reminds us, "When we approach the altar, we must, with God's help, prepare ourselves with all our power and search into every corner of our souls lest any sin be hidden therein. For then, if Christ sees us clothed in the light of grace, He will give us His Flesh and Blood, not to our condemnation, but to our salvation."

Saint Catherine of Siena tells us that even when we are not conscious of any personal mortal sins, the minimal disposition we must have in order to receive Holy Communion without committing a sacrilege (1 Cor 11:27), we still should feel unworthy of the Lord: "Of course you are unworthy. But when do you hope to be worthy? You are no more worthy at the end than at the beginning. All the good works that we could ever do would never make us worthy of Holy Communion. God alone is worthy of Himself. He alone can make us worthy of Him, and He alone can make us worthy with His own worthiness."

PLEDGE

In speaking about the "eschatological thrust" of the Holy Eucharist (no. 18), Pope John Paul II uses again the phrase of Saint Thomas Aquinas, namely, that the "holy banquet" is a "pledge of future glory". The Holy Father calls Holy Communion under this aspect a "straining towards the goal", a "foretaste of the fullness of joy promised by Christ", an "anticipation of heaven", the "first-fruits of a future fullness", and "a pledge of our bodily resurrection" (Jn 6:54 and 15:11; 1 Cor 11:26). The Supreme Pontiff, calling the Holy Eucharist "the secret of the resurrection", quotes Saint Ignatius of Antioch, who "rightly defined the Eucharistic Bread as 'a medicine of immortality, an antidote to death'".

The Pope recalls for us that "the Eucharist is truly a glimpse of heaven appearing on earth. It is a glorious ray of the heavenly Jerusalem which pierces the clouds of our history and lights up our journey" (no. 19). "In celebrating the sacrifice of the Lamb, we are united to the heavenly 'liturgy' and become part of the great multitude (Rev 7:10)" (no. 19). "The eschatological tension kindled by the Eucharist *expresses and reinforces our communion with the Church in heaven*" (no. 19). However, the Pope also notes, "A significant consequence of the eschatological tension inherent in the Eucharist is also the fact that it spurs us on our journey through history and plants a seed of living hope in our daily commitment to the work before us" (no. 20).

JULY 11, 2003

Eucharistic Encyclical
VIII

WORSHIP

In his encyclical letter of last April 17 (*Ecclesia de Eucharistia*), our Holy Father, Pope John Paul II, writes:

> The *worship of the Eucharist outside of the Mass* is of inestimable value for the life of the Church. This worship is strictly linked to the celebration of the Eucharistic Sacrifice. The presence of Christ under the sacred species reserved after Mass—a presence which lasts as long as the species of bread and wine remain— derives from the celebration of the Sacrifice and is directed towards communion, both sacramental and spiritual. It is the responsibility of Pastors to encourage, also by their personal witness, the practice of Eucharistic adoration, and exposition of the Blessed Sacrament in particular, as well as prayer of adoration before Christ present under the Eucharistic species. (no. 25)

In an earlier apostolic letter, entitled *On the Mystery and Worship of the Holy Eucharist*, our Holy Father remarks: "Worship directed to the Trinity, Father, Son, and Holy Spirit, accompanies and pervades above all the celebration of the Eucharistic liturgy. But, this should also fill our sanctuaries even outside the hours of Mass. Since the Eucharist was instituted by love and renders Christ present sacramentally, it is indeed worthy of thanksgiving and worship."[9]

Modern, postconciliar liturgical documents urge the faithful to see in the exposed Blessed Sacrament, especially when placed in the monstrance (ostensarium), an extension of the elevation of the Mass, which always follows the solemn Consecration in the Eucharistic liturgy in the Latin Rite.

DOCUMENTS

Other official documents of the Church's teaching authority ("Magisterium") likewise speak along those same lines. For instance, the *Catechism of the Catholic Church*, quoting an encyclical letter of Pope Paul VI (*Mysterium fidei*, no. 56), says: "The Catholic Church has always offered and still offers to the sacrament of the Eucharist the cult of adoration [*latria*, that worship which may be given to God alone], not only during Mass, but also outside of it, reserving the consecrated hosts with the utmost care, exposing them to the solemn veneration of the faithful, and carrying them in processions" (CCC 1378).

The *Catechism* explains,

> The tabernacle was first intended for the reservation of the
> Eucharist in a worthy place so that it could be brought to the sick
> and those absent, outside of Mass. As faith in the real presence of
> Christ in his Eucharist deepened, the Church became conscious of
> the meaning of silent adoration of the Lord present under the
> Eucharistic species. It is for this reason that the tabernacle should
> be located in an especially worthy place in the church and should
> be constructed in such a way that it emphasizes and manifests the
> truth of the real presence of Christ in the Blessed Sacrament. (CCC
> 1379)

SAINTS

Our present Pope writes in that same apostolic letter, "The Church and the world
have a great need for Eucharistic worship, Jesus awaits us in this sacrament of
love. Let us not refuse the time to go to meet Him in adoration, in contemplation
full of faith, and open to making amends for the serious offenses and crimes of the
world. Let our adoration never cease."[10] In his teaching our Holy Father echoes
the sentiments and thoughts of many of the saints who constantly reminded all to
whom they spoke that the Holy Eucharist is actually "heaven in our midst".

Saint Mary Pelletier says, "The Blessed Sacrament is the first and supreme object
of our worship. We must preserve in the depths of our hearts a constant,
uninterrupted, profound adoration of this precious pledge of divine love." Saint
Augustine of Hippo says, "O sacrament of love, O sign of unity, O bond of charity…
Whoever would have life finds here indeed a life to live in and a life to live by. God
in His omnipotence could not give us more; in His wisdom He knew not how to
give more; in His riches He had not more to give than the Eucharist."

Saint John Bosco says, "Do you want our Lord to give you many graces? Then
visit Him often. Visits to the Blessed Sacrament are a powerful and indispensable
means of overcoming the attacks of the devil. Make frequent visits to Jesus in the
Blessed Sacrament and then the devil will be powerless against you." Saint
Alphonsus Liguori says, "All can go to converse with Jesus whenever they wish.
He desires that we speak to Him with unbounded confidence. It is for this purpose
that He remains with us under the species of bread." Saint John Vianney (the Curé
of Ars) says, "We should consider the moments spent before the Blessed Sacrament
as the happiest of our lives." Saint Thérèse of Lisieux says, "Kneeling before the
tabernacle, I can think of only one thing to say to our Lord: My God, You know
that I love You. And, I feel that my prayer does not weary Jesus. Knowing my
weakness, He is satisfied with my good will."

Biographers of Saint Francis of Assisi relate that he often spent whole nights on his knees before the Blessed Sacrament in reparation for the world's sins, simply saying over and over again: "Love is not loved."

LOOKING

A former American Protestant minister told me this story. He was struggling with his faith a few years ago and approached a Catholic priest for some help. The priest kindly offered to give him some spiritual advice but also told him that it was important for him, while receiving this advice, to go into a Catholic church from time to time and pray in front of the Blessed Sacrament. The minister was a bit shocked at that counsel, but he went into a nearby Catholic church for the first time in his life. He said he carried along his Bible for protection. He sat down in the church and wondered what praying in front of the Blessed Sacrament meant and why he should do it.

He casually flipped open his Bible, and, as it happened, it fell open at the sixth chapter of the Gospel according to Saint John. He let his finger slip down the page, and it alighted on verse forty, where Jesus says, "For this is the will of my Father Who sent Me, that whoever looks at (beholds) the Son and believes in Him shall have everlasting life, and I will raise him up on the last day." So, thought the minister, praying in front of the Blessed Sacrament makes it really possible for someone to "look at" or "behold" the Son. That first visit of that minister to the Blessed Sacrament was a life-changing experience for him. He became a Catholic and, needless to say, is very devoted to visiting our Lord in the Blessed Sacrament. May his devotion inspire ours, especially as we read and study *Ecclesia de Eucharistia*.

JULY 25, 2003

2

ANOINTING OF THE SICK

SACRAMENT

In the New Testament we read about the Sacrament of the Anointing of the Sick. "Is any among you sick? Let him call for the elders of the church, and let them pray over him, anointing him with oil in the name of the Lord; and the prayer of faith will save the sick man, and the Lord will raise him up; and if he has committed sins, he will be forgiven" (Jas 5:14–15). The Catholic Church teaches in the Council of Trent: "This sacred anointing of the sick was instituted by Christ our Lord as a true and proper sacrament of the New Testament. It is alluded to indeed by Mark [Mk 6:13], but is recommended to the faithful and promulgated by James the apostle and brother of the Lord" (DS 1695).

Because this sacrament frequently in the past was given near to the end of one's life, it received the name "Extreme Unction". Its purpose, however, was always to give strength to a seriously ill person. This strength is mainly spiritual strength, but the sacrament also includes the prayer that the person will receive as well physical strength and even healing, if that is God's will for him.

The *Catechism of the Catholic Church* states, "The Anointing of the Sick 'is not a sacrament for those only who are at the point of death. Hence, as soon as anyone of the faithful begins to be in danger of death from sickness or old age, the fitting time for him to receive this sacrament has certainly already arrived'." [11]

RITE

The Anointing of the Sick, under the direction of the Second Vatican Council, was modified somewhat in its ritual by Pope Paul VI in 1972, retaining, of course, the essential elements that always marked this efficacious sign of grace. The Pope wrote: "The sacrament of Anointing of the Sick is given to those who are seriously ill by anointing them on the forehead and hands with duly blessed oil—pressed from olives or other plants—saying, only once: 'Through this holy anointing may the Lord in his love and mercy help you with the grace of the Holy Spirit. May the Lord who frees you from sin save you and raise you up'." [12]

Only Bishops or priests can validly and licitly be the ministers of this sacrament. The sacrament can be administered in private homes, hospitals, churches, on battlefields, on warships, and so on. It can be given to an individual person or be a communal rite, bestowed on a number of people at the same time. When possible, its celebration should be in the context of other sacraments, preceded by the Sacrament of Penance and then administered in the context of Holy Mass. When a dying person receives our Lord in Holy Communion for the last time, this is called "Viaticum", which means a "passing over" and "Food for the journey".

The actual rite of the Anointing of the Sick includes prayers, some readings from Sacred Scripture, a period of silence, a laying on of hands, followed by the special prayer of the sacrament that accompanies the act of anointing.

Effects

The Sacrament of the Anointing of the Sick is generally a "sacrament of the living", that is, it must be received only when one is in the state of grace. This is why confession of sins must usually precede its celebration. However, if a person is incapable of confessing his sins (for instance, because of unconsciousness, the necessary presence of others in the room, and so on), it can become a "sacrament of the dead", that is, it can remit even unforgiven mortal sins, provided the person has at least imperfect contrition (for instance, before unconsciousness set in). Because clinical death is not necessarily always the same as theological death (the separation of the body and soul), sometimes the Sacrament of the Anointing can be given conditionally ("if you are alive ... through this holy anointing ...") for a brief time even after apparent death has occurred.

In addition to greatly increasing sanctifying grace, this sacrament bestows the special sacramental graces that enable a person to be better resigned to God's will in this regard: to regain physical strength and health, if that is God's will; to receive spiritual strength to pass successfully through death to eternal life with God, which is our human destiny, if that is God's will; and to go directly to heaven, without passing through purgatory, when all venial sins and temporal punishment due to sin are remitted. Among the effects that the *Catechism* lists are a special union with the Passion of Christ, a special union with the works of the whole Catholic Church, and the best preparation for the final and most important journey of one's life (see CCC 1520–23).

Last Rites

The term "last rites" of the Church includes a person's final confession and absolution of sins, the Anointing of the Sick, Holy Viaticum, the apostolic blessing of the Pope (which comes, by means of the priest, to the deathbed of every Catholic) and the plenary indulgence, along with the prayers for the dying. The Anointing of the Sick, of course, can be bestowed, as can these other sacraments and prayers, even apart from the "last rites".

Even if we are still young and healthy, it is a good practice to ask God in prayer often for the grace of a happy death, for final perseverance in grace and in our Catholic faith, and for the happiness of having a priest with us when our time comes to die.

It is always better to have a person receive these sacraments when he is still conscious and can take part, along with family members and loved ones, in the rites themselves. It is the highest folly to put off calling a priest for someone seriously ill, for instance, out of fear that the presence of a priest might unduly frighten or upset the sick person. Priests are highly trained professionals and know well how to deal with people in various stages of sickness and old age. When there is doubt about the suitability of summoning a priest, call him anyway, and let him judge which, if any, sacraments the sick person should receive. Even before we find it useful or necessary to receive this Sacrament of the Anointing of the Sick, let us thank Jesus for instituting this gift and sign for us.

SEPTEMBER 12, 1997

[1] Pius XII, encyclical *Humani generis* (August 12, 1950), nos. 20-21.
[2] *Sacrosanctum concilium*, no. 7.
[3] *Presbyterorum ordinis*, no. 2,§ 4, quoted by CCC 1369.
[4] Saint Gregory the Great, *Dialogues* 4.
[5] Leo XIII, encyclical *Caritatis studuim* (July 25, 1898), no. 10.
[6] John Henry Newman, discourse 13, "Mysteries of Nature and Grace", *Discourses to Mixed Congregations* (1849)
[7] Saint Cyril of Jerusalem, *Catechetical Lectures*, lecture 22, "On the Body and Blood of Christ", nos. 1, 3.
[8] Paul VI, *Solemn Profession of Faith*, June 30, 1968.
[9] John Paul II, letter *Dominicae cenae* (February 24, 1980), no. 3.
[10] Ibid.
[11] CCC 1514, quoting *Sacrosanctum concilium*, no. 73; cf. CIC can. 1004, §1;1005; 1007; CCEO, can. 738.
[12] Cf. CIC, Can. 847 #1

Part Two

VOCATIONS

1

THE PRIESTHOOD

Eternal Priesthood

IMMINENT ORDINATIONS

Once again our Diocese of Lincoln approaches the beautiful time of year when, by God's grace, the prayers and sacrifices of many people are rewarded by experiencing new ordinations to the transitional diaconate and the priesthood. Through the hands of legitimate apostolic succession, Jesus Christ once again shares His one and only priesthood of the New Testament with frail human beings, giving them a participation in His ineffable and unique mediatorship with God the Father (1 Tim 2:5) for the Father's glory and the salvation of souls.

The *Catechism of the Catholic Church* says, "In the ecclesial service of the ordained minister, it is Christ himself who is present to his Church as Head of his Body, Shepherd of his flock, high priest of the redemptive sacrifice, Teacher of truth. This is what the Church means by saying that the priest, by virtue of the sacrament of Holy Orders, acts *in persona Christi Capitis* [in the person of Christ the Head]."[1] Pope Pius XII writes, "It is the same priest, Christ Jesus, whose sacred person his minister truly represents. Now the minister, by reason of the sacerdotal consecration which he has received, is truly made like to the high priest and possesses the authority to act in the power and place of the person of Christ himself."[2] Saint Thomas Aquinas observed, "Christ is the source of all priesthood: the priest of the old law was a figure of Christ, and the priest of the new law acts in the person of Christ."[3]

ORDERS

The Catechism explains,

> The word *order* in Roman antiquity designated an established civil body, especially a governing body. *Ordinatio* means incorporation into an *ordo*. In the Church there are established bodies which Tradition, not without a basis in Sacred Scripture [cf. Heb 5:6; 7:11; Ps 110:4], has, since ancient times, called *taxeis*

(Greek) or *ordines*. And so the liturgy speaks of the *ordo episcoporum* [order of Bishops], the *ordo presbyterorum* [order of priests], the *ordo diaconorum* [order of deacons] ... .

Integration into one of these bodies in the Church was accomplished by a rite called *ordinatio*, a religious and liturgical act which was a consecration, a blessing or a sacrament. Today the word *"ordination"* is reserved for the sacramental act which integrates a man into the order of bishops, presbyters, or deacons, and goes beyond a simple *election, designation, delegation,* or *institution* by the community, for it confers a gift of the Holy Spirit that permits the exercise of a "sacred power" (*sacra potestas*) [cf. *Lumen gentium*, no. 10], which can come only from Christ himself through his Church. Ordination is also called *consecratio*, for it is a setting apart and an investiture by Christ himself for his Church. The *laying on of hands* by the bishop, with the consecratory prayer, constitutes the visible sign of this ordination. (CCC 1537–38)

Pope John Paul II says, "[The priesthood] is not to be considered as a purely human reality, as if it were the expression of a community which democratically elects its Pastor. Rather, it is to be seen in the light of the *sovereign will of God who freely chooses his pastors*. Christ wanted his Church to be sacramentally and hierarchically structured, and for this reason no one has the right to change what the divine Founder has established." [4]

GRACE

Grace, an undeserved gift from God in every sense, is bestowed in abundance on anyone who receives any sacrament, including the Sacrament of Holy Orders. First, there is a vast increase in the ordained priest's soul of sanctifying grace, the created share in the very life and nature of God (1 Pet 1:4), which is initially received in Baptism. Then, there are the particular or sacramental graces proper for men who are ordained. Pope John Paul II says these graces give them *"a deeper configuration to Christ the Priest*, who makes them his active ministers in the official worship of God and in sanctifying their brothers and sisters; [they are given] ministerial powers to be exercised in the name of Christ, the Head and Shepherd." [5] The two most awesome powers that a priest receives are that to bestow the forgiveness of sins in the Sacrament of Reconciliation (Jn 20:22–23) and that to confect the Holy Eucharist, making present the dying and rising of our Savior in the transubstantiated Species (1 Cor 11:23–29).

The Pope goes on to note,

The whole Church garners the fruit of the sanctification resulting from the ministry of [priests] ... . The profound ontology of the consecration received in Orders and the dynamism of sanctification that it entails in the ministry certainly exclude any secularized interpretation of the priestly ministry, as if the presbyter were simply dedicated to establishing justice or spreading love in the world. The presbyter participates ontologically in the priesthood of Christ. He is truly consecrated, a "man of the sacred," designated like Christ to the worship that ascends to the Father and to the evangelizing mission by which he spreads and distributes sacred realities —the truth, the grace of God,— to his brothers and sisters. This is the priest's true identity.[6]

PRAY

We know that it is very important for all Catholics to obey our Lord's command to pray for an increase in vocations to the priesthood (Mt 9:38). However, it is equally important to pray for those who are already our priests. Cardinal Richard Cushing says,

Catholics should beg God to shield their priests from every danger, to drive far from them the onslaughts of the infernal enemy. They should ask that each priest may daily increase in virtue, that his imperfections may melt away in the heat of divine love. They should pray that the way of the Lord may be made smooth for the blessed feet of those who preach and bring the good news of peace. They ought to pray that their priests may be, not only in the eyes of Catholics, but before all the world truly men of God, that Christ may live in them and in them walk this world once more.

A pious layman has remarked, "Catholics, watching the faith and fervor with which a young priest offers his first Mass, instinctively pray for him, that he may persevere to the end as their priest and shepherd. They know the road before him is difficult and beset with danger. Their prayer is touched with pity and tenderness for they know that their priest belongs to them and they have a duty toward him ... They pray because they know he needs the help of their prayers to fulfill his high vocation."

MAY 16, 2003

A Good Priest

Saint Vincent de Paul once exclaimed, "How great is a good priest!" His saying is emphasized in the latest encyclical letter of Pope John Paul II (*Ecclesia de Eucharistia*), in which our Holy Father extensively writes about the order of priests. "If the Eucharist is the center and summit of the Church's life, it is likewise the center and summit of priestly ministry. For this reason, ... I repeat that the Eucharist 'is the principal and central raison d'être of the sacrament of priesthood, which effectively came into being at the moment of the institution of the Eucharist' " (no. 31, quoting his apostolic letter *Dominicae cenae*, no. 2). "The fact that the power of consecrating the Eucharist has been entrusted only to Bishops and priests does not represent any kind of belittlement of the rest of the People of God, for in the communion of the one body of Christ which is the Church this gift redounds to the benefit of all" (no. 30).

The Supreme Pontiff remarks, "As the Second Vatican Council teaches, 'the faithful join in the offering of the Eucharist by virtue of their royal priesthood' [*Lumen gentium*, no. 10], yet it is the ordained priest who, 'acting in the person of Christ, brings about the Eucharistic Sacrifice and offers it to God in the name of all the people' [ibid.]. For this reason, the Roman Missal prescribes that only the priest should recite the Eucharistic Prayer, while the people participate in faith and in silence" (no. 28).

Pope John Paul II (no. 59) cites the words of Pope Pius XII, "The minister of the altar acts in the person of Christ inasmuch as he is head, making an offering in the name of all the members." He also cites writings of Pope Saint Pius X and Pope Pius XI along the same lines. He notes,

> The expression repeatedly employed by the Second Vatican Council, according to which "the ministerial priest, acting in the person of Christ, brings about the Eucharistic Sacrifice" [*Lumen gentium*, nos. 10 and 28; *Presbyterorum ordinis*, no. 2], was already firmly rooted in papal teaching. As I have pointed out on other occasions, the phrase in persona Christi "means more than offering 'in the name of' or 'in the place of' Christ. *In persona* means in specific sacramental identification with the eternal High Priest who is the author and principal subject of this sacrifice of his, a sacrifice in which, in truth, nobody can take his place" [*Dominicae cenae*,

no. 8]. The ministry of priests who have received the sacrament of Holy Orders, in the economy of salvation chosen by Christ, makes clear that the Eucharist which they celebrate is *a gift which radically transcends the power of the assembly* and is in any event essential for validly linking the Eucharistic consecration to the sacrifice of the Cross and to the Last Supper. The assembly gathered together for the celebration of the Eucharist, if it is to be a truly Eucharistic assembly, absolutely requires the presence of an ordained priest as its president. On the other hand, the community is by itself incapable of providing an ordained minister. This minister is a gift which the assembly *receives through the episcopal succession going back to the Apostles*. It is the Bishop who, through the Sacrament of Holy Orders, makes a new presbyter by conferring on him the power to consecrate the Eucharist. Consequently, "the Eucharistic mystery cannot be celebrated in any community except by an ordained priest, as the Fourth Lateran Council expressly taught" [Congregation for the Doctrine of the Faith, letter *Sacerdotium Ministeriale*, III, 4]. (no. 29)

THE OFFICE

In the old ritual, the Bishop at the time of ordination would remind the deacons who were about to be ordained as priests that "the office of a priest is to offer sacrifice, to bless, to govern, to forgive sins, to preach, and to baptize." The Roman Catechism said priests are given the duty to participate in the teaching mission of Christ (1 Tim 5:17), in the sanctifying work of our Savior (Acts 19:4–6; Jas 5:14; 1 Cor 1:16), and in caring for the flock of the Good Shepherd (Heb 13:17; 1 Pet 5:1–4; 1 Tim 3:1–6).

The *Catechism of the Catholic Church* says,

"It is in Eucharistic cult or in the *Eucharistic assembly* of the faithful ... that [priests] exercise in a supreme degree their sacred office; there, ... they unite the votive offerings of the faithful to the sacrifice of Christ their head, and in the sacrifice of the Mass they make present again and apply, until the coming of the Lord, the unique sacrifice of the New Testament, that namely of Christ offering himself once for all a spotless victim to the Father" [*Lumen gentium*, no. 28; cf. 1 Cor 11:26]. From this unique sacrifice their whole priestly ministry draws its strength [cf. *Presbyterorum ordinis*, no. 2]. (CCC 1566)

PROCLAMATION

The Second Vatican Council teaches that the "primary duty" of every priest is to proclaim the Gospel of God to all humanity (Mk 16:15; Rom 10:17). The Council says that "this ministry of the Word is carried out in many ways according to the various needs of those who hear and the special gifts of those who preach."[7] However, the Council goes on to say that the Eucharist is "the source and the apex of the whole work of preaching the Gospel".[8]

Although, as the *Catechism* points out, the fact that a priest is "chosen from among men of faith" (CCC 1579) and "'appointed to act on behalf of men in relation to God'"[9] does not exempt him from "all human weaknesses, the spirit of domination, error, even sin" (CCC 1550), we must still try to see our priests as "icons" of Christ, however flawed and imperfect, and we always should pray for them that they ever might be for all of us living homilies and sermons, God's servants and ours, preaching to us by the eloquence of their lives.

The great French priest Father Jean-Baptiste Lacordaire, who lived from 1802 to 1861, describes the Catholic priest in now famous words: "To live in the midst of the world without wishing its pleasures, to be a member of every family yet belonging to none, to share all sufferings, to penetrate all secrets, to heal all wounds, to go from men to God and offer Him their prayers, to return from God to men to bring pardon and hope, to have a heart of fire for charity and a heart of bronze for chastity, to teach, to pardon, to console, to bless always."

"One does not take this honor upon himself, but he is called by God just as Aaron was" (Heb 5:4). "He who does not enter the sheepfold by the door but climbs in by another way, that man is a thief and a robber; but he who enters by the door is the shepherd of the sheep" (Jn 10:1). "Only those can be sure they are called by God who are called by the lawful Bishops of His Church" (*Catechism of the Council of Trent*).

2

RELIGIOUS LIFE

Ripe Harvest

VOCATIONS

A vocation is a "call", a summons from God. Respecting the liberty in which He created us and which He gives us as a gift, God issues an invitation to all of His rational creatures to separate themselves freely from sin and join themselves to Him, in and through His divine Son, Jesus, by means of Christ's Body and Bride, which is the Catholic Church. An affirmative and permanent answer to this call is a guarantee for every sincere respondent of unending happiness. The entire human race has a vocation to join the Catholic Church. Every human being is called to faith and repentance. Pope John Paul II says that there is a "vocation which constitutes the horizon of every human heart, eternal life".[10]

The Church herself has a vocation to hope and love, a call to worship, to preach, to serve, to care, and to provide, especially in a spiritual way, for all humanity. Also, the Second Vatican Council, in its Dogmatic Constitution on the Church, speaks eloquently of the "universal vocation or call" of the whole Church and of each of her members, no matter what their personal vocations may be, to holiness. It is only within the context of these general and universal vocations that vocations to various states of life, various occupations and activities, and various specialized life-styles and work can be correctly understood.

FOURTH SUNDAY

Because it is the Sunday when the liturgical calendar calls for Bible readings at Mass that depict our Lord as the Good Shepherd, the Fourth Sunday of Easter is called Good Shepherd Sunday and has become, by rather recent custom (the last thirty-six years), an occasion when the entire Church is asked to pray in a particular way for an increase in vocations to the ordained ministry and to the consecrated life. This prayer, of course, should include a petition to God that His sovereign grace will also give to those called to the priesthood, the diaconate, and the religious life the gifts of perseverance and holiness in their vocations. This observance is one of the ways in which our Catholic Church obeys the command of her divine Founder: "Pray therefore the Lord of the harvest to send out laborers into his harvest" (Mt 9:38).

Recent Popes, including our present Holy Father, have used this occasion to issue an annual "vocation message" and to proclaim the Fourth Sunday of Easter as "World Day of Prayer for Vocations". Pope John XIII once remarked "The problem of ecclesiastical and religious vocations is a daily concern of the Pope. It is the subject of his prayer, the ardent hope of his soul." This concern should also be the subject of our own constant prayers and hope.

VATICAN II

The Second Vatican Council explicitly places the obligation to discover and promote vocations to lives of special consecration to God upon the entire Christian community. It teaches that certain special kinds of duties in this regard are given by divine providence to Catholic families, to Catholic teachers, to Catholic lay organizations, and, most of all, to religious themselves, as well as to Bishops and priests. However, no Catholic, including any with a vocation to the laity, can, without responsibility for serious neglect, fail to foster vocations to the priesthood and religious life. The Council says that it "gives primary commendation to the traditional means for this joint effort, such as persistent prayer and Christian mortification".[11]

ANNUAL MESSAGE

In his message to the Church for this year's celebration of the "World Day of Prayer for Vocations", the Supreme Pontiff takes note of our dedication of this year, 1999, to God the Father, in preparation for the Great Jubilee. The Pope says that we should see vocations to the priesthood and to the consecrated life as coming down from our heavenly Father, the Father of lights, from Whom "every good endowment and every perfect gift" derives (Jas 1:17), and Who gives these vocations to "enrich his Church".

He says,

> The Father has poured out his Spirit in abundance on his adopted children, manifesting in the various forms of consecrated life his Fatherly love, which he wishes to extend to the whole of humanity. His love is a love that awaits with patience and welcomes with rejoicing the person who has been far away; which educates and corrects; which satisfies every person's hunger for love. He continues to point out the expectations of eternal life which open the heart to hope, even in the midst of difficulties, pain and death, especially by means of those who leave everything to follow Christ, dedicating themselves totally to the establishment of his Kingdom.[12]

Our Holy Father beautifully uses the Lord's Prayer in this year's appeal as the vehicle for the major part of his message, applying each invocation and petition to the idea of vocations to the priesthood and religious life. He concludes by asking, "How can we fail to stress that the promotion of vocations to the ordained ministry and the consecrated life must become the harmonious commitment of the whole Church and of individual believers?"[13]

As he often does, the Pope composed a fine prayer to end this year's message. Among other things, he prays to God the Father, "You call us to be holy as you are holy. We pray you, never allow your Church to lack holy ministers and apostles who, with the word and the sacraments, may open the way to the encounter with you... Give to lost humanity men and women who, through the witness of a life transfigured to the image of your Son, may walk joyfully with their other brothers and sisters towards our heavenly homeland."[14]

God seems to have chosen to make the number and quality of our priests and religious dependent upon our prayers and efforts as well as upon the call of Jesus. Let us do all we can to allow that call to be heard and followed by many young people, that laborers might be found and sent out into the harvest. The fields of the world truly are ripe for an abundant harvest of souls at end of this century and this millennium.

APRIL 23, 1999

The Religious Vocation
I

BIG THREE

If a mythical visitor from another planet were to visit earth and note our American and Western European culture, view and listen to our media, and inquire about our life-styles, he might go away believing that for us the purposes of human existence are money, sex, and independence. These could be seen as the driving forces for all our activities and, far from being merely the means to an end, the very goals of our lives. How utterly counter-cultural, then, are the characteristics of consecrated religious life, marked by the three great vows of poverty, chastity, and obedience!

The *Catechism of the Catholic Church* says, "Religious life derives from the mystery of the Church. It is a gift she has received from her Lord, a gift she offers as a stable way of life to the faithful called by God to profess the counsels. Thus, the Church can both show forth Christ and acknowledge herself to be the Savior's bride. Religious life in its various forms is called to signify the very charity of God in the language of our time" (CCC 926).

Religious life is a subdivision of a larger category within the Catholic Church called "consecrated life". The Second Vatican Council calls consecrated life in the Church "the state of life... constituted by the profession of the evangelical counsels, [which,] while not entering into the hierarchical structure of the Church, belongs undeniably to her life and holiness."[15]

COUNSELS

Jesus instructs all of us who are His disciples to strive for perfection (Mt 5:48) within the Church He founded. There are certain minimal requirements that our Lord has set in place for all of His followers. However, there are those among us who are somewhat special disciples, whom God calls to go beyond the basics, to excel and not merely to qualify. As the Second Vatican Council teaches, "The state of consecrated life is a way of experiencing a 'more intimate' consecration, rooted in Baptism and dedicated totally to God."[16] The current *Code of Canon Law* says, "In the consecrated life, Christ's faithful, moved by the Holy Spirit, propose to follow Christ more nearly, to give themselves to God, who is loved above all and, pursuing the perfection of charity in the service of the Kingdom, to signify and proclaim in the Church the glory of the world to come."[17]

Speaking of vowed religious life, Saint Thomas Aquinas says, "Three stages have to be passed in order to reach perfect friendship with God. External goods have to be renounced. Carnal thoughts have to be left behind. Life has to be given up, either by suffering death for Christ or by denying one's own will. Whoever binds his whole life by vow to these works of perfection assumes the status of perfection. Such is religious life."

THE VOWS

Writing about the three vows that mark religious consecration, Pope John Paul II says,

> The *chastity* of celibates and virgins, as a manifestation of dedication to God with *an undivided heart* (cf. 1 Cor 7:32–34), is a reflection of the *infinite love* which links the three Divine Persons in the mysterious depths of the life of the Trinity, the love to which the Incarnate Word bears witness even to the point of giving his life, the love "poured into our hearts through the Holy Spirit" (Rom 5:5), which evokes a response of total love for God and the brethren. *Poverty* proclaims that God is man's only real treasure. When

poverty is lived according to the example of Christ, who, "though he was rich... became poor" (2 Cor 8:9), it becomes an expression of that *total gift of self* which the three Divine Persons make to one another. This gift overflows into creation and is fully revealed in the Incarnation of the Word and in his redemptive death. *Obedience*, practiced in imitation of Christ, whose food was to do the Father's will (cf. Jn 4:34), shows the liberating beauty of a *dependence which is not servile but filial*, marked by a deep sense of responsibility and animated by mutual trust, which is a reflection in history of the loving *harmony* between the three Divine Persons.[18]

LIFE OF GRACE

Saint Francis de Sales wrote extensively about consecrated religious life. In his works one finds such expressions as: "The religious life is not a natural life. It is above nature and its soul is given and formed by grace." "Religious orders are not formed for the purpose of gathering together perfect people, but they are for those who have the courage to aim at perfection." "When God calls any man or woman to be a religious, He binds Himself to bestow on that person all that is needed for perfection in his vocation."

Thomas Merton, in *The Waters of Siloe*, writes, "The final end proposed to the religious Orders is nothing else but God Himself: which means that their function is to bring their members, in one way or another, to the vision and possession of God, Who is the summit of all reality and the perfection of infinite Truth and the unending fullness of all joy."[19] Our Holy Father, the Bishop of Rome, says,

> The direct point of reference in [any religious] vocation is the living person of Jesus Christ. The call to the way of perfection takes shape from Him and through Him in the Holy Spirit, who continually "recalls" to new people, men and women, at different times in their lives but especially in their youth, all that Christ "has said" (Jn 14:26), especially what He "said" to the young man who asked him, "Teacher what good deed must I do to have eternal life?" (Mt 19:21; Mk 10:21; Lk 18:22). Through the reply of Christ, who looks upon His questioner "with love", the strong leaven of the mystery of the redemption penetrates the consciousness, heart and will of a person who is searching with truth and sincerity.[20]

In talking to young people who might be trying to discern a religious vocation, Blessed Pope John XXIII said, "Consult not your fears, but your hopes and dreams. Think not about your frustrations, but about your unfulfilled potential. Concern yourself not with what you tried and failed in, but with what it is still possible to do." All of us should constantly pray for an increase in vocations to the religious life and for holiness and perseverance for those so called.

JANUARY 26, 2001

The Religious Vocation
II

VARIETY

Within the Catholic Church there are many types of special, consecrated life. These include secular institutes, orders of men and women hermits, orders of consecrated virgins and widows, and societies of apostolic life. However, the form of consecrated life that is most familiar to the proverbial "man in the pew" and that is most commonly experienced among the faithful, as well as that which has the most members, is called consecrated religious life.

The Second Vatican Council notes that consecrated religious life is "based on the words and example of the Lord", that it has been commended by the Apostles, Fathers, and other teachers and shepherds of the Church through the centuries, and that the Church preserves it as a "divine gift" received from her Lord. The Council says, "Church authority has the duty, under the inspiration of the Holy Spirit, of interpreting the evangelical counsels, of regulating their practice, and finally of establishing stable forms of living according to them."[21]

All the faithful, and consequently all consecrated religious persons, have the duty to place into their lives some activity for Christ and His Church but also to maintain there a prayerful and contemplative dimension, which our Savior called "the better part" (Lk 10:42). Communities and orders of consecrated religious are basically divided into three groups on that basis: those that are predominantly contemplative, those that are predominantly active, and those that combine both aspects and are sometimes called semi-contemplative. Each of these three forms of religious life is valid, and all are an important part of the Church.

CHARISMS

A "charism" is a free gift that a person receives from God, the Holy Spirit, not for his own benefit, but for the good of the entire Church. Founders and foundresses of religious orders and communities throughout the years are the recipients of charisms and the channels of many of God's graces to His People. Of course, the ultimate judgment about the authenticity of a charism in the matter of religious communities, as in all ecclesial matters, rests with the Bishops of the Catholic Church.

The Second Vatican Council remarks:

> that by a Divine Plan a wonderful variety of religious communities grew up. This variety contributed mightily toward making the Church experienced in every good deed (see 2 Tim 3:17) and ready for a ministry of service in the building up of Christ's Body (see Eph 4:12). Not only this, but being adorned by the various gifts of her children, our Mother, the Church, becomes radiant like a Bride made beautiful for her Spouse (see Rev 21:2), and through her God's manifold wisdom can reveal itself to the world (see Eph 3:10).
>
> But, whatever the diversity of their spiritual endowments, all who are called by God to practice the evangelical counsels, and who do so faithfully, devote themselves in a special way to the Lord. They imitate Christ, chaste and poor (see Mt 8:20; Lk 9:58), Who, by an obedience which carried Him even to death on the Cross (see Phil 2:8), redeemed men and made them holy. As a consequence, impelled by a love which the Holy Spirit has poured into their hearts (see Rom 5:5), those Christians who are consecrated in religious vows spend themselves ever increasingly for Christ and for His Body, the Church (see Col 1:24).[22]

STATUS

Consecrated religious life can include the clergy as well as the laity. The Second Vatican Council teaches, "From the point of view of the divine and hierarchical structure of the Church, the religious state of life is not an intermediate one between the clerical and the lay states. Rather, the faithful of Christ are called by God from both these latter states of life so that they may enjoy this particular gift in the life of the Church and thus each in his own way can forward the saving mission of the Church."[23]

Consecrated religious who are laymen and women vowed to observe the evangelical counsels of poverty, chastity, and obedience are sometimes referred to as "lay sisters" or "lay brothers". The majority of priests in the Church are diocesan clergy (sometimes called secular priests). The diocesan clergy, even more than ordinary lay people, are required to observe the "spirit" of the evangelical counsels, even if they are not specifically bound to them by vows. Diocesan priests in the Latin Rite, of course, are bound by a solemn promise to God to observe sacred celibacy for the sake of God's kingdom (see Mt 19:12) and by a similar solemn promise of obedience to their Bishop. Although they can acquire and own their own property, diocesan priests must live in simplicity and detachment and give away their surplus wealth to the Church or to the poor.

However, there are other priests who belong to religious orders or communities. Some are canons regular, monks, clerks regular, mendicants, and so on. ("regular" here means those who follow a specific "rule of life," from the Latin word for rule, *regula*). Some religious communities, lay, clerical, or combined, are under the jurisdiction of a local Bishop and are called communities "of diocesan right". Others are exempt from the jurisdiction of a local Bishop in their religious and community life and come directly under the jurisdiction of the Pope. They are called communities "of pontifical right". A local Bishop, of course, has the right and duty to supervise and control all aspects of the external apostolate in his diocese, including that exercised by exempt religious. Consecrated life in general and consecrated religious life specifically is regulated by many Church laws found in the Code of Canon Law.

The *Catechism of the Catholic Church* says,

> All religious, whether exempt or not, take their place among the collaborators of the diocesan bishop in his pastoral duty [cf. *Christus Dominus*, nos. 33–35; CIC, can. 591]. From the outset of the work of evangelization, the missionary "planting" and expansion of the Church require the presence of the religious life in all its forms [cf. *Ad gentes*, nos 18; 40]. "History witnesses to the outstanding service rendered by religious families in the propagation of the faith and in the formation of new Churches: from the ancient monastic institutions to the medieval orders, all the way to the more recent congregations [John Paul II, encyclical *Redemptoris missio* (December 7, 1990), no. 69]. (CCC 927)

FEBRUARY 2, 2001

3

FAMILY LIFE

The Rights of Families
I

THE CHARTER

Just over twenty years ago an international synod of Bishops was held in Rome that treated the theme "The Role of the Christian Family in the Modern World". The Bishops at that 1980 synod asked Pope John Paul II to study their presentations, synthesize them, critique them, and then issue an appropriate document, in his name, concerning the issues they raised. The result was an apostolic exhortation, dated November 22, 1981, entitled in Latin *Familiaris consortio.*

The apostolic exhortation, a document of significant moral, theological, and pastoral importance, continues to have an important impact on the way that Catholic doctrine regarding families is presented and taught. However, the Holy See, at the direction of the Pope, also wanted some of the matters presented by the synodal fathers to be presented to a wider audience than only the Catholic faithful. Therefore, the Holy See also published a *Charter of the Rights of the Family*, presented "to all persons, institutions, and authorities concerned with the mission of the family in today's world". The *Charter* aimed at presenting "to all ..., be they Christian or not, a formulation—as complete and ordered as possible—of the fundamental rights that are inherent in that natural and universal society which is the family".[24]

AUDIENCE

The *Charter* is meant to express what should be in every human conscience about family rights and to set out values common to all humanity. It does this, of course, from a Christian vision in which supernatural, divine revelation enlightens and clarifies the natural reality of the family. It is intended to defend the essential rights of every human family and to be a point of reference for the drawing up of legislation and civil-law family policy.

The *Charter* is meant for all people of goodwill, including certainly all the members of the Catholic Church. In fact, it states that it is meant to bear clear witness to Christian convictions concerning the irreplaceable mission of the family and to see that families and parents receive the necessary support and encouragement to carry out their God-given tasks.

In our times, when family life and family values are held up to constant ridicule and scorn, when sexual promiscuity and perversion are exalted and flaunted, when the institution of marriage is disdained, and when divorce and multiple remarriages are usual, it seems more important than ever for sincere Catholics to be aware of the apostolic exhortation and to become familiar with the *Charter*. This is especially true for those who are called to the vocation of marriage and parenting. In the general population of the United States at the present time, half of all first-time births are to unwed mothers, millions of couples cohabit without marriage, and the birthrate among unmarrieds has climbed more than 15 percent since 1990. This neopaganism affects us all. Even the healthiest fish cannot last too long when forced to swim in poisoned waters.

STRUCTURE

The *Charter* is divided into a preamble and twelve articles of varying length. The thirteen sections of the preamble set forth the basis on which the rest of the *Charter* rests. It says, among other things, that "the family is based on marriage, that intimate union of life in complementarity between a man and a woman which is constituted in the freely contracted and publicly expressed indissoluble bond of matrimony and is open to the transmission of life" (B). What gives every marriage its irrevocable character is the fact that each marriage is a three-way contract between a man, a woman, and God. If it were merely an agreement between a man and a woman and both agreed to dissolve the contract, this could be done. However, God, being the third party to the contract, makes a marriage union permanent (see Mk 10:2–12). "Marriage is the natural institution to which the mission of transmitting life is exclusively entrusted" (C).

Pope Leo XIII writes that the family, the society of a man's house, is "a true society and one older than any state. Consequently, it has rights and duties peculiar to itself which are quite independent of any government." Pope Pius XI states, "The family is more sacred than the state, and humans are brought into existence, not for the earth and for time, but rather for heaven and for eternity." It is not governments that bring families into existence, but God Himself.

This is set out in the *Charter*, "The family, a natural society, exists prior to the State or any other community and possesses inherent rights which are inalienable. The family constitutes, much more than a mere juridical, social, and economic unit, a community of love and solidarity, which is uniquely suited to teach and transmit cultural, ethical, social, spiritual, and religious values, essential for the development and well-being of its own members and of all society" (D–E).

Some Rights

The *Charter* says, "The spouses have the inalienable right to found a family and to decide on the spacing of births and the number of children to be born, taking into full consideration their duties towards themselves, their children already born, the family and society, in a just hierarchy of values and in accordance with the objective moral order, which excludes recourse to contraception, sterilization, and abortion" (art. 3). It goes on to say, "In international relations, economic aid for the advancement of peoples must not be conditioned on acceptance of programs of contraception, sterilization, or abortion. The family has a right to assistance by society in the bearing and rearing of children. Those married couples who have a large family have a right to adequate aid and should not be subjected to discrimination" (art. 3, nos. 2–3).

The *Charter* states, "Human life must be respected and protected absolutely from the moment of conception. Abortion is a direct violation of the fundamental right to life of the human being. Respect for the dignity of the human being excludes all experimental manipulation or exploitation of the human embryo" (art. 4, a–b). The *Charter* surely deserves study and energetic application to our culture and times by every conscientious Catholic adult.

JANUARY 5, 2001

The Rights of Families
II

The Institution

Our Holy Father, Pope John Paul II, teaches, "The Church... finds in the family, born from the sacrament [of Matrimony], the cradle and setting in which she can enter the human generations and where these in their turn can enter the Church."[25] The Pope goes on to say, "The family has the mission to guard, reveal, and communicate love, and this is a living reflection of and a real sharing in God's love for humanity and the love of Christ the Lord for the Church, His Bride... . Thus,... [there are] four general tasks for a family: forming a community of persons; serving life; participating in the development of society; [and] sharing in the life and mission of the Church."[26]

G. K. Chesterton observes, "Round the family do indeed gather the sanctities that separate men from ants and bees. Decency is the curtain of that tent; liberty is the wall of that city; property is but the family farm; and honour is the family flag."[27] Father R. H. Benson notes, "The union of a family lies in love, because love is the only place where there can be a balance between authority and liberty."

FAMILY PRAYER

Everyone probably remembers the slogan of Father Patrick Peyton, "The family that prays together, stays together." In that same vein, Pope John Paul II says,

> Family prayer [is important because it] is offered in common by husband and wife together, parents and children... Joys and sorrows, hopes and disappointments, births and birthday celebrations, wedding anniversaries..., departures, separations and homecomings, important and far-reaching decisions, the death of those who are dear, and so on — all of these mark God's loving intervention in the family's history. They should be seen as suitable moments for thanksgiving, for petition, for trusting abandonment of the family into the hands of their common Father in heaven. The dignity and responsibility of the Christian family as the domestic Church can be achieved only with God's unceasing aid, which will surely be granted if it is humbly and trustingly petitioned in prayer.[28]

The Supreme Pontiff teaches, "By reason of their dignity and mission, Christian parents have the specific responsibility of educating their children in prayer, introducing them to gradual discovery of the mystery of God and to personal dialogue with Him."[29] The Second Vatican Council teaches, "It is particularly in the Christian family, enriched by the grace and office of the sacrament of Matrimony, that, from their earliest years, children must be taught, according to the faith received in Baptism, to have a knowledge of God, to worship Him, and love to their neighbor."[30]

VOCATIONS

In many ways the Catholic family is the place where the call of Christ to a vocation to a life of special consecration to God can be discovered and grow. Catholic spouses should always consider one of the highest honors a family can receive from God would be to have a priest-son or a daughter-nun. A good Catholic family is, as the Holy See has often pointed out, a "first seminary" or a "first convent". Parents have a duty to advise their children about such things as the choice of a spouse or about discerning a vocation to the priesthood or religious life. However, it is wrong, and could even be seriously sinful, for parents to try to force or coerce their children, even their minor children, in these matters.

Our Holy Father remarks,

> Virginity or celibacy for the sake of the Kingdom of God not only does not contradict the dignity of marriage but presupposes it.... When marriage is not esteemed, neither can consecrated virginity or celibacy exist; when human sexuality is not regarded as a great value given by the Creator, the renunciation of it for the sake of the Kingdom of Heaven loses its meaning... In virginity and celibacy, the human being is awaiting, also in a bodily way, the eschatological marriage of Christ with the Church.[31]

CHARTER

The 1981 *Charter of the Rights of the Family*, issued to "all people of goodwill" by the Holy See, has some important articles that touch on many of these topics. For instance, it says, "With due respect for the traditional role of families in certain cultures in guiding the decisions of their children, all pressure which would impede the choice of a specific person as spouse is to be avoided" (art. 1, no. 2b). "All persons have the right to the free choice of their state in life and thus to marry and establish a family or to remain single" (art. 1).

The *Charter* speaks to many issues relevant to our American situation. For instance, it addresses the matter of our godless public school system: "The rights of parents are violated when a compulsory system of education is imposed by the State from which all religious formation is excluded" (art. 5d). Parents have the right to ensure that their children are not compelled to attend classes which are not in agreement with their own moral and religious convictions. In particular, sex education is a basic right of the parents and must always be carried out under their close supervision, whether at home or in educational centers chosen and controlled by them" (art. 5c). The *Charter* notes, "Parents have the right to freely choose schools or other means necessary to educate their children in keeping with their convictions. Public authorities must ensure that public subsidies are so allocated that parents are truly free to exercise this right without incurring unjust burdens. Parents should not have to sustain, directly or indirectly, extra charges which would deny or unjustly limit the exercise of this freedom" (art. 5b).

Also found in the *Charter*: "The institutional value of marriage should be upheld by the public authorities. The situation of non-married couples must not be placed on the same level as marriage duly contracted" (art. 1c). "Public authorities must respect and foster the dignity, lawful independence, privacy, integrity, and stability of every family" (art. 6a). "Every family has the right to live freely its own domestic religious life under the guidance of the parents, as well as a right to profess publicly and to propagate the faith, to take part in public worship and in freely chosen programs of religious instruction, without suffering discrimination" (art. 7).

Pope John Paul II said, "The future of humanity passes by way of the family. It is therefore indispensable and urgent that every person of good will should endeavor to save and foster the values and requirements of the family."[32]

JANUARY 12, 2001

The Rights of Families
III

CATECHISM

In its consideration of the fourth commandment, the *Catechism of the Catholic Church* has a rather extensive treatment of the "Christian Family". It notes, "The Christian family is a communion of persons, a sign and image of the communion of the Father and the Son in the Holy Spirit. In the procreation and education of children it reflects the Father's work of creation. It is called to partake of the prayer and sacrifice of Christ. Daily prayer and the reading of the Word of God strengthen it in charity. The Christian family has an evangelizing and missionary task" (CCC 2205).

The *Catechism* also observes, citing the Second Vatican Council, "The relationships within the family bring an affinity of feelings, affections, and interests, arising above all from the members' respect for one another. The family is a *privileged community* called to achieve a 'sharing of thought and common deliberation by the spouses as well as their eager cooperation as parents in the children's upbringing'."[33]

SOCIAL JUSTICE

The 1981 *Charter of the Rights of the Family*, issued by the Holy See, sets forth some social justice requirements due to all families, some of which rights were subsequently reiterated in the *Catechism*. "Families have the right to economic conditions which assure them a standard of living appropriate to their dignity and full development. They should not be impeded from acquiring and maintaining private possessions which would favor stable family life; the laws concerning inheritance or transmission of property must respect the needs and rights of family members."[34] The *Charter* says, "Families have a right to measures in the social domain which take into account their needs, especially in the event of the premature death of one or both parents, of the abandonment of one of the spouses, of accident or sickness or invalidity, in the case of unemployment, or whenever the family has to bear extra burdens on behalf of its members for reasons of old age, physical or mental handicaps, or the education of the children" (art.9b).

The Holy See asserts in the *Charter*,

> Remuneration for work must be sufficient for establishing and maintaining a family with dignity, either through a suitable salary called a "family wage", or through other social measures such as family allowances or the remuneration of the work in the home of one of the parents; it should be such that mothers will not be obliged to work outside the home to the detriment of family life and especially of the training of the children. The work of a mother in the home must be recognized and respected because of its value for the family and for society. (art. 10 a–b)

OTHER RIGHTS

Sometimes certain aspects of family life are not clearly seen by us, even when thinking about the fourth commandment, particularly if these do not directly touch upon our own immediate experiences. However, from time to time it is useful to reflect upon the ensemble of family rights and about our own duty to foster and protect these rights. The *Catechism* teaches, "Where families cannot fulfill their responsibilities, other social bodies have the duty of helping them and of supporting the institution of the family. Following the principle of subsidiarity, larger communities should take care not to usurp the family's prerogatives or interfere in its life" (CCC 2209).

The *Charter* mentions, "The elderly have the right to find within their own family or, when this is not possible, in suitable institutions, an environment which will enable them to live their later years of life in serenity while pursuing those activities which are compatible with their age and which will enable them to participate in social life" (art. 9c). Our Holy Father notes that the elderly in a family "carry out the important mission of being a witness to the past and being a source of wisdom for the young". [35] The *Charter* adds, "The extended family system, where it exists, should be held in esteem and helped to carry out better its traditional role of solidarity and mutual assistance, while at the same time respecting the rights of the nuclear family and the personal dignity of each member" (art. 6c).

TEACHING

Following the doctrine about family life found in Sacred Scripture (Eph 5:21—

6:4; Col 3:18–21; 1 Pet 3:1–7: Sir 3:2–14; Lk 2:51–52), Pope John Paul II has said, "The Christian family constitutes a specific revelation and realization of ecclesial communion, and for this reason too it can and should be called 'the domestic Church'."[36] "It is a community of faith, hope, and charity; it assumes singular importance in the Church, as is evident in the New Testament" (CCC 2204).[37]

The Pope teaches that,

> the equal dignity and responsibility of men and women fully justifies women's access to public functions. On the other hand, the true advancement of women requires that clear recognition be given to the value of their maternal and family role, by comparison with all other public roles and all other professions... All of this does not mean for women a renunciation of their femininity or an imitation of the male role, but the fullness of a true feminine humanity which should be expressed in their activity, whether in the family or outside of it.[38]

The Roman Pontiff, speaking to husbands, quotes Saint Ambrose, "You are not [your wife's] master, but her husband; she was not given to you to be your slave, but your wife.... Reciprocate her attentiveness to you and be grateful to her for her love."[39] The Pope says, "As for the Christian [husband], he is called upon to develop a new attitude of love, manifesting towards his wife a charity that is both gentle and strong like that which Christ has for the Church [Eph 5:25]."[40]

Our Holy Father says,

> By proclaiming the word of God, the Church reveals to the Christian family its true identity, what it is and should be according to the Lord's plan; by celebrating the sacraments, the Church enriches and strengthens the Christian family with the grace of Christ... By the continuous proclamation of the new commandment of love, the Church encourages and guides the Christian family to the service of love, so that it may imitate and relive the same self-giving and sacrificial love that the Lord Jesus has for the whole human race.[41]

JANUARY 19, 2001

Fatherhood

CRISIS

In modern society, especially in our own country, there appears to be a growing crisis in the matter of fatherhood. The recent rise of feminism, some of which has a certain validity in its concerns, but much of which is radical, ugly, aggressive, and even irrational, has contributed to the crisis in fatherhood. The lack of any objective moral standards in the area of sex, the widespread promulgation of pornography even in prime-time television, the plague of cheap and easy divorce, the use of contraception, the practice of abortion, the scourge of narcotic and other addictions, the general atmosphere of depraved hedonism and sordid materialism, all seem to be contributing to the absence of fathers in American homes, along with a frivolous disregard on the part of many men for the vows, promises, and commitments they once made. It is estimated that by the year 2000 more than half of all American children will find themselves being raised in homes without a father.

Children raised in homes without fathers statistically are shown to be more prone to receiving and later bestowing physical and sexual abuse, to juvenile delinquency and other forms of antisocial behavior, to economic destitution, to promiscuity, to future marital instability and divorce, and to poor academic performance in school.

GOD'S WORD

As Father's Day draws near, it is useful to remember the high vocation that is involved in being a father and the grave responsibility that accompanies it. Saint Paul writes in the Bible, "I bow my knees before the Father [of our Lord Jesus Christ], from whom every family in heaven and on earth is named" (Eph 3:14). When Jesus instructs us (Mt 23:9) to "call no man your Father on earth, for you have one Father, who is in heaven", He is not forbidding us to use the term "father" for our physical progenitor or for our spiritual fathers, our priests. But, rather, He is reminding us that their fatherhood is only a participation in the unique fatherhood of God Himself and must ever be seen as such.

A singular part of Christ's revelation is His teaching that we are permitted to call God "our Father" (Mt 6:9 and Lk 11:2). This kind of intimacy is possible for us, without committing the sin of blasphemy, because we actually share the very life and nature of God when we are in the state of sanctifying grace (2 Pet 1:4). Created grace brings with it always Uncreated Grace, which is the Holy Spirit, God Himself. This presence of God in those who are justified and sanctified makes it possible for them to use a family word in speaking to and about their almighty Creator, the word "Abba" (Rom 8:15 and Gal 4:5–6).

SAINT JOSEPH

The holy husband of Mary and the foster father of Jesus is surely an important role model for every Catholic husband and father. Because it is assumed from further lack of mention of Saint Joseph after Christ began His public life that he had earlier died, he is held out as an example of a person experiencing a happy death (with Jesus and Mary at his deathbed). We know he was a carpenter and humbly supported the Holy Family with the work of his hands. A "just man", he is depicted by Sacred Scripture as sensitive to the feelings of others, utterly responsive and obedient to God, and bravely facing life's vicissitudes, especially in the trip to Bethlehem, the flight into Egypt, and the loss of the Child Jesus in the Jewish Temple.

The old hymn says, "O Blessed Saint Joseph, how great was thy worth, that God deigned to call thee His father on earth!" We know little about this "just man". Some speculate that he was a widower when he became betrothed to Mary and that this accounts for the "brothers and sisters" of Jesus mentioned in the New Testament. Mary, of course, perpetually was a virgin, before, during, and after the birth of Christ. It is also possible that the "brothers and sisters" were simply cousins or kinsfolk of our Savior. We can only guess about such things. However, the value of Saint Joseph's example and prayers for Catholic husbands and fathers is unquestionable.

ADVICE

Recently, the Bishop of Peoria, John Myers, wrote a pastoral letter to his people about "Fathers and Fatherhood". In it he gave some points of advice to those who have received the vocation of being fathers. His points are worth repeating here. First, fathers should trust in the Lord and the heavenly Father's providence for themselves and their families. Such trust comes from the practice of prayer, the sacraments, study of Sacred Scripture, and recollection.

Second, fathers should cultivate those virtues they need as a spouse, disciple, and father, such as humility, compassion, faith, fidelity to one's word, and so on. Third, fathers should share their faith and prayer life with their family and love the Catholic Church, staying close to her always. Fourth, fathers should remember that their marriage covenant will give them the necessary actual graces to enable them to know how to impart their moral and religious values and principles to their children.

Fifth, fathers should love their wives, support them, affirm them, esteem them as equal and responsible partners in the marriage bond and in the task of child rearing, and by action and word they should constantly communicate the fact of their love to their spouses. Sixth, fathers must spend time with their families, not only in recreation and leisure, but also in worship and in catechetical and religious formation of their children all the way through high school. Seventh, fathers should not abandon the task of discipline and, when necessary, punishment of children to their wives; rather, they should always undertake these duties together with them, not harming their children by being too severe and demanding or by being too permissive and indulgent.

Fathers are responsible for the protection and support of their families. This must include, of course, moral and spiritual protection and support as much as material, financial, and physical support and protection. Saint Joseph, pray for those called by God to be fathers!

JUNE 6, 1997

Children

RIGHTS

It can sometimes be forgotten that children have certain rights. As they grow older, of course, these rights have corresponding duties attached to them. Pope John Paul II says, "In the family, which is a community of persons, special attention must be devoted to the children by developing a profound esteem for their personal dignity and a great respect and generous concern for their rights."[42] Our Holy Father goes on to say, "Acceptance, love, esteem, many-sided and united material, emotional, educational, and spiritual concern for every child that comes into this world should always constitute a distinctive, essential characteristic of all Christians, in particular of the Christian family."[43] The Pope mentions that children "offer their own precious contribution to building up the family community and even to the sanctification of their parents".[44]

The vocation of parenthood, which is cooperation with God in bringing new human life into this world, requires that parents accept the awesome responsibility not only for the bodily well-being of their offspring, but also for their spiritual formation, education, and welfare.

DISCIPLINE

It is clearly one of the rights of children to be brought up in a family where balanced discipline is part of everyday life. Parents who are too permissive and indulgent toward children are as bad as parents who are too severe. Sometimes misguided parents try to buy the affection of their children by shirking their obligation to rebuke and even punish inappropriate behavior or language. Sometimes, especially if there is some tension in the parents' relationship with each other, one parent will cast the other in the role of punisher or naysayer, while trying to retain his own popularity with the children.

As children grow older and get closer toward emancipation from their God-given duty of obedience (Ex 20:12; Deut 5:16; Eph 6:1–3; Prov 6:20), they deserve and need more trust, privacy, and personal autonomy. Nevertheless, even teenage youngsters require and have a right to clearly set boundaries, rules, and limits, as well as their fair enforcement by their parents (Sir 30:1–2). Indeed, even children over eighteen years of age who continue to live in their parents' home are morally obliged to obey their parents in those matters that pertain to the good order of the household.

EDUCATION

The Holy See, in the *Charter of the Rights of the Family*, issued on October 22, 1983, asserted again what the Catholic Church has always taught: "Since they have conferred life on their children, parents have the original, primary, and inalienable right to educate them; hence, they must be acknowledged as the first and foremost educators of their children" (art. 5). Children have a right to an education not only in secular and profane knowledge, but also, before all else, in matters spiritual. Physical or material child abuse or neglect is a heinous thing, but spiritual abuse or neglect of children is even worse, since that can have eternal consequences.

Modern Catholic parents should themselves be familiar with the *Catechism of the Catholic Church* and should ensure that their children in Catholic schools (which is highly preferable) or in parish CCD programs truly know, understand, and accept the teaching of Jesus Christ, as this comes to us in its fullness and beauty through the Catholic Church. The Catholic home should be, as the *Catechism* says, the place where children are taught to "be generous and tireless in forgiving one another for offenses, quarrels, [and] injustices" (CCC 2227). As much by example as by words, parents must teach their children to pray, to love the Mass and the sacraments, to respect the Church and her ministers, and to support and participate in the local parish.

Of course, a solid foundation for supernatural virtue must be laid in the natural virtues, such as honesty, modesty, courtesy, toleration, respect for people who are different, and consideration for the handicapped and for those materially less fortunate. This kind of education in a home is more frequently "caught" by children rather than formally "taught" to them. Parents must be careful that their children are not learning contrary values from their friends and from the media.

CHOICE OF LIFE

One of the important rights that children have is that of choosing their profession and state of life. However, as the *Catechism* puts it, "They should assume their new responsibilities within a trusting relationship with their parents, willingly asking and receiving their advice and counsel. Parents should be careful not to exert pressure on their children either in the choice of a profession or in that of a spouse. This necessary restraint does not prevent them—quite the contrary—from giving their children judicious advice" (CCC 2230).

Surely if Christ honors a family by giving one of its children a vocation to the priesthood or religious life, parents should never try to influence a child for or against such a call, but rather with prayer and affection they should assist a child to discern God's will.

Parents are not morally bound to provide for a child's postsecondary education. Many parents help with their children's college education, if they are able to do so, but there is no requirement to do that. While retaining strong family ties of affection and interest, parents, of course, should not interfere with the lives of their adult children or with their families or lay upon them unnecessary "guilt trips". Children, of course, even when they no longer must obey their parents, are obliged always to show them love and respect. Children also must take care of their parents in their old age, if they become needy, but, naturally, a person's own spouse and children have priority.

OCTOBER 25, 1996

The Lay Vocation

RIGHTS

In the columns about the lay vocation that I wrote in September 1992 and last May, there was a significant amount of information about the duties and obligations as well as about the dignity of the lay vocation in the Catholic Church. Situated in the universal call to holiness, which was reemphasized by the Second Vatican Council, the lay vocation is very important and very noble.

Laymen and laywomen are called upon to sanctify the secular world, especially the home, family, workplace, the field of culture, business, commerce, art, entertainment, politics, economics, and the like. They are called and commissioned to promote Catholic missions and missionary effort and to foster vocations to the priesthood and religious life. They are to be spiritual "yeast and salt" for the world, bringing Christ to every area of human life and activity.

It is interesting to note, however, that the Second Vatican Council also speaks about the rights of the laity in the Church. These rights, which are set forth in the Dogmatic Constitution on the Church issued by that Council, are specified in its decree on the laity and also promulgated in the 1983 Code of Canon Law for the Church.

PRIESTHOOD

Saint Peter, the first Pope, teaches us that we constitute a "royal priesthood" (1 Pet 2:9). The indelible character that each Catholic receives in Baptism (and Confirmation) is a share in the unique priesthood of Jesus Christ, Who is the only Mediator between God and man (1Tim 2:5). The share in Christ's priesthood, of course, that is possessed by the laity is different not only in degree but also in essence from that which is possessed by a man who has received Holy Orders.

Nevertheless, this share in the priesthood of Jesus, which bestows many obligations and duties upon Catholic lay people, also gives to each lay person certain rights, such as the right to worship God by receiving the sacraments and, in the case of matrimony, of administering a sacrament. Only an ordained priest can confect the Holy Eucharist, making present the paschal mystery and substantial presence of Christ in the Blessed Sacrament. However, at Mass, once transubstantiation has occurred, all the baptized participate in the "offering" of the spotless Victim to the Father, not as mere onlookers, but as genuine participants. This is why lay people not only attend Mass but also participate in the Mass.

WORD AND LITURGY

The Second Vatican Council states that lay people have a right to receive the Word of God. This right, commentators inform us, means the fullness of God's revelation, as contained in Sacred Scripture and Sacred Tradition. The Word of God in words of men, as proclaimed by the Church both in "kerygma" and in catechesis, must be imparted to the laity in all its integrity and purity.

Because the sacred liturgy is the worshipping of God the Father by the Whole Christ, Head and members, in the Holy Spirit, it is not the private action of any individual or group. In this regard the Second Vatican Council teaches that "... no other person [except Bishops], not even a priest, may add, remove, or change anything in the liturgy on his own authority."[45] Within the limits allowed by some lawful options, the objectivity of the liturgy must be maintained. Lay people have the right to participate in legal and lawfully conducted liturgical actions, and it is a violation of their rights, even if they were to acquiesce in or agree to such a violation, to disobey the directives of the Second Vatican Council in this regard.

NEEDS AND DESIRES

Another right that lay people have always had in the Church but that has received an explicit endorsement by the Second Vatican Council is the right to make known to the leaders of the Church their spiritual needs and desires. The exercise of this right, of course, does not impose a corresponding duty on the leaders necessarily to satisfy what lay people may discern as their needs and desires. However, their duty to listen appears implicit in the lay person's right to "make known".

In the same direction the Second Vatican Council talks about a right that is linked with an obligation on the part of lay people to give their opinion and advice when they have special skills and knowledge or particular competence in some matters pertaining to the good of the Church. Once again, this does not necessarily mean that "those whom the Holy Spirit has raised up to shepherd the Church" necessarily must heed the advice or accept the opinions expressed. Nonetheless, lay people should be conscious of this right and, indeed, this duty that may sometimes come to them. Obviously, the exercise of these rights must not prescind from those qualities that should always mark Christian conduct in such matters, namely, reverence, respect, humility, prudence, courage, and, above all, charity.

SYNOD

The coming synod here in our Lincoln Diocese has already provided an excellent opportunity for the laity in southern Nebraska to exercise their rights and duties as members of the Family of God. The discussions and listening sessions in the thirteen deaneries were wonderful occasions of ecclesial life and vigor. The celebration of the Synod itself will be a time when the elected and appointed lay delegates will be able to represent the views of the almost ninety thousand Catholics in our Diocese, as they join with the priest delegates and religious delegates to help our Diocesan Family prepare for the next century and the next millennium.

May the synod truly be a "walking together down the same road" and "a journey of faith into the twenty-first century". Let us pray and work to that end so that we may contribute substantially to God's glory and the salvation of souls. After the conclusion of the synod there will be the vital aspect of applying its work effectively. In this, once more, the laity of the Diocese will have to play an essential role.

AUGUST 2, 1996

The Dignity of Women

EVANGELIZERS

In this Easter season it is appropriate to remember that God's providence arranged that the first human witnesses to Christ's Resurrection, aside perhaps from the terrified soldiers guarding the sepulcher of Jesus (Mt 28:4), were holy women. Instructed by angels and by the risen Christ Himself, they were commissioned "to go and tell", that is, to be evangelizers (Mt 28:7–10; Mk16:7–8; Lk 24:1–10; Jn 20:1–18). In effect, those devoted and loyal women, some of whom remained at the foot of the Cross (Jn 19:25) even when other cowardly disciples of our Lord had fled, were commissioned to be the first to carry "the good news", that is, the gospel or the "evangel" to others, specifically to the apostles. Some commentators suggest that it is even possible to imagine that one of the two disciples whom the risen Lord met on the road to Emmaus may have been a woman. Only the name of one man, Cleopas (Lk 24:13–35), is mentioned. It might be that the two were a married couple.

IN THE GOSPELS

In His earthly life, Jesus willingly accepted assistance and financial support from His feminine disciples (Lk 8:1–3). When He thought it fitting, He easily broke the conventions and customs of the time in dealing with women (Jn 4:7–9). He had a special affection for Martha and Mary (Lk 10:38–42; Jn 11:1–45). Women were sometimes the objects of His miraculous work (Lk 8:40–56; 7:11–15; 13:10–13; Mk 7:24–30; 1:29–31). As is well known, He saved an adulteress from death (Jn 8:3–11) and He accepted the homage of the woman who was known as a "public sinner" (Lk 7:37–47).

He had special words of exhortation and instruction for those dedicated women who accompanied Him on His way of the Cross (Lk 23:28). In His parables He often spoke to and about women. For instance, He spoke about the lost coin (Lk 15:8–10), about yeast and dough (Mt 13:33), about bridesmaids (Mt 25:1–13), and about the widow's mite (Lk 21:1–4).

COMPREHENSIVE

An exceptionally fine treatment of women's dignity, as seen and taught by the Catholic Church, can be found in the apostolic letter of Pope John Paul II entitled *Mulieris dignitatem*, dated August 15, 1988. In that important document, which deserves the reading and study of all Christians, our Holy Father approvingly quotes part of the "closing message" of the Second Vatican Council: "The hour is coming, in fact has come, when the vocation of women is being acknowledged in its fullness, the hour in which women acquire in the world an influence, an effect and a power never hitherto achieved. That is why, at this moment when the human race is undergoing so deep a transformation, women imbued with the spirit of the Gospel can do so much to aid humanity in not falling."[46]

As she has through her two thousand years of history, the Catholic Church has brought true Christian liberation to women. One only need look at the situation in which non-Christian lands and cultures place women even today to illustrate this fact.

HISTORY

The great feminine figures of the Old Testament, Sarah, Rebekah, Rachel, Ruth, Judith, Deborah, and so on, are, of course, surpassed by the most magnificent creature God created, the "Woman" of the New Testament, the Blessed Virgin Mary (Gal 4:4–6; Jn 2:4; 19:26).

Pope John Paul II notes that the two grand vocations that can come to women are motherhood and virginity. He says, "In the light of the Gospel, [these vocations] acquire their full meaning and value in Mary, who as a virgin became the Mother of the Son of God. These *two dimensions of the female vocation* were united in her in an exceptional manner, in such a way that one did not exclude the other but wonderfully complemented it."[47]

IN THE CHURCH

In addition to valid and legitimate modern concerns about female equality, we all know that there currently exists another kind "feminism" in our culture and sometimes even within the Church, a false kind, seeking to coarsen and "masculinize" women, trying to defy and reconfigure nature itself, sometimes even advocating sexual perversion, the right to kill babies before birth, and other monstrous activities. Capitalizing on and often exaggerating past injustices, this wicked form of feminism can occasionally assume grotesque forms.

For example, some people, forgetting or denying the truth of the spousal relationship between Christ and His Catholic Church, teach the erroneous and evil doctrine that women could be ordained to the priesthood. Gender equality is not the same as gender interchangeability. Such people also overlook the fact that the greatest and most important people in the Church are not those who have power and authority but those who are holy. The Church's grand history is not made by prelates; rather it is composed of saints.

Woman are utterly necessary in this history, which contains Doctors of our Church, such as Saint Catherine of Siena, Saint Teresa of Avila, Saint Thérèse of Lisieux, and great women such as Saint Monica, Saint Hedwig, Saint Olga, Saint Frances

Cabrini, Saint Elizabeth Ann Seton, Saint Joan of Arc, Saint Elizabeth of Hungary, Saint Mary Ward, Saint Rose Philippine Duchesne, Saint Edith Stein, Blessed Kateri Tekakwitha, Blessed Katherine Drexel, and many others. The fortitude of our magnificent women martyrs was as great as that of any others. Think of Saint Lucy, Saint Barbara, Saint Perpetua, Saint Felicity, Saint Maria Goretti, Saint Cecilia, Saint Agnes, and many more.

As our Holy Father says, "In our own days too the Church is constantly enriched by the witness of the many women who fulfill their vocation to holiness. Holy women are an incarnation of the feminine ideal; they are also a model for all Christians, a model of the "sequela Christi" [following of Christ], an example of how the Bride must respond with love to the love of the Bridegroom."[48]

APRIL 9, 1999

Older Persons

U. N. - YEAR

Each year in October the United Nations celebrates a "World Day of Older Persons". On the occasion of last year's celebration of that "World Day", the present Secretary General of the UN, Kofi Annan, announced that this year of 1999 would be an "International Year of Older Persons", with the theme "Towards a Society for All Ages".

The Pontifical Council for the Laity of the Holy See has noted that such a "society for all ages is, therefore, a multigenerational society committed to creating the conditions of life able to fulfill the great potential that older people still have."[49] The Pontifical Council went on to say that the Holy See supports the creation of such a society and that the Council itself wishes to contribute to the celebration of the International Year of Older Persons.

The UN considers as older persons (in America we usually use the term "senior citizens") those in the "third age", that is, between sixty-five and seventy-five years old, as well as those in the "fourth age", those who are over seventy-five years old. The UN groups the principles concerning older persons, which it studies from an international perspective, under five headings: independence, participation, care, self-fulfillment, and dignity. The organization is busy now formulating "global objectives relating to aging for the year 2001".[50]

THE POPE

Our Holy Father has spoken frequently to and about older persons and in the context of the ongoing UN celebration, has made more remarks than usual about them. He says, "Old age is also a gift for which we are called to give thanks, a gift for the person on in years, for society, and for the Church."[51] On another occasion he says, "Brothers and sisters of the older generation, you are a treasure for the Church, you are a blessing for the world."[52]

Addressing the elderly, Pope John Paul II says,

> Do not be surprised by the temptation of interior solitude. Notwithstanding the complexity of your problems... and the forces which gradually wear you down, and despite the inadequacies of social organizations, the delays of official legislation, and a selfish society's failure to understand, you are not... on the margins of the life of the Church, passive elements in a world of excessive motion, but active subjects of a period in human existence which is rich in spirituality and humanity. You still have a mission to fulfill and a contribution to make.[53]

LOOKING BACK

The Supreme Pontiff says on another occasion to a group of seniors,

> As you look back on your lives you may remember sufferings and personal failures. It is important to think about these experiences, so as to see them in the light of the whole of life's journey. ... I am speaking of the important *spiritual healing that restores inner freedom* to the elderly. This kind of healing is gained through an awareness and appreciation of the ways in which God works through human weakness as well as through human virtue. Even the memory of our sins does not discourage us any longer, because we realize that *God's mercy is greater than our sins* and that *God's pardon is a proof of his faithful love for us.*[54]

In his apostolic exhortation *Christifideles laici* (December 30, 1988), the Pope writes:

> I remind older people that the Church calls and expects them to continue to exercise their mission in apostolic and missionary life. This is not only a possibility for them, but it is their duty even in this time of their life when age itself might provide opportunities in some specific and basic way.
>
> The Bible delights in presenting the older person as the symbol of someone rich in wisdom and fear of the Lord (cf. Sir 25:4–6).

In this sense the "gift" of older people can be specifically that of being the witness to tradition in the faith both in the Church and in society (cf. Ps 44:4; Ex 12:26–27), the teacher of the lessons of life (cf. Sir 6:34; 8:11–12), and the worker of charity. ...I said during the celebration of the Older People's Jubilee: "Arriving at an older age is to be considered a privilege: not simply because not everyone has the good fortune to reach this stage in life, but also, and above all, because this period provides real possibilities for better evaluating the past, for knowing and living more deeply the Paschal Mystery, for becoming an example in the Church for the whole People of God." (no. 48)

THE FATHER

In this year of 1999, dedicated to God the Father, we are told that we should look upon the entirety of human history as well as the totality of our individual lives as a "great pilgrimage to the home of our Father". The celebration of the Great Jubilee calls us all to recognize the need to be forgiven and to forgive. As those nearing the completion of their individual pilgrimages to the Father, the elderly can teach us how to approach the end of a century and a millennium and the beginning of another millennium and century in the spirit of Robert Browning, "Grow old along with me; the best is yet to be ... the last of life, for which the first was made."

The Pontifical Council for the Laity has issued a document, dated October 1, 1998, entitled *The Dignity of Older People and Their Mission in the Church and in the World*. It deserves the respectful reading not only of those Catholics who are senior citizens and those who are their caregivers, but it can be profitably studied by all. It "can provide the younger generations an occasion to reflect on and re-establish their relations with the older generations. It can also provide those who are no longer young with an occasion to reexamine their own existence and to place it in [a] joyful perspective."[55]

Pope John Paul II said recently to some older persons, "Do not lose heart: life does not end here on earth, but instead only starts here. We must be witnesses to the resurrection! Joy must be a characteristic of the elderly."[56] Of course, it is an ongoing task for all of us to "create an environment in which communion can thrive between the various generations and a spiritual climate that helps older people to maintain their spiritual vitality and youthfulness".[57]

APRIL 16, 1999

Marital Fidelity

Marriage

One of the characteristics of every permanent and happy marriage is fidelity. The marriage of anyone must contain this element. However, the marriage of Christians should contain it to an eminent degree. This is because Christian marriage is more than a sacred contract between a man, a woman, and God, binding the covenanting couple for life. Christian marriage is such a contract, but much more.

For Christians, marriage is a sign, that is, a sacrament or holy mystery, symbolizing the union of Christ with His Catholic Church (Eph 5:32). The union of Christ and His Church is one of self-giving love, which is perpetual and indefectible (Mt 28:20 and Eph 5:21–33). Christian marriage, then, must have these same attributes. When a spouse says "yes" to the other spouse, he at the same time says "no" to every other person in the world. In a certain sense marriage is utterly exclusive. On the other hand, this does not mean that marriage is "closed" in a selfish way; rather, it means that the exclusive marital love of husband and wife is meant to enable them to bestow love of a different and sublimated kind upon their children, upon neighbors in need, and upon the world.

Two Kinds

Fidelity in marriage is both interior and exterior. Indeed, the external observance of marital fidelity is simply the exteriorization of that which is already present in the mind and heart. Jesus was very clear about that (Mt 5:27–30). Human beings are made of both body and soul. In maintaining fidelity to any lifelong commitments, the intellect, will, and internal senses are the first to come into operation. Unfaithfulness in marriage first begins in the mind and heart and then goes on to external acts. Married couples are obliged to control their imaginations and desires in order to preserve the fidelity they have vowed to each other.

A Chinese proverb says that if you do not want to take the trip, do not take the first step, or, as we might say, do not sit on the edge of the precipice, and then you will not fall off the cliff. A married person in heart and conscience must be able to recognize what constitutes that first step, that sitting on the edge. In itself this may mean some inherently innocent action or words, but in the context of the marriage vows, a tender conscience will tell a person, No, I cannot comport myself with someone of the opposite sex, now that I am married, in the same way I could were I not married. It is very simple to rationalize and excuse our behavior and to forget what is owed in justice as well as in conjugal purity to the wedding covenant.

TEMPTATION

All of us, save the Blessed Virgin Mary, have within us the effects of original sin. Even when the sin itself is washed from our souls by the waters of Baptism, concupiscence remains. It is impossible to walk through life without internal as well as external temptations. Those who stand must take heed lest they fall. The humble realization of our weakness and our being prone to error is the first step toward ensuring our practice of the necessary cautions, which are vital to the preservation of chastity and purity in our lives.

Sexual self-control and responsibility are essential for everyone. Married people, especially during times of necessary separation or illness or of the tensions that sometimes enter into human relationships, must be always mindful of the exclusive love to which they have committed themselves on their wedding day. Each day should be, for a married couple, a time for the renewal of their wedding vows.

Prayer, particularly family prayer, and the devout and frequent reception of the Sacraments of the Holy Eucharist and Penance are indispensable for maintaining marital fidelity. Avoiding unnecessary occasions of sin, that is, the persons, places, and situations that usually lead to sin, is an important element in the practice of the virtue of prudence to which we all are bound.

MODERN CULTURE

Our world and our culture treat marital fidelity very lightly. The communications and entertainment media do their best to make it appear "everybody does it" (Così fan tutti). Alcoholic beverages, fine in themselves, can sometimes loosen inhibitions and make it easier to succumb to temptations to adultery. Some people are perpetual adolescents who cannot understand how the exclusiveness of marriage is, not confining or restricting, but really liberating and a source of true freedom for the spouses.

Sometimes in middle age there arises a sense of insecurity about one's appearance or attractiveness, and this, too, can lead to foolish toying with temptation. Also middle age with an "empty nest" can lead to a feeling of boredom and ennui and a weariness with the sacrifices that are always required to make a marriage "work". Coupled with our modern world's contempt for purity and conjugal faithfulness, this can be a source of great temptation for some married people.

BIBLE

Jesus, in His infinite mercy, forgave the woman taken in adultery (Jn 8:1–10), but He warned her not to commit that sin again. Our Lord made His own the commandment of the Old Testament "You shall not commit adultery" (Mk 10:19). Adultery is a sin not only against chastity, but also against justice, and it requires restitution, even after being forgiven. Since God (Yahweh) was espoused to His People in the Old Testament, the prophets depicted their idolatry as a form of adultery. In the New Testament, those who have bestowed and received the Sacrament of Matrimony upon and from each other have an even more serious obligation to symbolize in their lives the unbreakable and love-filled union of Jesus with the Chosen People of the New Testament, Christ's Catholic Church.

APRIL 18, 1997

Defend Marriage
I

REFERENDUM

A small minority of people are attempting to redefine marriage and to make civil marriages or their equivalent (called civil unions) possible between people of the same sex. Behind scare words like discrimination and the ugly neologism "homophobia", there is currently among us a well-financed and loud effort to persuade the people of Nebraska that it is in their interest not to forbid civil recognition of "same-sex marriages" or civil unions.

However, it is the right and probably the duty of Christians to see to it that civil laws recognize the promotion and defense of families, founded on monogamous, heterosexual marriage. This is vitally necessary for the common good. The civil government should not be allowed, with the acquiescence of Christians, to deprive itself of the healthy social fabric that is necessary not only for a harmonious human society, but for the continuation of human civilization. A Christian, and certainly a Catholic, has an obligation to oppose the homosexual culture, which means not simply a person who is tragically inclined to homosexuality, but rather a collection of individuals who publicly adopt a homosexual life-style and are committed to having such a life-style accepted by society as fully legitimate in civil law.

THE PLAN

The Vatican's semi-official newspaper, *L'Osservatore Romano*, observes that justifiable opposition to offenses and discrimination that violate a person's rights cannot be confused with the unjust demands of homosexuals to promote their agenda in civil law. The paper says, "In fact, a systematic plan for the public justification and glorification of homosexuality is taking shape, starting with the attempt to make it fully accepted in the mind of society. It aims, through increasing pressure, at a change in legislation so that homosexual unions may enjoy the same rights as marriage, including that of adoption."[58] The plan is evil and must be vigorously opposed.

Keen observers note that homosexuals and their liberal-left supporters have an eight-point program underway: First, redefine homosexuality as an inborn, genetic condition, and persuade people that it is irreversible. Second, get the focus off the acts that homosexuals do, and emphasize who they are. Try to cast them as objects of unjust discrimination like African Americans. Play the civil-rights card. Third, create a new positive language to influence public opinion in their favor, using phrases such as "domestic partners, alternate life styles, gay", and so on. Fourth, make new laws and repeal any standing laws that conflict with their goals. Fifth, portray the homosexual community as normal and natural. Sixth, organize parades and demonstrations and try to intimidate lawmakers and any religious people who disagree with their perversions. Seventh, get homosexual propaganda into all the public schools, and there form clubs, alliances, and so on. Play the multi-cultural card. Eighth, through the entertainment and information media make homosexual acts seem acceptable to the public as normal and good, getting the liberals who control these media to be on the homosexual side. Anyone who has not been living in a cave recently can see this program now unfolding.

CATECHISM

The *Catechism of the Catholic Church* teaches, "Basing itself on Sacred Scripture, which presents homosexual acts as acts of grave depravity [cf. Gen 19:1–29; Rom 1:24–27; 1 Cor 6:10; 1 Tim 1:10), tradition has always declared that 'homosexual acts are intrinsically disordered' [Congregation for the Doctrine of the Faith, *Persona humana*, no. 8]. They are contrary to the natural law. They close the sexual act to the gift of life. They do not proceed from a genuine affective and sexual complementarity. Under no circumstances can they be approved" (CCC 2357).

The *Catechism* goes on to say,

> The number of men and women who have deep-seated homosexual tendencies is not negligible. This inclination, which is objectively disordered, constitutes for most of them a trial. They must be accepted with respect, compassion, and

sensitivity. Every sign of unjust discrimination in their regard should be avoided. These persons are called to fulfill God's will in their lives and, if they are Christians, to unite to the sacrifice of the Lord's Cross the difficulties they may encounter from their condition. Homosexual persons are called to chastity. (CCC 2358–59)

It has always been the teaching of the Catholic Church and remains so today that any homosexual act that is done with free will and due deliberation is a mortal sin.

INTRINSIC EVIL

The Holy See points out that, although one can distinguish the homosexual inclination or orientation from homosexual acts themselves, the orientation cannot be considered "neutral or good"; rather, it must be seen as "a more or less strong tendency ordered toward an intrinsic moral evil; and thus the inclination itself must be seen as an objective disorder."[59] The Congregation for the Doctrine of the Faith says that there must be care lest people with homosexual tendencies "be led to believe that the living out of this orientation in homosexual activity is a morally acceptable option. It is not."[60] Catholic teaching on this issue is clear: "The Church, obedient to the Lord who founded her and gave to her the sacramental life, celebrates the divine plan of the loving and life-giving union of men and women in the sacrament of marriage. It is only in the marital relationship that the use of the sexual faculty can be morally good. A person engaging in homosexual behavior therefore acts immorally."[61]

"As in every moral disorder, homosexual activity prevents one's own fulfillment and happiness by acting contrary to the creative wisdom of God. The Church, in rejecting erroneous opinions regarding homosexuality, does not limit but rather defends personal freedom and dignity realistically and authentically understood."[62] "Same-sex marriage" is not marriage at all and is morally illicit, even when it is given another name like "civil union". In God's eyes it is a deviant and perverted violation of His law and His love. Vote in favor of defending true and genuine marriage. Do not be frightened. Despite some screams and shouts, this referendum, if it passes, will actually be a blessing to our state, our country, and our world. Vote yes on 416.

NOVEMBER 6, 2000

Defend Marriage
II

Voting Yes

Despite negative shrieks from opponents, the good citizens who vote in favor of the defense of marriage referendum (416) are not only acting in a correct and moral way, but also are in no way offending or violating the human and civil rights of anybody. Human society and civilization itself are placed in serious jeopardy when a tiny group of people can succeed in making certain kinds of immoral sexual arrangements the equivalent of marriage. Preventing the destruction of families and family life is a noble task. Destruction will surely follow in large measure if there is civil, public glorification and justification for homosexual conduct through a lack of appropriate civil constitutional and legislative arrangements.

To favor the defense of marriage referendum does not say that one favors violence or harm to homosexual people. All decent folks are opposed to those things. But rather, voting yes is a service to truth. The Holy See says, "The promotion of errors and ambiguities is not consistent with a Christian attitude of true respect and compassion: persons who are struggling with homosexuality no less than any others have the right to receive the authentic teachings of the Church from those who minister to them."[63]

Stop the Church

Unfortunately, many homosexual people hate the Catholic Church, mainly because the Church refuses to bless and approve their "life-style". To illustrate: several years ago at one of the regular homosexual film festivals at the University of Nebraska in Lincoln (your tax dollars at work?), a film was presented entitled *Stop the Church*. It showed the plotting and carrying out of an attack at Saint Patrick's Cathedral in New York while Cardinal O'Connor was offering Mass. The plot and attack were the work of homosexual groups calling themselves things like "Act Up" and "Everyone Out". Homosexuals interrupted the Cardinal's Mass with screaming and shouting. They spit sacred Hosts onto the floor and did unspeakable things to desecrate our Lord's Body, while also doing impure things with each other in the aisles and pews. While the film was running, people at the UNL homosexual festival (there was an NCC observer present who saw it all) joined in shouting blasphemies and cursing Catholics. We Catholic Bishops of Nebraska protested about this to the university officials, who, of course, brushed us off and strongly supported their festival.

During homosexual parades in New York City, it has become a usual practice for some homosexuals in the parade to walk naked down Fifth Avenue in front of Saint Patrick's Cathedral and to throw condoms at the Cathedral facade.

FRIGHTENING

Undoubtedly, there are some gentle and nonviolent people who have homosexual tendencies. Courage, a Catholic organization for people who believe in and want to follow the teachings of the Church about homosexual morality, has many such members. However, there is another (and larger?) group of a different type. For instance, there are homosexual men ("drag queens") who call themselves "Sisters of Perpetual Indulgence". Clothed in fake nuns' habits, they go about in homosexual parades around our country, mocking, ridiculing, and scoffing at Catholics, while they viciously sow hatred for the Catholic Church.

Recently, in a "multi-culturalism" class at UNL, a female professor, who proclaimed she was a lesbian, told her class that if there were "any Catholics or recovering Catholics" among them, they would have a difficult time passing the course.

Michael Swift, a homosexual "activist", makes the agenda of large numbers of homosexuals quite clear: "We shall sodomize your sons, emblems of your feeble masculinity, of your shallow dreams and vulgar lies. We shall seduce them in your schools, in your dormitories, in your gymnasiums, in your seminaries, in your youth groups, in your movie theater bathrooms, in your houses of Congress, wherever young men are with men together. Your sons shall become our minions and do our bidding. They shall be recast in our image. They will come to crave and adore us."

SCRIPTURE

The theology of creation, which derives from the first book of the Bible, provides a fine starting point for knowing God's will in regard to any discussion of homosexuality. In the Book of Genesis, God in His infinite wisdom and love is seen as the One Who brings all reality into existence as a reflection of His goodness. He fashioned the human race, male and female, in His very image. Therefore, human beings are a work of God, and this includes the complementarity of the sexes. They are meant to reflect the inner unity of the Creator, and this is to be done in a striking way in the mutual self-giving found in marriage and in their openness to the transmission of human life. Homosexual acts have no self-giving in them. They are simply selfish pleasure seeking and, of course, cannot have any openness to new human life. Thus, they are seriously sinful.

In the nineteenth chapter of the Book of Genesis, the effects of original sin are seen in the sins of the men of Sodom. Although there may have been several components of those sins, it is clear from the text that they are more than offenses against hospitality; rather, they are evil insofar as they are homosexual acts. The Mosaic Law found in the Book of Leviticus (18:22) corroborates this.

In the New Testament, Saint Paul says that those who engage in homosexual acts

Vocations

cannot enter heaven (1 Cor 6), and he lists sodomites among the worst kinds of sinners (1 Tim 1:10). The Apostle of the Gentiles also mentions homosexual behavior as the prime example of human degeneracy and debauchery, leading to that spiritual blindness that characterizes atheism. "For this reason God gave them up to dishonorable passions. Their women exchanged natural relations for unnatural, and the men likewise, gave up natural relations with women and were consumed with passion for one another, men committing shameless acts with men and receiving in their own persons the due penalty for their error" (Rom 1:26–27).

OCTOBER 13, 2000

Defend Marriage
III

CONSTITUTION

Although American civil laws regarding marriage are not always in harmony with God's law (and therefore with the laws of the Catholic Church), nevertheless, to the greatest extent possible every effort should be made by conscientious Catholics not to allow a greater and growing discrepancy between our civil and constitutional arrangements and God's will. This is why we Catholic Bishops of Nebraska say: "We call on Catholic Nebraskans and all our fellow citizens to join us in supporting this (Defense of Marriage) amendment and voting for it on election day." Marriage as a union of a man and woman holds a unique position in our culture and in our law. This should be affirmed in our public policy, and we should never cooperate in allowing the government to view a union of two persons of the same sex in a civil union, domestic partnership, or similar association to have the same recognition as marriage in our state laws.

We Bishops say: "We urge that the uniqueness of marriage be upheld, retained, and perpetuated." The Catholic Church teaches: "To choose someone of the same sex for one's sexual activity is to annul the rich symbolism and meaning, not to mention the goals, of the Creator's sexual design. Homosexual activity is not a complementary union."[64]

PROMISCUITY

Livio Melina, professor of moral theology at the Pontifical Lateran University in Rome, recently said,

In the homosexual act, ... that true reciprocity which makes the gift of self and the acceptance of the other possible cannot take place. By lacking complementarity, each one of the partners remains locked in himself and experiences contact with the other's body merely as an opportunity for selfish enjoyment. At the same time, homosexual activity also involves the illusion of false intimacy that is obsessively sought and constantly lacking. The other is not really "other"; he is like the self: in reality, he is only the mirror of the self, which confirms it in its own solitude, exactly when the encounter is sought. This pathological "narcissism" has been identified in the homosexual personality by the studies of many psychologists. ... Hence, great instability and promiscuity prevail in the most widespread model of homosexual life, which is why the view advanced by some of encouraging "stable" and institutionalized unions seems completely unrealistic.[65]

It is interesting that clinical experience shows that often when authentic personal friendship forms between male homosexuals, they find themselves unable to engage in homosexual acts with each other.

POLITICAL

In 1973 pressure from the politically rich and powerful homosexual movement persuaded the American Psychiatric Association to declare that homosexuality is no longer a mental disease. Countless experienced and learned psychiatrists vehemently disagree with this view, however, and insist that this was done on absolutely no scientific basis. Many of them claim that a high percentage of their homosexual patients obtain a permanent cure and that most of the others gather great benefit from various proven therapies.

Neither the Catholic Church nor organizations such as Courage has any opinion about these issues one way or another. Also, the Church has no opinion about whether homosexual tendencies are inborn and genetic or are (semi-consciously) acquired, although, of course, at the present time there is not a shred of scientific evidence for the "inborn or genetic theory". However people obtain these tendencies, they must be considered always as morally disordered, and, if acted upon with freedom and knowledge, they are lethal sins, separating one from God's sanctifying grace and placing one in immediate danger of eternal damnation.

SOCIAL COLLAPSE

The late great Doctor Herbert Ratner used to say, "God forgives, but nature doesn't." Although certain diseases can be found in many populations, it is a well-known fact that a prime source for HIV-AIDS, genital herpes, hepatitis, syphilis, gonorrhea, gay bowel syndrome, and other such illnesses is the homosexual community.

Despite claims that homosexuals àre only looking for their civil rights (which our voting yes on the Defense of Marriage referendum will not deny them), there are certain past events that point to a wider agenda, which can only open the door to social depravity and degeneracy. In New York, for instance, the public schools, deeply influenced by the homosexual lobby, gave the little children who were starting to learn to read homosexual primers, with such names as "Daddy's Roommate", "Heather Has Two Mommies", "Gloria Goes to Gay Pride", and so on.

The Holy See says,

> The proper reaction to crimes committed against homosexual persons [which the Church strongly condemns] should not be to claim that the homosexual condition is not disordered. When such a claim is made and when homosexual activity is consequently condoned, or when civil legislation is introduced to protect behavior to which no one has any conceivable right, neither the Church nor society at large should be surprised when other distorted notions and practices gain ground, and irrational and violent reactions increase.[66]

JUST DISCRIMINATION

Unjust discrimination is sinful. However, there can be such a thing as "just" discrimination. For example, if someone has a tendency to pyromania or kleptomania or pedophilia, even if the tendency itself might not be a sin because it is not the result of a negative moral decision, it is "just" to keep a pyromaniac from guarding a gasoline storage facility, a kleptomaniac from being a bank teller, or a pedophile from a child's care. Certain kinds of "discrimination" in regard to people with homosexual tendencies can be just in some circumstances, although all people are entitled to basic human rights. For instance, a Christian can justly refuse to rent apartments or rooms to persons (heterosexual or homosexual) who are obviously in an intrinsically disordered arrangement in their sexual lives. Thus, it is right and just for Christians and all people of goodwill to vote yes on the Defense of Marriage referendum and to be undaunted by the clever propaganda to the contrary.

As Pope John Paul II says, "Acting is morally good when the choices of freedom are *in conformity with man's true good* [corresponding to the wise design of God, indicated by His commandments].... *Only the act in conformity with the good can be a path that leads to life*."[67]

[1] CCC 1548; cf. *Lumen gentium*, nos. 10; 28; *Sacrosanctum concilium*, no. 33; *Christus Dominus*, no. 11; *Presbyterorum ordinis*, nos. 2, 6.

[2] Pius XII, encyclical *Mediator Dei*: AAS 39 (1947), 548; quoted by CCC 1548.

[3] Saint Thomas Aquinas, *Summa Theologiae* III, 22, 4c; quoted by CCC 1548.

[4] John Paul II, "Priestly Identity Shines in Eucharist", audience of October 22, 1993, *L'Osservatore Romano*, no. 44 (November 3, 1993): 9, no. 7.

[5] John Paul II, "Presbyters Share in Christ's Priesthood", General Audience of March 31, 1993, *L'Osservatore Romano*, no. 14 (April 7, 1993): 11, no. 6.

[6] Ibid., nos. 7–8.

[7] *Presbyterorum ordinis*, no. 4.

[8] Ibid., no. 5.

[9] CCC 1539, quoting Heb 5:1; cf. Ex 29:1–30, Lev 8.

[10] John Paul II, "The Father Calls to Eternal Life", *L'Osservatore Romano*, no. 48 (December 2, 1998): 5.

[11] *Optatam totius*, no. 2.

[12] John Paul II, "The Father Calls to Eternal Life".

[13] Ibid.

[14] Ibid.

[15] *Lumen gentium*, no. 44

[16] CCC 916, with reference to *Perfectae caritatis*, no. 5.

[17] CCC 916, with reference to CIC, can. 573.

[18] John Paul II, postsynodal apostolic exhortation *Vita consecrata* (March 25, 1996), no. 21.

[19] Thomas Merton, *The Waters of Siloe*, (New York: Harcourt, Brace and Co., 1949), p. xxxiii.

[20] John Paul II, apostolic exhortation *Redemptionis donum* (March 25, 1984), no. 6.

[21] *Lumen gentium*, no. 43.

[22] *Perfectae caritatis*, no. 1.

[23] *Lumen gentium*, no. 43.

[24] *Charter of the Rights of the Family* (October 22, 1983), introduction by the United States Conference of Catholic Bishops, Secretariat for Family, Laity, Women and Youth.

[25] John Paul II, apostolic exhortation *Familiaris consortio* (November 22, 1981), no. 15.

[26] Ibid., no. 17.

[27] G. K. Chesterton, *The Everlasting Man*, vol. 2 of *The Collected Works of G. K. Chesterton* (San Francisco: Ignatius Press, 1986), p. 186.

[28] John Paul II, *Familiaris consortio*, no. 59.

[29] Ibid., no. 60.

[30] *Gravissimum educationis*, no. 3.

[31] John Paul II, *Familiaris consortio*, no. 16.

[32] Ibid., no. 86.

[33] CCC 2206 quoting *Gaudium et spes*, § 1.

[34] *Charter of the Rights of the Family*, art. 9a.

[35] John Paul II, *Familiaris consortio*, no. 27.

[36] Ibid., no. 21, quoting *Lumen gentium*, no. 11.

[37] Cf. Eph. 5:21-6:4; Col. 3:18-21, 1 Pet. 3:1-7.

[38] John Paul II, *Familiaris consortio*, no. 23.

[39] Ibid., no. 25.

[40] Ibid.
[41] Ibid., no. 49.
[42] Ibid., no. 26.
[43] Ibid.
[44] Ibid.
[45] *Sacrosanctum concilium*, no. 22, § 3.
[46] John Paul II, letter *Mulieris dignitatem* (August 15, 1988), no. 1, quoting the Council's Message to Women (December 8, 1965).
[47] John Paul II, *Mulieris dignitatem*, no. 17.
[48] Ibid., no. 27.
[49] Pontifical Council for the Laity, *The Dignity of Older People and Their Mission* (October 1, 1998), introduction.
[50] Ibid., no. 3.
[51] John Paul II, "Age Does Not Prevent Elderly from Devoting Themselves to Needs of Community or Parish", General Audience of September 7, 1994, *L'Osservatore Romano*, no. 37 (September 14, 1994): 11, no. 7.
[52] John Paul II, "In Your Old Age, Accompany Christ to the Cross", address to the elderly in Munich, November 19, 1980, *L'Osservatore Romano*, no. 51 (December 22, 1980): 7, no. 2.
[53] John Paul II, General Audience of March 23, 1984, quoted in Pontifical Council for the Laity, *Dignity of Older People*, introduction.
[54] John Paul II, "Old Age Is Also a Time of Responsibility for the Future", address to the elderly, Perth, Australia, November 30, 1986, *L'Osservatore Romano*, no. 49 (December 9, 1986): 2, nos. 5–6.
[55] Pontifical Council for the Laity, *Dignity of Older People*, conclusion.
[56] John Paul II, "No Authority Can Justify Euthanasia", address of October 31, 1998, *L'Osservatore Romano*, no. 47 (November 25, 1998): 7, no. 9.
[57] Pontifical Council for the Laity, *Dignity of Older People*, no. 4.
[58] Livio Melina, "Moral Criteria for Evaluating Homosexuality", Christian Anthropology and Homosexuality, no. 13, *L'Osservatore Romano*, no. 24 (June 11, 1997): 8.
[59] Congregation for the Doctrine of the Faith, *Letter to the Bishops of the Catholic Church on the Pastoral Care of Homosexual Persons* (October 1, 1986), no. 3.
[60] Ibid.
[61] Ibid., no. 7.
[62] Ibid.
[63] Congregation for the Doctrine of the Faith, "Notification regarding Sister Jeannine Gramick, SSND, and Father Robert Nugent, SDS" (May 31, 1999).
[64] Congregation for the Doctrine of the Faith, *Letter on Pastoral Care of Homosexual Persons*, no. 7.
[65] Melina, "Moral Criteria for Evaluating Homosexuality", 7.
[66] Congregation for the Doctrine of the Faith, *Letter on Pastoral Care of Homosexual Persons*, no. 10.
[67] John Paul II, encyclical *Veritatis splendor* (August 6, 1993), no. 72.

Part Three

FAITH

1

DOCTRINE

Doctrinal Development
I

ENDED

In Jesus Christ God has spoken His final and definitive Word to our world. Our Savior, in His entire life, death, and Resurrection, was and is the culmination of all God's revelation, the total and exhaustive self-giving of the Almighty. When the echo of the "Christ-event" faded away with the death of the last apostle, public revelation ended. The faith was "once and for all delivered to the saints" (Jude 3). Nothing more can be added to the "deposit of faith", and it is the obligation of the Catholic Church, founded by our Redeemer, to carry and preach that faith to the end of time, unmutilated, undiluted, and unsullied.

The Second Vatican Council teaches what the Church has always taught: "The Christian dispensation, therefore, as the new and definitive covenant, will never pass away, and now we await no further new public revelation before the glorious manifestation of our Lord Jesus Christ (see 1 Tim 6:14; Tit 2:13)".[1] Our Holy Father, Pope John Paul II, says, "Guarding the deposit of faith is the mission which the Lord entrusted to his Church, and which she fulfills in every age."[2] There is, without any doubt, a "once-and-for-allness" about divine revelation. Public revelation is ended until the end of the world. Private revelations, visions, apparitions, locutions, whatever they may be (most of them are spurious and false), can add nothing to the deposit of faith or to public revelation, nor can they compel our belief. The constitutive period of revelation is ended.

HOLY SPIRIT

Christ promised to remain with His Church until the end of time (Mt 28:20). He also promised that the Holy Spirit, God Himself, would abide in a special way in the Catholic Church. He said, "He will teach you all things, and bring to your remembrance all that I have said to you" (Jn 14:26). In this way, Jesus promised that He would not "leave us orphans" (see Jn 14:15–18).

There are three attributes of the Church: authority, indefectibility, and infallibility. All, in large measure, depend not only upon the divine origin of the Church, but also on the continuing presence of the Holy Spirit within her. Christ said, "I have yet many things to say to you, but you cannot bear them now. When the Spirit of truth, comes, he will guide you into the truth" (Jn 16:12–13). In this year dedicated to the Holy Spirit in preparation for the Great Jubilee, it is appropriate to reflect on the mystery, meaning, and fact of the abiding presence of God, the Holy Spirit, in the Church, as He is the divine Soul of the Mystical Body of Christ, of Which we are the members. One of the clear manifestations of this presence is in the development of doctrine.

TRUE AND FALSE

There is a notion of doctrinal development that is false. Modernists and other heretics down through the centuries have confused authentic doctrinal development with that which is aberrant. Doctrinal development is not innovation. It does not mean that there is no clear and stable dogma to anchor our faith. Doctrinal relativism is not an acceptable Christian philosophy.

Interestingly enough, many heresies begin as reaction and then proceed to innovation. How many people in Christian history have determined to "get back to the original kernel", back to an earlier and more pristine and unpolluted religion, but have ended in a new man-made church or religion! "Archaism" has its dangers. Some great historical figures have indeed recaptured various aspects of the Gospel that were not being emphasized at one time or another. Saint Francis of Assisi would be an example of this. Others, such as Luther, did not succeed in their quest.

NEWMAN

The finding that captivated the mind of John Henry Newman in the last century almost always fascinates those who delve deeply into Christian history. He recognized many similarities between the Church of the earliest centuries, the Church of the Fathers, and the nineteenth-century Catholic Church. As he studied the Fathers more and more, he remarked, "To be deep in history is to cease to be Protestant." However, he also noticed dissimilarities, which troubled him in his search for religious truth. It was the discovery that the oak tree is the same as yet different from its previous stage as sapling or as an acorn, and yet maintains an identity with it, that persuaded him finally that the credentials of the Catholic Church as the true Church, founded by Jesus, were worthy of acceptance.

In his searches and struggles, Newman decided to put his thoughts on paper. In particular he wanted to try to discern how true development could be distinguished from false or erroneous doctrinal development and how this could be reconciled with the final and definitive nature of public divine revelation. He completed his *Essay on the Development of Christian Doctrine*, set down his pen, and said, "Now I must be received into the Catholic Church." He became a Catholic on October 9, 1845.

Newman's *Essay* along with his *Apologia pro Vita Sua* and his *Grammar of Assent* constitute a most brilliant defense of Catholicism and stand as monuments of English literature as well. He concludes his *Essay* with the words, "Wrap not yourself round in the associations of years past, nor determine that to be truth, which you wish to be so, nor make an idol of cherished anticipations. Time is short, eternity is long."

The Second Vatican Council states, "God ... uninterruptedly converses with the bride of His beloved Son; and the Holy Spirit through whom the living voice of the Gospel resounds in the Church, ... leads unto all truth those who believe."[3] This does not mean any new revelation or any addition or subtraction from revelation. It means what is called "doctrinal development".

JUNE 19, 1998

Doctrinal Development
II

HOLY SPIRIT

Preparing ourselves for the Great Jubilee of the year 2000, we have been asked by our Holy Father to dedicate this present year to contemplating the action and works of the third Person of the Most Blessed Trinity. One of the great functions of the Holy Spirit is to preside, as the Soul of the Mystical Body of Christ, over the unsullied preservation of the complete, integral, and beautiful doctrine of Jesus in the Catholic Church and over the development of doctrine in that Church. The Second Vatican Council teaches, "God, who spoke of old, uninterruptedly converses with the bride of His beloved Son, and the Holy Spirit, through whom the living voice of the Gospel resounds in the Church, and through her, in the world, leads unto all truth those who believe and makes the word of Christ dwell abundantly in them (see Col 3:16)."[4]

Pope John Paul II says, "In our own day too, the Spirit is *the principal agent of the new evangelization.* Hence it will be important to gain a renewed appreciation of the Spirit as the One who builds the Kingdom of God within the course of history and prepares its full manifestation in Jesus Christ, stirring peoples' hearts and quickening in our world the seeds of the full salvation which will come at the end of time."[5]

IMPULSES

A brief reflection on Church history will indicate to a perceptive reader the impulses under which doctrine develops. Dogmas, which are intrinsically immutable, can develop under the impulse of heresy, which occasions, but does not cause, doctrinal development. Heretical errors and their challenges often represent the circumstances in which significant doctrinal development occurs. Theological reflection and advances in such sciences as exegesis, profane culture, archaeology, linguistics, religious sociology, religious phenomenology, and religious anthropology, *and so on*, are impulses that frequently drive doctrinal development.

The sacred liturgy (under the axiom *the law of prayer is the law of belief*) and charisms, special gifts of the Holy Spirit for the good of the Church, are also such impulses. Of course, charisms can be within or outside the Magisterium of the Church, but their authenticity can only be truly judged by that teaching authority of the Catholic Church, just as the Second Vatican Council teaches that the Holy See and the Bishops alone are competent to regulate the liturgy of the Church.

Also it must not be forgotten that there is a natural, God-given dynamism of the human intellect that strives to pass from one type of knowledge to higher types. There is also a flux in human culture accompanied by a natural desire in every rational man to find universal and absolute truths, which often are imbedded in certain cultural forms and expressions, and to set them out in perennial, viable language. These, too, are such impulses.

MOST IMPORTANT

The most important "impulse" in doctrinal development, certainly, is the Holy Spirit, Who constantly guides the Church and assists her consciousness. This makes development of doctrine more than merely logically drawn conclusions taken from revealed premises. Our divine Lord told us: "the Father ... will give you another Counselor,... the Spirit of truth" (Jn 14:16–17). And, again He said, "But the Counselor, the Holy Spirit, whom the Father will send in my name, he will teach you all things and bring to your remembrance all that I have said to you" (Jn 14:26).

Speaking of the Holy Spirit, Who is the personification of the Love between the almighty Father and the only begotten Son, Christ said: "Nevertheless I tell you the truth; it is to your advantage that I go away, for if I do not go away, the Counselor will not come to you; but if I go, I will send him to you" (Jn 16:7). Our Redeemer also said, "When the Spirit of truth comes, he will guide you into all truth" (Jn 16:13).

Four Ways

Doctrine, all of which is found in Sacred Scripture and Sacred Tradition, the fonts of revelation, despite the fact that it is irrevocable and incapable of alteration, nevertheless develops in four ways: objectively, subjectively, estimatively, and hermeneutically. Doctrine develops objectively in two ways: first, when the things expressed in the fonts of revelation in prescientific, affective, and catechetical language are set out in scientific terms, which appeal more to the intellect than to feelings; second, when there is gathered into one phrase or word what is oftentimes stated in the fonts of revelation in a scattered and nontechnical way. Words such as purgatory, bible, assumption, immaculate conception, and so on are examples of objective development of doctrine.

Keep in Mind

In considering the development of doctrine, it is vital to remember that God cannot contradict Himself. Therefore, correct doctrinal development, as distinct from doctrinal corruption and error, must be homogeneous and consistent with what has gone before. It must always include and affirm and never contradict what the Church has set down as doctrinally necessary to be accepted in order to be saved. In no sense is it "new revelation", nor can it be seen as a species of the philosophical falsehood called relativism. To be correct, doctrinal development must always be in accord with the teaching of the Magisterium of the Church.

The Second Vatican Council says, "This tradition which comes from the Apostles develops in the Church with the help of the Holy Spirit. For there is a growth in the understanding of the realities and the words which have been handed down... For as the centuries succeed one another, the Church constantly moves forward toward the fullness of divine truth until the words of God reach their complete fulfillment in her."[6]

JULY 3, 1998

Doctrinal Development
III

Subjectively

Under the guidance of God Himself, the Holy Spirit, Whom Jesus promised to the Catholic Church (Jn 16:13), dogmas and doctrines "develop" in the Church. This is not in any sense a "new revelation", nor is it something "added" to divine revelation, which is contained definitively in Sacred Scripture and Sacred Tradition. Subjective development of doctrine takes place under the impulse of the human intellect, created by God in such a way that it strives to make explicit what is only implicit, to pass from knowing "about something" to knowing the "something in itself". Of course subjective development also strives to express what God has revealed in language that is permanent and understandable to all people of all times and places.

Each Sunday when we recite the Creed at Mass, we remember that God the Holy Spirit is the "Lord and Giver of Life". In this year of 1998 dedicated especially to Him, it is well to recall how He continues the work of Jesus in the Church, the Mystical Body of the risen Christ, in an infinite variety of ways, including His care for the "consciousness of the Church" in her possession and knowledge of the doctrine of her divine Founder.

ESTIMATIVELY

Christian doctrine also is capable of developing "reflectively" or estimatively. Human minds are made by God in such a way that they can "reflect back" on their own development. In this kind of "reflection" there also is the possibility of "directing" or even in a certain sense "controlling" this development. As a human person progresses from infancy to old age, he can reflect along the way on his own change and development. This can be done as well by a collectivity, especially a living organism such as the Catholic Church.

It should be noted, however, that growth in knowledge and doctrinal development does not necessarily mean a growth in faith or in supernatural wisdom. The faith of a first communicant could be as rich and full as that of a learned theologian. Thomas à Kempis, in *The Imitation of Christ*, says, "Better it is to be a humble rustic who loves God than a proud philosopher, who can chart the course of the stars, but yet loses his soul" (bk. 1, chap 2).

HERMENEUTICALLY

Human beings can never be perfectly objective. They bring to every encounter the "baggage" of their personal experience, knowledge, modes of thought, and so forth. Water poured into a container assumes the shape of the container. In a certain sense, the encounter of a human being with divine revelation is always conditioned by the human part of such a "dialogue". True it is that the word of God can penetrate and transform the person it encounters. However, as human beings perfect their categories of thought and their modes of understanding, their ability to hear the word of God as true is also perfected. Thus they can pass not only from heterodoxy to orthodoxy, but also from a simpler way of knowing to a more profound way.

Prescinding temporarily from the elements of grace and sin, we can see from history how two men can hear the word of God, but one hears it as true and the other not. Saint Athanasius and Arius both read the Gospel according to Saint John. However, the former saw clearly that the "Word" was identical with the Creator, but the latter saw the "Word" only as a creature and was condemned as a heretic.

CONTEMPORARY

In the recent apostolic letter of our Holy Father entitled *To Defend the Faith* and in the authoritative and official commentary that accompanied its publication, there are several striking examples of doctrinal development discussed.

For example, it is seen how the Church from her beginning saw the primacy of Saint Peter and his legitimate successors as divinely revealed and therefore requiring of all Catholics the assent of faith. The infallibility of the Pope, when speaking *ex cathedra* about faith and morals, was also universally and clearly held by the Church and had to be assented to by Catholics. However, until the First Vatican Council defined the dogma, namely, that this infallibility is part of divine revelation, it was open to discussion whether papal infallibility was a logical consequence of revelation or part of such revelation itself.

ANOTHER MATTER

In a similar way the reservation of priestly ordination to males is a Catholic belief that is infallible and irrevocable. It is present in the consciousness of the Church as a true doctrine and must be held definitively. A Catholic who would doubt or deny such a doctrine would be in the state of serious sin, would not be in full communion with the Church, and (as a result of the Pope's apostolic letter) would be subject to ecclesiastical censures.

"This doctrine [of the Church]", says the commentary, "is to be held definitively, since, founded on the written Word of God, constantly preserved and applied in the Tradition of the Church, it has been set forth infallibly by the ordinary and universal Magisterium... This does not foreclose the possibility that, in the future, the consciousness of the Church might progress to the point where this teaching could be defined as a doctrine to be believed as divinely revealed."[7] Of course, the Church, which cannot err in such doctrine, could never "reverse herself" about the matter. It is precisely to preserve her from such corruption in doctrine that the Holy Spirit was given to her (see Jn 16:12–15) by our Redeemer.

Sometimes theological and religious themes might seem somewhat abstract and separated from the realities of our everyday lives. However, consideration of the development of Christian doctrine has great significance for the life of the Church, in the lives of many individuals (witness the conversion in the last century of John Henry Newman), and in our contemporary theological and ecclesial situation. It is consoling to remind ourselves often about the Holy Spirit, Whom Jesus promised would abide with us and be in us (Jn 14:15–17) and Who will lead us to all truth, that is, to Him Who is, in His very Person, the Truth.

JULY 17, 1998

Doctrinal Development
IV

ALWAYS THE SAME

Sometimes when a family returns to a homestead for Thanksgiving or Christmas, the grandparents, who may not have seen their grandchildren for awhile, will remark, "My, how they have grown!" They are the same grandchildren they have always been; yet there is growth and development. Such an incident can serve as an analogy for what is called the development of doctrine.

Jesus Christ founded the Catholic Church and entrusted to her the deposit of faith, that is, the fullness and totality of His teaching. He charged her to preserve His doctrine unmutilated and undamaged until He returns in glory. Furthermore, He gave His Church the Holy Spirit to abide with her, along with His gifts of infallibility and indefectibility, to ensure that she would carry out her mission. In this way our Redeemer Himself is "with" His Church until the end of time (Mt 28:20). Saint Vincent of Lerins said that we can be sure of the faith, which is believed by all Catholics everywhere and always (*Quod semper, quod ubique, quod ab omnibus*). This is "the faith which was once for all delivered to the saints" (Jude 3). It is impossible, therefore, for the Catholic Church to defect from the faith, although through the centuries various individual Catholics have left or lapsed from true belief.

NEWMAN

On his way to becoming a Catholic, John Henry Newman wrote in splendid prose a book entitled *An Essay on the Development of Christian Doctrine*. He said, "Considering the high gifts and the strong claims of the Church of Rome and her dependencies on our admiration, reverence, love, and gratitude, how could we withstand her... how could we refrain from being melted into tenderness, and rushing into communion with her...?"[8] He had initially thought, however, that he had found an obstacle to his conversion in the history of the Catholic Church, that is, some differences between the early Church and the Church of the nineteenth century.

In the course of composing his *Essay*, he changed his mind. He saw the "obstacle" as "a specious objection". He wrote,

> Granting that some large variations of teaching in its long course of eighteen hundred years exist, nevertheless, these, on examination will be found to arise from the nature of the case, and to proceed on a law, and with a harmony and a definite drift, and with an analogy to Scripture revelations, which, instead of telling to their disadvantage, actually constitute an argument in their favour, as witnessing to a superintending Providence and a great Design in the mode and in the circumstances of their occurrence.[9]

He said, "He little thought [when he began his book] that the time would ever come when he should feel the obstacle, which he spoke of as lying in the way of communion with the Church of Rome, to be destitute of solid foundation."[10]

IDENTITY

Just as the grandparents mentioned above would be able to recognize the identical grandchildren, although they had grown and developed, so Newman was able to conclude, "The doctrine [of the Catholic Church] is where it was, *and usage, and precedence, and principle, and policy*; there may be changes, but they are consolidations or adaptations; all is unequivocal and determinate, with an identity which there is no disputing."[11] Father Gustave Weigel says, "Of course, Newman accepted the proposition that the Church of Christ endures and is identical with the Catholic Church."

Weigel notes that Newman, a great historian, knew that if the Church of Christ were to continue through history, she would have to experience some change. However, Newman set out a number of qualities that he perceived would make such a change without the Church becoming something other than what she always was and will be. "For Newman the Church of Christ and the Catholic Church were identical."

CORRUPTIONS

The biggest problem in studying the development of doctrine is how to distinguish genuine and correct development from corruption and decay. How, the question may be put, can we see the doctrine that comes from the apostles undergo development without error, dilution, or mutilation? Heresy, religious falsehood, doctrinal error, and immoral teaching always exist, and these flourish in the world and among some calling themselves Christians even today.

Certainly, we know that the true faith is safeguarded by the divinely constituted teaching authority (Magisterium) of the Church herself and by Christ's guarantees to His Body and Bride. As we gaze back over the Church's history, moreover, we can join Newman (who later became a Cardinal of the Holy Roman Church) in seeing seven notes as marking the difference between genuine development and corruption of doctrine. He names these notes as: preservation of type; continuity of principles; power of assimilation; logical sequence; anticipation of the future; conservative upon the past; and chronic vigor.

God is the God of truth and can never contradict Himself. Jesus not only taught the truth (Jn 18:37), but declared that in His divine Person He is the Truth itself (Jn 14:6). Therefore, what is true in revelation today was true yesterday and will be true tomorrow. Philosophical relativism is not compatible with Christianity. At the same time, there is a continual development in Catholic doctrine (Jn 16:12–14) that, of course, does not constitute any new revelation or contradict the past authoritative teaching of the Church.

The Second Vatican Council teaches: "God, who spoke of old, uninterruptedly converses with the bride of His beloved Son, and the Holy Spirit, through whom the living voice of the Gospel resounds in the Church, and through her, in the world, leads unto all truth those who believe and makes the word of Christ dwell abundantly in them (see Col 3:16)."[12] The Dogmatic Constitution on Divine Revelation *Dei Verbum* of the Second Vatican Council and the grand work of Cardinal Newman are the best sources for more information about the vital subject of doctrinal development.

NOVEMBER 13, 1998

Liberalism In Religion

CARDINAL NEWMAN

The last century produced few converts to the Catholic faith who could match

Cardinal John Henry Newman in intellectual vigor and no one who could equal his superb ability to write English prose. He became a Catholic in the crucible of nineteenth-century British politics and in the turmoil of the Oxford Movement.

When he was named a Cardinal of the Holy Roman Church in 1879, at quite an advanced age, he remarked that "For thirty, forty, fifty years I have resisted to the best of my powers the spirit of liberalism in religion."[13] On that occasion, he called liberalism in religion "an error overspreading as a snare the whole earth."[14] Although he acknowledged that there was some interpenetration of philosophical and political liberalism into religious liberalism, he was careful to distinguish precisely that what he opposed was liberalism in religion. Of course, liberalism as a general attitude and temperament can have a bearing on a person's total outlook, including religion.

TERM

The word *liberal* derives from the Latin word *libertas*, which means freedom. Plato in the *Republic* wrote about the "liberal arts", meaning the studies considered worthy of a free man. Liberal education, which includes the traditional seven liberal arts, was (and in many places still is) always considered an important part of a person's rational formation in Western culture and civilization. The term *liberal*, however, began to take on a totally different meaning during the French Revolution. Liberalism then began to mean a philosophy that exalted human freedom to the point of denying the rights and laws of God, the rejection of the rights of religion, of the Church, and sometimes the rights of organized society itself. In this sense, Pope Pius IX in the famous Syllabus of Errors condemned liberalism.

Today, in various countries and sections of countries, the term politically can have a variety of meanings, from total libertarian views ("that government governs best which governs least"), which denies such a thing as the common good, to the advocacy of types of statism and even socialism. In Protestantism, liberalism means a type of rationalism that denies divine revelation, insists upon a religion based solely on human reason, and is relativistic in its philosophy. The heresy of "Modernism", which was condemned by Pope Saint Pius X in the early part of our century, contains many elements of Protestant liberalism, especially in its treatment of Sacred Scripture. The doctrines of the contemporary theologian Hans Küng, who may not teach any longer as a Catholic, were called by the Jesuit scholar Karl Rahner indistinguishable from liberal Protestantism.

IN RELIGION

Cardinal Newman said,

> Liberalism in religion is the doctrine that there is no truth in religion, but that one creed is as good as another... It is inconsistent with any recognition of any religion, as *true*. It teaches that all are to be tolerated, for all are matters of opinion. Revealed religion is not a truth, but a sentiment and a taste; not an objective fact, miraculous; and it is the right of each individual to make it say just what strikes his fancy. Devotion is not necessarily founded on faith. Men may go to Protestant Churches and to Catholic, may get good from both and belong to neither. They may fraternise together in spiritual thoughts and feelings, without having any views at all of doctrines in common, or seeing the need of them... If a man puts on a new religion every morning, what is that to you? It is as impertinent to think about a man's religion as about his sources of income or his management of his family.[15]

It does not take much inquiry or insight to see how liberalism in religion has captured the mind and outlook of many people in our time. The season of Lent is a precious time when not only our sins and failings should become more apparent to us in the course of our penance and self-denial. Our attitudes, our outlook on life, our doctrinal and moral convictions, and our knowledge of our faith should also undergo a careful evaluation to be certain that liberalism has not crept into our hearts subtly, even unknowingly. Newman states, "Liberalism then is the mistake of subjecting to human judgment those revealed doctrines which are in their nature beyond and independent of it, and of claiming to determine on intrinsic grounds the truth and value of propositions which rest for their reception simply on the authority of the Divine Word."[16]

DOGMA

Opposing the principle of liberalism in religion, Newman sets forth what he called the "dogmatical principle". It was finding this principle in the Catholic Church that was decisive in Newman's experience of conversion:

> That there is a truth then; that there is one truth; that religious error is in itself of an immoral nature; that its maintainers, unless involuntarily such, are guilty in maintaining it;... that the mind is below truth, not above it, and is bound, not to descant upon it, but to venerate it; that truth and falsehood are set before us for the trial of our hearts; that our choice is an awful giving forth of lots on which salvation or rejection is inscribed; that "before all things it is necessary to hold the Catholic faith;" that "he who would be

saved must thus think," and not otherwise;... this is the dogmatical principle.[17]

The "principle of philosophies and heresies" (liberalism in religion) is described by Newman as the view "that the Governor of the world does not intend that we should gain the truth; that there is no truth; that we are not more acceptable to God by believing this than by believing that; that no one is answerable for his opinions;... that it is enough if we sincerely hold what we profess;... that it is a duty to follow what seems to us to be true, without a fear lest it should not be true;... that we may safely trust to ourselves in matters of Faith, and ourselves in need no other guide."[18]

Perhaps our Lenten prayers and our reading and listening to Sacred Scripture and the *Catechism of the Catholic Church* will enable us in this holy season to purge from our hearts and minds all traces of liberalism in religion.

MARCH 6, 1998

2

SOCIAL DOCTRINE

Social Doctrine - I

SOCIAL SIN

The *Catechism of the Catholic Church*, as has been the custom in religious education now for many generations, treats the social doctrine of the Church under the rubric of the seventh commandment. Since the manifestation and growth of the industrial revolution, especially in the middle of the nineteenth century in the West, a huge body of moral literature and of doctrinal pronouncements regarding the social teaching of the Church has developed that deserves serious study. Immersed in this, one often finds the term "social sin", and that idea needs clarification, particularly when dealing with issues in the virtue of justice and those concerning moral imputability.

Pope John Paul II says,

> There is one meaning sometimes given to social sin that is not legitimate or acceptable, even though it is very common in certain quarters today. This usage contrasts social sin and personal sin, not without ambiguity, in a way that leads more or less unconsciously to the watering down and almost abolition of personal sin, with the recognition only of social guilt and responsibilities. According to this usage, which can readily be seen to derive from non-Christian ideologies and systems,... practically every sin is a social sin, in the sense that blame for it is placed not so much on the moral conscience of an individual, but rather on some vague entity or anonymous collectivity, such as the situation, the system, society, structures, or institutions.[19]

PERSONAL

Our Holy Father explains in his apostolic exhortation entitled *Reconciliation and Penance*,

> Sin, in the proper sense, is always a personal act, since it is an act of freedom on the part of an individual person and not properly

of a group or community. The individual may be conditioned, incited, and influenced by numerous and powerful external factors. He may also be subjected to tendencies, defects, and habits linked with his personal condition. In not a few cases such external and internal factors may attenuate, to a greater or lesser degree, the person's freedom and therefore his responsibility and guilt. But it is a truth of faith, also confirmed by our experience and reason, that the human person is free. This truth cannot be disregarded in order to place the blame for individuals' sins on external factors such as structures, systems, or other people... Hence there is nothing so personal and untransferable in each individual as merit for virtue or responsibility for sin.

As a personal act, sin has its first and most important consequences in the sinner himself: that is, in his relationship with God, who is the very foundation of human life; and also in his spirit, weakening his will and clouding his intellect. (no. 16)

How Then?

Setting forth the perennial teaching of the Church on these matters, Pope John Paul II states that in one sense every sin is a social sin because "a soul that lowers itself through sin drags down with itself the Church and, in some way, the whole world. In other words, there is no sin, not even the most intimate and secret one, the most strictly individual one, that exclusively concerns the person committing it...According to this first meaning of the term, every sin can undoubtedly be considered as social sin" (no. 16).

The Supreme Pontiff also notes that some sins of individuals directly constitute an attack on one's neighbor or his property or rights. Such sins that violate the love that God demands we must have for our neighbor are rightly called "social sins". "Likewise the term social applies to every sin against justice in interpersonal relationships, committed either by the individual against the community or by the community against the individual. Also social is every sin against the rights of the human person, beginning with the right to life and including the life of the unborn or against a person's physical integrity" (no. 16).

Leaders' Duties

The Holy Father continues:

Likewise social is every sin against others' freedom, especially against the supreme freedom to believe in God and adore him; social is every sin against the dignity and honor of one's neighbor...against

the common good and its exigencies in relation to the whole broad
spectrum of the rights and duties of citizens. The term social can
be applied to sins of commission or omission—on the part of
political, economic, or trade union leaders who, though in a position
to do so, do not work diligently and wisely for the improvement
and transformation of society according to the requirements and
potential of the given historical moment, as also on the part of
workers who through absenteeism or non-cooperation fail to ensure
that their industries can continue to advance the well-being of the
workers themselves, of their families, and of the whole of society.
(no. 16)

The term social sin can also apply to relationships between human communities
that "are not always in accordance with the plan of God, who intends that there be
justice in the world and freedom and peace between individuals, groups, and peoples.
Thus the class struggle, whoever the person who leads it or on occasion seeks to
give it a theoretical justification, is a social evil" as also is any "obstinate
confrontation between blocs of nations, between one nation and another, [or]
between different groups within the same nation" (no. 16).

ANALOGOUS

As the Pope remarks, there are some modern social realities and contemporary
situations that have such vast proportions and are so complex and anonymous that,
when one speaks of "social sins" in their regard, one can only give the expression
an "analogical meaning". However, he cautions, "to speak even analogically of
social sins must not cause us to underestimate the responsibility of the individuals
involved" (no. 16). This occasional analogical usage of the term "social sins" by
Church authorities "is meant to be an appeal to the consciences of all, so that each
may shoulder his or her responsibility seriously and courageously in order to change
those disastrous conditions and intolerable situations" (no. 16).

Someone once observed that working for social justice requires not only getting
people out of the slums, but also getting the slums out of people. Then too, there is
sometimes a strong temptation to try to disguise or minimize or even rationalize
personal sins, by claiming (or feigning) activity and devotion in the cause of social
justice, thus trying to salve a troubled conscience. It is always easier to point out
and criticize the sins of others or the wrongdoing of some collectivity than to own
up with humility and contrition to our own personal moral shortcomings, just as it
is always easier to criticize the creed of another than to formulate and express
one's own.

NOVEMBER 8, 2002

Social Doctrine
II

USURY

The sin of usury is usually considered under the seventh commandment. It is seen as a violation of commutative justice and thus forbidden by the natural law. In its deepest meaning it means taking incorrect advantage of another who is in serious need, and thus it violates charity, the love of neighbor that Jesus requires all His followers to practice (Jn 13:34; Mk 12:29–31; Lk 10:25–28; Deut 6:4–5). In Christian moral law (and sometimes in modern civil law as well) the sin and crime of usury today means taking exorbitant and excessive interest on a loan.

Through the centuries the nature and use of money drastically changed and, consequently, so did what constituted usury. In ancient times, there was no such thing as a market rate of interest; rather this was determined by bargaining between private lenders and borrowers. It was only in the fourteenth and fifteenth centuries in Europe that capitalism was born, and money was no longer considered a "fungible good". Until the close of the Middle Ages, almost any interest on a loan of money was considered usury, but with a change in the nature and use of money around that time, reasonable interest from then on has been legitimately and morally considered the "price of a loan".

SCRIPTURE

The Chosen People of the Old Testament were explicitly forbidden to charge interest on loans to the poor. While they were permitted to loan money to Gentiles for interest, they were prohibited from demanding interest on loans made to their fellow Hebrews (Lev 25:35–37; Ex 22:25). God, already in the Old Testament, explicitly condemned greed and the amassing of riches by means of oppressing the poor by usury.

Some famous pagan thinkers, such as Plato, Cicero, Seneca, and Cato, often wrote and spoke against the practice of taking interest on loans as something detrimental to the welfare of the State. Greek and Roman laws usually permitted but strictly regulated interest on money loans in their ancient empires.

In New Testament times, the Church has always been loyal to the teaching of her divine Founder. Christ did not seem to condemn getting interest on monetary investments as intrinsically evil, according to His parable of the talents (Mt 25:27), but at the same time He also spoke about the desirability of some loans being gratuitous (Lk 6:30; Mt 5:42). Of course, our Lord condemned greed and those who were devoted to riches rather than to God (Mt 6:19–21; 19:24).

CHURCH

At least from the fifth century to the eighteenth, there were laws of the Church that considered taking interest on loans as a type of usury. At first this practice was forbidden for the clergy, but later the prohibition was extended to the laity as well. Yet, the Catholic Church never taught that interest in itself and under all conditions was to be considered usury and a violation of justice. Theologians such as Saint Thomas Aquinas along with some prominent canonists held that there could exist factors permitting the taking of interest on loans, such as actual damage to or loss of the loan, risk in regard to the loan, loss of profit from the use of the loan, and danger of delay in repayment.

In various places in Christian Europe in earlier times, there arose institutions that were a sort of credit union for humbler and simpler folks, which accepted savings and dispensed loans at low interest. These were often founded by religious orders and dioceses and were praised by the authorities of the Church. In the Middle Ages and slightly later, the Church laws forbidding usury for Christians led to moneylending falling almost entirely into the hands of non-Christians (with consequent dislike and sometimes hatred of moneylenders: "Loan oft loses both itself and friend"). However, when Church authorities recognized the evolutionary process that was changing the nature and use of money, they then clearly taught that requiring moderate amounts of interest for loaned money was a justified and permitted practice for Christians. As one contemporary Catholic theologian puts it, "The Church's basic teaching on this subject did not change. Injustice surrounding money lending was and remains condemned. What changed was the economic system. As this changed the circumstances under which injustice is committed changed. The Church permitted what was no longer unjust." Of course, in modern times amounts, types, and regulation of interest on loans are not exclusively matters of commutative justice; rather they must also be seen as concerns of social justice as well.

HUMAN PERSONS

The *Catechism of the Catholic Church* states, "Society ensures social justice when it provides the conditions that allow associations and individuals to obtain what is their due, according to their nature and their vocation. Social justice is linked to the common good and the exercise of authority" (CCC 1928). Not only in matters of commerce, banking, moneylending, and so on, but in all matters of social relationships the *Catechism* insists that the human person must be seen as the ultimate end and purpose of human society. Social justice can only be found where there is respect for "the transcendent dignity of man" (CCC 1929).

Pope John Paul II says, "What is at stake is the dignity of the human person."[20]

The *Catechism* reminds us that the rights that flow from a human being's dignity as a creature of God are prior to the existence and rights of any human society and must be recognized by it. By flouting these rights "or refusing to recognize them in its positive legislation, a society undermines its own moral legitimacy [cf. John XXIII, *Pacem in terris*, no. 65]. If it does not respect them, authority can rely only on force or violence to obtain obedience from its subjects. It is the Church's role to remind men of good will of these rights and to distinguish them from unwarranted false claims" (CCC 1930).

The Second Vatican Council teaches that "everyone should look upon his neighbor ... as 'another self', above all bearing in mind his life and the means necessary for living it with dignity."[21] The *Catechism* says, "No legislation could by itself do away with the fears, prejudices, and attitudes of pride and selfishness which obstruct the establishment of truly fraternal societies. Such behavior will cease only through the charity that finds in every man a 'neighbor', a brother [Mt 25:40]. The duty of making oneself a neighbor to others and actively serving them becomes even more urgent when it involves the disadvantaged" (CCC 1931–32).

Social Doctrine
III

Forty, Eighty, and One Hundred

On May 15, 1891, Pope Leo XIII published an encyclical letter entitled *Rerum novarum* ("About New Things") and subtitled "On the Condition of Human Labor". It was a ground-breaking event, in which the Holy Father attempted for the first time since the start of the Industrial Revolution to use his teaching authority to apply the traditions and principles of Christian morality to the spectrum of social, economic, and political realities then existing in the world, especially in Europe. That document's significance has been emphasized by the fact that the successors of Pope Leo XIII in the See of Peter have seen fit to commemorate that historic and important encyclical on its fortieth anniversary (*Quadragesimo anno*, by Pope Pius XI), on its eightieth anniversary (*Octogesima adveniens*, by Pope Paul VI), and on its hundredth anniversary (*Centesimus annus*, by Pope John Paul II).

The Bishops of Rome also have issued many adjacent documents over recent years treating political, economic, and social questions. Some of the more notable ones are the 1937 encyclical *Divini Redemptoris*, of Pope Pius XI, condemning Communism, Socialism, and other forms of Marxism, that same Pope's condemnation of Fascism (*Non abbiamo bisogno*) and Nazism (*Mit brennender sorge*), the writings of Pope John XXIII (*Mater et Magistra*, *Pacem in terris*), of Pope Paul VI (*Populorum progressio*), and of Pope John Paul II (*Laborem exercens and Sollicitudo rei socialis*). No one can claim to have a correct and comprehensive grasp of the social doctrine of the Catholic Church without a thorough knowledge of these papal teachings.

A RIGHT

It is not the mission, duty, or right of the Church to establish or endorse any particular social, economic, or political system. The Popes have constantly asserted that the Catholic Church, throughout her history, has found herself at home in a large variety of different systems and cultural situations. Pope John Paul II has said, "The Church does not propose economic or political systems or programs, nor does she show preference for one or the other, provided that human dignity is properly respected and promoted, and provided she herself is allowed the room she needs to exercise her ministry in the world."[22] However, it is the mission, duty, right of the teaching authority of the Church to proclaim the gospel in its integrity, which includes its moral requirements, and to apply Catholic moral principles to all areas of human life and activity. Pope Pius XI states that "the principle which Leo XIII so clearly established must be laid down at the outset here, namely that there resides in Us the right and duty to pronounce with supreme authority upon social and economic matters. Certainly the Church was not given the commission to guide men to an only fleeting and perishable happiness but to that which is eternal."[23]

The Pope goes on to remark, "Indeed 'the Church holds that it is unlawful for her to mix without cause in these temporal concerns'; however, she can in no wise renounce the duty God entrusted to her to interpose her authority, not of course in matters of technique for which she is neither suitably equipped nor endowed by office, but in all things that are connected with the moral law."[24]

MORALS

From the time of Pope Leo XIII to the present age, there are (and presumably will always be) some people who are surprised, shocked, and amazed that any ecclesiastical pronouncements and Church teaching should touch upon such worldly matters as politics, social arrangements, or economic concerns. Some would say the Church should confine her work only to the sacristy, to the church building, and to merely spiritual matters, or, at most, limit herself simply to urging the poor to resignation, the rich to generosity, and politicians to basic honesty.

However, Pope Pius XI says what his successors have often repeated.

> Even though economics and moral science employs each its own
> principles in its own sphere, it is, nevertheless, an error to say that
> the economic and moral orders are so distinct from and alien to
> each other that the former depends in no way on the latter. Certainly
> the laws of economics, as they are termed, being based on the very
> nature of material things and on the capacities of the human body
> and mind, determine the limits of what productive human effort
> cannot, and of what it can attain in the economic field and by what
> means. Yet it is reason itself that clearly shows, on the basis of the
> individual and social nature of things and of men, the purpose
> which God ordained for all economic life.
>
> But it is only the moral law which, just as it commands us to
> seek our supreme and last end in the whole scheme of our activity,
> so likewise commands us to seek directly in each kind of activity
> those purposes which we know that nature, or rather God the Author
> of nature, established for that kind of action, and in orderly
> relationship to subordinate such immediate purposes to our supreme
> and last end. If we faithfully observe this law, then it will follow
> that the particular purposes, both individual and social, that are
> sought in the economic field will fall in their proper place in the
> universal order of purposes, and We, in ascending through them,
> as it were by steps, shall attain the final end of all things, that is
> God, to Himself and to us, the supreme and inexhaustible Good.[25]

JOHN PAUL II

Our present Holy Father, in explaining the entry of the Church's Magisterium in
the area of social teaching, says,

> The Church's social doctrine is not a "third way" between liberal
> capitalism and Marxist collectivism, nor even a possible alternative
> to other solutions less radically opposed to one another: rather, it
> constitutes a category of its own. Nor is it an ideology, but rather
> an accurate formulation of the results of a careful reflection on the
> realities of human existence, in society and in the international
> order, in the light of faith and of the Church's tradition. Its main
> aim is to interpret these realities, determining their conformity with
> or divergence from the lines of the Gospel teaching on man and
> his vocation, a vocation which is at once earthly and transcendent;
> its aim is thus to guide Christian behavior. It therefore belongs to

the field, not of ideology, but of theology and particularly moral theology.

The teaching and spreading of her social doctrine are part of the Church's evangelizing mission. And, since it is a doctrine aimed at guiding people's behavior, it consequently gives rise to a "commitment to justice", according to each individual's role, vocation, and circumstances. The condemnation of evils and injustices is also part of that ministry of evangelization in the social field which is an aspect of the Church's prophetic role.[26]

JANUARY 31, 2003

Social Doctrine
IV

THE POOR

Our Holy Father, Pope John Paul II, says, "The Church's love for the poor … is part of her constant tradition."[27] The *Catechism of the Catholic Church* goes on to say, "This love is inspired by the Gospel of the Beatitudes, of the poverty of Jesus, and of his concern for the poor [cf. Lk 6:20–22; Mt 8:20; Mk 12:41–44] …It extends not only to material poverty but also to the many forms of cultural and religious poverty" (CCC 2444). The New Testament is very clear about the duty of Christ's disciples toward the poor (Mt 5:42). When the poor have the gospel preached to them, it is a special sign of Christ's presence (Lk 4:18). How we have helped the poor during our lifetime will be a major factor in how we will be judged by Jesus at the end of the world (Mt 25:31–36). One of the motives for our work should be to enable us to assist the needy out of our income (Eph 4:28).

Although we shall always have the poor with us (Jn 12:8) and although poverty in spirit and a lack of riches can facilitate (or even make possible) one's journey to heaven (Mt 5:3; 19:23–26), we must take moral care that the misery and penury of others are not due to our selfishness, to our participation in any ongoing injustice, to our immoderate use or desire for this world's goods, or to our unconcern (Jas 5:1–6). Like it or not, we are by God's design our "brother's keeper". Saint John Chrysostom said that failing to help the poor is "stealing from them", and Saint Gregory the Great said that for Christians helping the poor is merely "paying a debt of justice".

SOME CAUSES

I recall a basement recreation room in the house of one of my uncles where there was a sign near the bar saying "If you are so smart, why aren't you rich?" Although humorous, the sign did prompt me to reflect on why people are rich or poor. This kind of reflection can be significant especially in our present American culture, where sometimes the worth and importance of people are mistakenly measured almost solely by their material wealth and where "having and enjoying" are given a vast priority over "being and growing" in knowledge, concern for justice, acquisition of wisdom, and charity.

It is true that sometimes people are poor because of their flaws, defects, or sins. There are some who are impoverished because they engage in self-destructive behavior (dope, alcoholism, laziness, gambling, extravagant living, reckless conduct of various kinds, and so on). However, the great majority of people in our country and in our world who are in material poverty are in that condition, not because of their own fault, but because of matters out of their control (sickness, injury, unemployment, market or investment failures, currency collapses, natural or man-made catastrophes, irresponsible parents, racial or ethnic discrimination, and so on). In the same way, many rich people come to their fortunes by personal hard work, cleverness, or good use of their gifts, but others are wealthy only or mainly because of fortuitous circumstances, such as inheritance, special unearned talents of mind or body, different kinds of luck, and so on. Indeed, some even become rich through dishonesty or through the exploitation of their fellow human beings.

VARIETY OF POVERTIES

It should be remembered that some people freely renounce the personal possession of goods and property, purposely being poor for the sake of the kingdom of heaven, following the evangelical counsel of poverty (Mk 10:21). While some rich people are like "Dives", the rich man in our Lord's parable (Lk 16:19–31), callously indifferent to the plight of the downtrodden, there are others who correctly use their wealth in socially and spiritually responsible ways marked by justice and charity. In a similar way, some poor people can be consumed by envy and greed and thus be poor materially but not "in spirit", while other poor people, despite their pains and struggles to "get ahead", can be saintly models for all to devote themselves principally to following our Savior's advice to "lay up treasures in heaven" rather than on earth and to become "rich in regard to God" (see Mt 6:19–21; Lk 12:21).

The *Catechism of the Catholic Church* teaches,
"In its various forms—material deprivation, unjust oppression,

physical and psychological illness and death—*human misery* is the obvious sign of an inherited condition of frailty and need for salvation in which man finds himself as a consequence of original sin. This misery elicited the compassion of Christ the Savior, who willingly took it upon himself and identified himself with the least of his brethren. Hence, those who are oppressed by poverty are the object of a *preferential love* on the part of the Church which, since her origin and in spite of the failings of many of her members, has not ceased to work for their relief, defense, and liberation through numerous works of charity which remain indispensable always and everywhere."[28]

LOCAL WORK

Some of my fondest boyhood recollections are of accompanying my father, who for years was the president of my native parish's Saint Vincent de Paul group, as he made his weekly rounds to bring food and relief to poor households in our old neighborhood in Milwaukee. Even when my widowed mother retired and acted as my part-time housekeeper while I was a pastor in Wauwatosa, she eagerly took a monthly turn serving at a "meals for the poor" distribution place, and she inspired me to have a huge area food pantry for the hungry as well as to have our parish participate with some neighboring parishes in a homeless shelter arrangement in the inner city of Milwaukee. She often told me heart-wrenching stories of the hungry and poorly clad little children she encountered in her charitable work.

Here in our Diocese of Lincoln, Catholic Social Services and the Saint Vincent de Paul Society do great and constant work in our name for the poor. Also, many wonderful initiatives to help the poor have been undertaken and are underway by many Catholic families, individuals, and parishes. Our emphasis on Medicaid patients at Madonna Rehabilitation Hospital and our affordable housing arrangements are aimed toward those in need. Of course, most of our almsgiving must and should be kept secret and be known only to our heavenly Father (Mt 6:2–4). Perhaps only a little bit of what we do in that regard should be revealed in order to inspire others and to "give glory to God" (Mt 5:16). Our works of charity, however, should not preclude or substitute for our equally important work for justice. Also, we must never forget that continuous charity for us Christians is not an option but an obligation if we want to follow and obey Christ.

FEBRUARY 7, 2003

Social Doctrine
V

NOT MONEY

One of the most misquoted (and misunderstood) Scripture passages is what Saint Paul wrote to Saint Timothy about money (1 Tim 6:10). The root of all evil is not money itself, according to Saint Paul, but rather "the love of money". The Apostle to the Gentiles wrote, "It is through this craving that some have wandered away from the faith and pierced their hearts with many pangs." Being rich is not wrong, but our Lord has warned us that wealth easily can be a serious danger to salvation (Mt 6:24; Lk 12:13–21; 18:24–27) and a source of woe (Lk 6:24–25).

The principal peril consists in the fact that money, necessary as it is, or an inordinate seeking for money, can become an idol, replacing God in the first place in one's life, and riches, or a quest for them, often can inspire temptations to commit sins, such as envy, greed, quarreling, unconcern for the sufferings of other human beings, injustice, dishonesty, neglect of family or other duties, sloth, and so on (Jas 5:1–6).

Our Holy Father, Pope John Paul II, says,

> Our age, regrettably, is particularly susceptible to the temptation toward selfishness which always lurks within the human heart. In society generally, and in the media, people are bombarded by messages which more or less openly exalt the ephemeral and the hedonistic. Concern for others is certainly shown whenever natural disasters, war, and other emergencies strike, but in general it is difficult to build a culture of solidarity. The spirit of the world affects our inner propensity to give ourselves unselfishly to others and drives us to satisfy our own particular interests.[29]

PROFIT

It is certain that people of means can make possible out of their wealth great works of charity, missions, Church undertakings, education, art, literature, and science, and many such persons in the past commendably and generously have done so. Even now, when much investment in some such fields is carried out as well by governments out of tax funds, there is still an important and irreplaceable need for those who are able to expend some of their possessions in those undertakings to provide for things that enhance the Church and the general public's well-being and that serve to improve and uplift the minds and hearts of others. Wealth that is properly used and rich people themselves can certainly be a source of much good.

It appears clear that it is entirely proper sometimes to see profit and monetary gain as legitimate motivations for human labor in order to fulfill the moral duty each one has to support oneself and one's dependents (2 Thess 3:6–15). It also seems moral and proper to visualize a hope for possible profits as a legitimate motive for promoting investments and similar property risks (Mt 25: 19–28). Pope John Paul II says in his encyclical *Centesimus annus* (May 1, 1991) that "it appears that, on the level of individual nations and of international relations, the *free market* is the most efficient instrument for utilizing resources and effectively responding to needs" (no. 34). The Pope also asserts that "the modern *business economy* has positive aspects" (no. 32). However, it must be pointed out that those important statements of the Bishop of Rome are surrounded by many qualifying elements and should not be read and cannot be correctly understood apart from their total context.

TAKING IT ALONG

It is well, moreover, to bear in mind another perspective. It is an ironic paradox that the only money and possessions that human beings can take with them when they leave this world to journey through the doorway of death into eternity are those things that they have given away while living on earth. This undoubtedly is why our Savior taught us that "it is more blessed to give than to receive" (Acts 20:35). Saint Francis of Assisi, paraphrasing the Gospel (Lk 6:38), says, "It is in giving that we receive." Christians in the light of faith should reflect readily on the fact that all earthly goods are, strictly speaking, not "owned", but only held in stewardship, and one day an accounting of the stewardship will have to be made to the real "Owner", Who is the Creator and Redeemer.

The saints through the ages have provided us with their teaching and example in that direction. "God loves the poor, all of whom are His friends, and consequently He loves those who have an affection for the poor because when we love anyone very much, we also love his friends" (Saint Vincent de Paul). "Love the poor tenderly, regarding them as your masters, and you yourselves as their servants" (Saint John of God). "The poor stretch out their hands, but it is God Who receives what we give" (Saint Peter Chrysologus). "Charity is the form, mover, mother, and root of all other virtues" (Saint Thomas Aquinas). "Be diligent in serving the poor. Love the poor. Honor them as you would Christ Himself" (Saint Louise de Marillac).

MOTHER TERESA

Next October, on Mission Sunday (World Mission Day), our Holy Father has scheduled the beatification of Venerable Mother Teresa of Calcutta. This great contemporary of ours has much to teach us about Catholic social doctrine. She says,

> Many people think, especially in the West, that having money makes you happy. I think it must be harder to be happy if you are wealthy because you may find it difficult to see God. You'll have too many other things to think about. However, if God has given you this gift of wealth, then use it for His purposes—help others, help the poor, create jobs, give work to others. Don't waste your wealth. Having food, a home, dignity, freedom, health, and an education are all of God's gifts too, which is why we must help those who are less fortunate than ourselves.[30]

She also says,

> Works of love are works of peace and purity. Works of love are always a means of becoming closer to God, so, the more we help each other, the more we really love God…Jesus very clearly said, "Love one another as I have loved you." Love in action is what gives us grace. We pray and, if we are able to love with a whole heart, then we will see the need. Those who are unwanted, unloved, and uncared for become just a throwaway of society…This kind of love begins at home. We cannot give to the outside what we do not have on the inside. This is very important. If I can't see God's love in my brother and sister then…how can I give it to someone else?[31]

"If we pray and love with our whole heart, we will see the needs and will work to fill them. Jesus said, 'What you did to the least of my brethren, you did it to Me.'… When we hurt the poor, and hurt each other, we're hurting God. Everything is God's to give and to take away, so share what you have been given, and that includes yourself."[32]

FEBRUARY 14, 2003

Social Doctrine
VI

DARWIN-ECONOMICS

The publication in 1858 of Charles Darwin's *The Origin of Species* coincided with the rising Industrial Revolution in which large sections of the world, especially Europe and North America, were undergoing drastic social changes, emerging from a basically agrarian society mostly controlled by landowners into a situation where a growing middle class of people, who owned factories, mines, and other "means of production", along with groups in the service professions, began to be on the top of the social order. Consciously or unconsciously, many wealthy people of that period began to apply Darwin's biological theories to economic life. Some, claiming that there existed iron-clad economic laws akin to those in biology, even used Darwinian expressions, such as "survival of the fittest", "allow only the strongest to survive", "favorable variations (in economic life) to be preserved and others to be destroyed", and so on. Something of that spirit can sometimes be discerned even today in the fact that many extremely wealthy people (Buffet, Gates, and so on) appear to be enthusiastic supporters of population control and birth prevention.

It is not surprising that in such an atmosphere, reinforced by the theories and concepts of *laissez-faire* capitalism and libertarian liberalism, working people were often cruelly exploited and their fundamental humanity and human needs often ignored. Workers were frequently lumped together by the term "labor" and were looked upon as a mere commodity to be bought, traded, sold, or disposed of, like "things" instead of "persons".

UNJUST CAPITAL

It was to address the growing problems of grave injustice in these areas that Pope Leo XIII wrote his famous encyclical *Rerum novarum* in 1891. Commenting on that encyclical with one of his own in 1931 (*Quadragesimo anno*), Pope Pius XI speaks about "unjust claims" in the social order, both on the part of capital and on the part of labor.

> Property, that is, "capital", has undoubtedly long been able to appropriate too much to itself. Whatever was produced, whatever returns accrued, capital claimed for itself, hardly leaving to the worker enough to restore and renew his strength. For the doctrine was preached that all accumulation of capital

falls by an absolutely insuperable economic law to the rich, and that by the same law the workers are given over and bound to perpetual want, to the scantiest of livelihoods. It is true, indeed, that things have not always and everywhere corresponded with this sort of teaching of the so-called Manchesterian Liberals; yet it cannot be denied that economic social institutions have moved steadily in that direction. That these false ideas, these erroneous suppositions, have been vigorously assailed, and not by those alone who through them were being deprived of their innate right to obtain better conditions, will surprise no one. (no. 54)

Unjust Labor

That Pope goes on to condemn some unjust claims of labor.

To the harassed workers there have come "intellectuals," as they are called, setting up in opposition to a fictitious law the equally fictitious moral principle that all products and profits, save only enough to repair and renew capital, belong by very right to the workers. This error, much more specious than that of certain of the Socialists ...is consequently all the more dangerous and the more apt to deceive the unwary. It is an alluring poison which many have eagerly drunk, even some whom open Socialism had not been able to deceive. (no. 55)

Those, therefore, are doing a work that is truly salutary and worthy of all praise who, while preserving harmony among themselves and the integrity of the traditional teaching of the Church, seek to define the inner nature of these duties and their limits whereby either the right of property itself or its use, that is, the exercise of ownership, is circumscribed by the necessities of social living. On the other hand, those who seek to restrict the individual character of ownership to such a degree that in fact they destroy it are mistaken and in error. (no. 48)

Wage Contracts

Provided that a wage arrangement is just to begin with, the Catholic Church teaches that its observance is binding under the seventh commandment (Ex 20:15; Deut 5:19; Mt 19:18) upon those who enter into such a contract. An employee is required to do all the work agreed to in an honest way, to respect the property of his employer, to obey the just orders of the owners, managers, or their agents, to participate as far as possible in improving production and such things as product design, and to use his gifts and strength for the general betterment of the enterprise or firm.

The employer, on the other hand, also has many moral obligations. Normally he must give the laborer a just compensation for his work and the products of his labor, the right to join a union or workers' association, a reasonably safe working environment, and, as far as possible, the opportunity to have adequate housing and medical care, as well as opportunities for rest and cultural or educational growth.

JUST WAGE

The *Catechism of the Catholic Church* says,

> A *just wage* is the legitimate fruit of work. To refuse or withhold it can be a grave injustice [cf. Lev 19:31; Deut 24:14–15; Jas 5:4]. In determining fair pay both the needs and the contributions of each person must be taken into account. [The Second Vatican Council says,] "Remuneration for work should guarantee man the opportunity to provide a dignified livelihood for himself and his family on the material, social, cultural, and spiritual level, taking into account the role and productivity of each, the state of the business, and the common good" [*Gaudium et spes*, no. 67, §2]. Agreement between the parties is not sufficient to justify morally the amount to be received in wages. (CCC 2434)

The *Catechism* also teaches, "Those *responsible for business enterprises* are responsible to society for the economic and ecological effects of their operations [cf. John Paul II, *Centesimus annus*, no. 37]. They have an obligation to consider the good of persons and not only the increase of *profits*. Profits are necessary, however. They make possible the investments that ensure the future of a business and they guarantee employment" (CCC 2432). It also states, "Efforts should be made to reduce these [economic] conflicts by negotiation that respects the rights and duties of each social partner: those responsible for business enterprises, representatives of wage-earners (for example, trade unions), and public authorities when appropriate" (CCC 2430).

3

SUNDAY

Sunday - I

NEW DOCUMENT

When he died in 1978, after a very brief pontificate of only one month, Pope John Paul I had on his desk a document he was preparing for early publication. It was concerned with restoring the proper Catholic observance of Sunday as the weekly "day of the Lord". This year our present Holy Father has issued a document on the same important subject, no doubt incorporating many of the ideas initially outlined by his immediate predecessor in the See of Peter.

The document is in the form of an "apostolic letter", entitled *The Day of the Lord* (*Dies Domini,* in Latin), from its first words. It is dated May 31, 1998, the Solemnity of Pentecost, but it was made public only in recent weeks. The Pope inserts this "apostolic letter" of his into the context of the coming year 2000. He writes:

> Dear Brothers and Sisters, the imminence of the Jubilee invites us to a deeper spiritual and pastoral commitment. Indeed, this is its true purpose. In the Jubilee year, much will be done to give it the particular stamp demanded by the ending of the Second Millennium and the beginning of the Third since the Incarnation of the Word of God. But this year and this special time will pass, as we look to other jubilees and other solemn events. As the weekly "solemnity", however, Sunday will continue to shape the time of the Church's pilgrimage, until that Sunday which will know no evening. (no. 87)

The Supreme Pontiff also says, "The coming of the Third Millennium, which calls believers to reflect upon the course of history in the light of Christ, also invites them to rediscover with new intensity the meaning of Sunday: its 'mystery', its celebration, its significance for Christian and human life" (no. 3).

IMPORTANCE

Sunday is the day that marks the beginning of God's work of creation. It is also the day that celebrates the anniversary of the coming of the Holy Spirit on the infant Catholic Church on Pentecost. However, its greatest meaning connects it with the pivotal event of all human history, the greatest of miracles, the Resurrection of Jesus from the dead. The Second Vatican Council teaches, "Every seven days, the Church celebrates the Easter mystery. This is a tradition going back to the Apostles, taking its origin from the actual day of Christ's Resurrection—a day thus appropriately designated the Lord's Day."[33]   The Bishop of Rome says, "[Sunday] is the day which recalls in grateful adoration the world's first day and looks forward in active hope to 'the last day' ... (Acts 11; 1 Thess 4:13–17) [when] all things will be made new (Rev 21:5)."[34]   He goes on to quote a fourth-century homily that calls the Lord's Day the "lord of days" and also Saint Jerome, who says, "Sunday is the day of the Resurrection. It is the day of Christians, it is our day."[35]   Pope John Paul II says, "For Christians, Sunday is the 'fundamental feastday', established not only to mark the succession of time but to reveal time's deeper meaning."[36]

SOCIAL CHANGE

It is obvious to any objective observer that, with the decline of genuine Christian civilization, there is change in our culture that often makes Sunday just another day of commerce, business, industry, agriculture, and labor. Continuing his apostolic letter, the Pope says,

> Until quite recently, it was easier in traditionally Christian countries to keep Sunday holy because it was almost universal practice and because, even in the organization of civil society, Sunday rest was considered a fixed part of the work schedule. Today, however, even in those countries which give legal sanction to the festive character of Sunday, changes in socioeconomic conditions have often led to profound modifications of social behavior and hence of the character of Sunday. (no. 4)

Our Holy Father states,

> The disciples of Christ, however, are asked to avoid any confusion between the celebration of Sunday, which should truly be a way of keeping the Lord's Day holy, and the "weekend", understood as a time of simple rest and relaxation. This will require a genuine spiritual maturity, which will enable Christians to "be what they are", in full accordance with the

gift of faith, always ready to give an account of the hope which is in them (cf. 1 Pet 3:15). In this way, they will be led to a deeper understanding of Sunday, with the result that, even in difficult situations, they will be able to live it in complete docility to the Holy Spirit. (no. 4)

Echoing what he said to the world at the commencement of his pontificate, almost twenty years ago, the Pope writes,

> *Do not be afraid to give your time to Christ*! Yes, let us open our time to Christ, that he may cast light upon it and give it direction. He is the One who knows the secret of time and the secret of eternity, and he gives "his day" as an ever new gift of his love. The rediscovery of this day is a grace which we must implore, not only so that we may live the demands of faith to the full, but also so that we may respond concretely to the deepest human yearnings. Time given to Christ is never time lost, but is rather time gained, so that our relationships and indeed our whole life may become more profoundly human. (no. 7)

LITTLE EASTER

In the very first years of the existence of the Catholic Church, there was only one feast day. This was Easter, and every Sunday was considered by the earliest Fathers of the Church a "little Easter". The entirety of the Christ-event and of all human existence was always looked upon through the lens of the Resurrection of our Savior. We too must adopt this perspective and look upon our observance of the third commandment of God and our obedience to the first precept of the Church, not merely as our obligation and duty, but, most of all, as a joyful privilege, which enriches us spiritually and physically each week.

Saint Ignatius of Antioch, the successor of Saint Peter in that See, wrote (sometime before A.D. 112, when he was martyred), "If those who were living in the former state of things have come to a new hope, no longer observing the Sabbath but keeping the Lord's Day, the day on which our life has appeared through him and his death,...how could we then live without him?"[37] May each Sunday fill us with hope and bring us closer to our Redeemer and His eternal love.

SEPTEMBER 18, 1998

Sunday
II

New Creation

The New Testament teaches us that Jesus was profoundly involved in the initial work of creation, which is attributed in the Old Testament to God, the almighty Father (Jn 1:3 and Col 1:16). Pope John Paul II writes in his apostolic letter: "In order to grasp fully the meaning of Sunday,...we must re-read the great story of creation [Genesis, chaps. 1–3) and deepen our understanding of the theology of the 'Sabbath'" (no. 8). Sunday, in the words of our Pope, "is the festival of the new creation" (no. 8). It is "above all an Easter celebration, wholly illuminated by the glory of the risen Christ.... Yet, when understood in depth, this aspect is inseparable from what the first pages of Scripture tell us of the plan of God in the creation of the world" (no. 8). We Christians observe Sunday as the Lord's Day because we see Christ, Whose Resurrection occurred on Sunday, as the origin and end of the universe. It was by His rising from the dead that He began the new creation (Col 1:15–18), which He will bring to completion when He comes again in triumph at the end of the world (1 Cor 15:24–28). Each Sunday recalls the beginning both of the first creation by God the Father and of the new creation by our divine Savior.

Eighth Day

Every Sunday should be for us a celebration of our Creator's work. The poetic language of the Book of Genesis ought to convey to us a weekly feeling of awe "before the immensity of creation and the resulting sense of adoration of the One who brought all things into being from nothing" (no. 9). Each Sunday should be in our lives "a hymn to the Creator of the universe, pointing to him as the only Lord in the face of recurring temptations to divinize the world itself ... a hymn to the goodness of creation, all fashioned by the mighty and merciful hand of God" (no. 9). Our Holy Father, in his apostolic letter *The Day of the Lord*, talks about the "unique connection between the Resurrection and Creation" (no. 24), that is, the link between the greatest of all miracles, which took place on the first day of the week (Mt 28:1), and the first day of the cosmic week, which saw the creation of light (Gen 1:1–5).

The Fathers of the Church spoke about Sunday, not merely as the first day of the week, but also as the eighth day, which symbolizes, not the commencement of time alone, but also the end of time "in the age to come". They saw Sunday as unique and transcendent, both the first and the eighth day, symbolizing "the day without end which will know neither evening nor morning, the imperishable age which will never grow old;... the ceaseless foretelling of life without end which renews the hope of Christians and encourages them on their way".[38] Saint Augustine saw this eighth day as "the peace of quietness, the peace of the Sabbath, a peace with no evening".[39]

DAY OF THE SUN

It has been and continues to be the practice of the Catholic Church to "baptize" certain pagan practices and celebrations, provided they are not intrinsically evil, and bring them into the orbit of Christian life. The ancient heathen Romans named the first day of the week after the sun. The Christianization of Sunday served "to draw the faithful away from the seduction of cults which worshipped the sun and to direct the celebration of the day to Christ, humanity's true 'sun'".[40]

Saint Justin the Martyr, who died in A.D. 165, wrote,

> On the day named after the sun, all believers who live in cities or in the countryside gather together in one place where the memoirs of the Apostles and the writings of the prophets are read as long as time permits. Sunday is the day on which we hold our common assembly because it is the day on which God brought light out of darkness and created the world, and it is the same day of the week when Jesus Christ, our Savior, rose from the dead.[41]

Christ is clearly designated in Sacred Scripture as the "light of the world" (Jn 1:4–9 and 9:5). Jesus is called the "dawn" for those in darkness (Lk 1:78–79) and the "light for revelation to the Gentiles" (Lk 2:32). His disciples celebrate Sunday as His special day to commemorate His Resurrection, which the Pope calls in his apostolic letter, "the enduring reflection of the epiphany of his glory" (no. 27).

DAY OF FIRE

In this year of 1998, dedicated to the Holy Spirit in preparation for the Great Jubilee of the year 2000, it is also important to see every Sunday as a "day of fire" in reference to the third Person of the Blessed Trinity. Sunday, our Supreme Pontiff tells us, is not just a weekly Easter but also a weekly Pentecost, in which we Christians relive the apostles' joyful encounter with the risen Lord and also receive anew the life-giving breath of His Spirit.

It was on the evening of the first day of the week that Christ first breathed the Holy Spirit upon the Catholic Church, which He had founded (Jn 20:22–23). Fifty days later it was again on a Sunday when the Holy Spirit descended in wind and fire and great power upon the nascent Church, gathered around Mary, the Mother of Jesus (Acts 2:2–3). God, the Holy Spirit, always remains with us as the living "Memory" of the Church (Jn 14:26). The Pope observes, "Pentecost is not only the founding event of the Church, but is also the mystery which for ever gives life to the Church. Such an event has its own powerful liturgical moment in the annual celebration which concludes 'the great Sunday', but it also remains a part of the deep meaning of every Sunday, because of its intimate bond with the Paschal Mystery" (no. 28).

Pope John Paul II writes, "Given its many meanings and aspects, and its link to the very foundations of the faith, the celebration of the Christian Sunday remains, on the threshold of the Third Millennium, an indispensable element of our Christian identity" (no. 30). It is our day of the sun, our day of fire, and the first day of the old and new creation. Sunday must be for us totally different from the other six days of the week. It is a day that is ours, but most of all it is a day that belongs to the Lord.

SEPTEMBER 25, 1998

Sunday
III

NEW PRACTICE

Saint Ignatius of Antioch, writing about A.D. 110. says, "those who were living in the former state of things have come to a new hope, no longer observing [Saturday], but keeping the Lord's Day, the day on which our life has appeared through him."[42] The earliest Christians always kept the first day of week as that day on which they gathered together for the "breaking of the bread" (Acts 20:7–12). Even before the New Testament was completely written, the Catholic Church called Sunday the Lord's Day (Rev 1:10).

Using the power of binding and loosing that Jesus gave to His Church (Mt 18:18 and 16:19) and based on the clear indications not only of Sacred Tradition, but also of Sacred Scripture (1 Cor 16:2; Jn 20:19 and 20:26), there was a distinction made by the apostles between the Old Testament observance of Saturday and the New Testament observance of Sunday. Early Christians who were converts from Judaism and the apostles themselves sometimes initially observed both days as "the Sabbath" (Acts 13:27). The Maronite Liturgy of the Catholic Church still emphasizes the link between Saturday and Sunday, derived from the connection of Holy Saturday with Easter Sunday. Pope John Paul II says, "The celebration of the day of the

Resurrection acquired a doctrinal and symbolic value capable of expressing the entire Christian mystery in all its newness" (no. 22).

OBLIGATION

In his apostolic letter *The Day of the Lord*, our Holy Father states, "Since the Eucharist is the very heart of Sunday, it is clear why, from the earliest centuries, the Pastors of the Church have not ceased to remind the faithful of *the need to take part in the liturgical assembly*" (no. 46). The Pope cites a third-century document (the *Didascalia*), "Leave everything on the Lord's Day and run diligently to your assembly, because it is your praise of God. Otherwise, what excuse will they make to God, those who do not come together on the Lord's Day to hear the word of life and feed on the divine nourishment which lasts forever?" (no. 46).

The martyrs of Abitina in Africa in the early third century said, "Without fear of any kind we have celebrated the Lord's Supper, because it cannot be missed; that is our law. We cannot live without the Lord's Supper."[43] Beginning in the fourth century there were penalties in Church Law for Catholics who missed Sunday Mass. The present *Code of Canon Law* for the Church reads, "On Sundays and other holy days of obligation the faithful are bound to participate in the Mass."[44] The *Catechism of the Catholic Church* says, "Those who deliberately fail in this obligation commit a grave sin" (CCC 2181). In his apostolic letter, our Supreme Pontiff observes that "it is crucially important for the life of faith that [Catholics] should come together with [their fellow Catholics] on Sundays to celebrate the Passover of the Lord in the sacrament of the New Covenant" (no. 48).

WHAT KIND OF DAY

Holy Mass not only is a remembrance of the dying and rising of Christ in the past, but it is the time and place when the risen Lord Himself is present once again in the midst of His people. This is particularly true when the parish community gathers on Sunday around the altar, which represents the two tables by which they are fed, the table of God's Word and the table of the Holy Eucharist, the Body and Blood of our Savior. In the first part of Mass, the liturgy of the Word, there is a dialogue between God and His people, an exchange of words. In the more important second part, the liturgy of the Eucharist, there is an exchange of gifts, in the middle of which our human, created gifts are "transubstantiated" by Jesus into His gift of Himself to His heavenly Father and His gift of Himself to us.

The Sunday Mass experience is meant also to be the weekly time and place where and when Catholics are renewed and strengthened by Christ and the Holy Spirit to carry out their ordinary tasks and duties in life as well as to evangelize and bear witness to the truths of the faith. Like the disciples of Emmaus, who hurried to bring the news of Christ's Resurrection to their brothers and sisters as soon as they recognized Him in the "breaking of the bread" (Lk 24:20–35), Catholics are to understand themselves as "sent" on "mission" at the end of every Mass, where the dismissal (from which we get our English word "Mass") does not just announce the obvious ("The Mass is ended"), but is a new "sending" of our Lord's disciples to proclaim the "good news" by word and example to all.

OTHER ASPECTS

There certainly is nothing wrong with spending some time on Sunday in recreation and relaxation. However, devout people should make Sunday the Lord's Day not only at Mass, but also at other moments throughout the day. The sacred liturgy should spill over into our family and private lives. Pope John Paul II suggests that all Catholics spend some extra time in personal or group prayer each Sunday. He also urges parents to make Sunday a special time to teach children their catechism, perhaps reading to them from the *Catechism of the Catholic Church.*

He says, "This rather traditional way of keeping Sunday holy has perhaps become more difficult for many people; but the Church shows her faith in the strength of the Risen Lord and the power of the Holy Spirit by making it known that, today more than ever, she is unwilling to settle for minimalism and mediocrity at the level of faith. She wants to help Christians to do what is most correct and pleasing to the Lord" (no. 52).

Each Sunday, as the convoked and assembled People of God, the Chosen People of the New Testament, we are supposed to experience an Easter banquet and a fraternal gathering. Every Sunday should be for each Christian a day of faith, a day of hope, and a day of supernatural love. On Sunday even more than on any other day of the week, we ought to "wait in joyful hope for the coming of our Savior, Jesus Christ". Sunday itself, with Mass at its heart, must be an encounter with our Redeemer under the signs of word and sacrament, to prepare for His loving embrace at the climax and conclusion of our earthly existence.

OCTOBER 2, 1998

Sunday
IV

SABBATH

In its basic significance, "sabbath" means rest. In the Old Testament this rest was strictly associated with the seventh day of the week (Ex 20:8–10; Deut 5:12–15). In the New Testament this rest is associated with the first day of the week (Mk 2:27–28; Jn 9:16; Mt 12:5; Mk 1:21). In the Old Testament the sabbath rest was linked to creation (Ex 20:11) and the third commandment of the Decalogue (Ex 31:15). It was also linked to the liberation of Israel from bondage and was set forth as a sign of the Old Covenant with God (Ex 31:16). A weekly day of rest is presented in Sacred Scripture, according to the *Catechism of the Catholic Church*, as a "model for human action" (CCC 2172). Just as God is said to have rested on the seventh day, so "man too ought to 'rest' and should let others, especially the poor, 'be refreshed' [Ex 31:17; cf. 23:12]. The sabbath brings everyday work to a halt and provides a respite. It is a day of protest against the servitude of work and the worship of money [cf. Neh 13:15–22; 2 Chron 36:12]" (CCC 2172).

Of course, the "rest" of God (Gen 1:31) is an anthropomorphism. Jesus told us that both He and His heavenly Father work even on the sabbath (Jn 5:17). Pope John Paul II notes, "The divine rest of the seventh day does not allude to an inactive God, but emphasizes the fullness of what has been accomplished."[45]

REST

In his apostolic letter *The Day of the Lord*, our Holy Father mentions that each Sunday is supposed to be not only a day of the Lord, but also a day for man, that is to say, a day of joy, of human solidarity, and of rest. He recalls that the law of the Church says that Christians "are obliged in conscience to arrange their Sunday rest in a way which allows them to take part in the Eucharist, refraining from work and activities which are incompatible with the sanctification of the Lord's Day, with its characteristic joy and necessary rest for spirit and body" (no. 67). Pope Leo XIII, in his great social encyclical *Rerum novarum*, taught that Sunday rest is a right owed to Christian workers and that civil governments are obligated to guarantee that right.

Our present Pope teaches,

> In our own historical context there remains the obligation to ensure that everyone can enjoy the freedom, rest, and relaxation which human dignity requires, together with the associated religious, family, cultural, and interpersonal needs which are difficult to meet if there is no guarantee of at least one day of the week on which people can *both* rest and celebrate.... Through Sunday rest, daily concerns and tasks can find their proper perspective: the material things about which we worry give way to spiritual values; in a moment of encounter and less pressured exchange, we see the true face of the people with whom we live.

Even the beauties of nature—too often marred by the desire to exploit, which turns man against himself—can be rediscovered and enjoyed to the full. (nos. 66–67)

The *Catechism of the Catholic Church* tells us, "Family needs or important social service can legitimately excuse from the obligation of Sunday rest. [However] the faithful should see to it that legitimate excuses do not lead to habits prejudicial to religion, family life, and health" (CCC 2185). It also says, "Every Christian should avoid making unnecessary demands on others that would hinder them from observing the Lord's Day" (CCC 2187).

What Else

Nature abhors a vacuum, according to the famous cliché. Sunday rest could easily become a mere "nothing-space" in a Christian's week. This is why the Bishop of Rome cautions,

> In order that [Sunday] rest may not degenerate into emptiness or boredom, it must offer spiritual enrichment, greater freedom, opportunities for contemplation and fraternal communion. Therefore, among the forms of culture and entertainment which society offers, the faithful should choose those which are most in keeping with a life lived in obedience to the precepts of the Gospel. Sunday rest then becomes "prophetic", affirming not only the absolute primacy of God, but also the primacy and dignity of the person with respect to the demands of social and economic life, and anticipating in a certain sense the "new heavens" and the "new earth", in which liberation from slavery to needs will be final and complete. In short, the Lord's Day thus becomes in the truest sense *the day of man* as well. (no. 68)

The Second Vatican Council teaches that our obligation to participate in the Sunday Eucharist and to observe the Sunday rest does not absolve Christians from their duties of charity, but commits them even more "to all the works of charity, of mercy, of apostolic outreach, by means of which it is seen that the faithful of Christ are not of this world and yet are the light of the world, giving glory to the Father in the presence of men".[46] From the earliest days of the Catholic Church, Sunday was kept as a day for special sharing with the poor (1 Cor 16:2). With Holy Mass at its center, "the whole of Sunday becomes a great school of charity, justice, and peace",[47] when Sunday rest is spent as it is supposed to be.

Joy

Pope John Paul II says,

Certainly, Christian joy must mark the whole of life, and not just one day of the week. But in virtue of its significance as *the day of the risen Lord*, celebrating God's work of creation and [celebrating the] "new creation", Sunday is the day of joy in a very special way, indeed the day most suitable for learning how to rejoice and rediscover the true nature and deep roots of joy. This joy should never be confused with shallow feelings of satisfaction and pleasure, which inebriate the senses and emotions for a brief moment, but then leave the heart unfulfilled and perhaps even embittered. In the Christian view, joy is much more enduring and consoling; as the saints attest, it can hold firm even in the dark night of suffering. It is, in a certain sense, a "virtue" to be nurtured.

Yet, there is no conflict whatever between Christian joy and true human joys, which in fact are exalted and find their ultimate foundation precisely in the joy of the glorified Christ...This vision of faith shows the Christian Sunday to be a true "time for celebration", a day given by God to men and women for their full human and spiritual growth.[48]

OCTOBER 9, 1998

[1] *Dei Verbum*, no. 4.

[2] John Paul II, apostolic constitution *Fidei depositum* (October 11, 1992).

[3] *Dei Verbum*, no. 8.

[4] Ibid.

[5] John Paul II, apostolic letter *Tertio millennio adveniente* (November 10, 1994), no. 45.

[6] *Dei Verbum*, no. 8.

[7] Congregation for the Doctrine of the Faith, "Commentary on the Concluding Formula of the 'Professio fidei'", *L'Osservatore Romano*, no. 28 (July 15, 1998): 4.

[8] John Henry Newman, *An Essay on the Development of Christine Doctrine*, advertisement to the first edition.

[9] Ibid., preface to the edition of 1878.

[10] Ibid., advertisement to the first edition.

[11] Ibid., chap. 12, no. 9.

[12] *Dei Verbum*, no. 8.

[13] John Henry Newman, "Biglietto Speech", May 12, 1879.

[14] Ibid.

[15] Ibid.

[16] John Henry Newman, *Apologia pro Vita Sua*, note A, "Liberalism".

[17] Newman, *Essay on the Development of Christian Doctrine*, chap. 8, sec 1, §1.

[18] Ibid.

[19] John Paul II, postsynodal apostolic exhortation *Reconciliation and Penance* (December 2, 1984), no. 16.

[20] John Paul II, encyclical *Sollicitudo rei socialis* (December 30, 1987), no. 47.

[21] *Gaudium et spes*, no. 27, § 1.

[22] John Paul II, *Sollicitudo rei socialis*, no. 41.

[23] Pius XI, encyclical *Quadragesimo anno* (May 15, 1931), no. 41.

[24] Ibid.

[25] Ibid., no. 42–43.

[26] John Paul II, *Sollicitudo rei socialis*, no. 41.

[27] John Paul II, encyclical *Centesimus annus* (May 1, 1991), no. 57.

[28] CCC 2448, quoting the Congregation for the Doctrine of the Faith, instruction *Libertatis conscientia* (March 22, 1986), no. 68. See also Lk 3:11; 11:41; Gal 2:10; Jas 2:15–16.

[29] John Paul II, Message for Lent 2003 (January 7, 2003), no. 2.

[30] Mother Teresa, *A Simple Path*, comp. Lucinda Vardey (New York: Ballantine Books, 1995), p. 179.

[31] Ibid., back cover.

[32] Ibid., p. 180.

[33] *Sacrosanctum concilium*, no. 106.

[34] John Paul II, *Dies Domini*, no. 1.

[35] Ibid., no. 2, quoting Jerome, *In Die Dominica Paschae* II, 52.

[36] John Paul II, *Dies Domini*, no. 2.

[37] Saint Ignatius of Antioch, *To the Magnesians*, 9, 1–2; quoted by ibid., no. 23.

[38] Ibid., no. 26, quoting Saint Basil, *On the Holy Spirit* 27, 66.

[39] *Dies Domini*, no. 26, quoting Saint Augustine, *Confessions* 13, 50.

[40] *Dies Domini*, no. 27.

[41] Saint Justin the Martyr, *First Apology*, chap. 67.

[42] John Paul II, *Dies Domini*, no. 23, quoting Saint Ignatius of Antioch, *To the Magnesians* 9, 1–2.

[43] John Paul II, *Dies Domini*, no. 46, quoting *Acta SS. Saturnini, Dativi et aliorum plurimorum Martyrum in Africa* 7, 9, 10.

[44] Can. 1247.

[45] John Paul II, *Dies Domini*, no. 11.

[46] *Sacrosanctum concilium*, no. 9.

[47] John Paul II, *Dies Domini*, no. 73.

[48] Ibid., nos. 57–58.

Part Four

THE CATHOLIC CHURCH: CHRIST PRESENT IN THE WORLD

THE CHURCH

One and Only

LORD JESUS

The first Pope, Simon Peter, declared what the Catholic Church, founded by Christ, has always said and will ever say about Jesus, namely, "There is salvation in no one else, for there is no other name under heaven given among men by which we must be saved" (Acts 4:12). The recent, clear reassertion of this truth, among others, by the Holy See, with the approval and under the direction of the present successor of Saint Peter, however, seems to have aroused undue amazement in some circles. The declaration entitled The Lord Jesus (Dominus Iesus, in Latin), issued on August 6, 2000, says, "One can and must say that Jesus Christ has a significance and a value for the human race and its history which are unique and singular, proper to him alone, exclusive, universal, and absolute. Jesus is, in fact, the Word of God made man for the salvation of all."[1]

Although the Jews of Saint Peter's age, like some of the non-Christians of every era including our own, found "political incorrectness" in the word only when asserted of Jesus Christ, it is more than ever necessary in our world, which is befogged by religious indifference, dedicated to considering tolerance as more important than truth, and confused by religious relativism, that the *only* of our Christian Creed be spoken by us loudly and clearly. We believe "in Jesus Christ, His *only* Son, our Lord." Our Lord called Himself "the only-begotten Son" (Jn 3:16).

EXCLUSIVE

Our divine Savior set forth the dogma on this matter, which for two millennia has been cherished and taught by His Bride and Body, the Catholic Church. He said, "No one comes to the Father, but by me" (Jn 14:6). The Holy See's declaration states, "It must therefore be *firmly believed* as a truth of Catholic faith that the universal salvific will of the One and Triune God is offered and accomplished once for all in the mystery of the incarnation, death, and resurrection of the Son of God."[2]

Loyalty to our Baptismal vows and Confirmation commitments requires that we courageously proclaim this truth before the world. Jesus said, "For whoever is ashamed of me and of my words in this adulterous and sinful generation, of him will the Son of Man also be ashamed, when he comes in the glory of his Father with the holy angels" (Mk 8:38). The teaching of the Church, repeated in the declaration, is that the event of Jesus Christ and nothing else constitutes the complete and definitive revelation of God.

BELIEVING

In our English language, unfortunately, the term *to believe* sometimes has taken on the connotation of "to guess" or "to suppose". Nothing could be more alien to the Christian meaning of the term. To believe, for a Christian, means to know with absolute and total certainty. It means to know by means of the knowledge of God Himself, Who cannot deceive or be deceived. Knowledge obtained in any other way than by faith can be flawed or defective, even knowledge obtained through our personal observations or sense structure. The knowledge that comes from our Catholic Christian faith, although fully in accord with human reason and capable of genuine rational explanation, is more certain than any merely human knowledge.

It is this certitude that makes it impossible for Christians to permit sociologists, entertainment people (like those in the silly film *Oh, God*), and students of comparative religion to place our Redeemer on a par with some human "founders of great religions", such as Buddha, Muhammad, Moses, and so on. It seems that for a Christian to think in such terms or to allow others to do so represents an outrageous blasphemy.

RAT POISON

The *Declaration on the Relationship of the Church to Non-Christian Religions* of the Second Vatican Council remains in full effect. The declaration *Dominus Iesus* should be seen as supplementing and clarifying what the Council said and as applying the conciliar teaching to present day circumstances. Both documents should be read together, noting their differing but not contradicting focus. In the New Testament, Saint Paul, who fearlessly proclaimed Jesus as the one and only Mediator between God and man (1 Tim 2:4–6), dealt with the non-Christian world with great skill and zeal in a way that deserves imitation (Acts 17:16–31).

It is true that one can find elements of truth in some aspects of various pagan or heathen or other non-Christian religions. When such elements (the fullness of all religious truth being, of course, only found in the Catholic faith) are discovered, they are cause for rejoicing and can serve as the basis for dialogue and even for missionary work. However, as Cardinal John Henry Newman states in telling of his discovery of the Catholic faith,

> That there is a truth then; that there is one truth; that religious error is in itself of an immoral nature; that its maintainers, unless involuntarily such, are guilty in maintaining it;... that the mind is below the truth, not above it, and is bound, not to descant upon it, but to venerate it; that truth and falsehood are set before us for the trial of our hearts; that our choice is an awful giving forth of lots on which salvation or its rejection is inscribed; that "before all things it is necessary to hold the Catholic faith;" that "he that would be saved must thus think," and not otherwise.[3]

As an old farmer once said, effective rat poison is at least 90 percent good, wholesome, nourishing food. It is the 10 percent of arsenic and other chemicals in the mixture that does the killing. Buddhism, Hinduism, Judaism, Islam, New Age, Shintoism, Confucianism, and other non-Christian religions may have elements of truth in some of their aspects. However, their defects, flaws, and errors cannot be overlooked. The Council says, "The Catholic Church rejects nothing of what is true and holy in those religions."[4] However, the Council then goes on to say, "She [the Catholic Church] proclaims and must ever proclaim Christ as the way, the truth, and the life (Jn 14:6) in whom men find the fullness of religious life (2 Cor 5:18–19)."[5]

Pope John Paul II, in his encyclical letter *The Mission of the Redeemer*, quoted by *Dominus Iesus*, says, "No one, therefore, can enter into communion with God except through Christ, by the working of the Holy Spirit."[6] It is only in Jesus Christ that one can find the fullness of divinity (Col 2:9).

OCTOBER 27, 2000

Aspects of the Church
I

SEEN AND UNSEEN

The Catholic Church, founded by Jesus (Mt 16:18–20), is both visible and invisible. Like her divine Founder, there are aspects of the Church that are perceptible to the senses and other aspects that can be seen only with the eyes of faith. The *Catechism of the Catholic Church* tells us that it is with such eyes alone "that one can see her in her visible reality and at the same time in her spiritual reality as bearer of divine life" (CCC 770). The Second Vatican Council states, "The one mediator, Christ, established and ever sustains here on earth his holy Church, the community of faith, hope, and charity, as a visible organization, through which he communicates truth and grace to all men."[7]

Cardinal Henri de Lubac notes, "In her structure the Church shows not only a mixture of visible and invisible but also a mixture of the divine and the human."[8] The Second Vatican Council tells us that the Catholic Church is an "earthly Church and the Church endowed with heavenly riches".[9] The Council goes on to say, "The Church is essentially both human and divine, visible but endowed with invisible realities, zealous in action but dedicated to contemplation, present in the world, but as a pilgrim, so constituted that in her the human is directed toward and subordinated to the divine, the visible to the invisible, action to contemplation, and this present world to that city yet to come, the object of our quest [Heb 13:14]."[10]

SACRAMENT

The Second Vatican Council emphasized what many Fathers and Doctors of the Church have always taught, namely, that the Catholic Church is a kind of sacrament. She is an outward sign, instituted by Christ, to give grace. The Latin word *sacrament* is a translation of the Greek word *mystery*, something partly seen and partly unseen. The *Catechism* says, "The Church, then, both contains and communicates the invisible grace she signifies. It is in this analogical sense, that the Church is called a 'sacrament'" (CCC 774). In her the seven great signs or sacraments made by our Redeemer are rooted and found. She is their custodian, their guardian, and the only competent organization to set forth what makes them licit and valid.

Speaking of the Catholic Church as the only true religion, the fullness of Christianity on earth, and the one true Church, Saint Bernard of Clairvaux says, "O humility! O sublimity! Both tabernacle of cedar and sanctuary of God; earthly dwelling and celestial palace; house of clay and royal hall; body of death and temple of light; and at last both object of scorn to the proud and the bride of Christ! She is black but beautiful, ... for even if the labor and pain of her long exile may have discolored her, yet heaven's beauty has adorned her."[11]

HOLY SPIRIT

The Catholic Church is identical with the Mystical Body of Christ (1 Cor 12:4–30). In this year of 1998, dedicated to the Holy Spirit in preparation for the Great Jubilee of the year 2000, it is useful to recall the words of Saint Augustine of Hippo, "What the soul is to the human body, the Holy Spirit is to the Body of Christ, which is the Church."[12] Saint Irenaeus writes, "It is in [the Catholic Church] that communion with Christ has been deposited, that is to say: the Holy Spirit, the pledge of incorruptibility, the strengthening of our faith and the ladder of our ascent to God...For where the Church is, there also is God's Spirit; where God's Spirit is, there is the Church and every grace."[13]

Pope Pius XII says, "To this Spirit of Christ, as an invisible principle, is to be ascribed the fact that all parts of the body are joined one with the other and with their exalted head [Jesus Christ]; for the whole Spirit of Christ is in the head, the whole Spirit is in the body, and the whole Spirit is in each of the members."[14] It is the third Person of the most Blessed Trinity Who, in the words of the *Catechism*, is "the source of [the Church's] life, of its unity in diversity, and of the riches of its gifts and charisms" (CCC 809).

The Holy Spirit in the Church constantly works to build her up by means of God's word, the sacraments, the virtues, the hierarchy, and the various tasks and offices He assigns to her members.

THE HEAD

The external and hierarchical structure of the Church, by Christ's will, is vital. As Father Louis Bouyer notes, a totally invisible Church does not exist. To say, as some Protestants do, that the real and true Church is completely invisible is to say that there is no Church at all. However, we must always remember that the absolute Head of the Church is Christ (Col 1:18), Who now reigns in heaven and is visible in the sign of the Holy Eucharist. The Church as His Bride and Body extends Him through time and space. Saint Thomas Aquinas says, "Head and members form as it were one and the same mystical person."[15] Saint Gregory the Great writes, "Our redeemer has shown himself to be one person with the holy Church whom he has taken to himself."[16]

Saint Augustine of Hippo preached, "Let us rejoice then and give thanks that we have become not only Christians, but Christ himself. Do you understand and grasp, brethren, God's grace toward us? Marvel and rejoice: we have become Christ. For he is the head, we are the members; he and we together are the whole man. ... The fullness of Christ then is the head and the members. But what does 'head and members' mean? Christ and the Church."[17]

Saint Paul says that the union of a Christian bride and groom is a symbol of the union "in one flesh" of Christ and the Catholic Church (Eph 5:29–31). Although a married couple is two different persons, yet they are one in their conjugal union. Thus, says Saint Augustine, "*as head, [Christ] calls himself the bridegroom, as body, he calls himself 'bride'.*"[18] In loving and helping the Catholic Church, we are participating in the work of the Holy Spirit, and we are loving and helping Jesus Himself.

OCTOBER 16, 1998

Aspects of the Church
II

Marriage

One of the most important metaphors used to describe the Catholic Church is that which calls her the Bride of Christ. To be joined to Jesus in the Catholic Church is something far more sublime and profound than mere membership in some organization, club, labor union, association, or society. It means being united to Christ in a most intimate and living way, akin to the way a branch is joined to and dependent upon a tree or vine (Jn 15:5). In creation and in the institution of matrimony as a sacrament of the New Law, a suitable way to look at the mystery of Christ and His Church may be found (Eph 5:31–33).

Already in the Old Testament the ancient prophets sometimes spoke about the Chosen People as the Spouse of Yahweh. The Old Covenant, we know, was a shadow cast before the great realities that were to follow. The *Catechism of the Catholic Church* (CCC 796) tells us that the nuptial expressions of the prophets were meant to prepare the theme in the New and Everlasting Testament of Christ as the Bridegroom and the Church as His Bride. This theme, of course, was taken up eloquently by the last and greatest prophet of the Old Testament, Saint John the Baptist (Jn 3:29).

Jesus called Himself the Bridegroom (Mk 2:19). The Bible calls the Church the spotless Bride of the Spotless Lamb (Rev 22:17 and Eph 1:4; 5:27–29). Saint Paul teaches how Christ loves His Church and gives Himself up for her to sanctify her. He cares for the Church much as any normal man cares for his own body, which, he tells us, is the way a Christian husband is to care for his wife. He explains how Christian marriage must be indissoluble, love-filled, and involved with total self-giving by the spouses because it must be a reflection of the "great mystery", namely, the union of our Redeemer with His redeemed People.

With Mary

The month of October, dedicated to the holy rosary of the Blessed Virgin Mary, particularly in this year of 1998, which has been given over by our Holy Father to God, the Holy Spirit, in preparation for the Great Jubilee, is a very appropriate time to reflect on the connection between the Catholic Church and Mary, who is the archetype and supreme model of the Church as well as the daughter and mother of the Church. Both Mary and the Church are instruments of the Holy Spirit. This is well expressed in a sermon attributed to Saint Eusebius of Gaul and Saint Caesarius of Arles:

Let the Church of Christ rejoice—she who, in the likeness of blessed Mary, finds herself enriched by the operation of the Holy Spirit and becomes the Mother of a divine progeny!...Let us, if you will, compare these two mothers, whose motherhood is to fortify our faith.... The Spirit overshadowed Mary, and his blessing does the same to the Church at the baptismal fountain. Mary conceived her Son without sin, and the Church destroys all sin in those whom she regenerates. By Mary there was born he who was at the beginning; by the Church is reborn he who perished at the beginning. The first [mother] brought forth for many peoples, the second brings forth these peoples. The one gave us her Son, remaining a virgin; through this Son, who is her virgin Bridegroom, the other continually brings forth children [for God].[19]

A Father of the Church, Honorius of Autun, wrote:

The glorious Virgin Mary stands for the Church, who is also both virgin and mother. She is a mother because every day she presents God with new sons in baptism, being made fruitful by the Holy Spirit. At the same time she is virgin because she does not allow herself to be in any way corrupted by the defilement of heresy, preserving inviolate the integrity of the faith, just as in the same way Mary was mother in bringing forth Jesus, and virgin in remaining intact after bearing him.... Which is why everything which is written about the Church may also be read as applying to Mary.[20]

ACTIVE AND PASSIVE

The very word "Church" has an active and passive meaning. Both meanings are legitimate when applied to the Catholic Church. A study of the New Testament, especially the writings of Saint Paul, will easily show that "Church" means both "the divine calling together" and "the assembly of those called together". The Church is a convocation and a congregation. Just as the Catholic Church has a visible and social aspect, inasmuch as she was founded by Jesus Christ as a hierarchical society, and yet she also has a mystical and spiritual aspect as the Body of Christ, so she is convoked and assembled but then truly is also the constituted assembly, the totality of those who have answered the call.

Saint Cyril of Jerusalem says, "The Church is thus properly so called because she calls together all men and unites them in one single whole."[21] Saint Gregory the Great teaches, "The holy Church has two lives: one in time and the other in eternity."[22] And, according to Saint Augustine, we should not separate them, making the Church below a stranger to the Church above.[23]

THE CREED

Whenever we recite the Creed, we profess our belief in the holy Catholic Church; we profess that our Church is formed by the Holy Spirit and that "she is 'his own proper work', the instrument with which he sanctifies us."[24] It is in her and by her faith that she communicates to us forgiveness for our sins and hope in our ultimate resurrection, our destiny, and our glory. Saint Thomas Aquinas says that when we say the words about the Church in our Creed, we are professing our belief not only in her existence, but also in her supernatural reality, in her essential prerogatives, and in our realization that we cannot be saved unless joined to her, since there is no other way in which a human being can be joined to Christ.

In the Creed we profess that we see the Catholic Church as the inseparable Bride of Jesus, the pillar and mainstay of truth (1 Tim 3:15), the House of God, the Temple of His Holy Spirit. Let us always love her. She is our mother.

OCTOBER 23, 1998

Aspects of the Church
III

THE BODY

In the midst of the Second World War, on June 29, 1943, Pope Pius XII wrote a famous and splendid encyclical on the Catholic Church as the Mystical Body of Christ. In it he summarized with eloquence and clarity this apostolic doctrine, which always had been held and taught by the Church (1 Cor 12:12–26). This teaching, which he found often expressed in the work of his predecessors, was also taken up by his successors in the See of Peter and by the Second Vatican Council, which says, "By communicating his Spirit, Christ mystically constitutes as his body those brothers [and sisters] of his who are called together from every nation."[25]

The *Catechism of the Catholic Church* states, "The comparison of the Church with the body casts light on the intimate bond between Christ and his Church. Not only is she gathered *around him*; she is united *in him*, in his body" (CCC 789). Jesus, of course, is the invisible and abiding Head of this Body (Col 1:18). The *Catechism* notes, "[The Church] lives from him, in him, and for him; he lives with her and in her" (CCC 807). As a result of their union with Christ, the members of the Church are united to each other in His Body (Gal 3:27–28). The Catholic Church, the Body of Christ, is established, so the *Catechism* teaches, "through the Spirit and his action in the sacraments, above all the Eucharist" (CCC 805). Pope Pius XII remarks that it is well to remember that it is "[our divine Redeemer Himself] who through the Church baptizes, teaches, rules, looses, binds, offers, sacrifices".[26]

THE SOUL

Pope Leo XIII states, "Let it suffice to say that, as Christ is the Head of the Church, so is the Holy Spirit her soul."[27] As this year of 1998, dedicated to God the Holy Spirit in preparation for the Great Jubilee of the year 2000, draws to a close, it is well to cast a glance once again at some aspects of this truth. Pope Pius XII writes,

> To this Spirit of Christ … as to an invisible principle is to be ascribed the fact that all the parts of the Body are joined one with the other and with their exalted Head; for He is entire in the Head, entire in the Body, and entire in each of the members. To the members He is present and assists them in proportion to their various duties and offices, and the greater or less degree of the spiritual health which they enjoy. It is He who, through His heavenly grace, is the principle of every supernatural act in all parts of the Body....He yet refuses to dwell through sanctifying grace in those members that are wholly severed from the Body."[28]

"It is the Spirit of Christ that has made us adopted sons of God (Rom 8:14–17; Gal 4:6–7) in order that one day 'we all beholding the glory of the Lord with open face may be transformed into the same image from glory to glory' (2 Cor 3:18)."[29] The *Catechism* tells us, "The Church is the Temple of the Holy Spirit. The Spirit is the soul, as it were, of the Mystical Body, the source of its life, of its unity in diversity, and of the riches of its gifts and charisms" (CCC 809). The twelfth Pope to be called Pius says, "Christ is in us through His Spirit, whom He gives to us and through whom He acts within us in such a way that all divine activity of the Holy Spirit within our souls must also be attributed to Christ (Rom 8:9–10)."[30]

CHRIST RULES

Jesus Christ is the "Shepherd and Guardian of [our] souls" (1 Pet 2:25). Both directly and personally He continues to govern and guide the Catholic Church, that is, the Society he founded in order to extend Himself through the centuries until He comes again in majesty to judge the universe. However, He does not do this only in a hidden or extraordinary manner, but "[He] also governs His Mystical Body in a visible and normal way through His Vicar on earth...Since He was all wise, He could not leave the Body of the Church He had founded ... without a visible head...For Peter in virtue of his primacy is only Christ's Vicar, so that there is only one chief Head of this Body, namely Christ, who never ceases Himself to guide the Church invisibly, though at the same time He rules it visibly, through him who is His representative on earth."[31] Christ and His vicar constitute only one Head of the Church.

As the encyclical cited above says, "They ... walk in the path of dangerous error who believe they can accept Christ as the Head of the Church, while not adhering loyally to His Vicar on earth. They have taken away the visible head, broken the visible bonds of unity, and left the Mystical Body of the Redeemer so obscured and so maimed that those who are seeking the haven of eternal salvation can neither see it nor find it."[32]

New Eve

In the poetic account of creation in the Book of Genesis (Gen 2:18–24), the first woman was born from the side of the first man, Adam, as he slept. She was called Eve, which means "the mother of all the living". So, many of the Apostolic Fathers saw the Church as mystically being born from the pierced side of the New Adam, Jesus, as He slept in death on the Cross. In a supernatural sense, the Catholic Church truly is the new Eve, the mother of all the spiritually living.

Just as Christ, at the beginning of His three-year, public ministry of preaching, healing, founding the Church, calling the world to repentance, and revealing God as our Father, was made known by the outpouring of the Holy Spirit over Him in the form of a dove (Lk 3:22; Mk 1:10), so our Lord, after His Ascension, sitting at the right hand of the Father, publicly proclaimed the Catholic Church as His Bride and Body by the outpouring of the Holy Spirit on Pentecost with the mighty wind and the tongues of fire (Acts 2:1–4).

Pope Pius XII writes: "Nothing more glorious, nothing nobler, nothing surely more honorable can be imagined than to belong to the One, Holy, Catholic, Apostolic and Roman Church, in which we become members of One Body, as venerable as it is unique; are guided by one supreme Head; are filled with one divine Spirit; are nourished during our earthly exile by one doctrine and one heavenly Bread, until at last we enter into the one, unending blessedness of heaven."[33]

NOVEMBER 6, 1998

The Church
I

Deep Mystery

Cardinal Henri de Lubac says, "To a man who lives [the] mystery [of the Catholic Church] [Eph 5:22–32], she is always the city of precious stones, the heavenly Jerusalem, the Bride of the Lamb [Rev 21:2]. ... But the dark side of the mystery is there too, and just as surely.... For the unbeliever whom the Father has not begun to draw to him, the Church remains a stumbling block. And she can be a testing ground for the believer too, which is a good thing; perhaps the test is all the more strenuous in proportion as his faith is purer and more vital."[34] Saint Hippolytus says, "[The Church is] where the [Holy] Spirit flourishes."[35]

Saint Clement of Alexandria says, "Just as God's will is creation and is called 'the world,' so his intention is the salvation of men, and it is called 'the Church.'"[36] The Fathers of the early Church, including Saint Justin, Aristides, Tertullian, and Pastor Hermae, state boldly, "The world was created for the sake of the Church."[37] Saint Epiphanius preaches, "The Church is the goal of all things."[38] The *Catechism of the Catholic Church* states, "God created the world for the sake of communion with his divine life, a communion brought about by the 'convocation' of men in Christ, and this 'convocation' is the Church" (CCC 760). The Second Vatican Council teaches, "By her relationship with Christ, the Church is a kind of sacrament or sign of intimate union with God and of the unity of mankind. She is also the instrument for the achievement of such union and unity."[39]

The Sacrament

The old and standard catechetical definition of a sacrament is that it is "an outward sign, instituted by Christ, to give grace". The Catholic Church, of course, perfectly fits that definition, and this is why she is called "a sacrament", in which the seven great and efficacious divine mysteries or sacraments are rooted in order to sanctify and save humanity. The *Catechism* says, "The seven sacraments are the signs and instruments by which the Holy Spirit spreads the grace of Christ the head throughout the Church which is his Body. The Church, then, both contains and communicates the invisible grace she signifies. It is in this analogical sense, that the Church is called a 'sacrament'" (CCC 774).

The *Catechism* goes on to teach, "The Church's first purpose is to be the sacrament of the *inner union of man with God*. Because men's communion with one another is rooted in that union with God, the Church is also the sacrament of the *unity of the human race*" (CCC 775), gathering people into spiritual union "from every nation and from all tribes and peoples and tongues" (Rev 7:9). The Second Vatican Council calls the Catholic Church "'the universal sacrament of salvation,' by which Christ is 'at once manifesting and actualizing the mystery of God's love for men".[40] Pope Paul VI says, "'[The Church] is the visible plan of God's love for humanity,' because God desires 'that the whole human race may become one People of God, form one Body of Christ, and be built into one temple of the Holy Spirit.'"[41]

Both And

The Catholic Church, which is "the church of the living God, the pillar and bulwark of the truth" (1 Tim 3:15), is both visible and invisible, both spiritual and material. In the words of the *Catechism*, "The Church is in history, but at the same time she transcends it. It is only 'with the eyes of faith' [*Roman Catechism* I, 10, 20] that one can see her in her visible reality and at the same time in her spiritual reality as the bearer of divine life" (CCC 770). The Second Vatican Council says, "The one mediator, Christ, established and ever sustains here on earth his holy Church, the community of faith, hope, and charity, as a visible organization through which he communicates truth and grace to all men."[42]

The Council, citing the Epistle to the Hebrews (13:14), observes, "The Church is essentially both human and divine, visible but endowed with invisible realities, zealous in action and dedicated to contemplation, present in the world, but as a pilgrim, so constituted that in her the human is directed toward and subordinate to the divine, the visible to the invisible, action to contemplation, and this present world to that city yet to come, the object of our quest."[43] The Council says that "the earthly Church and the Church endowed with heavenly riches ... form one complex reality which comes together from a human and divine element."[44]

Testimony

In speaking about the Catholic Church, Saint Bernard of Clairvaux exclaims, "O humility, O sublimity! Both tabernacle of cedar and sanctuary of God; earthly dwelling and celestial palace; house of clay and royal hall; body of death and temple of light; and at last both object of scorn to the proud and bride of Christ! She is black but beautiful, O daughters of Jerusalem, for even if the labor and pain of her long exile may have discolored her, yet heaven's beauty has adorned her."[45]

Cardinal John Henry Newman says of the Catholic Church to which he was converted, "Oh, long sought after, tardily found, desire of the eyes, joy of the heart, the truth after many shadows, the fulness after many foretastes, the home after many storms, come to her, poor wanderers, for she it is, and she alone, who can unfold the meaning of your being and the secret of your destiny. She alone can open to you the gate of heaven, and put you on your way."[46]

Orestes Brownson, a famous American convert to the Catholic faith in the nineteenth century, says, "Founded on immutable and universal principles, the church can never grow old or obsolete, but is the church for all times and places, for all ranks and conditions of men. Man cannot change either the church or the dogmas of faith, for they are founded in the highest reality, which is above him, over him, and independent of him."[47]

Pope Paul VI says, "Love the Church. This, dear children, is the duty of the present hour. To love her is to esteem her and to be happy to belong to her. It means to know how to reconcile belonging to her visible and mystical company with an honest, generous love for every created reality that surrounds us and possesses us: life, family, society, truth, justice, liberty, and goodness." Pope Pius XII writes, "For nothing more glorious, nothing nobler, nothing surely more honorable can be imagined than to belong to the One, Holy, Catholic, Apostolic, and Roman Church, in which we become members of One Body as venerable as it is unique; are guided by one supreme Head; are filled with one divine Spirit; are nourished during our earthly exile by one doctrine and one heavenly Bread, until at last we enter into the one, unending blessedness of heaven."[48]

JANUARY 2, 2004

The Church
II

BELIEF

Pope John Paul II says, "In the Creed—both in the Apostles' Creed and in the Nicene-Constantinople Creed—we say: *I believe in the Church.* We place the Church on the same level as the Mystery of the Most Holy Trinity and the mysteries of the Incarnation and of the Redemption...Following the [Second Vatican] Council, we can say that we believe in the Church as in a mystery."[49]

It has been pointed out that there can seem to be something "scandalous" and "foolish" involved in believing in "a Church where the divine is not only united with the human but presents itself to us by way of the all-too-human, and that without any alternative. For...what some have called the Church is really Christ perpetuated among us, Christ 'spread abroad and passed on',"[50] "the permanent incarnation of the Son of God".[51] Yet, the Church, because she is utterly holy while still composed almost entirely of sinners, "is even more compact of contrast and paradox than Christ".[52]

The First Vatican Council, following Isaiah, called the Catholic Church a "standard raised among the nations"[53] The Fathers of the early centuries call her the "mountain visible from afar, the radiant city, the light set in a candlestick to illuminate the whole house, … the imperishable building of cedar and cypress, which defies the passage of time in its awe-inspiring massiveness and gives to our ephemeral individualities their measure of confidence,"[54] "'inviting those who as yet have no faith, and assuring her own children that the faith they profess has the firmest of foundations'".[55] She is "the 'continual miracle', always announcing to men the coming of their Savior…; the magnificent vaulting under which the saints, like so many stars, sing together the glory of the Redeemer".[56]

Two Yet One

The *Catechism of the Catholic Church* notes, "The Church is both visible and spiritual, a hierarchical society and the Mystical Body of Christ. She is one, yet formed of two components, human and divine. That is her mystery, which only faith can accept" (CCC 779). Because the Church is the prolongation of Christ through the centuries, so that the salvation He won for humanity by His dying and rising might be available for all men of all time, the Church partakes to some extent in the very reality of the Savior, Who unites in His one divine Personhood His divine nature with a true human nature, including a created human soul and a visible human body.

Saying that the Catholic Church is a supernatural "mystery" means that she is a "divine reality inserted into human history, which cannot be fully captured by any human thought or language."[57] Pope Paul VI says, "the Church is a mystery because she is a reality imbued with the hidden presence of God."[58] The Second Vatican Council teaches,

> The visible assembly and the spiritual community, the earthly Church and the Church enriched with heavenly things are not to be considered as two realities, but they form one interlocked reality which is comprised of a human and divine element. For this reason by an excellent analogy, this reality is compared to the mystery of the incarnate Word. Just as the assumed nature, inseparably united to the divine Word, serves Him as a living instrument of salvation, so in a similar way, does the communal structure of the Church serve Christ's Spirit, who vivifies it by way of building up the body (Eph 4:16).[59]

Dual Aspect

The Greek and Latin word for Church is ecclesia, which means in its root definition two things, a convocation and a congregation. The Church, then, is both "a divine calling together" and the "holy community of those called together".

Both meanings are found in the New Testament, especially the Epistles of Saint Paul, and both are used extensively by the Fathers and Doctors of the Church. "The active sense is primary, but the passive is no less necessary and no less important."[60]

The Catholic Church is both the entity that sanctifies and the assembly of those sanctified by the Holy Spirit, that is, those called to be saints, those called to incorporation into Christ, Who alone is "the Holy One". She is the reconciling power and the family of those who have been reconciled. She bestows baptismal regeneration and is at the same time the gathering of those who receive it.

The Catholic Church by God's specific and revealed design is a hierarchical society in which certain members are "in possession of sacred powers",[61] so they can perpetuate in the assembly the actual functions of Christ. But, at the same time, the Church possesses another hierarchy, that of grace, wholly interior, the hierarchy of sanctity. However, she is by no means merely an invisible society of the saints and the elect. Both hierarchies are united in an inseparable way, Church teaching and Church taught, Church ruling and Church governed. It should also be remembered that in her unity and unicity the Catholic Church is much more than the sum total of the pastors and flock, much more than some mere aggregate, for she is Christ's Body and Bride.

FULFILLMENT

The *Catechism* says, "It is in the Church that Christ fulfills and reveals his own mystery as the purpose of God's plan: to 'unite all things in him' [Eph 1:10]. St. Paul calls the nuptial union of Christ and the Church 'a great mystery'. Because she is united to Christ as to her bridegroom, she becomes a mystery in her turn [Eph 5:32; 3:9–11; 5:25–27]. Contemplating this mystery in her, Saint Paul exclaims: 'Christ in you, the hope of glory' [Col 1:27]" (CCC 772).

The Church's structure is totally ordered to the holiness of Christ's members. In the words of Pope John Paul II, "Holiness is measured according to the 'great mystery' in which the Bride responds with the gift of love to the gift of the Bridegroom."[62] The Second Vatican Council states, "Henceforward the Church, endowed with the gifts of her founder and faithfully observing his precepts of charity, humility and self-denial, receives the mission of proclaiming and establishing among all peoples the Kingdom of Christ and of God, and she is on earth the seed and beginning of that kingdom."[63] The *Catechism* asserts, "The Church is the Bride of Christ: he loved her and handed himself over for her. He has purified her by his blood and made her the fruitful mother of all God's children" (CCC 808).

JANUARY 9, 2004

The Church
III

IMAGES

Because the Catholic Church in her deepest aspect is a supernatural mystery, beyond the possibility of any full comprehension by a created intellect, every definition of the Church necessarily has a certain amount of inadequacy. This is why divine revelation sets forth the reality of the Church by means of various images. The Second Vatican Council reiterated many of these images or symbols of the Church. The *Catechism of the Catholic Church* states: "In Scripture, we find a host of interrelated images and figures through which Revelation speaks of the inexhaustible mystery of the Church. The images taken from the Old Testament are variations on a profound theme: the People of God. In the New Testament, all these images find a new center because Christ has become the head of this people, which henceforth is his Body [cf. Eph 1:22; Col 1:18; *Lumen gentium*, no. 9]" (CCC 753). Some of these figures and images were set forth in the Dogmatic Constitution on the Church by the Second Vatican Council.

To quote that Council, "The Church is ... a *sheepfold*, the sole and necessary gateway is Christ [Jn 10:1–10]. It is also the flock of which God himself foretold that he would be the shepherd [Is 40:11; Ezek 34:11–31], and whose sheep, even though governed by human shepherds, are unfailingly nourished and led by Christ himself, the Good Shepherd and Prince of Shepherds [Jn 10:11; 1 Pet 5:4], who gave his life for his sheep [Jn 10:11–16].[64]

THE COUNCIL

The Second Vatican Council goes on to teach, "The Church is a *cultivated field*, the tillage of God [1 Cor 3:9]. On that land the ancient olive tree grows whose holy roots were the prophets and in which the reconciliation of Jews and Gentiles has been brought about again [Rom 11:13–26]. ... That land, like a choice vineyard [Mt 21:33–43 and parallels; Is 5:1–7), has been planted by the heavenly cultivator. Yet, the true vine is Christ who gives life and fruitfulness to the branches [Jn 15:1–5], that is, to us, who through the Church remain in Christ, without whom we can do nothing."[65]

Another biblical image of the Catholic Church is "'that Jerusalem which is from above' and 'our mother' [cf. Gal 4:26; Rev 12:17], is described as the spotless spouse of the spotless lamb [Rev 19:7; 21:2, 9; 22:17]. It is she whom Christ 'loved and for whom he delivered himself up that he might sanctify her' [Eph 5:25–26]. It is she whom he unites to himself by an unbreakable alliance, and whom he constantly 'nourishes and cherishes' [Eph 5:29]."[66] The Council goes on, "[Jesus] filled [the Church] with heavenly gifts for all eternity, in order that we might know the love of God and of Christ for us, a love which surpasses all knowledge (Eph 3:19). The Church on earth, while journeying in a foreign land away from the Lord (2 Cor 5:6), regards herself as an exile. Hence she seeks and experiences those things which are above, where Christ is seated at the right hand of God the Father, where the life of the Church is hidden with Christ in God until the Church appears in glory with her Spouse (Col 3:1–4)."[67]

AN EDIFICE

One of the common images of the Church is that of a building. In fact, our ecclesiastical buildings receive the name of "church" because they are supposed to be a visible symbols of all Catholics who make up the assembly of God's Chosen People. The Council says, "Often...the Church is called the *building* of God [cf. 1Cor 3:9]. The Lord compared himself to the stone which the builders rejected, but which was made into the corner-stone [Mt 21:42 and parallels; Acts 4:11; 1 Pet 2:7; Ps 118:22]. On this foundation the Church is built by the apostles [1 Cor 3:11] and from it the Church receives solidity and unity. This edifice has many names to describe it: the house of God [1Tim 3:15] in which his *family* dwells; the household of God in the Spirit [Eph 2:19–22], the dwelling-place of God among men [Rev 21:3]."[68]

The image of the Catholic Church as God's edifice that has a very special scriptural, patristic, and traditional meaning is "the holy *temple*. This temple, symbolized in places of worship built out of stone, is praised by the Fathers and ... is compared in the liturgy to the Holy City, the New Jerusalem. As living stones we here on earth are built up along in it (1 Pet 2:5). It is this holy city that is seen by John as it comes down out of heaven from God when the world is made anew, prepared like a bride adorned for her husband [Rev 21:1–2]."[69]

COMMUNITY

One of the important elements in considering the Catholic Church in her supernatural character is to reflect on the "law of salvation in community". Christ founded the Church (Mt 16:18), not merely to address the social nature of human beings or only for some kind of psychological support for one's personal trust in the Lord, but as the fulfillment of God's eternal design, which remained the same from the day of creation, that is, to save human beings and give them everlasting happiness by forming them into a people, a community in which and through which alone they can be in contact with Him and be saved.

Father Louis Bouyer observes, "The Church is the final actualization of that people which God had been preparing through the course of history, from the first just man to the 'Holy and Just One Himself'... The Church of the New Testament must be understood as the final perfection of what the Hebrew Bible calls the 'Qahal Yahweh' (Ex 19:3–8; 2 Kings 23; Esdras 8)."

Saint Peter calls the *ecclesia* or Church of the New Testament, of which he was the first Pope, "a chosen race, a royal priesthood, a holy nation, God's own people... once you were no people but now you are God's people. Once you had not received mercy but now you have received mercy" (1 Pet 2:9–10). It is clear that God wills all the human race to be in solidarity in good and in evil with the first human being, Adam. Jesus is the New Adam (Rom 5:12–17), the new Head of redeemed humanity, elevating, at least potentially, the entire human race to union with God's nature (2 Pet 1:4) and thus to something even higher than mankind's original destiny. Father Cyprian Vagaggini notes that to be redeemed means to become an associate of Christ and to be united really but mystically to Him, and this can only be done by means of incorporation into the People He made into His Body, that is, through His Church.

JANUARY 16, 2004

The Church
IV

An Identity

One of the primary images of the Catholic Church, taken from divine revelation itself, is that of the Mystical Body of Christ (1 Cor 12:12–13). The *Catechism of the Catholic Church* states, "The comparison of the Church with the body casts light on the intimate bond between Christ and his Church. Not only is she gathered *around him*; she is united *in him*, in his body" (CCC 789).

Saint Augustine of Hippo says, "Let us rejoice then and give thanks that we have become not only Christians, but Christ himself. Do you understand and grasp, brethren, God's grace toward us? Marvel and rejoice: we have become Christ. For if he is the head, we are the members; he and we together are the whole man.... The fullness of Christ then is the head and the members. But, what does 'head and members' mean? Christ and the Church".[70] Saint Thomas Aquinas writes, "Head and members form as it were one and the same mystical person."[71] Pope Saint Gregory the Great says, "Our redeemer has shown himself to be one person with the holy Church whom he has taken to himself."[72] Saint Joan of Arc says, "About Jesus Christ and the Church, I simply know they're just one thing, and we shouldn't complicate the matter."[73]

Pope John Paul II says, "While the concept of 'People of God'... belongs to the Old Testament and is taken up again and enriched in the New, the image of the 'Body of Christ', which was also used by Vatican II in speaking about the Church, has no precedents in the Old Testament. ... The concept of Church as the 'Body of Christ' can be said to complement the concept of 'People of God'. It is the same reality expressed according to the two aspects of unity and multiplicity by two different analogies."[74]

LIKE HIM

Pope Pius XII writes, "The doctrine of the Mystical Body of Christ, which is the Church [Col 1:24], was first taught us by the Redeemer Himself."[75] That Pontiff goes on to say,

> It should be noted that the society established by the Redeemer of the human race resembles its divine Founder, who was persecuted, calumniated, and tortured by those very men whom He had undertaken to save. We cannot deny, rather from a heart filled with gratitude to God, we admit that even in our turbulent times there are many who, though outside the fold of Jesus Christ, look to the Church as the only haven of salvation; but we are also aware that the Church of God not only is despised and hated maliciously by those who shut their eyes to the light of Christian wisdom and miserably return to the teachings, customs, and practices of ancient paganism, but is ignored, neglected, and even at times looked upon as irksome by many Christians who are allured by specious error or caught in the meshes of the world's corruption.[76]

Quoting Pope Leo XIII, Pius XII says, "'The Church is visible because she is a body.' Hence, they err in a matter of divine truth, who imagine the Church to be invisible, intangible, a something merely 'pneumatological', as they say, by which many Christian communities, though they differ from each other in their profession of faith, are united by an invisible bond."[77]

Pope Pius XII writes again, "If we would define and describe this true Church of Jesus Christ—which is the One, Holy, Catholic, Apostolic, and Roman Church—we shall find nothing more noble, more sublime, or more divine than the expression, The Mystical Body of Christ—an expression which springs from and is, as it were, the fair flowering of the repeated teaching of the Sacred Scriptures and of the holy Fathers."[78]

INSEPARABLE

In the early 1990s Pope John Paul II gave a series of talks about the Church, in which, among other teaching, he emphasized the inseparable bond between Christ and His Body and how it is impossible to reject the Church and still be joined to Jesus. He says, for example, "One thing is certain—the life which Jesus Christ, and the Church with him, proposes to man is full of *moral demands* which bind him to what is good, even to the heights of heroism. It is necessary to observe whether, when one says '*no to the Church*', in reality one is not seeking to escape these demands. Here, more than in any other case, the '*no to the Church*' would be the equivalent of a '*no to Christ*'."[79]

Saint Augustine says, "No one can attain salvation and achieve eternal life unless one has Christ as his Head. But no one can have Christ as his Head, unless such a one is joined to His Body, which is the Church." Sometimes the very human defects, weaknesses, and sins of the Church's members are used as an excuse to overlook the inherent holiness of the Church's teachings, sacraments, devotions, institutions, organizations, and discipline and are used to overlook the abiding and divine presence of Christ in His Catholic Church (Mt 28:20; Jn 14:18; Acts 2:33).

The Holy Father also points out another reason why some reject the Church:

> At the bottom of this there is a psychology characterized by the *will for total autonomy*, originating in a sense of personal or collective self-sufficiency, by which one maintains independence from the superhuman Being, which is proposed—or interiorly discovered—as author and lord of life, of fundamental law, of the moral order, and so, as the ground of the distinction between good and evil. There are those who pretend to establish on their own what is good or bad, and thus refuse to be directed by another, either by a transcendent God or by a Church which represents him on earth.[80]

The Pope goes on to say,

> This position generally results from a great ignorance of reality. God is conceived as an enemy of human freedom, as a tyrannical master, even though he is actually the one who created freedom and is its most authentic friend. His commandments have no other purpose than to help men to avoid the worst and most shameful form of slavery, that of immorality, and to foster the development of true freedom. Without a trusting relationship with God, it is not possible for the human person to achieve fully his own spiritual growth.[81]

The Fourth Lateran Ecumenical Council teaches, "Who breaks away from the Church separates himself from Christ." Saint Cyprian often says, "Whoever does not have the Church for his Mother does not have God for his Father."[82]

JANUARY 23, 2004

The Church
V

THE HEAD

God's revelation tells us that Christ is ever the Head of the Catholic Church (Col 1:18). Furthermore, using the image of the Church as the Mystical Body of Christ, Saint Paul instructs us in the New Testament, "From [Him] the whole body, (joined and knit together by every joint with which it is supplied, when each part is working properly, makes bodily growth and upbuilds itself in love" (Eph 4:16).

Saint Thomas Aquinas states that Jesus is the abiding and invisible Head of the Church that He founded by reason of His preeminence and by reason of government. Echoing the Angelic Doctor, Pope Pius XII says, "[Our Savior] is to be called the head of the Church by reason of His singular pre-eminence, for the Head is in the highest place. But who is in a higher place than Christ God, who as the Word of the Eternal Father must be acknowledged to be the 'firstborn of every creature' [Col 1:15]? Who has reached more lofty heights than Christ Man who, though born of the Immaculate Virgin, is the true and natural Son of God, and, in virtue of His miraculous and glorious resurrection, a resurrection triumphant over death, has become the 'firstborn from the dead' [Col 1:18]?"[83]

The *Catechism of the Catholic Church* teaches, "[Christ] is the principle of creation and redemption. Raised to the Father's glory, 'in everything he [is] preeminent' [Col 1:18], especially in the Church, through whom he extends his reign over all things" (CCC 792).

GOVERNMENT

Pius XII considering the Catholic Church as the Mystical Body of Christ, remarks that one's head "is the 'royal citadel' of the body—to use the words of Ambrose—and all the members over whom it is placed for their good are naturally guided by it as being endowed with superior powers".[84] He goes on to say,

So the Divine Redeemer holds the helm of the universal Christian community and directs its course. And as to govern human society signifies to lead men to the end proposed by means that are expedient, just, and helpful, it is easy to see how our Savior, model and ideal of all good shepherds, performs these functions in a most striking way.

While still on earth, He instructed us by precept, counsel, and warning, in words that shall never pass away and will be spirit and life [cf. Jn 6:63] to all men of all times. Moreover He conferred a triple power on His Apostles and their successors, to teach, to govern, to lead men to holiness, making this power, defined by special ordinances, rights, and obligations, the fundamental law of the whole Church.[85]

THREE OTHERS

In his 1943 encyclical letter on the Church as the Mystical Body of Christ, Pope Pius XII mentions, "To the reasons thus far adduced to show that Christ our Lord should be called the Head of the Society which is His Body, there may be added three others which are closely related to one another."[86] The first of these reasons is similarity or solidarity. The Pope says, "It is the will of Jesus Christ that the whole body of the Church, no less than the individual members, should resemble Him. And we see this realized when, following in the footsteps of her Founder, the Church teaches, governs, and offers the divine Sacrifice…What wonder then, if, while on this earth, she, like Christ, suffers persecution, insults, and sorrows."[87]

The second of these reasons is plenitude, that is, the fact that Christ, the Head of the Church, has all supernatural gifts in their "fullness and perfection in Him."[88] In Jesus are "'all the treasures of wisdom and knowledge' [Col 2:3]…So full of grace and truth is He that of His inexhaustible fullness we have all received (cf. Jn 1:14–16)."[89]

The third reason why Christ is the Head of the Mystical Body is because of His communication of grace and power to the Catholic Church. "As the nerves extend from the head to all parts of the human body and give them power to feel and to move, in like manner our Savior communicates strength and power to His Church so that the things of God are understood more clearly and are more eagerly desired by the faithful. From Him streams into the body of the Church all the light with which those who believe are divinely illumined and all the grace by which they are made holy as He is holy."[90]

INTERDEPENDENCE

Saint Paul remarks about the human body, "The head [cannot say] to the feet, 'I have no need of you'" (1 Cor 12:21). It is clear that there is no possibility of salvation without Jesus Christ. He Himself declared, "Apart from me you can do nothing" (Jn 15:5). However, paradoxically our Lord in a certain sense "needs" the members of His Body. As God, of course, Jesus is almighty and does not need anyone or anything. However, He has willed that His members should be His instruments in applying His work of redemption to all people of all time until the end of the world.

Pope Pius XII observes:

> That is not because He is indigent and weak, but rather because He has so willed it for the greater glory of His spotless Spouse. Dying on the Cross, He left to His Church the immense treasury of the Redemption, towards which she contributed nothing. But when those graces come to be distributed, not only does He share this work of sanctification with His Church, but He wills that in some way it be due to her action. This is a deep mystery and an inexhaustible subject of meditation, that the salvation of many depends on the prayers and voluntary penances which the members of the Mystical Body of Jesus Christ offer for this intention [Col 1:24], and on the cooperation of pastors of souls and of the faithful, especially of fathers and mothers of families, a cooperation which they must offer to our Divine Savior as though they were His associates.[91]

The *Catechism* states, "Believers who respond to God's word and become members of Christ's Body, become intimately united with him" (CCC 790). The Second Vatican Council teaches, "In that body the life of Christ is communicated to those who believe, and who, through the sacraments, are united in a hidden and real way to Christ in his passion and glorification."[92] The *Catechism* (CCC 791) notes that the reality of the Mystical Body, properly lived, should triumph over all human divisions (Gal 3:27–28) and ought to stimulate the practice of mutual charity among the faithful (1 Cor 12:26).

JANUARY 30, 2004

The Church
VI

THE SOUL

Since one of the major biblical and traditional images of the Catholic Church is that of Christ's Mystical Body, with Jesus as the abiding and invisible Head, then the image of God, the Holy Spirit, as the Soul of the Church is of equal importance (Jn 16:12–14). The *Catechism of the Catholic Church* teaches, "The Holy Spirit, whom Christ the head pours out on his members, builds, animates, and sanctifies the Church" (CCC 747). Pope Leo XIII says, "Let it suffice to say that, as Christ is the Head of the Church, so is the Holy Spirit her Soul."[93]

Pope Pius XII states,

> To this Spirit of Christ,... as to an invisible principle, is to be ascribed the fact that all parts of the Body are joined one with the other and with their exalted Head; for He [the Holy Spirit] is entire in the Head, entire in the Body, and entire in each of the members. To the members He is present and assists them in proportion to their various duties and offices, and the greater or less degree of spiritual health which they enjoy. It is He who, through His heavenly grace, is the principle of every supernatural act in all parts of the Body. It is He who, while He is personally present and divinely active in all the members, nevertheless in the inferior members acts also through the ministry of the higher members. Finally, while by His grace He provides for the continual growth of the Church, He yet refuses to dwell through sanctifying grace in those members that are wholly severed from the Body.[94]

THE COUNCIL

In the Apostles' Creed the article about the Holy Spirit was originally joined to that of the Church. It was at first considered as one united article: I believe in the Holy Spirit in the Holy Catholic Church. This is illustrated by the teaching of the Second Vatican Council in its Dogmatic Constitution on the Church.

> When the work which the Father gave the Son to do on earth (cf. Jn 17:4) was accomplished, the Holy Spirit was sent on the day of Pentecost, in order that He might continually sanctify the Church, and thus, all those who believe would have access through Christ in one Spirit to the Father (cf. Eph 2:18). He is the Spirit of life, the fountain of water springing up to life eternal (cf. Jn 4:14; 7:38–39)...The Spirit dwells in the Church and in the hearts of the faithful as in a temple (cf. 1 Cor 3:16; 6:19). In them He prays on their behalf and bears witness to the fact that they are adopted sons (cf. Gal 4:6; Rom 8:15–16, 26). The Church, which the Spirit guides in the way of all truth (cf. Jn 16:13) and which He unified in

communion and in works of ministry, He both equips and directs with hierarchical and charismatic gifts and adorns with His fruits (cf. Eph 4:11–12; 1 Cor 12:4; Gal 5:22). By the power of the Gospel He makes the Church keep the freshness of youth. Uninterruptedly He renews it and leads it to perfect union with its Spouse. The Spirit and the Bride both say to Jesus, the Lord, "Come!" (Rev 22:17).[95]

Manifested

Pope Leo XIII notes, "The Church which, already conceived, came forth from the side of the second Adam in His sleep on the Cross, first showed Herself before the eyes of men on the great day of Pentecost."[96] Pius XII continues, "The Divine Redeemer began the building of the mystical temple of the Church when by His preaching He made known His Precepts; He completed it when He hung glorified on the Cross; and He manifested and proclaimed it when He sent the Holy Ghost as Paraclete in visible form on His disciples [Jn 20:22; Acts 2:1–39]."[97]

The *Catechism* remarks that it is in the Catholic Church that the mission of Jesus Christ and of the Holy Spirit is brought to completion. "The Spirit *prepares* men and goes out to them with [the Lord's] grace, in order to draw them to Christ. The Spirit *manifests* the risen Lord to them, recalls his word to them and opens their minds to the understanding of his Death and Resurrection. He *makes present* the mystery of Christ, supremely in the Eucharist, in order to reconcile them, to *bring them into communion* with God, that they might 'bear much fruit' [Jn 15:8, 16]" (CCC 737).

"Through the Church's sacraments, Christ communicates his Holy and sanctifying Spirit to the members of his Body. ...These 'mighty works of God', offered to believers in the sacraments of the Church, bear their fruit in the new life in Christ, according to the Spirit" (CCC 739–40).

Presence

As the divine Soul of Christ's Mystical Body, the Holy Spirit is particularly active in the most significant works of the Church. He ratifies the work of the hierarchy. Our Holy Father, Pope John Paul II, speaking about the work of the third Divine Person of the Blessed Trinity in the Church, recalls how the apostles in the Council of Jerusalem prefaced their resolutions by the phrase: "It has seemed good to the Holy Spirit and to us" (Acts 15:28). They, along with the whole early Catholic community, "enjoyed the increased consolation of the Holy Spirit" (Acts 9:31).

The Holy Spirit is invoked in the "epiclesis" at every Mass immediately before the words of consecration are spoken. In the Latin Rite, this is signified by the priest extending his hands over the bread and wine that are about to be consecrated. The Holy Spirit is invoked before the words of absolution are pronounced in the Sacrament of Penance (Jn 20:22–23). To the Holy Spirit are attributed the inspiration of the words of Sacred Scripture and the enlightenment of those who hear them, especially in the sacred liturgy. Although present in all the sacraments, it is the Holy Spirit Who comes in a special way with His sevenfold gifts (Is 11:2–3) in the Sacrament of Confirmation (Acts 8:14–17).

In Church history it is the Holy Spirit Who inspires and strengthens the martyrs (Acts 6:10; Mt 10:20) in their heroic witness to Christ. As the *Catechism* says, "Because the Holy Spirit is the anointing of Christ, it is Christ who, as the head of the Body, pours out the Spirit among his members to nourish, heal, and organize them in their mutual functions, to give them life, send them to bear witness, and associate them to his self-offering to the Father and to his intercession for the whole world" (CCC 739).

FEBRUARY 6, 2004

The Church
VII

THE COUNCIL

It is generally agreed by those who took part in the Second Vatican Council as well as by subsequent knowledgeable commentators that the primary documents of that twenty-first Ecumenical Council in the history of the Catholic Church were its ecclesiastical constitutions, namely, the Dogmatic Constitution on the Church, the Dogmatic Constitution on Divine Revelation, the Constitution on the Sacred Liturgy, and the Constitution on the Church in the Modern World. Of these, the document that almost everyone sees as being the most important of all is the first, the Dogmatic Constitution on the Church, which goes by its Latin title, that is, its first two words in Latin, *Lumen gentium*.

The Council, which began on October 11, 1962, and concluded on December 8, 1965, used most of the traditional, customary, and familiar images in speaking about the Catholic Church, but in *Lumen gentium* it seemed also to use, with special emphasis, the term the "new People of God" to describe the Church. Before speaking at some length about the institutional and hierarchical aspects of the Church that Jesus Christ founded and that He intends His Church to possess, the Council first devoted the second chapter of *Lumen gentium* to the designation of the Church as the "People of God". That image, of course, just like the other images, is firmly rooted in Sacred Scripture and provides a rich biblical source of inspiration for those who deeply love the Church.

In using the terms "People of God" and new "People of God", the Council clearly intended to include both the clergy and the laity, both pastors and the flock entrusted to their shepherds' care, those who are ordained by Christ as the official teachers and guardians of His people and those whom Jesus desires to be taught and guarded.

CHARACTERISTICS

The Council instructs us that God,

> has ... willed to make men holy and save them, not as individuals without any bond or link between them, but rather to make them into a people who might acknowledge Him and serve Him in holiness [1 Pet 2:9–10]. He therefore chose the Israelite race to be His own people and established a covenant with it...These things happened ... as a preparation for and figure of the new and perfect covenant which was to be ratified in Christ....[In the New Covenant in His blood],He called a race made up of Jews and Gentiles which would be one, not according to the flesh, but in the Spirit.[98]

The *Catechism of the Catholic Church* (CCC 782) notes that in using the image of the Catholic Church as the new "People of God", one can immediately see some special characteristics of the Church. Because the Catholic Church is "of God", she is fundamentally different from every other religious, ethnic, political, or cultural group found in human history (Acts 10:35; 1 Cor 11:25; 1 Pet 2:9). One becomes a member of this People, not by physical birth, but by Baptism and faith (Jn 3:3–5; 1 Pet 1:23). Jesus is the Head of this People, the anointed Messiah, and His Anointing is the Holy Spirit, Who flows into the members, making them into a messianic people (Eph 1:22).

The "new People of God" enjoy the dignity and freedom of being God's adopted children, and the Holy Spirit lives in them as in a temple (1 Jn 3:1–2; 2 Cor 6:16; Gal 4:31). They are guided by the new commandment of love (Jn 13:34; Rom 8:2; Gal 5:25). Their mission is to be salt and light for the world (Mt 5:13–16) and to be, in the words of the Council, the "most sure seed of unity, hope, and salvation for the whole human race."[99] Their destiny is to be the embryo of "the Kingdom of God which has been begun by God himself on earth and which must be further extended until it has been brought to perfection by Him at the end of time [Col 3:4]."[100]

Our Holy Father, Pope John Paul II, observes that "this teaching of the [Second Vatican] Council emphasizes, with St. Peter, the continuity of the People of God with that of the old covenant, but, it also brings out what in a certain sense is the absolute newness of the new people who are established in virtue of Christ's redemption, and set apart (i.e., purchased) by the blood of the Lamb [Eph 2:12–22]."[101]

POPE PAUL VI

Pope Paul VI, soon after the Council, remarked that it is not easy to grasp the supernatural reality of the Catholic Church, "an association of believers and of those who pray, a religious society which is both visible and spiritual, the Body of Christ". He went on to say that difficulties can arise because "the Church presents herself covered with images, forms, and signs which are not easy to understand. What is the meaning of her rites, vestments, habits, words, ministers, and forms of life?"

He said that the Council directs our attention and that of the whole world to the fact that "no one can really and truly meet Christ apart from or outside the Church. The Church is Christ's fold, where He, the Good Shepherd, makes His voice heard. The Church is Christ's theater where every believer may have a sense of the meaning and value of his own existence, and may feel himself called to give his own life a mission of its own, a destiny which is both human and superhuman at the same time."

CARDINAL DE LUBAC

Speaking of the Church and basing himself on the teachings of the Church Fathers, Cardinal Henri de Lubac says,

> The [Catholic Church] is [the] fulfillment and "fullness" [of Christ]. She is the tabernacle of his presence, the building of which he is both Architect and Cornerstone. She is the temple in which he teaches and into which he draws with him the whole Divinity. She is the ship and he the pilot, she the deep ark and he the central mast, assuring the communication of all those on board with the heavens above them. She is the paradise and he is its tree and well of life; she is the star and he the light that illuminates our night.[102]

Saint John Chrysostom says, "No power is as powerful as the Church. The Church is your hope. The Church is your salvation. The Church never ages, and her vitality is eternal." Saint Augustine of Hippo remarks, "It is in proportion as one loves the Church of Christ that one has within oneself the Holy Spirit." Saint Irenaeus says, "Where the Church is, there is the Spirit of

God and all grace." Cardinal de Lubac says, addressing the Church, "Each day you give us him who is the Way and the Truth. Through you we have hope of life in him."[103]

FEBRUARY 13, 2004

The Church
VIII

POPE'S CREDO

Pope Paul VI, during his pontificate in the second half of the last century, declared a special Holy Year of Faith from June 1967 to June 1968, to commemorate the anniversary of the martyrdom of Saints Peter and Paul in Rome, which had occurred in A.D. 67 under reign of the pagan emperor Nero. One of the purposes for which that Pope held such a Year of Faith was his desire to correct some serious misunderstandings about the Catholic faith that had arisen in various places due to some doctrinal, moral, and disciplinary confusion resulting from certain peoples' misreading and misinterpreting the Second Vatican Council, which had just concluded in December 1965.

On June 30, 1968, Pope Paul VI published his *Credo of the People of God* as part of the concluding rites of that Holy Year of Faith. He said that he did this to emphasize his "steadfast will to be faithful to the deposit of faith (1 Tim 6:20; Jude 1:3) which they transmitted to us, and that we might strengthen our desire to live by it in the historical circumstances in which the Church finds herself in her pilgrimage in the midst of the world."[104] He also said that he issued this *Credo* to carry out his ongoing responsibility as the successor of Saint Peter, confirming his brothers in the faith (Lk 22:32).

ABOUT CHURCH

The section of the *Credo of the People of God* regarding the Church says,

> We believe in one, holy, catholic, and apostolic Church, built by Jesus Christ on that rock which is Peter. She is the Mystical Body of Christ and, at the same time, a visible society, instituted with hierarchical organs, and a spiritual community, the Church on earth, the pilgrim People of God here below, and the Church filled with

heavenly blessings, the germ and the first fruits of the Kingdom of God, through which the work and the sufferings of Redemption are continued throughout human history, and which look for its perfect accomplishment beyond time in glory.

In the course of time, the Lord Jesus forms His Church by means of the sacraments emanating from His plenitude. By these she makes her members participants in the Mystery of the Death and Resurrection of Christ, in the grace of the Holy Spirit who gives her life and movement. She is therefore holy, though she has sinners in her bosom, because she herself has no other life but that of grace: it is by living by her life that her members are sanctified; it is by removing themselves from her life that they fall into sins and disorders that prevent the radiation of her sanctity. This is why she suffers and does penance for these offenses, of which she has the power to heal her children through the blood of Christ and the gift of the Holy Spirit.[105]

HEIRESS

The *Credo* goes on to say that the Catholic Church is the,

> heiress of the divine promises and daughter of Abraham according to the Spirit, through that Israel whose scriptures she lovingly guards, and whose patriarchs and prophets she venerates; founded upon the apostles and handing on from century to century their ever-living word and their powers as pastors in the successor of Peter and the bishops in communion with him; perpetually assisted by the Holy Spirit, she has charge of guarding, teaching, explaining, and spreading the Truth which God revealed in a then veiled manner by the prophets, and fully by the Lord Jesus...We believe that the Church founded by Jesus Christ and for which He prayed is indefectibly one in faith, worship, and the bond of hierarchical communion...We believe that the Church is necessary for salvation, because Christ, who is the sole mediator and way of salvation, renders Himself present for us in His body which the Church.[106]

The words of Pope Paul VI echo those of Saint Augustine of Hippo, who says, The Church, after all, is His Body, as the teaching of the Apostle confirms (Eph 1:22–23), and is also called His wife (Eph 5:28–33). So, while His Body consists of many parts (1 Cor 12:13–31) having different functions, He binds it tightly together with the knot of unity and love to give it its proper kind of health. But, during this age He trains and purges it with various kinds of salutary vexation and distress, so that once it has been snatched from this world, He may bind His wife, the Church, to Himself for ever, "not having any stain or wrinkle or any such thing."

DE LUBAC

Cardinal Henri de Lubac, addressing his words to the Catholic Church, has written:

> Praised may you be, Mother of love at its most lovely, of healthy fear, of divine knowledge, and holy hope! Without you our thoughts are diffuse and hazy; you gather them together into a firm body. You scatter the darkness in which men either slumber or despair or—pitifully—"shape as they please their fantasies of the infinite". Without discouraging us from any task, you protect us from deceptive myths; you spare us from the aberrations and the aversions of all churches made by the hand of man. You save us from destruction in the presence of our God! Living Ark, Gate of the East! Unflawed mirror of the activity of the Most High! You are the beloved of the Lord of the Universe, initiated into his secrets, and who teach us what pleases him. You whose supernatural splendor never fades, even in the darkest hours! It is thanks to you that our darkness is bathed in light! You through whom the priest goes up every day to the altar of God, who gives joy to his youth! The Glory of Libanus is in you, under the obscurity of your earthly covering. Each day you give us him who is the Way and the Truth. Through you we have hope of life in him. The memory of you is sweeter than honey, and he who hears you shall never be put to confusion [see Sir 24:17–21; Jud 13:25]. Holy Mother, unique Mother, immaculate Mother! O great Mother! Holy Church true Eve, sole true Mother of all the living![107]

The Second Vatican Council quoted Saint Augustine, saying,

> The Church, "like a stranger in a foreign land, presses forward amid the persecutions of the world and the consolations of God", announcing the cross and death of her risen Lord until He comes [cf. 1 Cor 11:26]. By the power of the risen Lord [the Catholic Church] is given strength that it might, in patience and in love,

overcome its sorrows and its challenges, both within itself and from without, and that it might reveal to the world, faithfully though darkly, the mystery of its Lord until, in the end, it will be manifested in full light [Rev 22:17].[108]

APRIL 23, 2004

The Church
IX

BOTH-AND

The Second Vatican Council teaches, "By her relationship with Christ, the Church is a kind of sacrament of intimate union with God and of the unity of all mankind, that is, she is a sign and an instrument of such union and unity."[109] A sacrament, we know, is first of all "an outward sign" indicating and causing spiritual and invisible reality. As an outward sign, then, the Catholic Church that Jesus founded certainly has an aspect that is perceptible to the senses, while yet "signifying" interior and spiritual things.

Pope Pius XII proclaims what Catholic doctrine has always said, namely, "They err in a matter of divine truth who imagine the Church to be invisible and intangible, a something merely pneumatalogical', as they say, by which many Christian communities, though they differ from each other in their profession of faith, are united by an invisible bond."[110]

The *Catechism of the Catholic Church* says, "The Church is in history, but at the same time she transcends it. It is only 'with the eyes of faith' [*Roman Catechism* I, 10, 20] that one can see her in her visible reality and at the same time in her spiritual reality as bearer of divine life" (CCC 770). The Second Vatican Council notes, "The Church is essentially both human and divine, visible but endowed with invisible realities, zealous in action and dedicated to contemplation, present in the world, but as a pilgrim, so constituted that in her the human is directed toward and subordinated to the divine, the visible to the invisible, action to contemplation, and this present world to that city yet to come, the object of our quest [cf. Heb 13:14]."[111]

SACRAMENT

We are instructed by the *Catechism*:

The Greek word *mysterion* was translated into Latin by two terms:

mysterium and *sacramentum*. In later usage the term *sacramentum* emphasizes the visible sign of the hidden reality of salvation which was indicated by the term *mysterium*. In this sense, Christ himself is the mystery of salvation: "For there is no other mystery of God, except Christ" [St. Augustine, *Ep.* 187, 11, 34: PL 33, 846]. The saving work of his holy and sanctifying humanity is the sacrament of salvation, which is revealed and active in the Church's sacraments (which the Eastern Churches also call "the holy mysteries"). The seven sacraments are the signs and instruments by which the Holy Spirit spreads the grace of Christ the head throughout the Church which is his Body. The Church, then, both contains and communicates the invisible grace she signifies. It is in this analogical sense, that the Church is called a "sacrament." (CCC 774)

The *Catechism* also tells us: "As a sacrament, the Catholic Church is Christ's instrument. 'She is taken up by him also as the instrument for the salvation of all' [*Lumen gentium*, no. 9, § 2], 'the universal sacrament of salvation' [*Lumen gentium* no. 48, § 2], by which Christ is 'at once manifesting and actualizing the mystery of God's love for men' [*Gaudium et spes*, no. 45, § 1]. The Church 'is the visible plan of God's love for humanity' [Paul VI, June 22, 1973], because God desires 'that the whole human race may become one People of God, form one Body of Christ, and be built up into one temple of the Holy Spirit' [*Ad gentes*, no. 7, § 2; cf. *Lumen gentium*, no. 17]" (CCC 776).

PROJECTING CHRIST

The twofold reality of the Church, this-worldly and other-worldly, institutional and mystical, charismatic and hierarchical, spiritual and authoritative, holy but composed of sinners, must never be dissociated in our hearts and thoughts. Whenever in history such dissociation between the visible and invisible has occurred, inevitably schism, heresy, and spiritual anarchy followed, to the detriment of the eternal salvation of many souls.

The Catholic Church extends Jesus and His salvation down the centuries until He comes again in glory. Like her Master and Founder, she participates in the incarnational economy or divine plan for human redemption. When Christ walked on earth as a carpenter and chose to be a carpenter's son, there was in Him much of what was unseen, namely, His human soul and His divine Nature and Divine Personhood, while there also was that which was "perceptible to the senses", His human Body, His words, gestures, actions, and so on. So the Church is a social reality, a visible and highly organized community, much of whose organization is unchangeable because it derives directly from and by the will of Jesus and from the continuous action of the Holy Spirit. However, at the same time the Church is profoundly spiritual, much more than anything that can be perceived or measured by any physical or material system or means.

Pope John Paul II notes that "the Holy Spirit's action in the Church, beginning with the day of Pentecost [is] an interior, saving work which is also expressed externally in the birth of a community and institution of salvation."[112]

DICHOTOMIES

Pope Pius XII remarks,

> One must not think, ... that this ordered or "organic" structure of the body of the Church contains only hierarchical elements and with them is complete; or, as an opposite opinion holds, that it is composed only of those who enjoy charismatic gifts.... That those who exercise sacred power in this Body are its chief members must be maintained uncompromisingly. It is through them, by commission of the Divine Redeemer Himself, that Christ's apostolate as Teacher, King and Priest is to endure. At the same time, when the Fathers of the Church sing the praises of this Mystical Body of Christ, with its ministries, its variety of ranks, its officers, it conditions, its orders, its duties, they are thinking not only of those who have received Holy Orders, but of all those too, who, following the evangelical counsels, pass their lives either actively among men, or hidden in the silence of the cloister, or who aim at combining the active and contemplative life according to their Institute; as also of those who, though living in the world, consecrate themselves wholeheartedly to spiritual or corporal works of mercy, and of those in the state of holy matrimony.[113]

Our present Holy Father says, "The Church, a priestly, sacramental, and prophetic community, was instituted by Jesus Christ as a structured, hierarchical, and ministerial society, to provide pastoral governance for the continual formation and growth of the community." The *Catechism* says, "The Church is both visible and spiritual, a hierarchical society and the Mystical Body of Christ. She is one, yet formed of two components, human and divine. That is her mystery, which only faith can accept" (CCC 779).

JUNE 4, 2004

The Church
X

THE CHURCH-WORD

It is sometimes asked from where we get the word "church". In English it probably comes from the Anglo-Saxon word *cirice*, which, like many words with German roots, comes originally from a Greek word, *kyriakon*, which means the house of the *Kyrios* or the Lord. Also, into the linguistic mix comes the Greek word *ekklein*, which means to "call out of". Thus, there was a jump to the term *ekklesia* which came to mean a convoked or summoned assembly of people, called out of the generality of the human race and gathered in an ordered way for a religious purpose.

In the Old Testament the assembly of the Chosen People was called in Hebrew the qahal *Yahweh*, and this was translated into Greek as the *ekklesia Kyriou*. This was especially the term used, as the *Catechism of the Catholic Church* tells us, when they were gathered at Mount Sinai to receive the Old Law and to be established by God as His specially loved nation and race (Ex 19). This was also the usage when they were summoned to renew their solemn covenant with God at various times in the course of their historical vicissitudes and development (Nehemiah, chap. 8–10; 2 Kings 23).

The *Catechism* notes, "By calling itself 'Church', the first community of Christian believers recognized itself as heir to that assembly. In the Church, God is 'calling together' his people from all the ends of the earth" (CCC 751). The Catholic Church then consists of the Chosen People, the elect, of the New Testament.

THE FULLNESS

We are also told by the *Catechism*,

> In Christian usage, the word "church" designates the liturgical assembly [cf. 1 Cor 11:18; 14:19; 28, 34, 35], but also the local community [1 Cor 1:2; 16:1] or the whole universal community of believers [cf. 1 Cor 15:9; Gal 1:13; Phil 3:6]. These three meanings are inseparable. "The Church" is the People that God gathers in the whole world. She exists in local communities and is made real as a liturgical, and above all a Eucharistic, assembly. She draws her life from the word and from the Body of Christ and so herself becomes Christ's Body. (CCC 752)

In Jesus Christ, we know, "The whole fullness of deity dwells bodily" (Col 2:9), and "in him all the fullness of God was pleased to dwell" (Col 1:19). This "fullness" (in Greek, *pleroma*) is now transferred to the Church in time and in the future (the "eschaton"). "He...has made him the head over all things for the church, which is his body, the fullness of him who fills all in all" (Eph 1:22–23). Father Louis Bouyer notes, "In this supreme vision, the Church appears as the fullness of Christ Who is Himself the One in Whom dwells the fullness of the Deity, because the mystery of the life of God in the communication of a special love ('agape') is revealed to mankind and made a reality in the Church." Saint Thomas Aquinas says that through the Catholic Church the very life of the Most Blessed Trinity (2 Pet 1:4) is extended from the Son of God made man to all of mankind.

FORESHADOWED

Saint Clement of Alexandria says, "Just as God's will is creation and is called 'the world', so his intention is the salvation of men, and it is called 'the Church'."[114] Echoing Saint Epiphanius, the *Catechism* observes that "the Church is the goal of all things,[115] and God permitted such painful upheavals as the angels' fall and man's sin only as occasions and means for displaying all the power of his arm and the whole measure of the love he wanted to give to the world" (CCC 760; see Jn 3:16). Several early Church Fathers, such as Tertullian, Saint Justin, and Aristides, often say that God created the world for the sake of the Church. The *Catechism* says, "God created the world for the sake of communion with his divine life, a communion brought about by the 'convocation' of men in Christ, and this 'convocation' is the Church" (CCC 760).

This "gathering together of the Church", says the *Catechism*, "is, as it were, God's reaction to the chaos provoked by sin. This reunification [of all human beings who have fallen from grace with God and with each other] is achieved secretly in the heart of all peoples. 'In every nation anyone who fears him and does what is right is acceptable' to God [Acts 10:35; cf. *Lumen gentium*, nos. 9; 13; 16]" (CCC 761).

The call of Abraham to be the ancestor of a select and numerous people (Gen 12:2; 15: 5–6) and Israel's vocation to prefigure the future gathering of all nations (Ex 19:5–6; Deut 7:6; Micah 4:1–4) paved the way to the prophetic foretelling of a future surpassing, new, and eternal covenant between God and His human creatures, which later came into being with Christ (Is 55:3; Hos 1; Jer 2:31, and so on).

THE BIRTH

With a reference to Saint Ambrose,[116] the *Catechism* states, "As Eve was formed from the sleeping Adam's side, so the Church was born from the pierced heart of Christ hanging dead on the cross" (CCC 766). The Second Vatican Council echoes this thought: "For it was from the side of Christ as he slept the sleep of death upon the cross that there came forth the 'wondrous sacrament of the whole Church'."[117] "The origin and growth of the Church are symbolized by the blood and water which flowed from the open side of the crucified Jesus."[118] The *Catechism* states, "The Church is born primarily of Christ's total self-giving for our salvation, anticipated in the institution of the Eucharist and fulfilled on the cross" (CCC 766).

The Catholic Church was then revealed to the world as the only divine instrument for the salvation of human souls by the coming of the Holy Spirit. The Second Vatican Council says, "When the work which the Father gave the Son to do on earth was accomplished, the Holy Spirit was sent on the day of Pentecost in order that he might continually sanctify the Church."[119] "The Church was openly displayed to the crowds and the spread of the Gospel among the nations, through preaching, was begun."[120] The *Catechism* goes on to say, "So that she can fulfill her mission, the Holy Spirit 'bestows upon [the Church] varied hierarchic and charismatic gifts, and in this way directs her' [*Lumen gentium*, no. 4]. 'Henceforward the Church, endowed with the gifts of her founder and faithfully observing his precepts of charity, humility and self-denial, receives the mission of proclaiming and establishing among all peoples the Kingdom of Christ and of God, and she is on earth the seed and the beginning of that kingdom' [*Lumen gentium*, no. 5]" (CCC 768).

JUNE 18, 2004

The Church
XI

KINGDOM

Jesus Christ founded the Catholic Church (Mt 16:18), which is the "pillar and bulwark of the truth" (1 Tim 3:15) and with which He continues to abide, according to His solemn promise, until the end of time (Mt 28:20). While He walked on earth, our Savior also often spoke about "the kingdom of God", comparing it, for instance, to a field in which there are both weeds and wheat, a dragnet taken in from a lake with good and bad things found in it, a huge treasure hidden in a field or a priceless pearl found by a searching pearl merchant, and so on (Mt 13:1–50). This "kingdom" Jesus spoke about as already here (Mt 12:28) but also, paradoxically, as "yet to come" (see Lk 11:2). The question arises, then, as to how this "kingdom" that Christ spoke about is related to the Church about which He also spoke.

The Second Vatican Council said, "The Lord Jesus inaugurated his Church by preaching the Good News, that is, the coming of the Reign of God, promised over the ages in the scriptures."[121] The "Church 'is the Reign of Christ already present in mystery."[122] This Kingdom shines out before men in the word, in the works and in the presence of Christ."[123] "To welcome Jesus' word is to welcome 'the Kingdom itself'."[124] The *Catechism of the Catholic Church* notes, "The seed and beginning of the Kingdom are the 'little flock' of those whom Jesus came to gather around him, the flock whose shepherd he is [Lk 12:32; cf. Mt 10:16, 26:31; Jn 10:1 – 21]....The Lord Jesus endowed his community with a structure that will remain until the Kingdom is fully achieved" (CCC 764–65).

EMBRYO

The Catholic Church, then, is the kingdom of God in embryo form. The Second Vatican Council observes, as we just noted, the mission of the Church is to proclaim and establish "among all peoples the Kingdom of Christ and of God, and she is on earth the seed and the beginning of that kingdom."[125] The recent declaration *Dominus Iesus* of the Holy See says,

> The Church is...the sign and instrument of the kingdom; she is called to announce and establish the kingdom...She is [as the Council says] "the kingdom of Christ already present in mystery".... The kingdom of God, in fact, has an eschatological dimension: it is a reality present in time, but its full realization will arrive only with the completion or fulfillment of history....One may not separate the kingdom from the Church....Those theses [that deny the unicity of the relationship that Christ and the Church have with the kingdom of God] are contrary to Catholic faith."[126]

Our Holy Father, Pope John Paul II writes,

> The kingdom of God [as we know it] cannot be detached either from Christ or from the Church....Christ not only proclaimed the kingdom, but in him the kingdom itself became present and was fulfilled. This happened not only through his words and his deeds: above all,...the kingdom is made manifest in the very person of Christ, Son of God and Son of Man, who came 'to serve and to give his life as a ransom for many' (Mk 10:45) [*Lumen gentium*, no. 5]. The kingdom of God is not a concept, a doctrine, or a program subject to free interpretation, but it is before all else *a person* with the face and name of Jesus of Nazareth, the image of

the invisible God....Likewise, one may not separate the kingdom from the Church...While remaining distinct from Christ and the kingdom, the Church is indissolubly united to both. Christ endowed the Church, his body, with the fullness of the benefits and means of salvation. The Holy Spirit dwells in her, enlivens her with his gifts and charisms, sanctifies, guides, and constantly renews her.[127]

CHURCH

The Supreme Pontiff goes on to say,

> The many dimensions of the kingdom of God do not weaken the foundations and purposes of missionary activity [of the Church], but rather strengthen and extend them. The [Catholic] Church is the sacrament of salvation for all mankind, and her activity is not limited only to those who accept her message. She is a dynamic force in mankind's journey toward the eschatological kingdom, and is the sign and promoter of gospel values...The Church serves the kingdom by her intercession, since the kingdom by its very nature is God's gift and work, as we are reminded by the gospel parables and by the prayer which Jesus taught us. We must ask for the kingdom, welcome it and make it grow within us; but we must also work together so that it will be welcomed and will grow among all people, until the time when Christ "delivers the kingdom to God the Father" and "God will be everything to everyone" [1 Cor 15:24–28].[128]

The *Catechism* tells us that, "'To carry out the will of the Father Christ inaugurated the kingdom of heaven on earth'"[129] by founding the Catholic Church. "Christ stands at the heart of this gathering of men into the 'family of God'. By his word, through signs that manifest the reign of God, and by sending out his disciples, Jesus calls all people to come together around him. But above all in the great Paschal mystery—his death on the cross and his Resurrection—he would accomplish the coming of his kingdom" (CCC 542).

ASPECTS

There are certain characteristics of the kingdom that Jesus proclaimed (Mk 1:14–15), which, of course, also mark the beginning of that kingdom, which is to say, the Catholic Church. First, everyone is called to enter, all human beings of every race and nation (Mt 8:11; 10:5–7; 28:19). Second, the kingdom belongs in a special way to the poor and lowly (Lk 4:18; Mt 5:3). It is particularly for the "little ones" (Mt 11:25). Third, sinners are especially invited (Mk 2:17; 1 Tim 1:15; Mt 26:28). Fourth, to enter one must be willing to sacrifice everything else (Mt 13:44–45) and words are not enough, since deeds are required (Mt 21:28–32). Fifth, those who enter the kingdom are privy to certain salvific "secrets" (Mt 13:11), while for those who remain outside, the ultimate meaning, goal, and purpose of human existence will always remain a perplexing puzzle (Mk 4:11).

The twelve Apostles and their successors have been placed by Jesus Himself in charge of His kingdom: "As my Father appointed a kingdom for me, so do I appoint for you that you may eat and drink at my table in my kingdom, and sit on thrones judging the twelve tribes of Israel" (Lk 22:29–30). The one whom our Lord installed as the chief of the apostles, the head of the apostolic college, of course, was Saint Peter and his contemporary successor, the Bishop of Rome. It was to Saint Peter alone and his successors in Rome that Christ, our divine Savior, entrusted "the keys of the kingdom of heaven" (Mt 16:19).

JULY 2, 2004

The Church
XII

BAD ADVICE

Sometimes one sees here and there in America on the back of trucks, on bumper stickers, in newspaper church notices, and in similar places the well-intended slogan, "Attend the Church of your choice." It is usually well-meant and implies an exhortation to practice religion and to acknowledge God, as well as to carry out our human duty to worship Him. This is certainly laudable. The slogan also implies commendable praise for the religious liberty we enjoy in our country, where we are relatively free from government intrusion or coercion in choosing our religious profession and practices.

However, as someone has long ago pointed out, the slogan in itself is gravely erroneous. The correct slogan should be, "Attend the Church of God's choice." While human beings can and should be free from external pressure and undue influence in following their conscience in their religious allegiance, it has to be pointed out that each person has a supreme obligation to form his conscience correctly in that area of life, since deliberately not to do so involves a horrible consequence, the forfeiture of one's eternal salvation. Jesus Christ, true Man and true God, founded one Church, the Catholic Church. God did not and does not leave it up to each person to decide for himself what Church to belong to or "to attend". To find and follow the truth revealed by God is a solemn moral duty, divinely imposed by God on every human being who has the use of reason. As Cardinal John Henry Newman puts it, "There is a truth then [in religion];…there is one truth; [and] religious error is in itself of an immoral nature; [and] its maintainers, unless involuntarily such, are guilty in maintaining it…. The mind is below the truth, not above it, and is bound, not to descant upon it, but to venerate it…Truth and falsehood are set before us for the trial of our hearts; [and] our choice is an awful giving forth of lots on which salvation or rejection is inscribed."[130]

COUNCIL

In its Declaration on Religious Freedom, the Second Vatican Council teaches,

> On their part all men are bound to seek the truth, especially in what concerns God and His Church, and to embrace the truth they come to know, and to hold fast to it. This Vatican Council professes its belief that it is upon human conscience that these obligations fall and exert their binding force. The truth cannot impose itself except by virtue of its own truth, as it makes its entrance into the mind at once quietly and with power. Religious freedom, in turn, which men demand as necessary to fulfill their duty to worship God, has to do with immunity from coercion in civil society. Therefore it leaves untouched traditional Catholic doctrine on the moral duty of all men and societies toward the true religion and toward the one Church of Christ.[131]

In the same document, the Council says, "First, the council professes its belief that God Himself has made known to mankind the way in which men are to serve Him, and thus be saved in Christ and come to blessedness. We believe that this one true religion subsists in the Catholic and Apostolic Church, to which the Lord Jesus committed the duty of spreading it abroad among all men [Mt 28:19–20]."[132]

OUR BELIEF

The 2000 declaration *Dominus Iesus* (The Lord Jesus), ratified and approved by Pope John Paul II, states,

> In connection with the unicity and universality of the salvific mediation of Jesus Christ, the unicity of the Church founded by him must be *firmly believed* as a truth of Catholic faith. Just as there is one Christ, so there exists a single body of Christ, a single

Bride of Christ: "a single Catholic and apostolic Church". Furthermore, the promises of the Lord that he would not abandon his church (cf. Mt 16:18; 28:20) and that he would guide her by his Spirit (cf. Jn 16:13) mean, according to Catholic faith, that the unicity and the unity of the Church—like everything that belongs to the Church's integrity—will never be lacking. The Catholic faithful *are required to profess* that there is an historical continuity—rooted in the apostolic succession—between the Church founded by Christ and the Catholic Church.[133]

The Second Vatican Council, in its Dogmatic Constitution on the Church, notes, "This is the single Church of Christ,...which our Savior, after his resurrection, entrusted to Peter's pastoral care (cf. Jn 21:17), commissioning him and the other Apostles to extend and rule her (cf. Mt 28:18–20), erected for all ages as 'the pillar and mainstay of the truth' (1 Tim 3:15). This Church, constituted and organized as a society in the present world, subsists in the Catholic Church, governed by the Successor of Peter and by the Bishops in communion with him."[134]

Subsists

The declaration *Dominus Iesus* remarks,

> The interpretation of those who would derive from the formula [*subsistit in*] the thesis that the one Church of Christ could subsist also in non-Catholic churches and ecclesial communities is...contrary to the authentic meaning of *Lumen genti*um [the Dogmatic Constitution on the Church of the Second Vatican Council]. The Council instead chose the word *subsistit* [subsist] precisely to clarify that there exists only one "subsistence" of the true Church, while outside her visible structure there only exist *elementa Ecclesiae* [ecclesial elements], which—being elements of that same Church—tend and lead toward the Catholic Church."[135]

> "With respect to these, it needs to be stated that 'they derive their efficacy from the very fullness of grace and truth entrusted to the Catholic Church.'"[136]

> The Lord Jesus, the only Savior, did not only establish a simple community of disciples, but constituted the Church as a *salvific mystery*: he himself is in the Church and the Church is in him (cf. Jn 15:1–26; Gal 3:28; Eph 4:15–16; Acts 9:5). Therefore, the fullness of Christ's salvific mystery belongs also to the Church,

inseparably united to her Lord. Indeed, Jesus Christ continues his presence and his work of salvation in the Church and by means of the Church (cf. Col 1:24–27), which is his body (1 Cor 12:12–13, 27; Col 1:18). And thus, just as the head and members of a living body, though not identical, are inseparable, so too Christ and the Church can neither be confused nor separated, and constitute a single "whole Christ". The same inseparability is also expressed in the New Testament by the analogy of the Church as the *Bride of Christ* (cf. 2 Cor 11:2; Eph 5:25–29; Rev 21:2, 9).[137]

It is clear that God does not will our choice of religion and Church to be a matter of mere human or personal "opinion or taste", despite so many facets of our contemporary culture that try to teach otherwise.

JULY 16, 2004

The Church
XIII

ROMAN?

Recently a Catholic in our area was asked, "Are you a Roman Catholic?" He correctly replied, "Actually, I am a Nebraska Catholic." In two Ecumenical Councils, Trent and Vatican One, the word "Roman" was inserted into the title of the only true Church founded by Jesus Christ. Those Councils taught the truth that the Church is One, Holy, Catholic, Apostolic, and Roman. However, it should be noticed that the word "Roman" is an adjective and modifies the word "Church". It is not an adverb modifying the adjective "Catholic".

As Father Edward Taylor notes, "The term Roman Catholic is correct, but it must be understood that both adjectives govern the one noun and both belong uniquely to the one Church of Christ. That is the only sense which the words can have in their Latin form and in their English equivalent." If the term means that we glory in our union with the See of Rome, where its Bishop, the Pope, is the only legitimate and valid Successor of Saint Peter, the Vicar of Christ on earth, we have no difficulty with that usage. However, if it implies something irreconcilable with Christian truth and thus with our principles, namely, that some other entities or churches that are separated from the ancient Catholic Church may still be allowed to use the title "Catholic", we must refuse to accept such usage, since that would be unhistorical and completely untrue.

FALSE THEORIES

When Martin Luther, a fallen priest, abandoned the Catholic Church in the sixteenth century to start his own religion, he ordered his followers to purge the word "Catholic" from their creeds and instead to insert the word "Christian". Then too, many early Protestants in Europe and in England started to use disparaging words such as "Roman, Romish, Papist", and so on, to refer to Catholics and the Catholic Church with opprobrium and to display their hatred. Soon, however, Protestant scholars and observers noted that Luther's idea was a pure invention of his, the word "Christian" historically referring to the followers of Jesus Christ, but not specifically to the title of His Church. In the ancient creeds the Church always was called "Catholic". This caused some Protestants groups to start using the term "Catholic" in their creeds and documents and to try to justify the use by inventing some new concepts of the "Church", as a shadowy, vague, and largely invisible entity. Such concepts, of course, are unscriptural and illogical.

The misnaming tendency probably reached its climax in the middle of the nineteenth century in the English Oxford Movement with the "branch theory". John Henry Newman, before he became a Catholic, and some other university professors had dedicated themselves to an intense study of the early centuries of Christianity. They soon came to the conclusion that whatever the Church of the early Christians was, it certainly was not Protestantism, which they viewed as nothing but a collection of largely man-made religious innovations. They then tried to concoct an idea of a Catholic Church made up of three branches: Anglicans, Eastern Orthodox, and Roman. Very quickly, however, they realized that their branch theory was untenable because it defied history and implied that the Church of Christ was a monster filled with irrational self-contradictions. Newman, with his keen intellect and profound knowledge of Christian history, was among the first to discard the branch theory, which was never taken seriously by either Catholics or the Eastern Orthodox.

ANTIOCH

God's providence evidently determined that the two words "Christian" and "Catholic" were to originate in the city of Antioch in Syria. The Bible tells us that it was at Antioch where the disciples of Jesus were first called "Christians" (Acts 11:26). It was also from the Bishop of Antioch, the successor there of Saint Peter, Saint Ignatius, that we have the first written evidence of the use of the term "Catholic" for the Church. Ignatius was condemned to death for being a Christian. As he was being taken to Rome for his martyrdom, which occurred in A.D. 110, he wrote seven letters during his journey addressed to various "particular Churches", or dioceses, which letters we still have. In his letter to the "Church of Smyrna" (Izimir in present day Turkey), he writes, "Where the Bishop appears, there let the people be; even as, wherever Jesus Christ is, there is the Catholic Church."[138] The way he uses the term "Catholic Church" leads scholars to agree that it was already in widespread usage, at least in Antioch but perhaps elsewhere as well, to distinguish the "great" or "universal" Church, the true Church, from various sects and denominations, especially Gnostics, that already had, from time to time, broken off and separated themselves from her.

The Greek word *Katholike* is made up of two words, *kata* and *holon*, which mean "over the whole world". The letters of Saint Ignatius show that he regarded each Bishop in a diocese as the nucleus of a living cell and all the dioceses of the world as a living organism, the Mystical Body of Christ. He considered the See of Rome as preeminent and called the Diocese of Rome the "president of charity over the Church" and clearly acknowledged the special authority of Rome.

OTHERS

Saint Patrick in fifth-century Ireland regularly told his converts, "As you are Christians, so you must also be Romans." Saint Ambrose in fourth-century Milan often stated, "Where Peter is, there is the Church, and where the Church is, there is everlasting life."[139] Saint Augustine, in the fifth century, said, "I am kept in the Church by the very name Catholic, which, in the midst of so many heresies, this Church has owned, not without cause, even though all the heretics would like to be called Catholics. Yet when a stranger asks, where is held the meeting of the Catholic Church, no heretic would dare to point out his own church or house."[140] Saint Pacian in fourth-century Barcelona said, "My name is Christian, but my surname is Catholic."[141]

After he became a Catholic, Cardinal John Henry Newman said, "[The Church's] every-day name, which was understood in the marketplace and used in the palace, which every chance comer knew, and which state-edicts recognized, was the 'Catholic' Church."[142] It was one which the sects could neither claim for themselves, nor hinder being enjoyed by the rightful owner."[143] We are Catholics, and that is enough for us to say (Mt 28:19). However, the Church to which we, all undeserving, are privileged to belong is also apostolic and therefore directly joined to Saint Peter and Saint Paul, and thus she also may be called Roman, since it was in Rome that both of those saints died for the Catholic faith and are buried to this present day.

JULY 30, 2004

The Church
XIV

COMMUNION

In 1992 the Holy See sent a circular letter to all the Catholic Bishops of the world entitled *On Some Aspects of the Church Understood0 as Communion*. That instructive and clarifying letter dealt with many issues, including the use of both the singular and plural form of the word "Church", as well as how these terms and realities are related. In the New Testament and in the earliest Church writings both usages can be seen (for example, 1 Tim 3:15; Col 1:18; Rev 1:4). The Catholic "Church" can be viewed as "particular" or "local", meaning a parish or a Diocese, at the same time that she can be seen as the one and undivided Universal Assembly of the Chosen People of the New Covenant, the Mystical Body of Christ Himself, the Bride of the Savior (Eph 5:25–32; Rev 21:2–4; 1 Cor 12:12–29).

Pope Paul VI teaches what has ever been the doctrine of Christ and the Church's experience in this regard. "Let us be very careful not to conceive of the universal Church as the simple sum or…the more or less anomalous federation of essentially different particular churches. In the mind of the Lord the Church is universal by vocation and mission, but when she puts down her roots in a variety of cultural, social, and human terrains, she takes on different external expressions and appearances in each part of the world."[144] The *Catechism of the Catholic Church*, citing the Second Vatican Council, notes that this concept is the origin of the various rites and sub-rites in the Church. "The rich variety of ecclesiastical disciplines, liturgical rites, and theological and spiritual heritages proper to the local churches 'unified in a common effort, shows all the more resplendently the catholicity of the undivided Church' [*Lumen gentium*], no. 23]" (CCC 835).

PARTICULAR

The *Catechism* says,

> The phrase "particular Church," which is first of all the diocese (or eparchy), refers to a community of the Christian faithful in communion of faith and sacraments with their bishop ordained in apostolic succession [cf. *Christus Dominus* II; CIC, cann. 368–69; CCEO, cann. 177; 178; 311, 1; 312]. These particular Churches "are constituted after the model of the universal Church; it is in these and formed out of them that the one and unique Catholic Church exists [*Lumen gentium*, no. 23].

Particular Churches are fully Catholic through their communion with one of them, the Church of Rome, "which [as Saint Ignatius of Antioch notes,] (*Ad Rom.* 1, 1: *Apostolic Fathers*, II/2, 192; cf. *Lumen gentium*, no. 13) presides in charity." (CCC 833–34)

Saint Irenaeus, the Bishop of Lyons in the second and beginning of the third century, says, "For with this church [of Rome], by reason of its pre-eminence, the whole Church, that is, the faithful everywhere, must necessarily be in accord."[145] Saint Maximus, a seventh-century abbot, observes, "From the time of the incarnate Word's descent to us, all Christian churches everywhere have held and hold the great Church, that is here [at Rome] to be their only basis and foundation since, according to the Savior's promise, the gates of hell have never prevailed against her [Mt 16:18]".[146]

INSIDE THE OTHER

A legitimately constituted "particular Church" makes the universal or whole Catholic Church truly present when properly assembled under the authority of a Bishop who is in peace and communion with the See of Peter. The Holy See's 1992 letter notes, "Among [the] manifold particular expressions of the saving presence of the one Church of Christ, there are to be found from the times of the Apostles on, those entities which are in themselves *Churches*, because, although they are particular, the universal Church becomes present in them with all its essential elements. They are therefore constituted '*after the model of the universal Church*' and each of them is '*a portion of the People of God entrusted to a bishop to be guided by him with the assistance of his clergy*.'"[147]

The Second Vatican Council teaches,

> The Church of Christ is really present in all legitimately organized local groups of the faithful, which, insofar as they are united to their pastors, are also quite appropriately called Churches in the New Testament.... In them the faithful are gathered together through the preaching of the Gospel of Christ, and the mystery of the Lord's Supper is celebrated....In these communities, though they may often be small and poor, or existing in the diaspora, Christ is present, through whose power and influence the One, Holy, Catholic, and Apostolic Church is constituted.[148]

INTERIORITY

The letter from the Holy See's Congregation for the Doctrine of the Faith explains,

The universal Church is the *Body of the Churches*. Hence, it is possible to apply the concept of communion in *analogous fashion* to the union existing among particular Churches, and to see the universal Church as a *Communion of Churches*. Sometimes, however, the idea of a "communion of particular Churches" is presented in such a way as to weaken the concept of the unity of the Church at the visible and institutional level....In order to grasp the true meaning of the analogical application of the term *communion* to the particular Churches taken as a whole, one must bear in mind above all that the particular Churches, insofar as they are "*part of the one Church of Christ*", have a special relationship of "*mutual interiority*" with the whole, that is, with the universal Church...For this reason [as has been asserted], "*the universal Church cannot be conceived as the sum of particular Churches, or as a federation of particular [individual] Churches*." [The universal Church] is not the result of a communion of the Churches, but, in its essential mystery, it is a reality *ontologically and temporally* prior to every *individual* particular Church....

Every member of the [Catholic] faithful, through faith and Baptism, is inserted into the one, holy, catholic, and apostolic Church. He or she does not belong to the universal Church in a *mediate* way, *through* belonging to a particular Church, but in an *immediate* way, even though entry into and life within the universal Church are necessarily brought about in a particular Church. From the point of view of the Church understood as a communion,...the universal *communion of the faithful* and the *communion of the Churches* are not consequences of one another, but constitute the same reality seen from different viewpoints.[149]

AUGUST 13, 2004

2

SCRIPTURE

New Bible Insights

WHAT DATE?

For more than one hundred years Scripture scholars have been debating about the dates of the New Testament writings. Under the leadership of various Protestant writers, especially from Germany, there has been a tendency to ignore the testimony of antiquity and to assign rather late dates particularly to the Gospels. This tendency seems to have arisen not from any external evidence, but rather from what these people have called the internal evidence of the texts. The idea was that the Gospels were the result of the reflection of the early Church on the events of the life and death of our Savior.

It became the fashion in the last century to maintain that the Gospel according to Saint Mark was the earliest Gospel written. Saint Matthew (or an author using his name) and Saint Luke, so they said, used the Gospel of Mark, plus another document that they called *Q,* to write their Gospels. Also, there was some original material in each Gospel for which their theory could not entirely account. Although there was a fragment of the fourth Gospel found in Egypt, dating from the year 120, the mode was to assign the writings of Saint John to as late a date as possible.

O'CALLAGHAN

Despite his Irish sounding name, José O'Callaghan is a renowned scholar of Spanish blood. In 1972 he discovered that in Cave Seven of the Qumran Caves among the Dead Sea Scrolls there is a fragment of the Gospel according to Saint Mark. This means that this text existed well before modern scholars maintained it could have been written, since the Dead Sea documents were all hidden before the fall of Jerusalem. The Dead Sea area was conquered by the Tenth Roman Legion in A.D. 68. This discovery set off an enormous controversy that continues today about the O'Callaghan fragment.

In 1976 an Anglican Bishop named John A. T. Robinson wrote a book maintaining, from his study of internal evidence, that the New Testament Gospels, at least the synoptics, were written before the fall of Jerusalem. That he should agree with the witness of history was surprising because he previously was known as a skeptic or even an unbeliever.

THIEDE

The most sensational modern development in this field, however, was published in *The Times* of London at the end of 1994. Carsten Thiede, the most famous and best papyrologist (student of ancient papyrus documents) in the world, found the most ancient extant fragment of the New Testament in a library at Oxford University. It is three little pieces of papyrus, written in Greek and containing portions of the Gospel according to Saint Matthew. This fragment dates, without any doubt, from the middle of the first century, about A.D. 50. There is a long scientific explanation of how this is known to be certain. Specialists would be able to understand all the aspects of the proof. Since it is also undisputed that the Gospel according to Saint Matthew was first written in Aramaic or Hebrew (there is a scientific way in which this can be shown), it is clear that Matthew's Gospel records an eyewitness to Jesus.

Many in the past, particularly Catholics through the centuries, have maintained that the Gospels were written by contemporaries or near contemporaries of Jesus. This modern evidence, however, corroborates this past testimony in a way that truly satisfies modern scientific minds. It proves that the Gospel according to Saint Matthew was written about a generation or less after the death and Resurrection of Jesus. The papyrus pieces were found in Upper Egypt in 1901 and donated to Oxford. Thiede guesses that these pieces may have been handled by some of the more than five hundred people (1 Cor 15:6) who saw the risen Christ with their own eyes.

DISPUTES

The modern, scientific findings of O'Callaghan and Thiede caused havoc to more than a century of modern Scripture study, some of which was partly valid, but some of which was based on rationalism and other errors. It is not surprising, therefore, that their discoveries have created a huge uproar in the scholarly world. If one admits the validity of their findings, as it appears unprejudiced minds must do, modern Bible scholars will have to discard their theory about the theoretical document named *Q*. Obviously, there also will have to be a serious and new examination of the synoptic question.

Briefly, the synoptic question is: *Which Gospel came first, and which depends on which?* If one takes the first three Gospels (the fourth Gospel appears to be in a category by itself) and places them (especially in the Greek text) alongside each other, it can be readily seen that they coincide with each other in many places, although there are subtle differences even where they seem to agree. Of course, there are some unique features to each, and Saint Matthew and Saint Luke seem to have some material in common, beyond what is contained in the

Gospel according to Saint Mark. The arrangement and the material in each of the Gospels also lend themselves to scholarly discussion about the synoptic question.

Christ of Faith

Protestant rationalists and modernist heretics among fallen-away Catholics have maintained for about a hundred years now that there is a difference between the Jesus of history and the Christ of faith. Perhaps as our century comes to a close, these new discoveries will help to dispel that falsehood, which has damaged the faith of so many over these past decades. The Christ of faith and the Jesus of history are one and the same. Along with some of the other nonsense and evils that our century has produced, such as the utopianism of Marxism and Socialism and the racism of the Nazis, maybe the errors of some so-called Bible scholars will also be consigned to the "dustbin of history".

Of course, our faith does not rest upon scientific evidence, even when this reinforces the rational aspects of our beliefs. Our intelligence and our reason can tell us that the Gospels are authentic. Our faith tells us that they are true. Whenever we read or hear the Gospel, we should say, at least in our hearts, as we do at every Mass, "Praise to You, Lord Jesus Christ!"

OCTOBER 10, 1997

Book of Revelation
I

Certain Difficulties

The last book in the Bible, the Book of Revelation, also called the Apocalypse, often has been a source of perplexity for people throughout the Christian era. Founders of false churches, heretics of various kinds, and inventors of religious fraud have always seemed to find in that book a rich source in their attempts to have the Bible corroborate and endorse their religious errors. In some instances they even have succeeded in instilling fear and confusion in the outlook of believers.

This book of the Bible can appear at times bizarre especially to modern men. As Father Bruce Vawter points out, "Its flamboyant imagery, its symbolisms, its almost exclusive preoccupation with the end time, and corresponding lack of interest in the world of history make it alien to our ways of thought."

Yet, the Book of Revelation is part of Sacred Scripture, the inspired word of God Himself, and, as such, deserves our respect, our affection, and our attentive reading and listening. The Magisterium of the Catholic Church has placed the Book of Revelation in the canon of Scripture.

How to Read

The Bible is not self-interpreting. To be correctly understood, Sacred Scripture has to be taken as a *whole*, and each part read and understood in its relationship to all the other parts as well as to Sacred Tradition and the Magisterium (official teaching authority) of the Catholic Church. The Second Vatican Council teaches, "It is clear [therefore] that sacred tradition, Sacred Scripture, and the teaching authority [Magisterium] of the Church in accord with God's most wise design, are so linked and joined together that one cannot stand without the others, and that all together and each in its own way under the action of the one Holy Spirit contribute effectively to the salvation of souls."[150]

Following the Second Vatican Council, the *Catechism of the Catholic Church* indicates three criteria for correct interpretation of Sacred Scripture: attention to the unity and content of the whole Bible; always reading within the living Tradition of the Church; and always being attentive to the analogy of faith, which is the coherence of the truths of faith among themselves and within the whole plan of salvation (see CCC 111–14).

Literary Form

A modern newspaper headline next week might read (being a Packer fan, I hope so): "Packers slay Broncos". Unless understood as the literary form of a sports page, an onlooker might conclude that the newspaper was informing us that some meat-packers killed some horses! We always speak and write in literary forms, generally assuming that our readers and listeners will easily "catch on". For instance, the teenage girl who announces to her parents, "I almost died", may be telling them, not about a near-death experience, but merely about her profound embarrassment at something.

The last book of the Bible is written in an ancient literary form, no longer used today, called "apocalyptic" (hence, the sometime title of the book). In order to understand the meaning of the Book of Revelation, it is necessary to try to understand something about this literary form.

The *Catechism of the Catholic Church* tells us, "In order to discover *the sacred authors' intention*, the reader must take into account the conditions of their time and culture, the literary genres in use at that time, and the modes of feeling, speaking, and narrating then current" (CCC 110).

Book Itself

Christian Tradition tells us that this book was written by Saint John the Evangelist in Greek while he was in exile on the island of Patmos probably before the end of the first century A.D. The Greek language used is somewhat more "rough and crude" than is the language of the other writings in the New Testament attributed to him, namely, the fourth Gospel and three of the "catholic" epistles. While the apocalyptic style marks the entire book and most of its content, there are elements of prophetic and epistolary writing that can be found in it as well.

The book is meant to foretell future events, in the sense of being a commentary on history or an "unraveling" of the same. It is a revelation given by God to Saint John through the agency of an intermediary angel. The apocalyptic style always includes awesome and fearsome cosmic portents as well as a profusion of symbolism. In the Book of Revelation some of the symbolism is explained in the text, but most is left to the knowledge and surmise of the reader. Fifty-four times in the book Saint John receives a distinct "vision", and sixty-seven times an angel explains or interprets things for him.

Numbers

In apocalyptic writings and literary forms, numbers are always extremely important. However, they are meant to be taken, never literally, but only symbolically. The number seven, for instance, occurs fifty-four times in the Book of Revelation. It is always a number that indicates completeness or fullness or totality or perfection. Sometimes it indicates all of these things together. In addressing the "seven churches of Asia", for example, the seer of the book means to address the entire Church throughout the world. The same applies to the seven seals, the seven trumpets, and the seven signs. By the number seven is always meant certain universality.

As we approach the end of a century and of a millennium, there will surely be a renewed interest in the interpretation of history. Let us be unafraid to read what God has written in the last book of the Bible, being ever mindful, however, in this year dedicated to the Holy Spirit, of what the Second Vatican Council says: "Sacred Scripture must be read and interpreted in the light of the same Spirit by whom it was written."[151]

January 23, 1998

Book of Revelation
II

LAST BOOK

The final book of Sacred Scripture, the Book of Revelation or the Apocalypse, was not the only apocalyptic writing that was circulating among Christians and non-Christians in the early years of the Church. Although it was written in the apocalyptic style, however, many Fathers of the Church recognized it from the first as being part of the inspired word of God. Saints Hilary, Ambrose, Augustine, Jerome, Athanasius, Cyril of Alexandria, Basil, and Gregory of Nyssa ascribed its authorship to Saint John the Apostle and Evangelist. Several Eastern Fathers disputed its inspired character, but the matter was definitively settled by the Catholic Church in the Councils of Hippo in A.D. 393 and the Council of Carthage in A.D. 397, when the content of the Bible was authoritatively proclaimed. The Bishop of Rome confirmed the work of these Councils.

Because the language in the Book of Revelation is extremely figurative and symbolic, it has often given rise to strange and erroneous interpretations and even, out of malice or ignorance, strange and false religious beliefs. Other parts of the Bible contain elements of apocalyptic writing (Mt 24:1–41; Mk 16:17–18; the Book of Daniel; the Book of Baruch and so on), but the final book is the only one written almost entirely in that style. Saint John does not quote any other apocalyptic writing in this book. However, of the 404 verses in the book, 278 of them touch upon the Old Testament, including the Book of Psalms, Isaiah, Ezekial, Zechariah, and the Book of Exodus.

SYMBOLIC

In addition to the number *seven*, which denotes fullness, totality, completeness, and the like, the book contains many other symbolic numbers. The number *twelve* occurs twenty-three times in the book and stands for the twelve tribes of Israel. It also stands for the apostles and the final completeness of the People of God, the Chosen Race of the New Testament. The number *four* occurs sixteen times and indicates the whole visible world (the four ancient "elements" of earth, air, fire, and water, as well as the four directions of the compass: east, west, north, and south) and seems also to have a reference to the four evangelists and to the beings of animated nature. Other important numbers in the book are *three*, *ten*, and *a thousand*, this last in multiples. The number *144,000* of those who follow the Lamb (Rev 7:4–8 and 14:1–5) is a symbol of an unaccounted number by human standards but one that is known to God, somewhat akin to the "myriads of myriads" mentioned in another place (Rev 5:11). The number of the beast or anti-Christ is *666* (Rev

13:18). This probably means total evil (falling short of seven, the number of perfection), but it may refer as well to the Roman numeral equivalent of the name of the emperor Nero.

OTHER MEANINGS

Some of the beasts and creatures described in the Book of Revelation are almost impossible to imagine and would most likely baffle any artist who would try to draw them. This is because they are symbolic and were not intended to be drawn or imagined. Eyes, for instance, are a symbol of knowing and of interior vision (Rev 1:14; 2:18; 4:6; 5:6). Horns are a symbol of power and strength (Rev 5:6; 12:3). The Church often applies the symbol of the woman clothed with the sun, crowned with twelve stars, and with the moon beneath her feet (Rev 12:1) to Mary. There is some justification for this reference because of the use by Saint John of the word *woman* in reference to her in other places in his writing (Jn 2:4 and 19:26). However, the term *woman* also refers to the People of God and to the City of God, which is to say, to the Catholic Church. But, of course, Mary is the model and archetype of the Catholic Church.

Colors are important symbols in the Book of Revelation. *White* means victory and joy; *black* means death and fear; *red* means war and tribulation; *purple* means luxury and royalty. *Palms* symbolize triumph; *crowns,* dominion and rule; *white robes*, the state of grace and of glory. The *sharp sword* means the word of God in its activity of judging and punishing.

CRISIS THEOLOGY

It appears that the occasion for Saint John writing the Book of Revelation, apart from his being directed to do so by God (Rev 1:1–3), was his desire to console and encourage the members of the Church who were undergoing a terrible persecution. He wanted to urge them to perseverance and to assure them that God would ultimately vindicate and reward them, at the same time that He would horribly punish the enemies of Christ and the Church. Down through the centuries, persecution has been almost the fifth "mark" of the true Church. Looking back from the threshold of the third Christian millennium, God's providential love in providing for His People the words in the Book of Revelation is more clear than ever, as is its application even to our own era.

While not a complete catechetical outline of Christian doctrine, the Book of Revelation is constructed on a set of important Catholic truths. In that sense, it does not provide any new revelation different from the Gospels and epistles of the New Testament, but rather it uses Catholic doctrine as a guide for an ongoing interpretation of history and for Christian conduct.

Saint John in the Book of Revelation explains that suffering, both collective and individual, can be understood as having a purpose and significance. In the last analysis, those presently suffering in union with Christ and for Him will emerge glorious and immortal. The book depicts the great battle between the ancient Roman Empire and the Catholic Church as a symbol of the great battle between God and Satan, which will end with the victory of Christ and, for those loyal always to Him, to citizenship in the new and heavenly Jerusalem. Not only the early Christians, but also we contemporary Christians need this reassurance, as we are about to witness the close of the twentieth century and the beginning of the twenty-first.

FEBRUARY 6, 1998

Book of Revelation
III

HISTORY

Salvador Allende, the former Marxist President of Chile, who was overthrown in a coup some years ago and either committed suicide or was murdered, once explained that Communism, although an international political party, an economic system, and a type of social arrangement, is, fundamentally and before all else, an interpretation of history. The last book of the Bible, the Book of Revelation, is undoubtedly intended, among other functions, to be an all-inclusive interpretation of history. While the false and evil doctrines of Marx, however, were based on an erroneous idea of materialism, some theoretical iron laws of economics, and Hegelian evolutionary philosophy, the interpretation of history given in the Apocalypse, on the contrary, is based upon the certain truths of Christianity and the divine laws that show forth God's dealing with His Church and with humanity.

It seems that Saint John, who wrote under the inspiration of the Holy Spirit, intended the Book of Revelation (and, if this is so, we must insist that God, too, intended it) to be, not a complete compendium or *Catechism* of the Catholic faith, but rather the setting out of certain truths that would enable the believing reader or listener to understand the past better in the light of divine providence and to confront the difficult present and uncertain future in that same light.

THEOLOGY

Through all the symbolism, metaphors, historical allusions, visions, beasts, monsters, and the maze of apocalyptic vocabulary and language, a careful reader can discern some of the principles that the Holy Spirit, through the sacred author, desired to enunciate in the book. Various authors and interpreters, including in modern times Father William Heidt, have commented on them.

One doctrine that is quite apparent is the identity of Christ with the Catholic Church. Saint John (Rev 1:10–16) here recalls what he earlier recorded Jesus as saying (Jn 15:1) in this regard. The Apocalypse seems to echo strongly what Saint Paul (1 Cor 12:12; Eph 1:22–23; Col 1:24) taught about the Church being the Mystical Body of Jesus. The nuptial images of the Book of Revelation (Rev 21:2) certainly recapitulate what is found in the doctrine of the Apostle of the Gentiles (Eph 5:21–33). The book shows Jesus in the midst of the lampstands holding the seven stars and breaking the seals of destiny, so that He is obviously and continuously linked with the Catholic Church as His Bride and Body (Mt 25:45; 28:20).

JUDGEMENT

Another very clear doctrinal principle contained in the final book in Sacred Scripture concerns the certainty of God's judgment upon the wicked. It appears beyond dispute that the book was composed in a crisis situation and was intended to assist the first Christians in the midst of their anxieties and torments brought about through the persecution of Christianity ordered by the authorities of the ancient Roman Empire. The book devotes a major portion to promising vividly severe punishment on those who are enemies of the Church, punishment that will be much greater than the intense sufferings that the incipient Catholic religion was undergoing at the time of the book's composition. The book encourages Christians always to take comfort from a heavenly and eternal perspective when viewing past history and present human affairs.

The Book of the Apocalypse also shows that even members of the Church can fall under God's judgment, indicating that there was (and is?) much within the Church that is not pleasing to the Lord (for instance, "lukewarm" Christians will be vomited out of the mouth of the Lord, according to Revelation 3:16). The holy Church of God is composed of sinful people, who must recollect always that only those members who remain absolutely faithful to Christ, even in times of persecution, will receive the reward of everlasting paradise.

INFERNO

The existence of the eternal hell of the damned is quite clearly set forth in the Book of Revelation. It is also clear that the Book teaches that the inhabitants of Gehenna are, not only the fallen angels, but also those human beings who die outside of the state of sanctifying grace (Rev 14:9–11). "The smoke of their torment goes up for ever and ever; and they have no rest, day or night." The book (Rev

20:14) speaks about hell as "the second death" and the "lake of fire".

Among those who will be thrown into hell according to the book (Rev 21:8) are: (there is no reason to suppose that this list is meant to be exhaustive or exclusive) the cowardly, unbelievers, idolaters, murderers, fornicators, those who do abominable things, sorcerers, and liars (Rev 21:8).

OTHER TEACHING

The Book of Revelation teaches that there is a clear connection between the salvation of a human being and his good works. "Blessed are the dead who die in the Lord....Their deeds follow them" (Rev 14:13). The book equates Christ with God the Father. *Yahweh* or *Elohim* or *Adonai*, the names of God in the Old Testament, translated into the Greek of the Septuagint, were rendered *Kyrios* or *Lord*. In the book Jesus is called "King of kings and Lord of lords" (Rev 19:16). Equal titles and praise are given in the book to God "who sits upon the throne" and to "the Lamb", Who, certainly, is Christ (Rev 5:13; 7:10).

Everyone who listens to or reads the Book of Revelation surely must notice how the sacred writer intends us to stand in awe before the almighty transcendence of God (Rev 4:1–11), Who is the thrice-holy Creator and Master of the universe and before Whom everything that exists must prostrate in adoration. He is the *Kyrios* of history "who was and is, and is to come" (Rev 4:8). At the end of the second millennium of Christianity, let this be proclaimed anew, by our words, our works, and our lives.

FEBRUARY 13, 1998

Book of Revelation
IV

STRUGGLE

The holy season of Lent is a most appropriate time to reflect on what Saint Paul tells us: "For we are not contending against flesh and blood, but against the principalities, against the powers, against the world rulers of this present darkness, against the spiritual forces of wickedness" (Eph 6:12). Our existence as Christians certainly can be cast in terms of warfare and struggle. The Apostle of the Gentiles instructs us to take up the "shield of faith" and the "sword of the Spirit, which is the word of God", and to protect ourselves with "the helmet of salvation" and the "breastplate of righteousness", girded with, "truth", and "shod...[with] the gospel of peace" (Eph 6:13–17).

The last book of the Bible, the Book of Revelation, can be quite useful for our Lenten reading and meditation, as we strive, in these forty days, to follow Jesus, our divine Master, in His penitential preparation for the battle that He was to wage (and still wages) against the enemy of our salvation (Lk 4:1–13). In the Book of the Apocalypse, the Catholic Church, the extension of Christ in time and space, is described in her great struggle with the city set on seven hills, that is, with the ancient Roman Empire (Rev 17:11), which in turn is a symbol and figure for all the historical enemies of Christ and His Church.

ONGOING

The Book of Revelation conjures up a large number of Old Testament allusions to convey to its readers and hearers the reassuring truth that all of history is under God's guidance and that He continues to intervene in history when it pleases Him to do so. The book alludes to the Exodus, to Babylon, to the military destruction of various biblical cities, to plagues, theophanies, and the like. It then goes on to cite many figures and symbols to announce that now as well as in the future, the Church and her members, although called upon to suffer in hope, can be certain of their ultimate vindication. (There are grasshoppers, colored horses, seals, harlots coming and going, beasts of all types, the ark, Jerusalem, the temple, lights, and so on.)

One of the clear teachings of the Book of Revelation is that the redemptive work of Jesus is not simply concluded when the souls of the just, after death, will enjoy the beatitude that comes from union with their Creator, but that its conclusion will only be reached when history itself, the universe as we know it, is consumed and transformed by Christ's Second Coming in glory, the Parousia.

LITURGY

It seems certain that Saint John meant the Book of the Apocalypse or Revelation to have a liturgical character. He doubtlessly intended that it be read in church during Mass. Those who are familiar with the Jewish liturgy in the Old Testament and the earlier forms of the Mass in the New Testament can recognize very easily the many liturgical allusions in the book. Saint John declares that his vision occurred initially on a Sunday, the Lord's Day (Rev 1:10), and it involved a type of universal liturgy (Rev 4; also see Is 4 and Ezekiel 1–3.) in heaven. Christians always saw (and still should see) the liturgy on earth as a pale reflection of the great cosmic liturgy going on in heaven at the same time.

Experts in Christian paleontology tell us that the hymns scattered throughout the book are taken from the hymns sung during Mass by our Catholic ancestors. There is also solid evidence to indicate that Saint John structured the entire Book of Revelation on a model or outline of the earliest form of the Mass. For instance, the throne surrounded by the twenty-four elders is almost a perfect image of the chair of the bishop, which was, in the earliest forms of the Mass, to be surrounded by twenty-four priests.

FORNICATION

Saint John paints a most lurid picture of the ancient Roman Empire and its emperor worship (Rev 17:1–18). He describes the prostitute (pagan Rome) drunk with the blood of the saints and martyrs of Jesus, riding on a beast that comes out of the sea (Caesar worship). His insistence on using the terminology of illicit sex (fornication and adultery) to describe the objects of God's wrath derives not only from those sins against the sixth commandment, but also from those against the first commandment. In the Old Testament, the Hebrew People were considered to be betrothed and wedded to Yahweh. When Israel worshipped idols and false gods, the prophets told them that they were violating their marriage covenant with God Himself. In Christ all of mankind was betrothed and wedded to God (either in fact or in potentiality), and thus idolatry and all its attendants and consequences are appropriately described by Saint John in terms of sexual immorality.

OUR IDOLS

We might think that our own lives are untainted by idolatry, but perhaps, more than we may suppose, a certain measure of false religion may have crept into them. Lent is a splendid time to examine our priorities. Do we love or prefer anyone or anything to Christ? If so, He tells us we are not worthy of Him (Mt 10:37). Reading or hearing the Book of Revelation during Lent can help us better ascertain if we have been guilty of some self-deception in regard to what might not appear to us as so bad, but which is in reality idolatry. It can also assist us to imitate Jesus, under the help of His grace, in His heroic resistance to the temptations of Lucifer to place pleasure, power, or possessions on a higher plane in our lives than God's law and God Himself (Mt 4:1–11).

Lent is also a most suitable time to contemplate our Savior, hanging on His Cross, and to recall, as we gaze upon Him in our minds, the titles given Him in the Book of Revelation: Faithful and True, the Word of God, the Name that is unknown, the Lord of lords and the King of kings, the Lamb of God (Rev 19:11–16). The Apocalypse is awesome at any time, but especially in Lent and Easter.

FEBRUARY 27, 1998

3

TEN COMMANDMENTS

Commandment
I

NEW LAW

Jesus gave to us who are His followers a "New Law", the Law of the Gospel, which the *Catechism of the Catholic Church* says "'fulfills', refines, surpasses, and leads the Old Law to its perfection" (cf. Mt 5:17–19)" (CCC 1967). Our Lord told us that if we keep His commandments, we will abide in His love (Jn 15:10). All of His commandments are summed up in His "new" commandment, that we love one another as He has loved us (Jn 13:34).

Our Savior proclaimed, quoting the Book of Deuteronomy (6:5) and the Book of Leviticus (19:18), that the "first and greatest" commandment is to love God with all one's ability and potential and then to love one's neighbor as oneself. He said that all the Law and the prophets "hang on" our doing this (Mt 22:37–40). The Epistle to the Hebrews talks about the "newness" of this covenantal arrangement of God (Heb 8:8), fulfilling the words of the Prophet Jeremiah (31:31–34).

Saint Augustine of Hippo says that Christ's Sermon on the Mount (Matthew, chaps. 5–7) "contains ... all the precepts needed to shape one's life".[152] The *Catechism of the Catholic Church* suggests that "it is fitting" to adjoin to the Sermon on the Mount the teaching of the apostles on moral issues that the Bible contains (especially Romans, chaps. 12–15; 1 Corinthians, chaps. 12–13; Colossians, chaps. 3–4; and Ephesians, chaps. 4–5), in order to grasp more fully the meaning of Christ's New Law (see CCC 1971).

VALIDITY

In announcing a "New Law", which includes a dimension of freedom, grace, and joy, Jesus explicitly asserted that this newness that He brings to our earth does not abolish but rather deepens the moral prescriptions of the ancient Ten Commandments (Mt 5:17). These commandments, written by the finger of God Himself (Ex 31:18; Deut 5:22), are found in the Books of Exodus (20:2–17) and Deuteronomy (5:6–21). In our New Testament times, all of the commandments, however, must be interpreted and incorporated into "the twofold yet single commandment of love"

(Rom 13:9–10), that is, love of God and love of neighbor as one's self.

Our Redeemer Himself quoted the Ten Commandments approvingly (Mt 19:16–19). The *Catechism of the Catholic Church* tells us: "By his life and preaching Jesus attested to the permanent validity of the Decalogue" (CCC 2076). "The Decalogue contains a privileged expression of the natural law. It is made known to us by divine revelation and by human reason" (CCC 2080). "In fidelity to Scripture and in conformity with Jesus' example, the tradition of the Church has always acknowledged the primordial importance and significance of the Decalogue" (CCC 2078).

OTHER ELEMENTS

The Law of God as revealed in the Old Testament was intended by Him to be a preparation for the Gospel. God cannot contradict Himself. He is perfect Truth. Therefore, there is a consistency and unity in His divine legislation. The natural law, written in all human hearts by the Creator, remains immutable and permanent and the only basis for moral rules and civil legislation, just as His revealed law in the Ten Commandments, some of which could also be naturally knowable by human beings even without revelation, cannot be contradicted by the New Testament. The New Law, however, must be seen as deeper, spiritual, interior, and not as something extrinsic for a Christian. As the *Catechism* puts it, "The New Law is the *grace of the Holy Spirit* given to the faithful through faith in Christ. It works through charity" (CCC 1966).

The New Law does not add external precepts, "but proceeds to reform the heart, the root of human acts, where man chooses between the pure and the impure [cf. Mt 15:18–19], where faith, hope, and charity are formed and with them the other virtues. The Gospel thus brings the Law to its fullness through imitation of the perfection of the heavenly Father, through forgiveness of enemies and prayer for persecutors, in emulation of the divine generosity [cf. Mt 5:44, 48]" (CCC 1968).

RESPONSE

A prominent moral theologian once observed that "commandment and law are and always must be central ideas in Christian moral teaching. The sermon or instruction on the commandments must be God centered and at the same time dialogical, that is to say, essentially based on the dialogue between man and God, on word and response, for the simple reason that commandment is an entirely religious concept."

Another author notes, "The very core of any moral decision is the spirit of obedience to God. It is saying yes to God's will. It is daring to answer God. A good moral decision requires humble and docile attention to the will of God, our Creator and Father. From the very beginning man bears the responsibility for his free decision in his own particular situation. His response is his responsibility. In every moral decision, and above all, when his moral integrity is endangered, man senses that his response to God involves his very existence, his salvation."

GRACE

Because of his fallen nature and the effects of original sin in him, a human being needs the grace of God to know and keep God's law. The *Catechism* states "The *preparation of man* for the reception of grace is already a work of grace" (CCC 2001). Quoting the Council of Trent, the *Catechism* teaches, "Moved by grace, man turns toward God and away from sin, thus accepting forgiveness and righteousness from on high. 'Justification is not only the remission of sins but also the sanctification and renewal of the interior man.'"[153] The Council of Trent also said, "Without God's grace, [man] cannot by his own free will move himself toward justice in God's sight."[154]

"The Council of Trent teaches that the Ten Commandments are obligatory for Christians" (CCC 2068), and this again is confirmed by the words of the Second Vatican Council, "The bishops, the successors of the apostles, receive from the Lord ... the mission of teaching all peoples, and of preaching the Gospel to every creature, so that all men may attain salvation through faith, Baptism, and the observance of the Commandments."[155]

OCTOBER 1, 1999

Commandments
II

OBEDIENCE

Jesus, our divine Savior, told us, "If you would enter life, keep the commandments" (Mt 19:17). Implied in these words of Christ, of course, is the real possibility of our keeping God's laws and our high duty to obey His laws, with dire and sad consequences for us if we knowingly do not observe His ordinances. Christ summed up our duties to God by telling us that we must love Him with all our heart, mind, soul, and strength (Mt 22:37 and Lk 10:27).

In the organization of our thoughts about the moral demands that flow from accepting the gospel of our Redeemer, it is customary to place the first three commandments of the Decalogue under this "first and greatest commandment" of love set forth by Jesus. This greatest commandment contains, then, the first mandate of God, the first commandments in the traditional list of ten. Christ said, "It is written, 'You shall worship the Lord your God and him only shall you serve" (Mt 4:10). Our Lord was undoubtedly referring to the Old Testament text, which said, "You shall fear the LORD your God; you shall serve him... You shall not go after other gods" (Deut 6:13–14).

First

The normal expression of the first commandment of the Decalogue is derived from what God revealed to Moses: "I am the LORD your God, who brought you out of the land of Egypt, out of the house of bondage. You shall have no other gods before me. You shall not make for yourself a graven image, or any likeness of anything that is in heaven above, or that is in the earth beneath, or that is in the water under the earth; you shall not bow down to them or serve them" (Ex 20:25 and Deut 5:6–9).

The duty to give exclusive worship and adoration to the one true God is the opening theme of the Ten Commandments. It is a solemn requirement given to humanity by God Himself, a requirement that is fundamentally immutable, obliging everyone, always, and everywhere. As also in the case of all the rest of the Ten Commandments, no one can ever be dispensed from the obligation to carry out this duty. As the *Catechism of the Catholic Church* phrases it, "The Ten Commandments are engraved by God in the human heart" (CCC 2072).

In a Sense

Each sin, in a certain sense, is a deliberate preference for some creature or some created good thing in place of God. Thus, in a general way, every sin touches the first commandment, since sin in essence is giving some other value, deed, omission, or thought a priority over our Creator and Redeemer.

Also, since the first commandment requires that we practice religion and, in that activity, that we practice faith, hope, and charity or love, and since every sin involves an offense against God's love for us, every sin, either directly or indirectly, violates the first commandment. God revealed that He made human beings in His "image" and "likeness" (Gen 1:26–27). The first commandment requires that human beings always act in conformity with the way they were created. All of God's moral law simply directs humans toward their true destiny and toward the final end their Maker intends for them. Deviation from God's law sets a human being on a path to frustration and endless unhappiness, even if such a deviation might initially appear to be satisfying and gratifying. As a wise man once noted, "Many poisons are sweet to the lips and tongue but deadly to the digestion."

IDOLS

In reading the Old Testament, one is struck by how often the Chosen People of the Old Covenant, in the course of salvation history, went astray and, in the vivid language of the prophets, went "whoring" after false gods, thus violating their marriage covenant with "Yahweh". Sometimes their idolatry did not involve an explicit rejection of God (called Elohim, El Shaddai, Adonai, and so on), but rather it consisted of an attempt to share their worship of Him with other deities.

In our times, too, there sometimes are, not explicit and overt rejections of God, but rather attempts to "share" His demanded first place in lives with other persons, ideologies, and considerations. Christians must often ask themselves in prayer the "great question": What would I be willing to give up entirely if God asked it of me? If the answer is not "everyone and everything", it is likely that we have placed a "false god" before Him.

In our culture so dominated by a search for comfort, pleasure, and material success, as well as by overweening pride, "consumerist fun", and shallow thought, it is possible, almost without realizing it, to find oneself "bowing down" in front of someone or something that is created rather than before the Creator. If King Solomon, with all his wisdom, all his conversation with God, and all the special graces God gave him, nevertheless fell into idolatry with comparative ease (1 Kings 11:1–40), how careful should we be in the environment in which we find ourselves, lest we violate the first commandment.

GOD FIRST

Before his martyrdom for upholding God's revealed truth, namely, that the Bishop of Rome, the Successor of Saint Peter, is Christ's Vicar on earth, Saint Thomas More said, "I die the king's good servant, but God's first." Thomas More gave up wealth, riches, family, earthly contentment, and his very life rather than give something other than God first place in his outlook. In this he followed the noble example of millions of our Christian forebears, the martyrs who willingly faced torture and death rather than give worship and adoration to false gods. In contemplating their sacrifices and sanctity, it is useful to compare our lives to their deaths. Are we worthy of their memory?

Wealth, enjoyment, and worldly success are not bad in themselves. However, even good persons and things can be made into idols in our lives. Our loved ones, too, could fall into this category unless we always put God first and above all. In fact, we cannot truly love our families and those close to us with the intensity we ought unless we first love God even more.

OCTOBER 22, 1999

Commandments
III

FAITH

The first commandment of the Decalogue (Mt 4:10; Ex 20:2–5) requires each human being both as an individual and as a social being to offer authentic worship to God. Thus, God enjoins on all humans who have the use of reason the practice of the theological and supernatural virtues, the first of which is faith. "Without faith it is impossible to please God" (Heb 11:6). The *Catechism of the Catholic Church* notes that "Saint Paul speaks of the 'obedience of faith' [Rom 1:5; 16:26] as our first obligation... Our duty toward God is to believe in him and to bear witness to him. The first commandment requires us to nourish and protect our faith with prudence and vigilance and to reject everything that is opposed to it" (CCC 2087–88).

"Faith is the assurance of things hoped for, the conviction of things not seen" (Heb 11:1). Faith is a supernatural and gratuitous gift of God, but its exercise and retention depend on the free will, operating under grace, of the one who receives this most precious gift. To be salvific, faith, however, needs to be "filled up" with the other two theological virtues, namely, hope and love (1 Cor 13:13). Saint Ignatius of Antioch said, "Faith is the beginning and love is the end, and in God the two of them are brought into unity."[156]

SINS

If God, Who can neither deceive nor be deceived, speaks, it is the absolute obligation of every rational creature, without hesitation, to hold as true what He says. Deliberately to doubt or deny what God says in divine revelation, which is contained in Sacred Scripture and Sacred Tradition, as mediated to us and authentically interpreted by the Magisterium (teaching authority) of the Catholic Church, is certainly gravely sinful. Willfully to neglect revealed truth, as proposed by the Church Christ founded, or to refuse assent to it is the mortal sin of infidelity.

To doubt or deny obstinately one or the other of some truths that must be held with divine and Catholic faith is the grave sin of heresy. To repudiate totally the contents of the Christian faith (which is sometimes simply called "the faith") is the lethal sin of apostasy. The *Catechism* notes also that schism is a mortal sin against the first commandment. It is the refusal of obedience and submission to the Roman Pontiff or of communion with the members of the Church subject to him. All sins injure faith, but those directly contrary to the faith destroy this gift of God and thus discard the foundation of the spiritual life and all hope of eternal salvation.

DANGERS

Just as children are warned not to play with matches or knives or other dangerous things, just as loving mothers keep their youngsters from sampling the contents of the various bottles in the family medicine cabinet, and just as concerned parents forbid their children to play in the road, so the Catholic Church warns her children against the many poisons and dangers to the faith that lurk in our culture and our world.

Scoffing and ridicule are often the tools used by the enemies of Christ and His Church to inculcate a hesitation about believing. Insinuating into the cultural climate a distaste for correct moral conduct, especially as done by the entertainment and communications media, will often persuade people to abandon faith, because they can see too readily that believing will lead them to know about certain unpleasant consequences resulting from their immoral life-styles. To place one's faith in jeopardy or unnecessary danger (even by such things as certain kinds of reading, frequenting non-Catholic religious programs or services, or toying with doctrinal or moral dissent from people who may be within the pale of the Church but outside of her faith) is surely a serious sin.

DIFFICULTIES

The old adage always should be remembered that "a million difficulties do not make even one sinful doubt". Every thinking person possesses within his intellect the encounter between faith and reason, both gifts of God, the one supernatural and the other natural. They are not incompatible or in any intrinsic conflict. However, tensions between them can and normally do arise.

When difficulties about faith or its contents are present, conscientious people should try to address them candidly and immediately. Good reading, which can be recommended by a parish priest, and inquiring of properly instructed and learned priests can be of great assistance in such matters. The priest one goes to confession to also should be able to help or at least to direct one to where help can be found.

Of course, prayer is exceptionally important in maintaining faith and growing in it. Prayers found in the New Testament are very useful when facing difficulties about the faith: "[Lord,] I believe; help my unbelief" (Mk 9:23); "[Lord,] increase our faith" (Lk 17:5).

IDEAS ABOUT FAITH

Cardinal John Henry Newman writes, "No one is a Martyr for a conclusion, no one is a Martyr for an opinion; it is faith that makes Martyrs."[157] Robert Hugh Benson says, "Faith, after all, is a divine operation, wrought in the dark, even though it may seem to be embodied in intellectual arguments and historical facts."

The First Vatican Council teaches, "Faith is that supernatural virtue by which, through the help of God and through the assistance of His grace, we believe what He has revealed to be true, not on account of the intrinsic truth perceived by the natural light of human reason, but because of the authority of God Himself, the Revealer."[158]

Saint Thomas More once stated, "A faint faith is better than a strong heresy." Saint Thomas Aquinas writes, "The virtue of faith causes the mind to assent to a truth which, transcending human understanding, is held in divine knowledge. Men accept God's knowledge by faith and are joined thereby to Him. Faith's principal object is God Himself. Other things are subsidiary and dependent."

NOVEMBER 12, 1999

Commandments
IV

HOPE

Hope or trust, which is commanded by the first commandment of the Decalogue, often overlaps and penetrates faith, so much so that hope and faith are sometimes words that are used interchangeably. Like faith, hope is an infused, supernatural virtue, a grace, a free gift of God, but its exercise and maintenance depend, by God's design, upon the free cooperation, under God's sovereign grace, of the receiver with the gift and with the divine Giver.

Sacred Scripture says, "Let us hold fast the confession of our hope without wavering, for he who promised is faithful" (Heb 10:23), and again, "The Holy Spirit ... he poured out upon us richly through Jesus Christ our Savior, so that we might be justified by his grace and become heirs in hope of eternal life" (Tit 3:6–7). Saint Paul in the Bible tells us about Abraham becoming the father of many nations because "in hope he believed against hope" (Rom 4:18).

The virtue of hope, just like the virtue of faith, must be shown forth by one who possesses it in "acts". If it is not "used", it can more easily be lost, and God, Who owes His creatures nothing, could even take it away.

WHAT IT IS

Hope, like faith, can be an individual act and always has a personal quality. However, to be "real and fruitful", it must be spiritually connected with the universal

Assembly of God's People, the Catholic Church. This is because the Church is Christ's Mystical Body and the instrument Jesus chose to make in order to prolong His salvation through time and space until He returns in glory.

Hope means total, absolute, and unreserved trust that God will supply a person with all the necessary means of salvation and that an eternal life of supernatural happiness in heaven will be available, not through any good works or merits of a person, (Rom 3:22 and Heb 11:6), but through the infinite merits of Jesus Christ. The *Catechism of the Catholic Church* teaches that hope "responds to the aspiration to happiness which God has placed in the heart of every man; it takes up the hopes that inspire men's activities and purifies them so as to order them to the Kingdom of heaven; it keeps man from discouragement; it sustains him during times of abandonment; it opens up his heart in expectation of eternal beatitude. Buoyed up by hope, he is preserved from selfishness and led to the happiness that flows from charity" (CCC 1818).

Nihilism

Because the dominant moral "values" in our current culture appear to be based on atheism, agnosticism, hedonism, and materialism (just watch American television for one evening), it is understandable that supernatural hope not only would be generally unknown to modern people, but, if it were known, would be bitterly opposed by a world that exalts hopelessness. Our Western culture promotes death and suicide with vigor, and it generally provides its young with no tools to oppose the utter emptiness of secular humanism. The Satanic rock-and-roll singer, Marilyn Manson, who is greatly admired by many current American teenage murderers, explains, "God is dead... You are your own god... It's the part of you that no longer has hope in mankind. And you realize that you are the only thing you believe in."

The *Catechism* says the first sin against hope is despair, when one "ceases to hope for his personal salvation from God, for help in attaining it or for the forgiveness of his sins. Despair is contrary to God's goodness, to his justice—for the Lord is faithful to his promises—and to his mercy" (CCC 2091). Sinful despair, of course, is not the same as emotional despondence.

Can Do

A person can violate the first commandment against hope also by supposing that God will save one without one's personal, grace-guided involvement in the process. Sometimes the fiduciary faith of Protestantism can have this aspect of presumption. It is forgetting that Saint Paul says we must "work out [our] salvation in fear and trembling" (Phil 2:12). There is such a thing as our merit and supernatural "reward" (Jas 2:24 and Mt 25:31–46) involved in our salvation. It is not enough simply "to believe on the Lord Jesus" or to appropriate Him "as my personal Savior".

An even more prevalent form of the mortal sin of presumption is that which resembles the building of the Tower of Babel (Gen 11). It is the folly of thinking that one can "get to heaven" without (or with a most minimum connection with) Christ, the Church, the sacraments, repentance, contrition, the virtues, prayer, and so on. "Being good" is thought adequate to enter the supernatural order. This is as foolish as if a goldfish were to suppose that by swimming well it could learn to go above its nature and get to enjoy chess. Forgetting that Jesus instructs us His followers, even when we do no wrong, to claim that before God we are nothing but "unworthy servants" (Lk 17:10), people who fall into this sin adopt the attitude of the famous Pharisee (Lk 18:9–14) in contrast with the "justified publican". As the poet said, "One nearer the altar trod; the other nearer the altar's God".

REJOICE

To make an act of supernatural hope is indeed a noble and grand undertaking. Saint Paul calls hope the "helmet" we must wear in the battle for salvation (1 Thess 5:8). He tells us to "rejoice in hope." (Rom 12:12). Sacred Writ says, "[Hope is the] sure and steadfast anchor of the soul." (Heb 6:19). The *Catechism* says, "In every circumstance, each one of us should hope, with the grace of God, to persevere 'to the end' [Mt 10:22, cf. Council of Trent: DS 1541] and to obtain the joy of heaven, as God's eternal reward for the good works accomplished with the grace of Christ" (CCC 1821).

Saint Teresa of Avila says, "Hope, O my soul, hope!"[159] Saint Thomas Aquinas writes, "No man is able of himself to grasp the supreme good of eternal life. He needs divine help. Hence, there is here a twofold object, the eternal life we hope for, and the divine help we hope by." John Beaumont writes, "Sweet hope is the sovereign comfort of our life, our joy in sorrow, and our peace in strife."

NOVEMBER 19, 1999

Commandments
V

HIM ONLY

Obeying the first commandment of the Decalogue requires, among other things, giving to God adoration, prayer, and sacrifice. In other words, it demands that human beings practice the virtue of religion. God has planted in all human nature a disposition or inclination in this regard. Men are naturally religious, and every known culture and civilization has a religious component. If human beings do not have the true religion, almost always they find or invent a false one or involve themselves in some types of pseudo-religion.

Since the first commandment enjoins all humans to practice the theological virtues of faith, hope, and charity, this commandment logically must also require the practice of the moral virtues, the cardinal ones of which are prudence, fortitude, temperance, and justice. It is usually under the title of justice that the virtue of religion is situated. Justice is the virtue that demands we give to everyone that which is due to him. Giving to God the worship and obedience that is due to Him is what true religion is all about. It is the virtue of charity that "informs and gives life" to the moral virtues. It is part of our highest duty as rational creatures of God to love Him with all our heart, soul, mind, and strength (Deut 6:4; Mt 22:37; Lk 10:27). Jesus told us "him only shall you serve" (Lk 4:8).

PRAYER

It is impossible to imagine that allowing an entire day to pass without prayer would not be a sin for a Christian. The *Catechism of the Catholic Church* tells us that "adoration is the first act of the virtue of religion" (CCC 2096), acknowledging God as Lord and Savior, Creator and Master. It means absolute submission to God as illustrated by the example of the Blessed Virgin Mary (Lk 1:46–49). The *Catechism* says, "The worship of the one God sets man free from turning in on himself, from the slavery of sin and the idolatry of the world" (CCC 2097).

Prayer is raising one's mind and heart to God. In addition to adoration, our prayer must include gratitude to God, repentance for sins, and petitioning Him for His gifts and grace. Not only in one's childhood, but throughout one's life, it is prudent and wise to set aside certain important times every day to pray, such as each morning and evening, before and after meals, and in times of temptation. Our Savior told us "always to pray" (Lk 18:1). Prayer, at His direction, should be both secret and private (Mt 6:5–6) and communal and social. In our current culture, regular family prayer seems especially needed.

SACRIFICE

The only perfect sacrifice is that which Jesus Christ offered to His Father on the Cross (Heb 9:13–14). All the sacrifices of the Old Testament were mere symbols and shadows leading up to this complete worship of God. As High Priest and Victim, our Redeemer effected our salvation in His perfect act of love for God and for all humanity. By uniting their human pains and sorrows as well as their joys to Christ's sacrifice, Christians can and should offer their own lives as a sacrifice to God and thus fulfill some of the duties imposed on them by the first commandment. Saint Augustine says, "Every action done so as to cling to God in communion of holiness, and thus achieve blessedness, is a true sacrifice."[160]

However, it should be remembered that every sacrifice, to have any supernatural value, may not be merely external but must be accompanied by a proper interior and internal disposition (Ps 51:17; Amos 5:21–25; Is1:10—20; Mt 9:13 and 12:7; Hos 6:6).

LUKEWARMNESS

Among the sins condemned by the first commandment is spiritual lukewarmness. The words of God in the Bible about this sin are astonishing. "Because you are lukewarm and neither cold nor hot, I will spew you out of my mouth" (Rev 3:16). In a culture that exalts riches, pleasure, and leisure, the temptation in that direction is quite acute.

Sometimes because of our precious and valuable religious liberty, that is, freedom from external or governmental coercion in religious matters, it is easy to slip into the fallacious view that religion is merely a matter of opinion or taste or "persuasion". A sort of unspoken conviction can arise that truth in religious and moral matters is either unattainable for most people or is nonexistent or that its attainment is either unimportant or irrelevant to salvation.

The Second Vatican Council, especially in its *Declaration on Religious Liberty*, while acknowledging that non-Catholic religions may have within them some aspects of truth and that it is very possible for people, through no fault of their own, to adhere to such faiths, nevertheless states, "All men are bound to seek the truth, especially in what concerns God and his Church, and to embrace it and hold on to it as they come to know it."[161] The *Catechism* says, "The right to religious liberty is neither a moral license to adhere to error, nor a supposed right to error [cf. Leo XIII, *Libertas praestantissimum* 18; Pius XII, AAS 1953, 799], but rather a natural right of the human person to civil liberty, i.e., immunity, within just limits, from external constraint in religious matters by political authorities" (CCC 2108). Freedom from civil punishment for deliberately following religious falsehood does not mean that there are not eternal consequences from such a decision, provided the decision is free and deliberate.

Saint Irenaeus says, "Through the Decalogue, God prepared man to become his friend and to live in harmony with his neighbor.... The words of the Decalogue remain likewise for us Christians. Far from being abolished, they have received amplification and development from the fact of the coming of the Lord in the flesh."[162] The *Catechism* states, "In fidelity to Scripture and in conformity with the example of Jesus, the tradition of the Church has acknowledged the primordial importance and significance of the Decalogue" (CCC 2064). The Council of Trent teaches that the Ten Commandments are obligatory for Christians and that the justified man is still bound to keep them."[163] Of course, this includes the first commandment in all its ramifications.

JANUARY 14, 2000

Commandments
VI

MAJESTIC

In the Bible the Psalmist says, "O LORD, our Lord, how majestic is your name in all the earth!" (Ps 8:1). Saint Paul tells us that "at the name of Jesus every knee should bow in heaven and on earth and under the earth", because "God ... bestowed on him the name which is above every name" (Phil 2:9–10). The second commandment of the Decalogue is echoed throughout divine revelation, "You shall not take the name of the LORD your God in vain" (Exs 20:7; Deut 5:11). This demand from God to respect His name is due, as the *Catechism of the Catholic Church* explains, to "the respect owed to the mystery of God himself and to the whole sacred reality it evokes" (CCC 2144).

Again and again God tells us in divine revelation that "His name is holy" (Zech 2:13; Ps 29:2; Ps 96:2; Ps 113:1–2). The *Catechism* says, "God confides his name to those who believe in him; he reveals himself to them in his personal mystery. The gift of a name belongs to the order of trust and intimacy.... For this reason man must not abuse [the Lord's name]. He must keep it in mind in silent, loving adoration. He [should not dare] to introduce it into his own speech except to bless, praise, and glorify it" (CCC 2143).

RECOLLECTIONS

When I was a lad the second Sunday of every month in my home parish was "Holy Name Sunday". On that day the parish Holy Name Society, Junior Holy Name Society, and Boy Scouts would have "corporate Communion" at the eight o'clock Mass, followed by a breakfast meeting. The procession in and out of church was impressive on those occasions, but even more impressive was the Holy Name Pledge. Immediately after the Gospel we would all stand up and promise never to use the Lord's name in vain and pledge ourselves to avoid and oppose "blasphemy, profanity, and obscene speech". My own father would be with me on those occasions and was, as I remember him, always most conscientious in following the Holy Name Pledge, teaching me that foul, filthy, or improper speech was no way to assert one's manhood and virility, but rather it was an indication of ignorance and of a distorted personality.

In those days the Holy Name Society was the major men's organization in every parish. It seems it was brought to our country from Europe, where it was promoted by such people as Blessed John of Vercelli.

I also remember in my home parish how the priests would always preface the "divine praises", the prayers then required and now still often said after Benediction with the Blessed Sacrament, with the words "An Act of Reparation for Profane Speech", which is the original title of and purpose for those invocations.

DETERIORATION

For many reasons in our post-Christian culture, common speech has descended into vulgarity and worse. The media, including films, television, and radio, have taken the lead in polluting our language with vile expressions. While, wicked slurs against certain racial and ethnic groups can result these days in serious reaction, at the same time worse slurs against God, Jesus Christ, the Blessed Virgin Mary, the Catholic Church, the saints, and sacred things are not only tolerated, but praised and defended by the current culture police, by self-appointed "free speech" extremists, and, of course, by the liberal media.

A cousin of mine who was drafted into the U.S. military some decades ago told me after he returned to civilian life that he had been pressured to go to an officer's training school and make a career in the military since he had an engineering degree and some obvious talent. However, he said he told those who were trying to persuade him that he was appalled at the constant and continuous abuse of the Lord's name, the endless curses, and the obscene invective he encountered in military life, and, therefore, he could not entertain any thought of such a career. He said the bad language was so common that those who used it did not even reflect for the most part on what they said or how they spoke, and he was afraid he himself would inadvertently fall into those patterns of speech. I am told that that kind of situation has recently improved in modern U.S. military service. I hope so.

HALLOWED

In the ancient world of the Old Testament, the name of God was often used as a respectful euphemism for God Himself. Praising His name meant praising Him. Knowing His name also meant being His intimate and being possessed by Him. Thus, Jesus taught us to pray that God's name be "hallowed" (Mt 6:9; Lk 11:2). The holy name that God revealed to Moses (Ex 3:14) was definitively and finally revealed in all its fullness by Jesus (Jn 17:6). The exact identity of Jesus Christ with Yahweh (Jn 8:58) makes our Redeemer's name utterly unique. "There is salvation in no one else, for there is no other name under heaven given among men by which we must be saved" (Acts 4:12). Our prayers to God the Father have value if they are joined to Christ and made into His prayer and if they are done in His name (see Jn 14:13).

Saint Peter Chrysologus says, "We ask God to hallow his name, which by its own holiness saves and makes holy all creation.... It is this name that gives salvation to a lost world. But we ask that this name of God should be hallowed in us through our actions. For God's name is blessed when we live well, but is blasphemed when we live wickedly... We ask then that, just as the name of God is holy, so we may obtain his holiness in our souls."[164]

The *Catechism* tells us, "The second commandment *forbids the abuse of God's name,* i.e., every improper use of the names of God, Jesus Christ, but also of the Virgin Mary and the saints" (CCC 2146). Each of us should actively purge from our own lives and speech the misuse of the sacred names and strive to eliminate the abuse of those names from our environment, making this Jubilee Year a moment of conversion in that regard. We would be impatiently intolerant of anyone abusing our name or that of our family members. Why should we tolerate the abuse of the name of our God and our Savior?

FEBRUARY 18, 2000

Commandments
VII

FOURTH

The *Catechism of the Catholic Church* reiterates the truth that the fourth commandment "opens the second table of the Decalogue" (CCC 2197). Just as the first three commandments pertain to the supreme obligation of every human being to "love the Lord your God with all your heart, and with all your soul, and with all your mind, and with all your strength" (Mk 12:29–31; Lk 10:25–28), so the last seven of the Ten Commandments come under the heading of the associated human duty to "love your neighbor as yourself" (Mt 22:34–40). Saint Paul makes this especially clear when he teaches that the last seven commandments are "summed up in this sentence; You shall love your neighbor as yourself....Love is the fulfilling of the law" (Rom13:8–10). Of course, this is specified by the command of our Savior Himself, "Love one another; even as I have loved you" (Jn 13:34).

The fourth commandment says, "Honor your father and your mother, that your days may be long in the land which the LORD your God gives you" (Ex 20:12; Deut 5:16). In the New Testament the great Apostle to the Gentiles, in repeating this commandment for Christians, notes that it is "the first commandment with a promise" (Eph 6:1-3).

OBEDIENCE

While the fourth commandment explicitly and directly regulates the relationship of children to parents, implicitly and indirectly it requires, among other things, the practice of the virtue of obedience, a virtue that God teaches must be practiced by all people of every age group. Obeying seems to be the only way one can prove and demonstrate one's love for Christ (Jn 14:15).

Saint Benedict writes, "The first degree of humility is obedience without delay." Saint Francis de Sales says, "When God puts any inspiration into a heart, the way we know that it is genuinely from Him and not from another source is that He first inspires us to obey." He also remarks, "Blessed are the obedient, for God will never suffer them to go astray." One author has noted, "The whole of the New Testament and all of true Christian living, through the commandment of charity, is reducible to obedience." The philosopher Jacques Maritain says, "The virtue of obedience is an exalted virtue, eminently reasonable. It is not in the least servile or blind, but requires on the contrary the greatest freedom of spirit and the strongest discernment."

AUTHORITY

Obedience is founded on the principle of authority. For a disciple of Jesus all true authority is divine. It is either directly divine, deriving from the natural law implanted by the Creator in the structure of nature or in the human heart or deriving from revelation by God in Sacred Scripture or Sacred Tradition as mediated through the Church Christ founded, or else it indirectly comes from God through the agency of men who are endowed by the Almighty with the responsibility of authority. Authority is expressed in "law", to which human conduct and human conscience are obligated to conform. The Bible tells us that to resist legitimate and valid authority means resisting the ordinances of God (Rom 13:1-2).

Obedience for a Christian is not genuine if it is founded on base motives such as selfish ambition, a refusal to assume responsibility, lack of courage, a sick need to depend on others, a psychological disposition to avoid personal decisions, and so on.

CHRIST

Without the grace of God as it comes to us through Christ, it is impossible for a human being, in the present condition of the human race (fallen and redeemed, with the abiding effects of original sin in everyone), to obey the fourth commandment and, indeed, to practice the virtue of obedience in any supernaturally meritorious way. In addition to giving His followers the capacity to obey and in doing so to obtain merit, Jesus also provides the supreme and most glorious example of obedience.

From His childhood He obeyed Mary and Joseph (Lk 2:51), although as God He had created them, kept them in existence, and, of course, was and is omniscient. The purpose of His Incarnation was to obey the will of God the Father (Heb 10:5–7), and His very "food" on earth was to do God's will (Jn 4:34). He taught us to pray "Thy will be done" (Mt 6:10) and told us those who do God's will are mother, brother, and sister to Him (Mt 12:50). The most important constituent of His work of redemption was His obedience (Lk 22:42; Jn 17:4). It was from His utter humility that His saving obedience originated, which led Him to the ignominy and later the glory of the Cross (Phil 2:8).

LIBERTY

In this Holy Year of the Great Jubilee the famous words of the Book of Leviticus (25:10) are often cited: "Proclaim liberty throughout the land to all its inhabitants; it shall be a jubilee for you." Ironically, as Pope Paul VI notes, liberty and authority enrich each other. Obedience, properly practiced and understood, is a liberating experience. Recall that Saint Paul teaches that the freedom of the children of God is only actual and real when it involves total submission to the will of God and obedience to those who hold authority from Him (Gal 5:13; Rom 6:13).

Pope Paul VI writes, "The Mosaic Law has been repealed, but the natural law remains with all its innate vigor and is supported by the New Testament. It does not deprive man of his freedom but is an intrinsically necessary guide for it. Positive law (including the Canon Law of the Church)... safeguards human goods... disposes and promotes the common good... and guarantees the inviolable and responsible autonomy of the individual by which a human being can give fruitful expression to his personality because the law prevents abuses and unjust interferences...What would liberty be worth to an individual if he were not protected by wise and suitable laws?"

Cardinal John Henry Newman says, "What God demands of us is to fulfill His law, or at least aim at fulfilling it; to be content with nothing short of perfect obedience,... to avail ourselves of the aids given us,... and throw ourselves, not first, but afterwards on God's mercy for our short-comings."[165]

AUGUST 25, 2000

Commandments
VIII

HONORING

The fourth commandment, which begins that part of the Decalogue pertaining to charity or love toward our "neighbor" (Mk 12:29–31; Jn 13:34), tells us that we must "honor" our father and our mother (Ex 20:12; Deut 5:16). Children, even after their "emancipation" from obedience (when they reach their "majority", which is eighteen years old in America), are still required to extend love and respect to their parents during their entire lifetime. The *Catechism of the Catholic Church* explains that, after God, we must honor our parents, "to whom we owe life and who have handed on to us the knowledge of God" (CCC 2197). This duty of love and respect does not hinge on the goodness or badness of the parents. Even sinful parents must be loved and respected by their children, who in such cases, of course, must follow the adage: hate the sin but love the sinner, and who must then specially pray for their parents and try to convert them.

Related to the duty of "honoring parents" is the corresponding obligation often to pray for them and to "take care of them" in their old age. Certainly, conscientious parents will try to provide for themselves as much as possible and not be a burden to their children, but if parents become needy, lonely, or otherwise afflicted, even adult children have a duty to attend to their needs. Adult children, however, often have a hierarchy of obligations, which should be observed. For instance, married persons have a first obligation to their spouses and then to their children, which must come before that owed to their parents. Unfortunately, aged parents in our culture are often neglected and even sinfully ignored by their children. On the other hand, aging parents must avoid unnecessary or selfish demands on the time, attention, and resources of their adult offspring.

OBEYING

Children under their "majority age" are morally required to obey their parents, and it is a sin for them to disobey. Usually, it is venially sinful, but disobedience could be seriously sinful if the matter commanded is grave or if the parents intend to oblige seriously by their order. Jesus Himself made this duty of obedience on the part of children to their parents very clear by His teaching (Mk 7:8–13) and by His example (Lk 2:51). The only exception to this duty would be if a child were commanded to commit a sin. In this case, disobedience is required. However, if a child is in doubt as to whether a parent's command is sinful, the benefit of the doubt must be given to the parent. In the New Testament, Saint Paul said, "Children, obey your parents in the Lord, for this is right conduct" (Eph 6:1).

Children who are over their "majority age" are no longer required to obey their parents. But, the exception to this is if such children continue to live in their parents' home. In that case they are still obligated to obey their parents in those matters pertaining to the good order of the household. The *Catechism* points out that the fourth commandment "likewise concerns the ties of kinship between members of the extended family. It requires honor, affection, and gratitude toward elders and ancestors. Finally, it extends to the duties of pupils to teachers, employees to employers, subordinates to leaders, citizens to their country, and to those who administer or govern it" (CCC 2199).

PARENTING

The *Catechism* notes that the fourth commandment "includes and presupposes" the duties of parents (CCC 2199). The vocation of parenthood, noble and beautiful, also involves some very serious moral duties. Parents, of course, must feed, clothe, and educate their children. (In our culture, this means seeing them through high school, there being no obligation on the part of parents to give their children a college education.) Permitting or engaging in physical neglect or abuse of children is gravely evil. However, spiritual neglect or abuse is an even worse evil.

Parents must see to it that their children are baptized as soon as reasonably possible after birth, that they are taught to know about God and to pray daily even at a tender age, and that they attend Catholic schools (if at all possible) or at least regularly attend Catechism (CCD) instructions through their high school years. It is not enough for parents to "send" their children to Catholic schools or CCD classes. Parents themselves, who have to answer to God for their children's souls as well as bodies, must remember that they are the primary and inalienable educators of their youngsters. By example as well as words, they personally must see to the Christian and Catholic upbringing of their children.

DISCIPLINE

Parents have no obligation to provide luxury items or an abundance of material goods for their children. As a matter of fact, doing so can be damaging to the children's spiritual welfare and thus morally wrong on the parents' part. Instead of material goods (by which parents sometimes try to assuage guilt feelings or to buy the children's affection), parents are obligated to give their children the precious gift of their time and attention. Loving their children, parents must avoid being too severe and at the same time being too indulgent or permissive. Permissive parents are often more cruel to their children than they imagine.

Clear rules fairly enforced and punishments meted out when needed, never in anger but in a cool way and for a pedagogic purpose, are very important in raising children. Teaching their youngsters self-restraint and unselfishness, parents should allow their children (especially teenagers) some privacy and autonomy, while at the same time always knowing what is going on in their children's lives, in their rooms, and in their relationships and always encouraging the good qualities and talents they find in them. As they journey toward "emancipation", children should receive from their thoughtful parents a solid education in how to live and act in a moral and responsible way, walking on this earth with their thoughts and hearts ultimately set on heaven and the vision of God.

The *Catechism* says that observing the fourth commandment provides, "along with spiritual fruits, temporal fruits of peace and prosperity. Conversely, failure to observe it brings great harm to communities and individuals" (CCC 2200). Sacred Scripture teaches us, "Whoever honors his father atones for sins, and preserves himself from them. He stores up riches who reveres his mother" (Sir 3:3–4).

NOVEMBER 10, 2000

Commandments
IX

AUTHORITY

The fourth commandment of God (Ex 20:12; Deuty 5:16) involves not only the moral obligation of obedience on the part of children and on the part of everyone who is subject to some lawful authority in Church and State, but it also involves some grave obligations on the part of those invested with authority. The *Catechism of the Catholic Church* states that "this commandment includes and presupposes the duties of parents, instructors, teachers, leaders, magistrates, those who govern, all who exercise authority over others or over a community of persons" (CCC 2199).

Despotism, tyranny, capricious domination, failure to respect the human dignity of one's subjects, imposing excessively severe punishments, or the unnecessary restriction of legitimate liberty by those in authority can be and usually are seriously sinful. On the other hand, permissiveness, abdication of duty, lack of due vigilance, refusal to correct, admonish, and discipline, or other failures to exercise the lawful authority with which one is entrusted can be and often are also seriously sinful, especially when such things are motivated by laziness, cowardice, or a desire for popularity. Someone, who often might be motivated by evil, will always "fill the vacuum" when those who legitimately hold authority fail to carry out their duties. Father Vincent McNabb said: "There are three theories of power and therefore of authority, to wit: the robber theory that all authority is for mastery; the hireling theory that all authority is for wealth; the good shepherd theory that all authority is for service."

SERVICE

For a Christian, the exercise of authority always must be seen as service. Jesus was very clear that a worldly view of authority is incompatible with His Gospel (Mt 20:25–28). Whether in family life, in the Church, or in any form of governance, the example of Christ must be followed by everyone in authority who claims the honor of being His follower, for "the Son of Man came not to be served but to serve, and to give his life as a ransom for many." For every Christian our Savior's teaching is that "whoever would be great among you must be your servant, and whoever would be first among you must be your slave." This is why, since the time of Pope Saint Gregory the Great (A.D. 600), each Pope has called himself the "servant of the servants of God".

Saint Thomas More says that it is wicked for men to desire authority for its own sake, "in order to rule, command, and control other men, while perhaps living uncommanded and uncontrolled themselves".[166]

Those who have the moral duty to command as well as those who have the moral duty to obey must see all authority as ultimately based only in God, and it is to God that all human beings must one day render an account both for their obedience as well as for their use of any authority they have been given. Pope Leo XIII says, "True and legitimate authority is void of sanction, unless it proceed from God, the supreme Ruler and Lord of all. The Almighty alone can commit power to a man over his fellow men."[167]

IN SOCIETY

The *Catechism of the Catholic Church* states,

> The fourth commandment *illuminates other relationships in society*. In our brothers and sisters we see the children of our parents; in our cousins, the descendants of our ancestors; in our fellow citizens, the children of our country; in the baptized, the children of our mother the Church; in every human person, a son or daughter of the One who wants to be called "our Father." In this way our relationships with our neighbors are recognized as personal in character. The neighbor is not a "unit" in the human

collective; he is "someone" who by his known origins deserves particular attention and respect. (CCC 2212)

The *Catechism* goes on to say, "Human communities are *made up of persons*. Governing them well is not limited to guaranteeing rights and fulfilling duties such as honoring contracts. Right relations between employers and employees, between those who govern and citizens, presuppose a natural good will in keeping with the dignity of human persons concerned for justice and fraternity" (CCC 2213).

It is a valid axiom that no authority has the lawful power to impose error. Pope Leo XIII says, "When anything is commanded which is plainly at variance with the will of God,... it is right not to obey" (see Acts 5:29).[168]

YOUTH

Pope Pius XII says, "Educate youth to obedience and respect for authority. This is simple when man is submissive to God and recognizes the absolute value of His commandments. For the unbeliever and the man who denies God, there cannot be any true, just, and ordered authority because there exists no authority except from God (Rom 13:1). Man can neither rule nor be ruled only by force and fear." Saint Augustine of Hippo remarks that authority is necessary for peace because peace is more than simply the absence of conflict. "[Peace is] the tranquility of order."[169] Pope Leo XIII says that one of the "highest human duties is to respect authority and obediently to submit to just laws."[170] He also notes, "Hallowed in the minds of Christians is the very idea of public authority [Rom 13:7; 1 Pet 2:13–16] in which they recognize the likeness and symbol as it were of the divine Majesty, even when exercised by one unworthy. A due reverence to just laws abides in them, not from force and threats, but from a consciousness of duty, 'for God has not given us a spirit of fear' (2 Tim 1:7)."[171]

Children and youth should be told repeatedly (since repetition is the mother of learning) what Sacred Scripture and, hence, the teaching of the Church instruct them to do. They must always show filial piety, that is, respect, to lawful authority, especially to their parents and to those who take the place of parents (such as teachers, sitters, and so on), which must manifest itself in docility and obedience. Parents themselves should know and read to their youngsters the important texts of the Bible about these matters (found in Col 3:20; Sir 7:27–28 and 3:2–6; Prov 13:1 and 6:20–22).

NOVEMBER 17, 2000

Commandments
X

THANKSGIVING

There are many thoughts and memories that usually crowd in on us and on our fellow American citizens when we gather around family tables to celebrate our national holiday of Thanksgiving. Occasionally, especially in gatherings of extended families, the beautiful words of Sacred Scripture can come to mind: "Grandchildren are the crown of the aged" (Prov 17:6).

In its treatment of the fourth commandment of God, the *Catechism of the Catholic Church* inserts an interesting paragraph regarding a duty of giving thanks, which that commandment places upon us. "For Christians a special gratitude is due to those from whom they have received the gift of faith, the grace of Baptism, and life in the Church. These may include parents, grandparents, other members of the family, pastors, catechists, and other teachers or friends" (CCC 2220). Of course, our primary thanks must always be directed to God, Who touches our lives with such persons. Our American holiday of Thanksgiving is certainly an appropriate moment each year to focus on our duties of gratitude.

PARENTS

Perhaps the most effective way to show our ongoing gratitude to God for all His natural and supernatural gifts to us, including the gift of Himself in Christ, is to obey carefully His commandments. This obedience of ours can be our kiss of love for Him (Jn 15:14). Those who have the vocation of parenthood must keep in mind what the fourth commandment requires of them when they have minor children and youth in their charge.

The *Catechism* says,

> Parents have the first responsibility for the education of their children. They bear witness to this responsibility first by *creating a home* where tenderness, forgiveness, respect, fidelity, and disinterested service are the rule. The home is well suited for *education in the virtues*. This requires an apprenticeship in self-denial, sound judgment, and self-mastery—the preconditions of true freedom. Parents should teach their children to subordinate the "material and instinctual dimensions to interior and spiritual ones" [John Paul II, encyclical *Centesimus annus* (May 1, 1991), no. 36, § 2]. (CCC 2223)

Parents are obliged to give their children good example and to guide and correct them (Sir 30:1–2; Eph 6:4).

PARALLEL SCHOOLS

Today, more than ever, parents have to be involved in the schoolwork of their children, forming a partnership with the teachers and administrators of the schools to which they confide their youngsters. The way this partnership is done in our Catholic schools is truly one of the glories of these schools and the secret of much of their extraordinary effectiveness. Parents should never allow their children or youth to "play off the school against them or vice versa", any more than they should permit their children to "play off one parent against the other". Certainly, parents must see to it that their children's growth in knowledge and mastery of profane and secular subjects is matched by their growing knowledge of the faith through catechesis and religious education. The *Catechism* notes that parents must be the "first evangelizers" of their children and the "first heralds" of the Gospel for them (see CCC 2225). Parents in this area, too, unless they are personally and exceptionally gifted, should make use of the professional help available to them in the Catholic schools and in various religious education programs.

In our contemporary culture, children and youth often actually learn more from their friends and from the media, especially from television and Internet connections, than they do from their parents and schools. Friends and media form a parallel school, and parents would be abdicating their "primordial and inalienable right and duty" as the educators of their offspring if they did not exercise vigilance and control over this aspect of the lives of their children and youth. Excessive hours of unsupervised television viewing by children or youth, which indoctrinate children with sex, violence, consumerism, hedonistic and pleasure-seeking values, which scoff at and ridicule religion, our Catholic beliefs, and Christian morality, which numb minds and sell useless junk as things children must have and own, do not constitute the kind of "school" that good Catholic parents should want their children to attend.

GOOD HEALTH

All decent parents want their children to enjoy good physical health. They usually are careful about what they allow their youngsters to eat. Yet, sometimes even conscientious parents are careless about their children's spiritual health and about what kind of philosophical and moral poison these children and youth ingest from their friends or from their computer or their television set. No thoughtful parents would tell their children to taste and eat whatever they might find in the bathroom medicine cabinet or under the kitchen sink, in the theory that children should be left alone to decide for themselves what their preferences might be and what is good or bad for them.

But, today many parents, with a nonchalance that is astonishing, often leave their children to decide for themselves, without proper instruction and devoted attention, momentous matters that have consequences that cause not merely physical harm, injury, and death, but, far worse, eternal misery and everlasting death.

GIVE THANKS

At each Mass we hear the priest say, "Let us give thanks to the Lord our God." This phrase, so pregnant with significance, should encourage us to make the entirety of our lives a "Eucharist", that is, a prayer of thanksgiving to God. Those who are called to be Catholic parents should certainly give thanks to God for this gift by their loving and responsible obedience to the duties of their vocation. All of us should be ever grateful to our Creator for the gifts of families, for our own parents, and for all our loved ones. Under God's grace, obeying the fourth commandment can bring to our lives and to our homes a beautiful abundance of peace and joy. The Psalmist says, "Teach me, O Lord, the way of your statutes; and I will keep it to the end. Give me understanding, that I may keep your law ... with my whole heart (Ps 119:33–34). Blessed are those...who walk in the law of the Lord!" (Ps 119:1).

NOVEMBER 24, 2000

Commandments
XI

MURDER

The fifth divine commandment ("You shall not kill") forbids murder (Ex 20:13; Deut 5:17). That commandment was strongly restated by Jesus when He added hatred, anger, and vengeance to its prohibitions (Mt 5:21–22). The Catholic Church teaches, "God alone is the Lord of life from its beginning until its end: no one can under any circumstance claim for himself the right directly to destroy an innocent human being."[172]

From the beginning of human history, murder was and continues to be rampant, contradicting God's law and opposing His precious gift of human life. From Cain's killing of his brother, Abel, up to our own times, which include the genocidal madness of Hitler, the brutal slaughter of more than fifty million innocents by

Lenin, Stalin, Mao, and Pol Pot, and the modern, ferocious killing of tens of millions of tiny, innocent human babies by abortion in the United States and in other "progressive countries", the murderous saga of humanity goes on.

Doctor Kevorkian and the euthanasia doctrines of the Hemlock Society and similar groups continue to excite the enthusiasm of liberals everywhere, especially their media toadies, who are ecstatic over the new laws in the Netherlands permitting medical doctors to kill their patients. They usually also are delighted about using chopped-up pieces of aborted human babies for "research", and remember the happiness of that "newsman" when he recently showed the mercy killing of a human being on live American television, announcing afterward that he and his wife were looking forward to being killed in the same way some day. The revival of approval for Nazi-like eugenics and social Darwinism in modern academic circles explains why certain sociologists and social biologists, who often regard human beings as less important than insects and mice, defend the views of people like Professor Peter Singer at Princeton, who advocates killing human babies after birth and not just before.

TEACHING

The law in the Old Testament forbidding murder is still valid today. "For your lifeblood I will surely require a reckoning.... Whoever sheds the blood of man, by man shall his blood be shed; for God made man in his own image" (Gen 9:5–6; quoted by CCC 2260). Commenting on the text "Do not slay the innocent and the righteous" (Ex 23:7), the *Catechism of the Catholic Church* says, "The deliberate murder of an innocent person is gravely contrary to the dignity of the human being, to the golden rule, and to the holiness of the Creator. The law forbidding it is universally valid: it obliges each and everyone, always and everywhere" (CCC 2261). The direct and intentional killing of an innocent person is gravely sinful. The *Catechism* notes, "The murderer and those who cooperate voluntarily in murder commit a sin that cries out to heaven for vengeance" (CCC 2268, cf. Gen 4:10).

The heinous nature of the sin of murder can be made even worse by certain circumstances. For instance, it is an additional sin, a sacrilege, to murder someone in Holy Orders or someone consecrated to God by religious vows. The *Catechism* also says, "Infanticide [cf. *Gaudium et spes*, no. 51, § 3], fratricide, parricide, and the murder of a spouse are especially grave crimes by reason of the natural bonds which they break. Concern for eugenics or public health cannot justify any murder, even if commanded by public authority" (CCC 2268).

INDIRECT KILLING

The unintentional killing of an innocent human person is "not morally imputable. But one is not exonerated from grave offense if, without proportionate reasons, he has acted in a way that brings about someone's death, even without the intention to do so" (CCC 2269). This would certainly include killing a person by driving a motor vehicle while drunk. "The moral law prohibits exposing someone to mortal danger [such as pointing a loaded gun at someone] without grave reason, as well as refusing assistance to a person in danger" (CCC 2269).

Social responsibility also requires attention to indifference or omissions that could make one complicit in indirect murder. The *Catechism* remarks, "The acceptance by human society of murderous famines, without efforts to remedy them, is a scandalous injustice and a grave offense. Those whose usurious and avaricious dealings lead to the hunger and death of their brethren in the human family indirectly commit homicide, which is imputable to them [cf. Amos 8:4–10]" (CCC 2269). Also, we should remember what the Second Vatican Council teaches and the *Catechism* quotes in its section on the fifth commandment, "The arms race is one of the greatest curses on the human race and the harm it inflicts on the poor is more than can be endured."[173]

DEATH CULTURE

It is not surprising that in our country children should recently in increasing numbers undertake to murder people in their schools. They are exhorted to do so by any number of rock-and-roll singers whose lyrics few parents know or care about, which lyrics are protected as free speech guaranteed by the First Amendment. That amendment, of course, in the lunatic interpretation of current civil jurisprudence and of various self-appointed defenders of the Constitution, also forbids any mention, much less teaching, of the Ten Commandments in the godless public schools. In the minds of the unfortunate children who are indoctrinated in the religion of secularism in the government-run schools, ethics and morality, if they even admit that there are such things, are mere inventions of school boards, Congress, the Supreme Court, politicians, and the entertainment media. In a recent survey almost 90 percent of U.S. public high-school students said that it is morally acceptable to lie and cheat "if you do not get caught". Something called "society" might claim to want them to be law-abiding citizens and people of moderation and refinement, but they often ask why not become liberals and defy the "conventions"? Moral relativism, the implied philosophical error taught in those places, says that what is a "value" for one person can be wrong for another, and what is bad today can be declared good tomorrow. A Russian author correctly stated that if there is no God and no heaven and no hell, everything is permitted and nothing is forbidden. The human race as a whole will survive only if the majority can be brought to remember, "In [God's] hand is the life of every living thing and the breath of all mankind" (Job 12:10). "Give me understanding, that I might keep your law" (Ps 119:34).

APRIL 27, 2001

Commandments
XII

Walk For Life

The approach of the anniversary of the U.S. Supreme Court's decision that the American Constitution includes a right to unlimited abortion should also be an annual occasion for every conscientious Catholic to remember the teaching of the Church, as enunciated by Pope John Paul II, "Abortion and euthanasia are...crimes which no human law can claim to legitimize" (see Ex 20:13, the fifth commandment).[174] As we participate in the walk for life at our State Capitol in Lincoln (or in Washington, D.C.), which is scheduled for 10 A.M. next Saturday, January 19, it is also good to remember that "To celebrate the Gospel of life means to celebrate the God of life, the God who gives life."[175]

As our Holy Father points out, "We must celebrate Eternal Life, from which every other life proceeds. From this, in proportion to its capacities, every being which in any way participates in life, receives life. This Divine Life, which is above every other life, gives and preserves life."[176]

Suicide

Although suicide and assisted suicide are not quite as prominent in the news as they were before the imprisonment of the evil doctor Kevorkian, they remain ongoing realities in our culture, and they were recently brought to significant international attention by the suicides and murders by the fanatics who attacked our country last September. Commentators currently dispute with each other about whether suicides, as carried out by those killers, are in conformity to the dogmas of any religion.

However, there can be no dispute about the doctrine of the Catholic Church concerning suicide. Pope John Paul II is unequivocal about the matter. "Suicide is always as morally objectionable as murder. The Church's tradition has always rejected it as a gravely evil choice... In its deepest reality, suicide represents a rejection of God's absolute sovereignty over life and death."[177] If carried out with full freedom of the will and with sufficient reflection, suicide is a particularly heinous mortal sin, since it precludes any possibility of repentance and contrition.

Interconnected

As our Supreme Pontiff teaches, especially in his great encyclical letter "*The Gospel of Life*", there are many aspects of "life morality" that are joined to each other. To be consistent, logical, and credible, it seems that we must be as opposed to those who promote suicide in our culture and society as we are to those who foster and permit abortion. This is one of the reasons why I included in the extra-synodal legislation that I enacted for the Diocese of Lincoln in 1996 (which was modified and codified by me in the synodal legislation that came into effect in 1998) ecclesiastical censures for any Catholics in this Diocese who might be members of the Hemlock Society as for those who are in the Planned Parenthood Association. The Hemlock Society (presumably named after the poison taken by Socrates, as Plato explains in the *Phaedo*) promotes a so-called "right" to human self-destruction.

The second largest number of suicides in the United States are by teenagers and young adults. Many of those adolescents are products of the nihilistic philosophy that pervades so many institutions of our neo-pagan society. Some are incited and urged to suicide by the lyrics of more rock-and-roll "artists" than unsuspecting adults might realize. Some are led to kill themselves by a reckless disregard for psychological and physical boundaries, especially in the area of drugs and sex. Some are just mentally and childishly ridiculous: "They'll be sorry when I'm gone."

RESPONSIBLE

Many people who commit suicide are mentally ill and so disturbed that they may not be fully responsible for their act. Pope John Paul II says, "Even though a certain psychological, cultural, and social conditioning may induce a person to carry out an action which so radically contradicts the innate inclination to life, thus lessening or removing subjective responsibility, suicide, when viewed objectively, is a gravely immoral act."[178] The pastoral practice of the Church has changed in modern times in regard to giving people who commit suicide a Christian burial. Previously, it was presumed that most people who killed themselves were morally culpable, while today greater weight is given to the possibility of mental illness impeding culpability in many cases, and a Christian funeral is more often not denied.

We live in what the Holy Father has often called "a culture of death". Implicitly and even explicitly, often today human beings are looked upon as nothing special or different from brute animals. The moral sensitivity that Shakespeare put into the mouth of Hamlet, in the famous soliloquy in which the Prince of Denmark ponders suicide ("For in that sleep of death what dreams may come when we have shuffled off this mortal coil, must give us pause"), would be incomprehensible to many of our contemporaries, because they deny or doubt the existence of immortal souls in human beings, just as they deny or doubt our eternal destiny planned and desired by God.

LARGEST

The largest numbers of suicides in the United States are by elderly people, who are often infirm or handicapped. Society in general and many families in particular bear a heavy responsibility for this. Not only is there frequent unconcern about loneliness and pain, but many senior citizens are "warehoused" ("out of sight and out of mind") and sometimes are made to feel guilty about their alleged uselessness, about the cost of their upkeep, and even about consuming the inheritance expected by children and grandchildren. The beauty of old age, the usefulness for younger people to know of their lives' experiences, and the precious salvific value of suffering endured willingly in union with Christ on His Cross are often ignored in a heathen atmosphere, which seeks youth, pleasure, and possessions in preference to all other human considerations.

The Pope says that family members should be reminded to treat their aged members with patience and love, and he cites the Second Vatican Council: "'It is in the face of death that the riddle of human existence becomes most acute', 'and yet man rightly follows the intuition of his heart when he abhors and repudiates the absolute ruin and total disappearance of his own person. Man rebels against death because he bears in himself an eternal seed which cannot be reduced to mere matter.'"[179]

JANUARY 18, 2002

Commandments
XIII

ANGER

God planted in each human being an irascible appetite. However, like other such appetites, it became wounded by original sin and thus can be misused, sometimes seriously. This is why anger is always listed as one of the seven capital sins, which are inclinations in every human person that are good in themselves but which in their distorted form are at the root of many immoral acts or omissions. Anger, both that which is just and that which is sinful, is connected with the great duty to love one's neighbor (Mt 5:21–26) and, consequently, is linked by Jesus Himself to obedience to the fifth commandment of the Decalogue (Ex 20:13 and Deut 5:17).

It is clear that anger, in some instances, can be good (Ex 32:15–19) and even holy, when it conforms to the laws of charity and is motivated by zeal for justice, the honor due to God and God's Church, or some other similarly important good. Saint Paul says, "Be angry but do not sin; do not let the sun go down on your anger" (Eph 4:26). But, of course, the Apostle of the Gentiles also remarks, "Be kind to one another, tenderhearted, forgiving one another, as God in Christ forgave you" (Eph 4:26–32).

Sin

Anger can be sinful and sometimes can constitute a grave offense against God's law. Saint Paul lists unjust "anger" and "wrath" along with "malice, slander, and foul talk" as sins that all followers of Christ must try to put out of their lives permanently (Col 3:8). The tentmaker Saint of Tarsus also teaches in the New Testament that it is sinful to provoke others deliberately to anger (Col 3:21).

Being angry is sinful if it is a result of an immoderate desire for vengeance, especially if this involves purposely allowing angry emotions and feelings to escape the control of one's intellect and will. Sinful anger is present when one wishes the undeserving to be punished or wishes the guilty to be punished excessively or punished in a manner that is cruel and illicit. In some of these situations anger could be a mortal sin, particularly if genuine hatred for another person is present or if a wish for revenge is permitted to overwhelm an otherwise correct desire for justice and right order. Anger could be a lethal sin, too, if it leads to serious cursing, blasphemy, or physical harm to others that a person foresees before he is aroused to anger.

Habit

In many (perhaps most) situations anger or consenting to unjust angry thoughts or words would be venially sinful. Some people have a quick temper that they must struggle to control, especially if they have grown into a habit of being angry. Even venially sinful anger, however, can lead to unnecessary quarreling, to damaging family ties, and to harming friendships and other human relationships, and thus it should not be taken lightly. We must remember that venial sins, too, offend our Creator, weaken our will, and must be repented and expiated before one can enter heaven.

With the help of God's grace, all Christians should strive throughout their lives to acquire and practice the virtues of meekness and patience (Mt 5:5). Saint Francis de Sales, the gentlest of saints, had a vicious temper that he spent his life keeping under control. Experienced spiritual directors usually urge people who are struggling to overcome tendencies to unjust anger to take several steps: to pray constantly for the strength to overcome such inclinations, especially using the pardoning words of the Lord's Prayer (Mt 6:12); to recognize their own faults and sins and often reflect on God's merciful and undeserved forgiveness extended to them (Mt 6:14 and 18:35); to think over the possible evil consequences of giving way to anger; to condition themselves to resist the first risings of anger; to cultivate the habit of silence when provoked; and to practice asking forgiveness of those who have been offended by their anger, or at least indicating repentance by the way they treat them later.

HATRED

Hate, which is a voluntary act by which one regards a person or thing with bitter aversion, also is a sin against the fifth commandment. The exception, of course, would be hatred directed to some evil quality in another but that does not touch the person himself. That is not sinful. However, to "hate the sin but love the sinner" is much easier to say than to practice in reality.

Sinful hate is usually far more damaging to the hater than to the one hated even in this world, and hatred most clearly and openly contradicts the teaching and example of Christ (Lk 10:27–28; 1 Jn 2:11). If the evil that one wishes to another out of hatred is only slight, the hatred would be a venial sin. But, if the evil is serious or the hatred abiding, then the sin is mortal. If one hates a virtue or a good quality in another, it is the equivalent of hating the person and thus a grave sin. Even slight or temporary hatred can be an opening for the hater to turn his face away from God permanently as well as the motivation for other serious sins.

ENVY

Another capital sin that is often considered under the fifth commandment is envy, which is deliberate sadness over another's goods (possessions, talents, accomplishments, and so on), when these are considered as an evil to oneself. It is not a sin of envy to be sad when seeing our neighbor's good fortune simply because we lament our own limitations, nor is it sinful to regret, when seeing another's virtue or talent, that we do not possess the same. Sinful envy can lead to other sins, such as hatred, pride, backbiting, and detraction.

Fraternal charity should induce a follower of Christ always to rejoice over the good things a neighbor has or does. This promotes peace in families and communities, helps one to rise above all pettiness and meanness, induces one to live within one's means, helps one never to pretend to be something more than one is, and persuades one to practice courtesy and politeness, not merely as part of civilized behavior, but also as a way of putting Christian love of neighbor into everyday action. The best remedy for envy is emulation, that is, trying to imitate the things that are admirable in others. For us Christians, this means, above all, striving to imitate Christ and, then, to emulate the saints whose lives reflected His.

FEBRUARY 1, 2002

Commandments
XIV

SEVENTH

The seventh commandment of God requires human beings to respect the goods of their neighbors and to practice "justice and charity in the care of earthly goods and the fruits of men's labor" (CCC 2401). This ancient commandment of God forbidding stealing (Ex 20:15; Deut 5:19) was reiterated by our Lord's own words in the course of His sojourn among us (Mt 19:18). The *Catechism of the Catholic Church* reminds us that God thus prohibits us from unjustly taking or keeping the goods of our neighbor. This commandment "for the sake of the common good,... requires respect for the universal destination of goods and respect for the right to private property" (CCC 2401). It demands of Christians, in addition, that they strive "to order this world's goods to God and to fraternal charity" (CCC 2401).

The seventh commandment also requires men to practice the cardinal virtue of justice, which is defined in simple terms as that virtue which inclines one to give to each what is his due. Scholars usually divide the concept of justice into individual (commutative justice) and social justice. Commutative justice regulates the relationships of one human being to another person, either another individual or some corporation or collectivity. Social justice is called legal justice when it concerns what an individual owes to the State, and is called distributive justice when it concerns what the State owes to individuals. Social justice also involves the wider picture of such things as the moral aspects of social living, of economic activity and arrangements, and so on. In a very broad sense the virtue of justice involves the virtue of religion, which is, of course, giving God the worship, obedience, consideration, and devotion that is due to the Creator and Redeemer of the human race.

THEFT

In a direct way, by the seventh commandment God forbids theft, which is the taking of another's goods against his reasonable wish. One type of theft is borrowing something without the owner's consent. Even if the borrower intends to give it back, it is still a sin of "temporary theft". The sin of theft also includes getting something on loan with the owner's consent, but then refusing to restore and repay the loan as agreed upon. It is also a sin of theft to run up a charge account that one foresees never being able to repay or living so extravagantly that it makes the repayment of just debts rendered impossible. It is also a sin of theft to engage in business fraud or purposely to write bad checks. It is permissible to borrow something with an owner's presumed consent, provided that the owner cannot conveniently be consulted and one could in good conscience assume that the owner would consent were he available. To act morally in such cases, however, the borrower could not conceal the loan and would be bound to tell the owner as soon as conveniently possible about the loan.

It should be remembered that authors and inventors have a right in the natural law to the fruits of their labors and genius and, hence, exclusive rights to their plans, songs, plays, manuscripts, designs, discoveries, and so on. It is a sin of theft to take, use, or publish such things without the owner's consent, even if they are not protected by civil laws with patents, copyrights, and so on. Like all sins of theft, such stealing or cheating requires previous restitution as a condition for forgiveness by God.

Not Keepers

Lost objects do not automatically become in Christian morality the property of the finder. One who finds a lost object is bound morally to make a good faith attempt to find the owner, with an expenditure of effort and expense proportionate to the value of the object. For instance, a found pencil worth twenty cents might require the finder only to ask a few persons nearby about it, while a precious diamond ring might require inquiries with the police, ads in newspapers, and so on. Before giving a lost object back to its owner, the finder would have a right to ascertain with reasonable certitude the authenticity of the claim and also to demand compensation for any expenses incurred in caring for the object and in searching for the owner. Usually it is morally safe to follow the civil laws in such matters.

Only after a reasonable amount of time and effort has been used may a finder be assumed to be the new owner of a lost object. However, even after any period of time, if the rightful owner appeared, his claim, if legitimate, would require the finder to surrender the object to him. The general moral principle is that "a thing always calls out to its rightful owner" (*res clamat ad dominum*).

Abandoned property, however, does not carry the same rights to a former owner as lost property. It can be legitimately appropriated by anyone who first comes upon it.

Possessor

One who does not actually steal but who knowingly possesses another's property unjustly is morally bound to restore the goods or their value (if they have been destroyed or lost) to the true owner at once. If one is in doubt about an object that is in his possession, even if it was purchased by the possessor, one must make a thorough and sincere investigation about the matter. If the doubt still persists, the possessor may licitly retain the article or goods.

One who knowingly cooperates in theft or in causing unjust damage to the property of others, even if he does not actually perform the evil action himself, commits a sin of theft and is morally bound to restitution along with the thief. This cooperation can consist in supplying another with the means, encouraging or urging him, advising him how to go about it, covering up for him, any kind of enabling, and so on.

All Christians should strive to develop and form a tender and correct conscience about property matters, that is, about obeying the seventh commandment and practicing justice. This is particularly difficult in our modern American culture, which is materialistic and hedonistic and in which cheating and stealing are not uncommon in schools, workplaces, offices, gambling events, sports fields, and so on.

SEPTEMBER 27, 2002

Commandments
XV

PROPERTY

To understand the correct Catholic Christian interpretation of the seventh commandment of the Decalogue, which forbids stealing, it is necessary to give serious consideration to two elements that must be held in careful equilibrium in our moral view, namely, the individual as well as the social character of property. These elements are what the *Catechism of the Catholic Church* calls "the universal destination of goods and the respect for the right to private property" (CCC 2401).

Recent Popes have strongly emphasized the natural right of human beings to own private property, while at same time, with equal emphasis, they have taught that "God entrusted the earth and its resources to the common stewardship of mankind to take care of them, master them by labor, and enjoy their fruits [cf. Gen 1:26–29]. The goods of creation are destined for the whole human race" (CCC 2402).

The *Catechism* states, "The *right to private prope*rty, acquired or received in a just way, does not do away with the original gift of the earth to the whole of mankind. The *universal destination of goods* remains primordial, even if the promotion of the common good requires respect for the right to private property and its exercise" (CCC 2403).

PRIVATE

Beginning in the middle of the nineteenth century, there were some powerful

European intellectual movements that denied the right to private property, especially anarchism and Marxism. Both of those utopian ideologies denied the existence of God, claimed to have a foresight into human destiny, denied the existence and effects of original sin, claimed that social distress and injustice were due to private ownership of property and wealth, and so on. The anarchists Pierre Proudhon and Mikhail Bakunin had as their slogan: "Property is theft." Karl Marx claimed that in his coming "paradise of the proletariat" all property would be held in common and would be gathered "from each according to his ability" and then distributed "to each according to his need". It was in opposition to such nice-sounding but erroneous views that Pope Leo XIII asserted the perennial Catholic teaching on the subject.

> With reason, then, the common opinion of mankind, little affected by the few dissentients who have contended for the opposite view, has found in the careful study of nature, and in the laws of nature, the foundations of the division of property, and the practice of all ages has consecrated the principle of private ownership, as being pre-eminently in conformity with human nature, and as conducing in the most unmistakable manner to the peace and tranquility of human existence... The authority of the divine law adds its sanction, forbidding us in severest terms even to covet that which is another's [Deut 5:21].[180]

THE USE

The same Pope Leo XIII, however, makes it very clear that private ownership of money and property, while perfectly licit, entails very serious moral obligations and duties on the part of owners. Also, he states that it must be remembered that the just ownership of wealth is distinct from the just use of wealth.[181] This is why the Second Vatican Council says, "In his use of things man should regard the external goods he legitimately owns not merely as exclusive to himself but common to others also, in the sense that they can benefit others as well as himself."[182]

The *Catechism* explains, "The ownership of any property makes its holder a steward of Providence, with the task of making it fruitful and communicating its benefits to others, first of all to his family. Goods of production—material or immaterial—such as land, factories, or practical or artistic skills, oblige their possessors to employ them in ways that will benefit the greatest number. Those who hold goods for use and consumption should use them with moderation, reserving the better part for guests, for the sick and the poor" (CCC 2404–5). Saint Rose of Lima says, "When we serve the poor and the sick, we serve Jesus. We must not fail to help our neighbors, because in them we serve Jesus"[183] (see Mt 25:40; Jas 2:15–16). Saint Gregory the Great says, "When we attend to the needs of those in want, we give them what is theirs, not ours. More than performing works of mercy, we are paying a debt of justice."[184]

A DUTY

Commenting on the teaching of Saint Thomas Aquinas that "no one is obliged to live unbecomingly", Pope Leo XIII, in his great 1891 encyclical *On Capital and Labor (Rerum novarum)*, teaches what is still valid and important today. "No one is commanded to distribute to others that which is required for his own needs and those of his household; or even to give away what is reasonably required to keep up becomingly his condition in life... But, when what necessity demands has been supplied..., it becomes a duty to give to the indigent out of what remains [Lk 3:11; 11:41]."[185]

The *Catechism* warns us that "the seventh commandment forbids acts or enterprises that for any reason—selfish or ideological, commercial, or totalitarian—lead to the *enslavement of human beings*, to their being bought, sold and exchanged like merchandise, in disregard for their personal dignity. It is a sin against the dignity of persons and their fundamental rights to reduce them by violence to their productive value or to a source of profit" (CCC 2414).

We are also told by the *Catechism* that, in addition to the practice of justice, that is, preserving our neighbor's property rights and rendering him what is his due, the seventh commandment also requires us to practice temperance in relationship to all economic and property matters, so as to moderate our attachment to worldly goods. Sacred Scripture does not say that money itself is a source of evil, but rather that an incorrect attitude toward it is, which is to say, "the love of money is the root of all evil" (1 Tim 6:10). To follow Jesus Christ demands that no matter what our material wealth might be, we must always strive to be "poor in spirit" in order to go to heaven (Mt 5:3; 6:24; Lk 6:24). The seventh commandment also tells us it is our duty to practice the virtue of solidarity with our fellow human beings, in accordance with the golden rule (Mt 7:12) and in imitation of our Lord's generosity to us (2 Cor 8:9).

OCTOBER 4, 2002

Commandments
XVI

SINFULNESS

Since it is clear that God forbids stealing another's property or money (Ex 20:15;

Deut 5:19; Mt 19:18), it is also plainly obvious that theft, usurping the goods of another against his reasonable desire, is a sin. The question can be asked about what degree of sinfulness is involved in the act of theft. Stealing is also usually a civil crime. Almost all human societies, cultures, and governments consider theft a crime against the public order, a threat to peace and property rights, and a contribution to a lessening among people of a desire to acquire goods and to earn a living by honest means. It should be noted that civil laws regarding property rights sometimes inform, overlap, and contribute to moral judgments about the observance of the seventh commandment, but civil laws in these matters do not always and invariably coincide with all Christian moral principles.

ELEMENTS

Catholic moral teaching, which always distinguishes mortal from venial sins (1 Jn 5:16–17), says that to ascertain correctly the kind of sin involved in theft, one must consider three elements: the value of the stolen property, the person who is the victim of the theft, and the time over which the theft is spread. There is such a thing as an "absolutely grave value", which is to say, a value or amount stolen that is a mortal sin, no matter how much it would not be missed or would not inconvenience someone. This usually is calculated as the equivalent of three day's wages or salary for a middle-class person in a culture. Thus, that amount of money or property stolen even from a very rich person or from the government or from a large business or corporation would be a mortal sin for the thief, provided it were done with free will and due deliberation.

A lesser amount stolen from a needy or poorer person could be a serious sin, because of the notable harm done to him. Usually stealing the equivalent of a day's earnings from such persons would constitute a grave sin. One of the sins always listed among those "calling to heaven for vengeance" is to deprive a worker of his day's wages. When a theft is not of absolutely or relatively grave value, the sin is venial. It should be remembered, however, that even venial sins of theft require complete restitution as a condition for forgiveness, and, if this is not done in this world, the restitution must be made in purgatory after death.

WHO AND WHEN

Certain circumstances can enter into consideration of the moral judgment about the sin of theft and may condition the nature of the sin. For instance, minor children who steal from their parents might not be committing as serious a sin as if they stole the equivalent amount from strangers, since sometimes "the reasonable wishes" of the parents might not exclude with totality their children's possible deeds. Also, taking small amounts spread over time might not coalesce into a mortal sin, since venial sins do not accumulate into mortal sins. However, if one's intention is to steal what is a grave amount, but to do it in small increments, that surely would be a mortal sin because, of course, sin resides in the intention in a person's will more than in the actual deed.

Petty thievery, moreover, is very bad. Apart from mortal sins, venial sins are the greatest evils in the world and deeply insult God and offend His justice. Also, God Himself demands restitution and retribution even for venial sins, or He will not forgive them. Then too, engaging in the vice of petty stealing or cheating causes a conscience to become callous and can put into a person's attitude toward life such wicked dispositions as selfishness, lying, shirking responsibility, and the like. Even petty theft can violate civil laws, too, with consequent embarrassment and scandal for one's family and community.

Occult Compensation

Sometimes it may happen that someone is owed something in strict, commutative justice, but he cannot claim it in civil court because it would be seriously injurious to him to try to do so. There are strict moral guidelines that must be observed, however, before such a person would be entitled to take the law into his own hands by occult compensation. For example, there must be no way that a request for justice from the debtor or the threat of lawsuit or some similar means could be effective, or else these things must be seen to be futile. A debt cannot be considered as contracted just because something is thought to be owed on account of alleged ingratitude or because something was promised, but the promisor did not intend to bind himself in justice.

In taking occult compensation, one must guard carefully against undue damage to the debtor or injury to a third party. Because almost everyone exaggerates the extent of any injustice done to him, occult compensation often can degenerate into a sin of theft, especially when one deceives oneself into believing that all other available means to collect the debt have been exhausted or that there is no good excuse for the delay of the payment of the debt. This is particularly frequent when employees feel they are underpaid and insufficiently compensated, and then they think they are permitted to steal, overrating their worth. Sometimes in those situations they feel entitled to take things home (steal) from the office, shop, store, and so on. Sometimes business executives arrange to overpay themselves to the detriment of their employees, their stockholders, and the common good. No one should ever take any occult compensation without first seeking the advice of his confessor or of a very competent Catholic moral theologian. Otherwise there would be too much danger of self-justification and rationalization for stealing. Even the best and most morally sensitive people are always bad judges in their own cases.

Extreme Need

The right to private property, an acquired right, occasionally must be ceded to the connatural right of other human beings to possess more important things. Therefore, in extreme need, when one's (or one's dependants') life, liberty, health, reputation, or something of similar, supreme value is in immediate and grave danger, and the owner of some absolutely necessary property unreasonably refuses the needed use of his property, the one in danger and need may seize what is necessary for survival without committing a sin of theft. However, the need must be extreme; what is taken can be only that which is strictly necessary; and it must be repaid as soon as possible. Civil laws often do not recognize this aspect of morality, and people who take the property of others even in extreme need sometimes can be liable to civil or criminal prosecution. Obviously, it is a situation that rarely happens in more advanced societies, but it is always possible.

OCTOBER 11, 2002

Commandments
XVII

Questions

Many questions from a variety of possible situations can arise from those who want to be careful about observing the seventh commandment (Ex 20:15; Deut 5:19; Mt 19:18). Over the years competent Catholic moral theologians have attempted to answer some of such questions out of the logical consequences that are derived from the nature of justice, as well as out of the age-old wisdom set out over the centuries by the Doctors of the Church.

One set of such questions can be raised about the possessions of minor children. Usually civil laws regulate such matters, and ordinarily these are in accord with sound moral principles and, therefore, must be followed. However, the general moral criteria state that a child's gifts are his possession but are in the administration of the parents, who have a duty to preserve and protect them until the child reaches legal maturity or at least is ready to use them. This is especially true for outright gifts. If a child were to use such gifts (edibles, money for amusement and recreation, and so forth) against the wishes of the parents, the child would commit a sin of disobedience against the fourth commandment but not necessarily a sin of injustice against the seventh. If a child were given gifts for a specific purpose (books, clothes, scholarship funds, and so on), the parents would have an additional duty to ensure that they were used only for the purposes intended by the donor.

Minor children who earn money, apart from carrying out the orders of their parents or from working around the home, are the morally legitimate owners of that money. In such cases, however, the parents have the right to require that the child compensate them for room, board, clothing, and other such expenses. The child then has a corresponding obligation in justice to pay the parents. Children also have an obligation in obedience to reveal to their parents the facts of their labor and their earnings. Children who have from some means (such as inheritance) the possession of substantial resources could also have an obligation (out of their duty to practice family piety) to assist other members of their family who might be in straitened circumstances.

OTHERS

Another question that is sometimes asked is about found treasure. In this area, too, the civil laws must be observed. If none of those apply, however, the moral principle is that a treasure or treasure trove (nuggets of gold, gems, pearls on a seashore, and so on) belongs to those who find it. Those who possess "mineral rights" are the moral owners of underground oil, coal, ores, and so forth. Otherwise, property owners have the right to what might be found on or under their property, for instance, buried money from so long ago that the owner cannot be known or found.

Wild game belongs to no one and, therefore, can be hunted. It is disputed whether it would be a simply penal matter to violate civil hunting laws and thus no sin, or whether poaching and the like should be considered a sin against the common good. Wild animals (not domestic) that escape from their confinement (for instance bees, pigeons, and so on) belong to those who capture them.

If there are "good faith" intrusions on property, the owner of the property owns what is on it but is required in strict justice to compensate fully the one who made the honest mistake. For example, someone sows a crop on land he mistakenly thinks is his, or someone builds a house on what he supposes to be his property, but then the title to the land turns out to belong to another, and so on.

DAMAGE

The seventh commandment also forbids deliberately causing unjust damage to the property of another, with the corresponding obligation to make restitution as a necessary moral condition for the pardon by God of such sins. The damage can sometimes be either material damage or another type of damage, for instance attacking a person's reputation by slander, contumely, detraction, or calumny, or hindering another from obtaining what is rightfully his by lying, cheating, force, fear, trickery, flattery, and so on. Deliberate negligence can also unjustly damage the property of another and thus be a sin against the seventh commandment. If negligence is present in a parent or employer or other superior and thus contributes to the damage, there would likely be a moral duty, no matter what the civil law might say, to participate in or be wholly responsible for all necessary restitution.

Bankruptcy that is juridically declared in civil law releases one's conscience almost always from the moral debt obligations involved, unless fraud or deceit is involved. The thinking is that, while there is always a moral requirement to honor and pay all just debts, lenders, creditors, depositors, and other business personages are supposed to know the law and, therefore, are supposed at least implicitly to be willing to assume the risk of losses because of the possible bankruptcy of those with whom they deal.

CONTRACTS

Personal and other legal contracts bind a person in conscience to observe them, provided they are about that which is morally lawful, about that which is possible for the parties, and about that which rightfully belongs to the contracting parties. Also, to be morally binding in justice they must be entered into deliberately and freely and be manifested externally in some way, for instance a handshake, a written covenant, and so forth. Even a verbal contract can bind one in conscience, notwithstanding the famous malapropism attributed to Samuel Goldwyn, "Verbal contracts aren't worth the paper they are written on." Contracts can include insurance arrangements, wage and salary agreements, and so on. Usually the civil laws that determine whether this or that contractual error is substantial and invalidates a contract or whether it is merely accidental and keeps the contract valid are morally binding for the contracting parties.

In striving under God's grace to follow the seventh as well as the other commandments, it is good to make one's own the prayer of the Psalmist addressed to the Lord: "I love your commandments above gold, above fine gold. Therefore I direct my steps by all your precepts; I hate every false way" (Ps 119:127–28). "Hold me up, that I may be safe and have regard for your statutes continually! You spurn all who go astray from your statutes; yea, their cunning is in vain" (Ps 119:117–18).

OCTOBER 17, 2002

Commandments
XVIII

MERCHANTS

Saint Paul tells us in the New Testament that serious violations of the seventh commandment (Ex 20:15; Deut 5:19) can exclude the violator from the kingdom of God (1 Cor 6:10). His admonition should prompt us as Christ's disciples to be very careful about observing the rules of justice in all our dealing with others.

Merchants and business people are obliged to reveal to potential customers any substantial defects in any articles or property they sell. This especially applies to any case that would make the article or property other than what it appears or that would render it useless for the purpose of the purchaser. The old pagan warning *caveat emptor* (let the buyer beware) is not a Christian moral principle. A merchant or salesperson would not be required to call attention to obvious minor defects but would be obligated to answer truthfully if asked about them. One morally could sell at a current price even if one were certain the price would soon fall, and one could charge more for something that is dear or has special sentimental value. However, it would be immoral to make an excessive profit simply because of the special or urgent need of the buyer.

Lies or serious misrepresentation either in advertising or about a competitor's products or services would be a violation of both the eighth and seventh commandments. To do work in such a way as to endanger the lives or safety of the workers (because of known poor equipment or a lack of standard safety measures) or of other people (because of deliberately faulty, negligent construction or defective material) could be a sin against the fifth as well as the seventh commandment. It is not adequate for a conscientious Christian to judge the morality of his business practices merely by what competitors might be doing or only by avoiding civil law violations or the censure of entities such as better-business bureaus.

ANIMALS

Under its treatment of the seventh commandment, the *Catechism of the Catholic Church* teaches that, by that mandate, God requires of us "respect for the integrity of creation". The "use of the mineral, vegetable, and animal resources of the universe" are placed by the Creator's will under human domination (Gen 1:28–31), but this domination is not absolute. "It is limited by concern for the quality of life of his neighbor, including generations to come" (CCC 2415). The *Catechism* tells us that human beings, who are made in the image of God, are entrusted by Him with the stewardship of animals (Gen 2:19–20; 9:1–4). "Hence it is legitimate to use animals for food and clothing. They may be domesticated to help man in his work and leisure. Medical and scientific experimentation on animals is a morally acceptable practice if it remains within reasonable limits and contributes to caring for or saving human lives. It is contrary to human dignity to cause animals to suffer or die needlessly. It is likewise unworthy to spend money on them that should as a priority go to the relief of human misery" (CCC 2417–18). One can like animals, but one should never direct to them the affection due only to human persons, since only human beings have immortal souls.

The *Catechism* exhorts us to see all brute animals as God's creatures that praise and glorify Him by their mere existence. It tells us to be kind to them, following the example of such saints as Francis of Assisi and Philip Neri (cf. CCC 2416).

RESTITUTION

Sins against the seventh commandment require complete restitution, made as soon as possible, as a necessary condition for their being forgiven. To confess such sins and to be absolved from them in the Sacrament of Reconciliation, which is also necessary, would not have any validity without full restitution. Restitution issues can be quite complicated, and it is generally wise for laypeople to consult their confessors about such matters. It is not necessary for the one who stole or caused unjust damage to reveal or denounce himself in making restitution, unless that is the only way it can be done.

Restitution must be done to the lawful owner and no one else. If the ill-gotten goods have been lost, destroyed, or consumed, their exact price at the time of the theft or damage is what is owed immediately to the owner. If the owner cannot be known or if it is absolutely impossible to locate him, the restitution must be made to the poor or to the works of the Church. Ill-gotten goods can never be morally retained. Moreover, it is not permitted to give to the poor or to the Church to avoid giving the property back to the legitimate owner, just as a business person is not morally allowed to give to his employees as charity what is their due in justice.

It is possible that the absolute inability to repay could allow a debtor morally to postpone restitution, since no one is bound to the impossible. But, this matter should be discussed with one's confessor, and a decision should not be made on one's own. Also, one could be excused from restitution if the owner or creditor freely gives up all claims. If one discovers that he has obtained ill-gotten goods but in good faith, one must still restore them immediately to their rightful owner. However, such a person can claim restitution from the person who may have deceived him. For instance, one buys something that a thief has stolen but thinks the thief is the rightful owner. Upon learning of the true rightful owner, the property must be restored, but the person who has been deceived certainly may claim back the purchase price from the thief.

The *Catechism* teaches that:

> In virtue of commutative justice, *reparation for injustice* committed requires restitution...
>
> Jesus blesses Zacchaeus for his pledge: "If I have defrauded anyone of anything, I restore it fourfold" [Lk 19:8]. Those who, directly or indirectly, have taken possession of the goods of another, are obliged to make restitution of them, or to return the equivalent in kind or in money, if the goods have disappeared, as well as the profit or advantages their owner would have legitimately obtained from them. Likewise, all who in some manner have taken part in a theft or who have knowingly benefited from it—for example, those who ordered it, assisted in it, or received the stolen goods—are obliged to make restitution in proportion to their responsibility and to their share of what was stolen. (CCC 2412)

NOVEMBER 1, 2002

Commandments
XIX

EIGHTH

Saint John the Evangelist says in his first epistle (2:4) that anyone who claims to know God but does not keep His commandments "is a liar, and the truth is not in him". Those who lie and deceive are in a special way imitators of Lucifer, the chief devil, whom our divine Lord Himself called "a liar and the father of lies" (Jn 8:44). The commandment of God by which our Creator enjoins human beings to tell the truth and to respect the good name of others is the eighth of the Decalogue, "You shall not bear false witness against your neighbor" (Ex 20:16; Deut 5:20). On more than one occasion Jesus personally repeated the binding force of this eighth commandment (Mt 5:33; Mk 10:19).

Saint Thomas Aquinas teaches the traditional doctrine of the Church in this matter, namely, that the requirement to obey the eighth commandment derives from human reason and human nature, even before it derives from the absolute need for all humans to obey the positive precept of God regarding the truth. "Men could not live with one another if there were not mutual confidence that they were being truthful to one another."[186] As the *Catechism* goes on to explain,

"The virtue of truth gives another his just due. Truthfulness keeps to the just mean between what ought to be expressed and what ought to be kept secret: it entails honesty and discretion. In justice, 'as a matter of honor, one man owes it to another to manifest the truth.'"[187]

SINS

In common language terms, men can "become what they do". For instance, those who fornicate "become fornicators". Likewise, those who lie "become liars". Sins have a way of penetrating into the very personality of the sinner.

Some of the violations of the eighth commandment that can be sins, if they are done with free will and sufficient reflection, are lying, detraction, calumny, cheating, contumely, rash judgment, giving away secrets, perjury, and so on.

The *Catechism of the Catholic Church*, quoting Sacred Scripture, states, "Christ's disciples have 'put on the new man created after the likeness of God in true righteousness and holiness' [Eph 4:24]. By 'putting away falsehood' (Eph 4:25), they are to 'put away all malice and all guile and insincerity and envy of all slander' [1 Pet 2:1]" (CCC 2475). The *Catechism* also states, "Since God is 'true', the members of his people are called to live in the truth [Rom 3:4; cf. Ps 119:30]" (CCC 2465).

CHRIST THE TRUTH

When God became incarnate in Jesus Christ, He came into our world "to bear witness to the truth" (Jn 18:37). He came to save us, being in Himself "full of grace and of truth" (Jn 1:14). He came to tell us the truth so that "the truth [would] make [us] free" (Jn 8:32), and He came so that the truth would "sanctify" us (Jn 17:17).

Scholastic philosophers tell us that all beings, reflecting the Supreme Being, are marked by the three characteristics of beauty, goodness, and truth. God, Who is totally simple, totally other, and totally spiritual, is identified with His attributes, and, therefore, one can legitimately say that God is Truth (Num 23:19). It is no surprise, then, for Christ's followers to hear our Savior say very clearly that, since He is one with God the Father (Jn 14:9–11), He not only proclaims the truth, but in His Divine Person He is Truth Itself (Jn 14:6); so much for the sneer of Pontius Pilate (Jn 18:38).

The Catholic Church, which is the Bride and Body of Christ, extending Him through time and space until He comes again in glory, participates in His divine truthfulness because the Church's Founder, Jesus, the risen Lord, continues to keep His promise made at the Last Supper and pours into her with the Father "the Spirit of truth" Who "guides ... into all truth" (Jn 16:13). The members of the Mystical Body of Christ (1 Cor 6:15), therefore, have an even stronger obligation to observe the eighth commandment than those others who do not possess the fullness of revealed truth.

NEWMAN

In the middle of the nineteenth century, the English writer Charles Kingsley, in an outburst of anti-Catholic bigotry, falsely accused John Henry Newman of lying and teaching systematic lying. This elicited from the accused scholar one of the great autobiographical works in the English language (although it has a Latin title), Newman's *Apologia pro Vita Sua*. At the end of his great work, the future Cardinal refutes in general and then in detail Kingsley's accusations against him and against the Catholic Church. In the course of his refutation, Newman gives an extensive and fascinating treatise on the teachings of many of the Fathers and Doctors of the Church, especially Saint Alphonsus of Liguori, about the morality of truth-telling.

While discoursing about some subtle aspects of mental reservation and about maintaining certain secrets intact, Newman reiterates with clarity the intrinsic evil of lying. Saint Augustine of Hippo says a "lie consists in speaking a falsehood with the intention of deceiving."[188] Newman's summary of the teaching of the Fathers and Doctors can be seen today in the words of the *Catechism*. "Lying is the most direct offense against the truth. To lie is to speak or act against the truth in order to lead someone into error. By injuring man's relation to truth and to his neighbor, a lie offends against the fundamental relation of man and of his word to the Lord" (CCC 2483).

The *Catechism* goes on to say, "Since it violates the virtue of truthfulness, a lie does real violence to another. It affects his ability to know, which is a condition of every judgment and decision. It contains the seed of discord and all consequent evils. Lying is destructive of society; it undermines trust among men and tears apart the fabric of social relationships" (CCC 2486). In the New Testament, Saint Paul instructs us, as members of Christ's true Church, to put away all "anger, wrath, malice, slander, and foul talk". Then he goes on to say with emphasis, "Do not lie to one another" (Col 3:8–9).

AUGUST 8, 2003

Commandments
XX

TRUTHFULNESS

Jesus Christ, our divine Lord Himself, on more than one occasion reiterated the necessity for His followers to avoid sins against the requirements of the eighth commandment of the Decalogue (Deut 5:20). He listed "deceit" in His catalogue of soul-destroying evils, which can come from within the fallen nature of human beings (Mk 7:22). The Apostle Saint Paul specifically gave instructions to all Christians to obey that commandment. "Therefore, putting away falsehood, let every one speak the truth with his neighbor." (Eph 4:25). "Do not lie to one another, seeing that you have put off the old nature with its practices" (Col 3:9).

The divine law that states "You shall not bear false witness against your neighbor" (Ex 20:16) requires humans to practice sincerity and candor, also known as "truthfulness". The *Catechism of the Catholic Church* says, "Truth or truthfulness is the virtue which consists in showing oneself true in deeds and truthful in words, and in guarding against duplicity, dissimulation, and hypocrisy" (CCC 2468). That law, forbidding "false witness", carries with it a corresponding duty always to bear "witness to the truth" (Jn 18:37).

Being a "witness to the truth" especially concerns the Catholic faith and the obligation of all Christians (asserted anew by the Second Vatican Council) by words and deeds to be "witnesses of the Gospel", to be unashamed of Christ and the truths of the faith, and to admire and, when necessary, to imitate the "witness of the martyrs", who gave the highest and "supreme witness... to the truth of the faith" (CCC 2473). (The word "martyr" means "witness" in the Greek language.)

JUSTICE

Not only do violations of the seventh commandment involve justice with the duty to make restitution and reparation, but also some violations of the eighth commandment can be offenses against justice and can require, as a condition for forgiveness of such sins, the obligation to make appropriate restitution. This especially has to do with sins of calumny and detraction. The general principle is that everyone has a right to his good name unless deliberately forfeited. This includes even the deceased as well as collectivities, organizations, and communities. To injure someone's good name purposely without a validly objective reason is a sin that demands restitution as condition for pardon from God. In themselves such sins must be considered mortal, although they sometimes can be venial because an exceptionally slight injury is done or because of thoughtlessness on the part of the sinner, and so on.

Calumny means harming the reputation of another by falsely imputing to him defects, sins, faults, failings, and so forth, or communicating contrary to the truth matters that give "occasion for false judgments concerning [him]" (CCC 2477). Detraction means disclosing to people who would not otherwise know them without sufficient reasons the faults, sins, failings, and so on, of others.

MEDIA

Politicians and people involved in the entertainment and news media are certainly bound to observe the ethical principles enjoined by God on the human race by the eighth commandment. The news media can morally report public crimes, but they are obligated to avoid doing it in a way that can induce others to sin. They may morally manifest crimes or evils that will soon become public, unless a premature revelation of that sort will cause serious harm to society or to individuals.

Politicians and the news media certainly are permitted to criticize mismanagement or the public defects of public officials, since that can be "a wholesome restraining influence on some persons".

Those who listen to or read calumny or detraction can be guilty of participating in the sin of the calumniator or detractor. This is especially the case if one deliberately provokes the sin (for instance, by purposely bringing up a name to obtain gossip) or if one rejoices and approves of the sin or if one has it in his power to put a stop to some calumny or detraction and fails to do so through human respect or timidity. It is not detraction to bring up the faults and failings of a person to his superiors (for instance, parents), and in some cases it may be obligatory to do this. However, it would be wrong to do this were one to foresee as a result some excessive or cruel punishment. Teachers, for instance, morally could tell parents that their child misbehaves in school, is lazy, and so on.

INTRINSIC

It is the perennial teaching of the Catholic Church that lying, communicating an untruth for the purpose of deception, is inherently and intrinsically evil. Therefore, a lie is always a sin, even if used to avert the gravest evil. Lying usually is venially sinful, but it can be mortally evil under certain circumstances, particularly, for example, if some other virtue besides veracity (charity or justice) would be involved. Malicious lies, those that injure another, are all usually gravely sinful. Officious lies, meant as excuses for one's own or another's advantage, can be either venial or mortal sins. Jocose lies are usually venially sinful, but are no sin at all if it can be reasonably assumed that a normal person would understand what is communicated is really a joke.

The *Catechism* states,

> The *gravity of a lie* is measured against the nature of the truth it deforms, the circumstances, the intention of the one who lies, and the harm suffered by its victims...
>
> By its very nature, lying is to be condemned. It is a profanation of speech, whereas the purpose of speech is to communicate known truth to others. The deliberate intention of leading a neighbor into error by saying things contrary to the truth constitutes a failure in justice and charity. The culpability is greater when the intention of deceiving entails the risk of deadly consequences for those who are led astray.
>
> ... A lie does real violence to another. It affects his ability to know, which is a condition of every judgment and decision. It contains the seeds of discord and all consequent evils. Lying is destructive of society. It undermines trust among men and tears apart the fabric of social relationships. (CCC 2484–86)

We should make our prayer to God: "I hate and abhore falsehood, but I love your law" (Ps 119:163).

SEPTEMBER 12, 2003

Commandments
XXI

RASH JUDGMENT

Jesus, our Savior, instructed us in His "sermon on the mount" not to judge others in order to avoid having the kind of judgment that we might use in doing this later fall back upon ourselves. Our Lord was very clear, saying that the judgment technique we use toward others will be used someday by God Himself in regard to us (Mt 7:1–5). The duty to avoid rash judgment is considered under the rubric of the eighth commandment (Ex 20:16). Observance of that divine law is required by all human beings who wish "to inherit eternal life" (Mk 10:17–19), as Christ Himself told us.

Rash judgment means giving an undoubting assent, without sufficient reason, to another's alleged sin. Rash judgment violates the right of every human being to appropriate esteem and to a good name, unless these have been forfeited by misconduct. While such rash judgments (suspicions or opinions), whether external or internal, are usually venially sinful, they could be mortal sins if they cause grave damage to another. By putting a charitable "spin" on the deeds, words, and omissions of another, one is usually correct in his evaluation of another. Also, doing so is a significant way to observe the "golden rule" laid down by our Lord in the Gospels (Mt 7:12).

The poet said, "Who made the heart, 'tis He alone // Decidedly can try us: \\ He knows each chord, its various tone,\\ each spring, its various bias.\\ Then at the balance let's be mute,\\ We never can adjust it;\\ What's done we partly may compute,\\ but know not what's resisted."[189] A saint's slogan, spoken or thought when observing apparent evil in other people, should be placed in our own hearts: "There, but for the grace of God, go I!"

GOSSIP

Almost everyone remembers the saintly advice given to a gossiping woman who was struggling with her vice. She was told to cut open a pillow and let the feathers fly out her window. Then the following week she was told to go out and gather them all up. Protesting that such a thing was impossible, she was then reminded that her gossip, wrecking the reputation of her neighbors, was like those feathers, spreading continuously and impossible to call back. Backbiting, slander, detraction, and calumny, as well as rash judgment, can be involved in gossip. In those kinds of sins, the readers and listeners ("enablers") can share in the guilt of the gossiping persons themselves.

Gossip and the sins it sometimes contains, such as calumny and detraction, can also be carried out by suggestion and innuendo as well as in nonverbal ways (sardonic grins, winks, lampoons, and so on). By talking about the real or imagined faults and shortcomings of others, especially if they involve persons deserving of some prestige and respect (such as priests, religious, and so on) or figures of authority, some people try thereby to exalt themselves or to justify (to themselves or others) their own sins and failings.

CONTUMELY

An act of unjustly dishonoring a person to his face is called the sin of contumely. It is any positive act that directly and unjustly expresses insult or contempt for another. By its nature the sin of contumely violates either justice or charity or both. It is an offense against the "great commandment" (Lk 10:25–27). If this wicked deed were gravely to injure someone's honor, it could be a mortal sin, but if the injury is slight, it would be a venial sin. Sins of contumely require restitution in order to obtain God's forgiveness even after the sinner repents of them (Mt

5:22).

The *Catechism of the Catholic Church* states,

> Every offense committed against justice and truth entails the *duty of reparation*, even if its author has been forgiven. When it is impossible publicly to make reparation for a wrong, it must be made secretly. If someone who has suffered harm cannot be directly compensated, he must be given moral satisfaction in the name of charity. This duty of reparation also concerns offenses against another's reputation. This reparation, moral and sometimes material, must be evaluated in terms of the extent of the damage inflicted. It obliges in conscience. (CCC 2487)

NOT EVERYONE ALWAYS

The *Catechism* teaches, "The *right to the communication* of the truth is not unconditional. Everyone must conform his life to the Gospel precept of fraternal love. This requires us in concrete situations to judge whether or not it is appropriate to reveal the truth to someone who asks for it" (CCC 2488).

The traditional case would be, for instance, beaming new parents asking someone if he did not think their baby was truly beautiful. It would be cruel and uncharitable in such a case to remark, even if true, that the child is really ugly. While it would always be wrong to lie, one could make some other comment in those circumstances, such as "All new babies are charming and sweet ..."

The *Catechism* sets out the traditional Catholic moral teaching in these matters. "Charity and respect for the truth should dictate the response to every *request for information or communication*. The good and safety of others, respect for privacy, and the common good are sufficient reasons for being silent about what ought not be known or for making use of discreet language. The duty to avoid scandal often commands strict discretion. No one is bound to reveal the truth to someone who does not have the right to know it" (CCC 2489, cf. Sir 27:16; Prov 25:9-10).

The *Catechism* says, "Everyone should observe an appropriate reserve concerning persons' private lives. Those in charge of communications should maintain a fair balance between the requirements of the common good and respect for individual rights. Interference by the media in the private lives of persons engaged in political or public activity is to be condemned to the extent that it infringes upon their privacy and freedom" (CCC 2492).

Although we always must be dedicated to the truth, for which we must have the greatest respect and devotion, we must not use the truth, especially regarding other people, as a bludgeon or instrument by which to cause unnecessary harm. We are not permitted by God ever to lie, but He does not oblige us to assuage an unjust desire on the part of some people to exercise a fallacious "right to know".

SEPTEMBER 19, 2003

Commandments
XXII

SECRETS

The eighth commandment (Ex 20:16) concerns the morality involved in keeping or revealing secrets. A secret is some hidden knowledge that may not be revealed unless some higher right intervenes. Secrets may involve such things as incidents or information as well as inventions or compositions. Generally, secrets can be natural, which the natural law forbids revealing, or promised, which derive from an assurance given to someone, or entrusted, that is, some information that comes through special circumstances. An example of a natural secret would be knowledge about a shameful youthful act of someone who is now a respected and respectable person. An example of a promised secret would be a pledge not to tell a family member about a traffic violation. An example of an entrusted secret would be professional knowledge obtained by a doctor about a patient or by an attorney about a client. An agreement to keep something secret can be implicit or explicit.

The highest and most binding of all human secrets is that of the confessional. The *Catechism of the Catholic Church* notes that "*the secret of the sacrament of reconciliation* is sacred, and cannot be violated under any pretext" (CCC 2490). A priest must be willing to suffer martyrdom, as did Saint John Nepomucene, rather than "'betray a penitent by word or in any other manner or for any reason.'"[190] The same obligation in regard to confessional secrecy also binds anyone who might accidentally overhear a confession or who might serve as a language interpreter for a confession. Any violation of confessional secrecy is not only a heinous mortal sin, but also a horrible ecclesiastical crime, punished with severe excommunication.

OBLIGING AND PRYING

On the principle that everyone has a right to the ownership of his secrets, to his good name, to his own thoughts, talents, and industry, it can be sinful to pry into the secrets of others by such acts as eavesdropping, bribing servants or employees for information, tricking someone into betraying secrets, opening others' mail, and so on. Revealing secrets can sometimes be mortal sins, sometimes venial sins, and sometimes no sin at all. If revealing a secret causes grave harm or involves a matter of serious importance, the revelation could be a mortal sin against justice or charity or both. This is usually the case with all natural and entrusted secrets, but could sometimes involve promised secrets as well.

Secrets may be revealed without moral guilt if the information already has become public knowledge or if one may justly, with reflection and sufficient reason, presume the permission of the party concerned that the secret be no longer kept or if it is revealed to others whom we know share the same secret (except, of course, the secret of the confessional). Secrets may also be revealed (except confessional matters) without moral culpability if keeping a secret were to cause grave harm or danger to the one who owns the secret, to the one who shares the secret, to an innocent third party, or to the Church, State, or community.

CHEATING AND READING

It is usually sinful to read the letters, notes, diaries, and the private papers of others without permission. However, this may be done without guilt if such action is necessary to avert grave harm to the State, to an innocent person, to one self, and so on. A nation during war may censor mail, and prison officials may do so for inmates. Provided there are proper safeguards (such as a need for search warrants), government officials may do what is needed in this field to protect a country or person from serious injury. Parents may read, without any sin, the letters, diaries, and private papers of their minor children if they have serious and sufficient cause to suspect this might be necessary for a child's welfare and good. In some of these matters the civil laws of a government may coincide with the moral law, and in other places not.

Cheating in games is a type of lie and is usually a sin. Ordinarily it is a venial sin, unless other circumstances intervene (such as professional sports, involving large sums of money, throwing games or moderating scores to accommodate gamblers, and so on). Cheating in school examinations is also a kind of lie and, therefore, usually is a sin as well. If cheating in school examinations deprives someone else of a scholarship, medal, or honor, the sin demands restitution. It could also, in some of those kinds of situations, be a mortal sin.

School cheating could also be seriously sinful if one were thus enabled to practice a profession or occupation without adequate knowledge and, therefore, be in a later position to cause unjust injury to others. Placing one self in danger of shame, embarrassment, expulsion from school, defamation of one's family or school, and so on could also add to the moral weight of determining the seriousness of any sin of cheating in school examinations.

Mass Media

Under the heading of the eighth commandment, the *Catechism of the Catholic Church* also treats issues concerning the mass media, saying, for instance, "The means of social communication (especially the mass media) can give rise to a certain passivity among users, making them less than vigilant consumers of what is said or shown. Users should practice moderation and discipline in their approach to the mass media. They will want to form enlightened and correct consciences the more easily to resist unwholesome influences" (CCC 2496).

"Moral judgment must condemn the plague of totalitarian states which systematically falsify the truth, exercise political control of opinion through the media, manipulate defendants and witnesses at public trials, and imagine that they secure their tyranny by strangling and repressing everything considered 'thought crimes'" (CCC 2499).

By the very nature of their profession, journalists have an obligation to serve the truth and not offend against charity in disseminating information. They should strive to respect, with equal care, the nature of the facts and the limits of critical judgment concerning individuals. They should not stoop to defamation...

Nothing can justify recourse to disinformation for manipulating public opinion through the media. Interventions by public authority should avoid injuring the freedom of individuals or groups. (CCC 2497–98)

SEPTEMBER 26, 2003

Commandments
XXIII

Athanasius

There is a well-known historical incident involving the fourth-century Bishop of Alexandria, Saint Athanasius, who at one time was in a boat on the Nile River fleeing a gang of heretics who were seeking to kill him. Seeing his persecutors pursuing him in boats, he ordered his men to turn his boat around and run straight to meet his pursuers. As they passed, the heretics called out, "Have you seen Athanasius?" The saint ordered his followers to answer, "Yes, he is close to you.

Keep going." This is an interesting application of the principle of "mental reservation" or "mental restriction". The eighth commandment (Ex 20:16; Deut 5:20; Mt 5:33) forbids lying, but in certain particular circumstances, it seems to allow equivocations, which permit persons to deceive themselves.

The early Christians, for instance, were allowed by the Church Fathers to conceal their Creed, although they were never permitted to deny it, even under pain of death. This was to prevent ridicule and misunderstanding by the pagans. The heathens would sometimes question them, "Do you believe in a Trinity?"; then they were permitted to answer, "We believe in one God and no other."

RESERVATIONS

Generally there are two types of mental reservations. Strict mental reservations are indistinguishable from lies and are immoral, the equivalent of crossing one's fingers while telling an untruth for the purpose of deceiving, which practice does not take away the sin. An example of such an illicit mental reservation would be telling someone, "I am going to New York next week", while thinking to one self "only in my dreams and imagination".

A broad mental reservation is one in which the real meaning of the words, which could be taken in several varied ways, could be inferred from the question, the answer, or customary usage. Although there are contrary opinions about the morality of using broad mental reservations, most Catholic moral theologians say that, if there is a sufficiently serious, justifying reason for doing so, they can be used without sinning.

The usual example in these cases is the conventional expression "not at home". In certain circles and certainly in Victorian times, to say that one was "at home" meant one was disposed to receive visitors, although it could also have referred to being physically present in one's house. Thus, today it is probably acceptable to say that someone is "not at home" when the person may be physically in the house but not disposed to receive visitors. The caller can be allowed to deceive himself by that expression.

In the same vein, criminals who might be guilty of a crime do not lie if they plead "not guilty" in court. Such a plea simply means that they are demanding that the state supply proof for the charges against them. On the other hand, if they lie while testifying under oath about what they did, they commit the grievous sin of perjury.

DISPUTES

There are theological disputes about the use of mental reservations and the observance of the eighth commandment. The traditional teaching as expressed here, which is well-founded, can be safely followed. There are some new theological theories that are interesting but probably not safe to follow. They derive mainly from wartime situations, involving spying and secret information. They sometimes try to divide human speech into "per se representation of one's knowledge" and "per accidens" speech. The idea is that this avoids unrealistic distinctions and definitions and the fiction that others actually "deceive themselves". These newer theories have not been well worked out yet and therefore should not be followed.

In Protestant England it was falsely thought that Catholics were taught to use mental reservations in taking oaths and, thus, were told not to be really loyal to their country, although they might swear the opposite. This is why British oaths even to this day contain the phrase "without any mental reservation whatever". The oaths for federal offices in the government of the United States (except that for president) copied this English usage, and so you can hear the phrase used today in our country.

CHILDREN

There are theological disputes as well about the morality of deceiving children. Several Fathers of the Church maintained that such deception was not a sin for parents, especially regarding little children and especially concerning "benevolent lies" (for example, about Santa Claus, the tooth fairy, babies being brought by storks, and so on). However, other Church Fathers and many theologians today have a contrary view, namely, that since lying is intrinsically evil, there really is no such thing as "benevolent lies" for children. Also, the practice might be giving the children scandal and teaching them a light regard for the truth. Since the matter appears to be disputed and the *magisterium* of the Church has not yet pronounced definitively on it, it seems that either opinion may be followed, since both are well-founded.

Even if lying to children were not a sin, it might not be prudent for parents to do so. Children today are quite precocious and will "find out" sooner or later, especially through the media and by means of their friends and schoolmates. Not being candid and frank with them could breed mistrust later on and cause them not to confide in their parents about important issues. On the other hand, conscientious parents also want to guard and preserve their children's happiness and innocence in their early years. Still it is better that children learn important things about reality from their parents rather than from other sources.

Also, the first evangelizers of children are (and should be) their family members, particularly their parents. It could be easy for children to suppose wrongly that if their parents deceived them about certain things, their parents might also be deceiving them about religious doctrines and the truths of divine revelation, information necessary for their eternal salvation.

One of the most famous biblical cases of deception was that of Jacob (Israel) obtaining the special blessing of Isaac, his blind father, in place of his older brother Esau (Gen 27). Although he had obtained earlier the right to the blessing in exchange for a "mess of pottage", Jacob appeared to lie when it came time to obtain it.

OCTOBER 3, 2003

Commandments
XXIV

INTERNAL SINS

The ninth and tenth commandments of God's law require human beings to control their interior dispositions, especially their intellects, wills, and imagination (Ex 20:17). The ninth commandment specifically forbids giving way to interior lust, a commandment reinforced by the clear teaching of Jesus, "Every one who looks at a woman lustfully has already committed adultery with her in his heart" (Mt 5:28). Our Lord tells us plainly that external sins, such as "fornication and adultery", always begin "from within" (Mt 15:19).

In our modern American culture, obedience to the ninth commandment can be exceptionally difficult. The world of commercial advertising and the entertainment media shamelessly use sexual depictions and words to manipulate and control vast sectors of public thought and action. Sometimes the public is largely unaware of how people are being "used". The Christian truth that there can be sins, and even serious sins, involved in consenting to impure and unchaste thoughts goes largely ignored or ridiculed by our culture of unrestricted and irresponsible pleasure-seeking, in which even the disgusting horrors of pornography and sexual perversions are part of the usual landscape. Unbidden and unprovoked "bad thoughts", of course, are not sins, unless they are sufficiently reflected upon and freely consented to.

The *Catechism of the Catholic Church* teaches, "Saint John distinguishes three kinds of covetousness or concupiscence: lust of the flesh, lust of the eyes, and pride of life [cf. 1 Jn 2:16]. In the Catholic catechetical tradition, the ninth commandment forbids carnal concupiscence" (CCC 2514).

PURE HEARTS

The sixth beatitude (Mt 5:8), as the *Catechism* tells us, involves, among other things, "chastity or sexual rectitude" (CC 2518, cf. 1 Thess 4:7; Col 3:5; Eph 4:19). It says, "Purity of heart is the precondition of the vision of God. Even now it enables us to see *according to* God, to accept others as 'neighbors"; it lets us perceive the human body—ours and our neighbor's—as a temple of the Holy Spirit, a manifestation of divine beauty [1 Cor 13:12; 1 Jn 3:2]" (CCC 2519).

To live a life of purity and chastity is not possible for us in our fallen human condition without the grace of God. Humbly acknowledging our human weaknesses and beseeching our almighty Father for His constant help is a vital prerequisite for being able to obey the ninth commandment. Pride, self-reliance, and self-righteousness are almost always a prelude to spiritual bankruptcy in this area of life. In his *Confessions* Saint Augustine addressed God in these words: "I thought that continence arose from one's own powers, which I did not recognize in myself. I was foolish enough not to know ... that no one can be continent unless you grant it. For you would surely have granted it if my inner groaning had reached your ears and I with firm faith had cast my cares on you."[191] Prayer, regular recourse to the sacraments of Confession and Holy Communion, and careful avoidance of the occasions of sin are essential to living a life of purity and chastity.

MODESTY

The gateway to purity is the virtue of modesty. The *Catechism* states,

> Modesty protects the intimate center of the person. It means refusing to unveil what should remain hidden. It is ordered to chastity to whose sensitivity it bears witness. It guides how one looks at others and behaves toward them in conformity with the dignity of persons and their solidarity...
>
> [Modesty] encourages patience and moderation in loving relationships; it requires that the conditions for the definitive giving and commitment of man and woman to one another be fulfilled. Modesty is decency. It inspires one's choice of clothing. It keeps silence or reserve where there is evident risk of unhealthy curiosity. It is discreet...
>
> [Modesty] protests, for example, against the voyeuristic explorations of the human body in certain advertisements, or against the solicitations of certain media that go too far in the exhibition of intimate things. Modesty inspires a way of life which makes it possible to resist the allurements of fashion and the pressures of prevailing ideologies...
>
> Everywhere; however, modesty exists as an intuition of the spiritual dignity proper to man. It is born with the awakening consciousness of being a subject. Teaching modesty to children and adolescents means awakening in them respect for the human person. (CCC 2521–24)

Social Climate

The social climate contributes greatly to a culture of purity or less than purity. Even the healthiest fish cannot last long in polluted water. Widespread eroticism, along with written, spoken, photographic smut, and "sex education" without any accompanying correct moral instruction often poison the cultural air of our time and place. The *Catechism* remarks, "So-called *moral permissiveness* rests on an erroneous conception of human freedom; the necessary precondition for the development of true freedom is to let oneself be educated in the moral law" (CCC 2526). "The baptized must continue to struggle against concupiscence of the flesh and disordered desires. With God's grace he will prevail" (CCC 2520).

Christ taught us, "If your eye is not sound, your whole body will be full of darkness. If then the light in you is darkness, how great is the darkness!" (Mt 6:23). Again our divine Lord said, "If your eye causes you to sin, pluck it out and throw it from you; it is better for you to enter life with one eye than with two eyes to be thrown into the hell of fire" (Mt 18:9). Perhaps we, who claim to be His followers, should take the matter of obeying the ninth commandment more seriously than we do.

The Second Vatican Council teaches, "The Good News of Christ continually renews the life and culture of fallen man; it combats and removes the error and evil which flow from the ever-present attraction of sin. It never ceases to purify and elevate the morality of peoples."[192]

OCTOBER 10, 2003

Commandments
XXV

Treasure

Jesus Christ instructed us, His disciples, to work to become rich, but rich with treasures that are not earthly but that are stored up for us in heaven (Mt 6:19–23). It is precisely because this effort requires so much expenditure of energy and labor that our Savior warns us about excessive concern regarding our material circumstances and acquisitions, which often can distract and even impede the far more important interests that should occupy our attention and direct our lives (Mt 6:24–34).

The tenth commandment of the Decalogue (Ex 20:17; Deut 5:21) orders us to avoid covetousness and the sins that derive from it. It tells us to control "the intentions of our heart", especially when we sometimes encounter higher prosperity and the greater wealth of others. Particularly, we are forbidden to indulge ourselves in avarice, greed, and envy, sins and vices that the *Catechism*, following the age-old catechetical tradition of the apostles, says are really forms of idolatry. Indeed, as I have already indicated, all sins have that characteristic, because sinning basically means placing some created thing higher than God in one's mind and will.

Because our human nature has been seriously wounded by original sin, whose effects always abide in us, interior control of our intellects, wills, and imagination requires the constant assistance of God's actual grace, for which we should regularly pray.

EARTHLY GOODS

There is nothing intrinsically wrong with a desire to acquire and possess earthly goods. This is especially true if the underlying purpose in doing this is to provide for one's dependents, to ensure some security for old age or future contingencies, or to use such goods to assist the poor and needy, to promote higher education, or to help institutions of charity and the Church. The sin of greed comes into existence when such a desire is inordinate, taking excessive possession of an exceptionally large portion of one's life. A wish to amass worldly goods without limit is usually venially sinful, but that kind of cupidity can easily lead to serious sins against charity. It certainly contradicts the first beatitude (Mt 5:3; Mk 10:17–31).

The *Catechism of the Catholic Church* states, "The sensitive appetite leads us to desire pleasant things we do not have, e.g., the desire to eat when we are hungry or to warm ourselves when we are cold. These desires are good in themselves; but often they exceed the limits of reason and drive us to covet unjustly what is not ours and belongs to another or is owed to him" (CCC 2535). The tenth commandment requires that we struggle against "a passion for riches and their attendant power" and that we do not indulge any "desire to commit injustice by harming our neighbor in his temporal goods" (CCC 2536). The *Roman Catechism* says, "Our thirst for another's goods is immense, infinite, never quenched. Thus it is written: 'He who loves money never has money enough' [cf. Sir 5:8]."[193] But, it is not avarice to desire to obtain another's goods by just means. However, it would be sinful for merchants, for example, to desire scarcity and higher prices so that the misfortune of others would give them greater profits or for doctors to desire a greater spread of disease so they could obtain more patients or for attorneys to wish for more crimes so they could have more clients, and so on.

ENVY

The capital sin of envy, which is also forbidden by the tenth commandment, "can lead to the worst crimes" [cf. Gen 4:3–7; 1 Kings 21:1–29] (CCC 2538). Saint Gregory the Great says that from envy are born hatred, detraction, calumny, illicit joy at another's misfortune, displeasure caused by another's prosperity, and many other evils.[194] The holy Bible tells us that "through the devil's envy death entered the world" (Wis 2:24). Envy is often a mortal sin. It is deliberate sadness purposely put into one's heart because of the good fortune of a fellowman, which is seen as a diminishing of one's own worth. It is begrudging one's neighbor something good (natural or supernatural) that one sincerely wishes he did not have.

It is not sinful envy merely to grieve that one does not have something (talent, virtue, and so on) another has or to be sad because someone has something he does not deserve or to be depressed at one's own lack of some goods because of one's limitations.

To counteract envious inclinations, a Christian should always strive to cultivate the virtue of emulation, trying to imitate the praiseworthy and good one sees in others. The highest form of emulation, of course, is our duty in our spiritual life to imitate Christ in all His human perfection (1 Cor 11:1).

REJOICING

Another important antidote to envy is to acquire the habit of rejoicing over the good fortune and possessions of our neighbor. A Catholic author notes that,

> such rejoicing is an indication of real charity, it promotes peace in families and communities, it makes one's life happier, and it helps one practice many other virtues. One who rejoices over a neighbor's success is not likely to live beyond his own means nor pretend to be something that he isn't. He will be cooperative and gracious in his dealings with others and will not be overly sensitive or imagine slights and offenses when none are intended. In short, he will be a magnanimous person who rises above the meanness, pettiness, backbiting, and brooding, which pervade so much of the human race.

The *Catechism of the Catholic Church* remarks, "Envy often comes from pride; the baptized person should train himself to live in humility" (CCC 2540). The *Catechism* quotes Saint John Chrysostom, "Would you like to see God glorified by you? Then rejoice in your brother's progress and you will immediately give glory to God. Because his servant could conquer envy by rejoicing in the merits of others, God will be praised."[195]

The *Catechism* reminds us that "The precept of detachment from riches is obligatory for entrance into the Kingdom of heaven" (CCC 2544). Saint Augustine says, "Let the proud seek and love earthly kingdoms, but blessed are the poor in spirit for theirs is the Kingdom of heaven."[196] Saint Paul tells us in the New Testament that "Our Lord Jesus Christ,... though he was rich, yet for your sake he became poor, so that by his poverty you might become rich" (2 Cor 8:9).

OCTOBER 17, 2003

[1] Congregation for the Doctrine of the Faith, declaration *Dominus Iesus*, no. 15.

[2] Ibid., no. 14.

[3] John Henry Newman, An Essay on the Development of Christian Doctrine, chap. 8, sec. 1, § 1.

[4] *Nostra aetate*, no. 2.

[5] Ibid.

[6] *Dominus Iesus*, no. 12, quoting John Paul II, encyclical *Redemptoris missio*, no. 5.

[7] *Lumen gentium*, no. 8, § 1; quoted by CCC 771.

[8] Henri de Lubac, *The Splendor of the Church*, trans. Michael Mason (San Francisco: Ignatius Press, 1999), p. 88. (Hereafter abbreviated LSC.)

[9] *Lumen gentium*, no. 8; quoted by CCC 771.

[10] *Sacrosanctum concilium*, no. 2; quoted by CCC 771.

[11] Saint Bernard of Clairvaux, *In Cant. Sermo* 27:14: PL 183:920D; quoted by CCC 771.

[12] Saint Augustine, *Sermo* 267, 4: PL 38, 1231D; quoted by CCC 797.

[13] Saint Irenaeus, *Adversus haereses* 3, 24, 1: PG 7/1, 966; quoted by CCC 797.

[14] Pius XII, encyclical *Mystici Corporis*: DS 3808; quoted by CCC 797.

[15] Saint Thomas Aquinas, *Summa Theologiae* III, 48, 2; quoted by CCC 795.

[16] Pope Saint Gregory the Great, *Moralia in Job, praef.*, 14: PL 75, 525 A; quoted by CCC 795.

[17] Saint Augustine, *In evangelium Johannis tractatus* 21, 8: PL 35, 1568; quoted by CCC 795.

[18] Saint Augustine, *Enarrationes in Psalmos* 74:4: PL 36, 948–49; quoted by CCC 796.

[19] *Hom.* 3 (PL, 1048b–c); quoted by LSC 325–26.

[20] Honorius of Autun, *Sigillum beatae Maria* (PL 172 499d); quoted by LSC 322–23.

[21] Saint Cyril of Jerusalem, *Catechesis* 18, chap. 24; quoted by LSC 103.

[22] Saint Gregory the Great, *In Ezech.*, bk. 2, no. 10; quoted by LSC 79.

[23] LSC 79, referring to Saint Augustine, *Sermo* 181, no. 7.

[24] LSC 31, quoting Saint Albert the Great, *De sacrificio Missae*, bk. 2, chap. 9, a. 9.

[25] *Lumen gentium*, no. 7; quoted by CCC 788.

[26] Pius XII, encyclical *Mystici Corporis Christi*, no. 54.

[27] Ibid., no. 57, quoting Leo XIII, *A.S.S.* 29:650.

[28] Pius XII, *Mystici Corporis Christi*, no. 57.

[29] Ibid., no. 56.

[30] Ibid., no. 76.

[31] Ibid., no. 40.

[32] Ibid., no. 41.

[33] Ibid., no. 91.

[34] LSC 47.

[35] Saint Hippolytus, *Traditio apostolica* 35: Sch 11, 118; quoted in CCC 749.

[36] Saint Clement of Alexandria, *Paedogogus* 1, 6, 27: PG 8, 281; quoted in CCC 760.

[37] *Pastor Hermae*, Vision 2, 4, 1: PG 2, 899; cf. Aristides, *Apol.* 16, 6; St. Justin, *Apol.* 2, 7: PG 6, 456; Tertullian, *Apol.* 31, 3; 32, 1: PL 1, 508–9; quoted in CCC 760.

[38] Cf. Saint Epiphanius, *Panarion* 1,1,5; PG 41, 181C; quoted in CCC 760.

[39] *Lumen gentium*, no. 1.

[40] CCC 776, quoting *Lumen gentium*, no. 9, § 2, no. 48, § 2; *Gaudium et spes*, no. 45, § 1.

[41] CCC 776, quoting Paul VI, June 22, 1973; *Ad gentes*, no. 7, § 2; cf. *Lumen gentium*, no. 17.

[42] *Lumen gentium*, no. 8, § 1; quoted by CCC 771.

[43] *Sacrosanctum concilium*, no. 2; quoted by CCC 771.

[44] *Lumen gentium*, no. 8.

[45] Saint Bernard of Clairvaux, *In Cant. Sermo* 27:14: PL 183:920D; quoted in CCC 771.

[46] John Henry Newman, Discourse 13, "Mysteries of Nature and of Grace", *Discourses Addressed to Mixed Congregations* (1849).

[47] Orestes Brownson, *The American Republic* (New York, 1866), chap. 15.

[48] Pius XII, *Mystici Corporis Christi*, no. 91.

[49] John Paul II, *Crossing the Threshold of Hope* (New York: Knopf, 1995), p. 174.

[50] LSC 49, quoting Bossuet.

[51] Ibid., no. 142.

[52] LSC 49–50.

[53] LSC 46, quoting the First Vatican Council, constitution *De fide catholica*, chap. 3.

[54] LSC 46.

[55] Ibid., quoting the First Vatican Council, constitution *De fide catholica*.

[56] Ibid., referring to Alain of Lille, *Sententiae*.

[57] *The Documents of Vatican II*, ed. By Walter M. Abbot (New York, 1966), *Lumen gentium*, chap. 1, no. 1.

[58] Paul VI, address at opening of the Second Session of the Second Vatican Council (September 29, 1963).

[59] *Lumen gentium*, no. 8.

[60] LSC 104.

[61] LSC 106, quoting *Mystici Corporis Christi*, no. 17.

[62] John Paul II, apostolic letter *Mulieris dignitatem* (August 15, 1988), no. 27, quoted in CCC 773.

[63] *Lumen gentium*, no. 5, quoted by CCC 768.

[64] *Lumen gentium*, no. 6; quoted by CCC 754.

[65] Ibid.; quoted by CCC 755.

[66] Ibid.; quoted by CCC 757.

[67] *Lumen gentium*, no. 6.

[68] Ibid.; quoted by CCC 756.

[69] Ibid.

[70] Saint Augustine, *In evangelium Johannis tractatus* 21, 8: PL 35, 1568; quoted by CCC 795.

[71] Saint Thomas Aquinas, *Summa Theologiae* III, 48, 2; quoted by CCC 795.

[72] Pope Saint Gregory the Great, *Moralia in Job, praef.*, 14: PL 75, 525 A; quoted by CCC 795.

[73] *Acts of the Trial of Joan of Arc*; quoted by CCC 795.

[74] John Paul II, "The Church Is the Body of Christ", General Audience of November 20, 1991, *L'Osservatore Romano*, no. 47 (November 25, 1991): 3, nos. 1, 5.

[75] Pius XII, *Mystici Corporis Christi*, no. 1.

[76] Ibid., no. 3.

[77] Ibid., no. 14, quoting Leo XIII, *Satis cognitum*, no. 3.

[78] Pius XII, *Mystici Corporis Christi*, no. 13.

[79] John Paul II, "Christ and Church are Inseparable", July 24, 1991, *L'Osservatore Romano*, no. 30 (July 29, 1991): 7, no. 3.

[80] Ibid., no. 6.

[81] Ibid.

[82] Saint Cyprian, *De unitate ecclesiae*, no. 6.

[83] Pius XII, *Mystici Corporis Christi*, no. 36.

[84] Ibid., no. 37.

[85] Ibid.

[86] Ibid., no. 45.

[87] Ibid., no. 47.

[88] Ibid., no. 48.

[89] Ibid.

[90] Ibid., no. 49.

[91] Ibid., no. 44.

[92] *Lumen gentium*, no. 7; quoted by CCC 790.

[93] Pius XII, encyclical *Mystici Corporis Christi*, no. 57, quoting Leo XIII, *A.S.S.* 29:650.

[94] Ibid., no. 57.

[95] *Lumen gentium*, no. 4.

[96] Leo XIII, encyclical *Divinum illud*; quoted by Pius XII, *Mystici Corporis Christi*, no. 26.

[97] Pius XII, *Mystici Corporis Christi*, no. 26.

[98] *Lumen gentium*, no. 9.

[99] Ibid.

[100] Ibid.

[101] John Paul II, "The Church Is the New People of God", General Audience of November 6, 1991, *L'Osservatore Romano*, no. 45 (November 11, 1991): 11, no. 5.

[102] LSC 209–10.

[103] LSC 278.

[104] Paul VI, motu propio *Credo of the People of God* (June 30, 1968), no. 1.

[105] Ibid., no. 19.

[106] Ibid., nos. 20–21, 23.

[107] LSC 278.

[108] *Lumen gentium*, no. 8, quoting Saint Augustine, *De civitate Dei* XVIII, 51, 2.

[109] Ibid., no. 1.

[110] Pope Pius XII, *Mystici Corporis Christi*, no. 14.

[111] *Sacrosanctum concilium*, no. 2; quoted by CCC 771.

[112] John Paul II, "The Birth of the Church at Pentecost", General Audience of October 2, 1991, *L'Osservatore Romano*, no. 40 (October 7, 1991): 11, no. 4.

[113] Pius XII, *Mystici Corporis Christi*, no. 17.

[114] Saint Clement of Alexandria, *Paedagogus* 1, 6, 27: PG 8, 281; quoted by CCC 760.

[115] Cf. Saint Epiphanius, *Panarion*, 1, 1, 5: PG 41, 181C.

[116] Cf. Saint Ambrose, *In Luc.* 2, 85–89: PL 15, 1666–68.

[117] *Sacrosanctum concilium*, no. 5; quoted by CCC 766.

[118] *Lumen gentium*, no. 3; cf. Jn 19:34; quoted by CCC 766.

[119] Ibid., no. 4; cf. Jn 17:4; quoted by CCC 767.

[120] *Ad gentes*, no. 4; quoted by CCC 767.

[121] *Lumen gentium*, no. 5; quoted by CCC 763.

[122] CCC 763, quoting *Lumen gentium*, no. 3.

[123] *Lumen gentium*, no. 5; quoted by CCC 764.

[124] CCC 764, quoting *Lumen gentium*, no. 5.

[125] *Lumen gentium*, no. 5.

[126] Congregation for the Doctrine of the Faith, declaration *Dominus Iesus* (August 6, 2000), nos. 18–19.

[127] John Paul II, encyclical *Redemptoris missio* (July 12, 1990), no. 18.

[128] Ibid., no. 20.

[129] *Lumen gentium*, no. 3; quoted by CCC 541.

[130] John Henry Newman, *Essay on the Development of Christian Doctrine*, chap. 8, sect.1, § 1.

[131] *Dignitatis humanae*, no. 1.

[132] Ibid.

[133] Congregation for the Doctrine of the Faith, *Dominus Iesus*, no. 16.

[134] *Lumen gentium*, no. 8.

[135] Congregation for the Doctrine of the Faith, *Dominus Iesus*, no. 56.

[136] Ibid., no. 16.

[137] Ibid.

[138] Saint Ignatius of Antioch, *Epistle to the Smyrnaeans*, chap. 8.

[139] Saint Ambrose, *Enarrationes in XII Psalmos Davidicos* 40, 30.

[140] Saint Augustine, *Contra epistolam Manichaei quam vocant fundamenti* 4.

[141] Saint Pacian, *First Letter to Sumronian*, no. 7.

[142] Newman, *Essay on the Development of Christian Doctrine*, chap. 6, sect. 2, no. 6.

[143] Ibid.

[144] Paul VI, apostolic exhortation *Evangelii nuntiandi* (December 8, 1975), no. 62; quoted by CCC 835.

[145] Saint Irenaeus, *Adversus haereses* 3, 3, 2: PG 7/1, 849; cf. Vatican Council I: DS 3057; quoted by CCC 834.

[146] Saint Maximus the Confessor, *Opuscula theo.*: PG 91: 137–40; quoted by CCC 834.

[147] Congregation for the Doctrine of the Faith, *Letter to the Bishops of the Catholic Church on Some Aspects of the Church Understood as Communion* (May 28, 1992), no. 7.

[148] *Lumen gentium*, no. 26; quoted by CCC 832.

[149] Congregation for the Doctrine of the Faith, *Letter to the Bishops*, nos. 8–10.

[150] *Dei Verbum*, no. 10.

[151] Ibid., no. 12, § 3, quoted by CCC 111.

[152] Saint Augustine, *De sermone Domini in monte* 1, 1: PL 34, 1229–30; quoted by CCC 1966.

[153] CCC 1989, quoting the Council of Trent (1547): DS 1528.

[154] Council of Trent (1547): DS 1525; quoted by CCC 1993.

[155] *Lumen gentium*, no. 24; quoted by CCC 2068.

[156] Saint Ignatius of Antioch, *Letter to the Ephesians*, chap. 14, no. 1.

[157] John Henry Newman, discourse 9, "Illuminating Grace", *Discourses to Mixed*

Congregations (1849).

[158] First Vatican Council, sess. 3, cap. 3.

[159] Saint Teresa of Avila, *Exclamaciones del alma a Dios* 15:3; quoted by CCC 1821.

[160] Saint Augustine, *De civitate Dei* 10, 6: PL 41, 283; quoted by CCC 2099.

[161] *Dignitatis humane*, no. 1, § 2; quoted by CCC 2104.

[162] Saint Irenaeus, *Adversus haereses* 4, 16, 3–4: PG 7/1, 1017–18; quoted by CCC 2063.

[163] CCC 2068; cf. DS 1569–70.

[164] Saint Peter Chrysologus, *Sermo* 71, 4: PL 52: 402A; cf. Rom 2:24; Ezek 36:20–22; quoted by CCC 2814.

[165] John Henry Newman, "The Strictness of the Law of Christ", *Parochial and Plain Sermons*, IV, 1 (San Francisco: Ignatius Press, 1997), p. 740.

[166] Saint Thomas More, *A Dialogue of Comfort against Tribulation* 3, 11.

[167] Leo XIII, encyclical *Sapientiae Christianae* (January 10, 1890), no. 8.

[168] Leo XIII, encyclical *Liberatas praestantissimum* (June 20, 1888), no. 30.

[169] Saint Augustine, *De civitate Dei* 19, 13, 1: PL 41, 640; quoted by CCC 2304.

[170] Leo XIII, *Libertas*, no. 13.

[171] Leo XIII, *Sapientiae*, no. 9.

[172] CCC 2258, quoting Congregation for the Doctrine of the Faith, instruction, *Donum vitae*, intro. 5.

[173] *Gaudium et spes*, no. 81, § 3; quoted by CCC 2329.

[174] John Paul II, encyclical *Evangelium vitae* (March 25, 1995), no. 73.

[175] Ibid., no. 84.

[176] Ibid.

[177] Ibid., no. 66.

[178] Ibid.

[179] Ibid., no. 67, quoting *Gaudium et spes*, no. 18.

[180] Leo XIII, encyclical *Rerum novarum* (May 15, 1891), no. 11.

[181] Ibid., no. 22.

[182] *Gaudium et spes*, no. 69, § 1; quoted by CCC 2404.

[183] Quoted in P. Hansen, *Vita mirabilis* (Louvain, 1668); quoted by CCC 2449.

[184] Saint Gregory the Great, *Regula Pastoralis* 3, 21: PL 77, 87; quoted by CCC 2446.

[185] Leo XIII, *Rerum novarum*, no. 22.

[186] Saint Thomas Aquinas, *Summa Theologiae* II–II, 109, 3 ad 1; quoted by CCC 2469.

[187] CCC 2469, quoting ibid., 3, corp. art.

[188] Saint Augustine, *De mendacio* 4, 5: PL 40, 491; quoted by CCC 2482.

[189] Robert Burns, "Address to the Unco Guid".

[190] CCC 2490, quoting CIC, can. 983 § 1.

[191] Saint Augustine, *Confessions* 6, 11, 20: PL 32, 729–30; quoted by CCC 2520.

[192] *Gaudium et spes*, no. 58, § 4; quoted by CCC 2527.

[193] *Roman Catechism* III, 37; quoted by CCC 2536.

[194] Cf. Pope Saint Gregory the Great, *Moralia in Job* 31, 45: PL 76, 621; quoted by CCC 2539.

[195] Saint John Chrysostom, *Homiliae in ad Romanos* 71, 5: PG 60, 448; quoted by CCC 2540.

[196] Saint Augustine, *De sermone Domini in monte* 1, 1, 3: PL 34, 1232; quoted by CCC 2547.

Part Five

CATECHETICS AND CATHOLIC SCHOOLS

CATECHETICS

Sound Catechetics
I

The beginning of the academic year for our Catholic schools and the coming celebration of Catechetical Sunday in the middle of this month make this time of year a fine occasion to recall to our Catholic community the vital necessity of imparting to our children and youth a solid and sound grasp of the truths of our Catholic faith. Not only priests, religious educators, and catechists, but above all Catholic parents must see to their responsibility, as an obligation in Christian charity and justice, to impart an appropriate knowledge of the contents of our faith to those in their care. The beautiful and important vocation of parenthood is accompanied by a serious duty before God to answer to Him not only for the material well-being of children and youth, but most of all for their spiritual health and for the safety and salvation of their souls.

The emptiness and deficiencies of so much catechesis in so many places in the past unfortunately have left many Catholic parents themselves gravely impaired and challenged in their own grasp of the doctrines and moral teaching of the Church, and thus they are not able to participate as they ought in the catechetical formation of their offspring.

CULTURAL

Religious illiteracy and catechetical ignorance seem to infect a significant number of contemporary Catholics in our country. It is amazing to encounter numbers of merely "cultural or nominal Catholics", even beyond the well-known "Easter and Christmas Catholics", who are unaware of enormous parts of the beautiful gospel message. Sometimes they imbibe what they know about religion from Protestant or other non-Catholic media presentations, but most often they have allowed themselves to be trained and formed by the secular culture in which they are immersed. Fear of offending and fear of excluding, tolerance of everything at any cost, an ardent desire to be modern and up-to-date, and a deep wish to be accepted by non-Catholic elements in society thought to be influential are frequently the motivation for them to bypass or ignore the fullness of religious truth. Sometimes, too, a sincere desire to inculturate truth actually results in their distorting or diluting truth.

Both the secular entertainment media and the information media in America are generally quite hostile to any concept of moral absolutes or to any claims of religious certitude. This clearly influences many Catholics, especially those for whom their religion is, at best, on the periphery of their daily lives. Unless Catholic adults, especially parents, are themselves converted and well catechized, even the best efforts of Catholic schoolteachers and CCD teachers will rarely have the good and needed effects in the lives and thoughts of Catholic children and youth that are indispensable for their eternal happiness.

INSTRUMENTS

One of the best means by which conscientious Catholic parents can inform themselves and thus equip themselves for carrying out their primary and indispensable role as the main educators of their children is the reading and study of the *Catechism of the Catholic Church*. When they themselves are well informed, parents will be in a better position to assist their children and youth in their catechetical formation. It is not enough for Catholic parents merely to entrust their children to Catholic schools or, where these are lacking, to the parish programs of the Confraternity of Christian Doctrine (CCD), important as that is, but they themselves should take a personal interest in their children's teachers and in what is being taught. Enrolling children and youth in catechetical programs and ensuring their regular attendance at the classes are so important that parents should not allow themselves to be persuaded (children and especially high-school age youngsters can be very persuasive in these matters) to refrain from insisting on these.

The Bishops of the United States a short time ago established a committee to "oversee the use of the *Catechism of the Catholic Church*". In checking on the conformity to Catholic truth of the various catechisms and other religious educational material currently used in our country, that committee found occasional errors, but more often they found "a pattern of doctrinal deficiencies", that is, a pattern of essential things "left out", or they discovered issues treated in insufficient completeness and depth. I believe that it is fair to say that those deficiencies are also imbedded in our American catechetical knowledge, that of both adults and children.

DEFICIENCIES

The Bishops' committee, headed by Archbishop Daniel Buechlein of Indianapolis, lists various areas where modern catechesis in our country seriously needs improvement.[1] The committee says, for a start that, "there is insufficient attention to the Trinity and the Trinitarian structure of Catholic belief and teaching." Some of this derives from an excessive "gender sensitivity", even a refusal to use the names given in divine revelation to the first and second Persons of the Most Blessed Trinity, thus obscuring the reality of God's revelation of His innermost life and making unclear the Trinitarian nature of our prayer, especially our liturgical prayer. The supernatural mystery of the relationship of the utter oneness of God with the three Persons of the Holy Trinity very often is inadequately contemplated and held.

The committee also notes a pattern of insufficiency in the teaching about original sin and its effects as well as about sin in general. It is often not seen how the doctrine of original sin alone makes comprehensible other doctrines, such as those regarding grace, Baptism, redemption, concupiscence, and so on. An understanding of the loss of holiness and original justice caused by original sin, of the transmission of this sin of our first parents in every human conception and birth, and of the profound spiritual wounds that it causes to abide in every human being is often lost in the fatuous and false modern idea of fallen humanity's capacity to reach perfection without redemption by Jesus Christ. Sometimes original sin in the popular imagination is reduced to a simple matter of "bad example", obscuring its true and ugly reality. A glance at these noted deficiencies could stimulate a personal interest in renewing and reviewing our catechetical knowledge.

SEPTEMBER 6, 2002

Sound Catechetics
II

CHRISTOCENTRIC

One of the serious deficiencies in contemporary American Catholic religious instruction often is a failure adequately to present Jesus Christ as the center of all Sacred Scripture and Sacred Tradition, the culmination of the Old Testament and the fulfillment of God's plan for human salvation, God's definitive, final Word, and the complete revelation and gift of Himself. Sometimes, too, there is a grave imbalance in teaching about our Lord, when His roles as our divine Savior is overshadowed excessively by His other role as our unique Teacher, Master, Model, Brother, and Friend.

Instruction about the liturgy, the official public worship of the Church, easily can be defective in these cases, since the liturgy, especially the core of the liturgy that is the Mass, only makes sense when seen as the adoration, praise, and thanksgiving offered to God the Father by the "whole Christ", Head and members, through the working of the Holy Spirit.   Not being fully aware of the ongoing supernatural and spiritual union of the members of the Catholic Church with Christ, the invisible and perennial Head of the Church that He founded, leads to "yawning at the Mass".

Also, the American Bishops have noticed a frequent modern insufficiency in the presentation of the Incarnation, the hypostatic union in the one Divine Person of Jesus of Nazareth of a truly human nature and a truly divine nature. Sometimes Jesus is not adequately presented as truly man, like us in all things but sin, but more often it is the case that His divinity, as the second Person of the Blessed Trinity, is not properly understood and taught. A kind of heretical neo-Arianism is not infrequent in the thought of some people, which is then imparted in faulty catechetics to children and youth.

ONE AND ONLY

In a society and culture that is pluralistic and tolerant, where we Catholics are in a minority, there is always a strong temptation to conform to the dominant attitude, to try to find acceptance and show liberal-mindedness, and to avoid offending Jews, Muslims, pagans, and other non-Christians among whom we must live and work by avoiding the mention of Jesus or by disclaiming Him as the one and only means of human salvation. Sometimes also there can be shame because of the noisy anti-intellectual and mistaken religious enthusiasms of some fundamentalist Protestants, leading to our embarrassment over accepting and proclaiming the vitally important words of our first Pope about Jesus: "And there is salvation in no one else, for there is no other name under heaven given among men by which we must be saved" (Acts 4:12).

Lukewarm faith and defective catechetics induce many modern Christians rather to imitate Peter at Christ's Passion when he denied our Lord: "I do not know this man of whom you speak!" (Mk 14:71). It is well known that public education in our country is rapidly becoming totally godless. While adverting to the right of freedom of speech allows the government schools to teach and discuss the doctrines of Hitler, Stalin, Marx, and so on, the ACLU and similar groups try to make sure that Jesus and the truths of the Gospel can never be mentioned favorably in those State-controlled institutions.

PELAGIANISM

The Bishops' committee on the use of the *Catechism*, headed by Archbishop

Daniel Buechlein, in criticizing some aspects of modern catechetics, also says, "There is a trend that gives insufficient emphasis to God's initiative in the world, with a corresponding overemphasis on human action." The English monk and heretic Pelagius (who lived from A.D. 355 to 425) taught that Jesus merely left us His teachings and a good example and that, using them, human beings had to get to heaven by their own doing, an old and enduring religious error. (See the story of Babel in Genesis 11:1–9.) There can be temptations even now in that direction, neglecting the human being's absolute need to have God's grace in order to be able to obey the commandments, in order to cooperate, as free creatures ought, with God's free and undeserved gift of salvation, and in order to persevere in it and thus get to heaven.

When there is a methodological imbalance in catechetics, the impression can be given to children and youth that God's action and initiatives only follow human experience and action and that God's initiative is somehow subordinate to the actions and undertakings of His creatures. There could be an eclipse of the reality of the revelation about the essential need for unearned actual grace in order to be saved. That revelation is found plentifully in the New Testament (Gal 5:4; Rom 3:24; 4:4; 5:12–21; 6:14; Eph 1:6; and so on).

DIVINE NATURE

Sanctifying grace, which is a created share in the life of God, a participation in His very nature (2 Pet 1:4), is not always properly and adequately explained. Sometimes simply called "God's love" or "God's favor", it is often not treated in catechetics as it should be, namely, in a central way, as a result of an initiative by God, through the death and Resurrection of Jesus, to introduce a human person into the deepest intimacy of the Holy Trinity. The relationship of sanctifying grace, its reception, retention, growth, and regaining in case of loss, and how all this is related to the paschal mystery of Christ, to the seven sacraments of the Church, and to obtaining eternal salvation often remains, unfortunately, too obscure in the minds and hearts of today's Catholic children and youth. The truth that the preparation of a human person for this sanctifying grace is in itself a work of actual grace often is not clearly presented.

The absolute and utter gratuity of the supernatural order, including the supernatural gift and act of faith, frequently is not presented well. At the same time, the need for apologetics, especially for older children and youths, presenting the rational and logical arguments for the truths of the Catholic faith and showing how reason, when correctly used, leads inevitably to the acceptance of these truths has not been seen in recent times, perhaps out of human respect. While logical and rational apologetic processes can and should lead a person to the brink of faith, showing it to be in accord with reason to believe and a violation of reason not to believe, the "leap of faith" itself must ever be seen, not as a "human work", but as a grace from God.

SEPTEMBER 13, 2002

Sound Catechetics
III

DOCUMENTS

Those who are or who ought to be concerned with imparting sound Catholic doctrine and correct Christian moral teaching should have some familiarity with the more important documents that have been issued by the Holy See in recent times touching on religious education. In addition to the *Catechism of the Catholic Church*, first issued in English in 1997 and issued in a second English-language edition in 2000, the *General Catechetical Directory*, published in English in 1997, along with the 1979 apostolic exhortation of Pope John Paul II *Catechesi tradendae* should probably lead any list of documents to be known, studied, and used for reference. The *General Catechetical Directory* also contains a rather thorough bibliography of other significant and helpful documents in catechetics.

The United States Conference of Catholic Bishops is currently working on producing a new *National Catechetical Directory* for our country as well as a new *Catechism for Adults*. Even before such work is finished, however, one can easily find an abundance of solid Catholic material available now, all updated in accordance with the Second Vatican Council, which should enable any previous defects or lack of completeness in catechesis to be remedied by conscientious Catholic parents and teachers.

CHURCH

It has been noticed that sometimes in previous catechetical presentations the emphasis on the Church's catholicity and diversity appeared to eclipse a needed emphasis on her unity in faith, government, and worship, as this is willed by Christ, her Founder, just as the emphasis on her as a uniquely warm and welcoming community often has eclipsed proper catechesis about her missionary and magisterial roles.

The attribute of Church authority, resting by divine design exclusively in the hierarchy of the Catholic Church, is sometimes not taught as the extension of the presence and mission of Jesus in the world. "He who hears you hears me, and he who rejects you rejects me, and he who rejects me rejects him who sent me" (Lk 10:16). For older children and youth, there is often no clear teaching, as there should be, about how intellectual dissent from Church doctrine, moral instruction, and Church order can be a serious sin against Church unity, against faith, and a source of scandal, or about the fact that such dissent serves to place the dissenter in grave peril of his eternal salvation.

MORALS

A meager exposition of Christian moral life and the moral demands of following the Gospel has sometimes marred catechetical work in the recent past. Personal identity, self-esteem, self respect, and pragmatism were too often falsely supposed to be primary sources of morality. The supreme objective criteria for morality, that is, natural, positive, divine, and Church laws, as well as the binding force for Catholic consciences of the Church's moral teaching in certain areas were often inadequately treated. The need for human beings to use their free will to cooperate with God's grace and to obey those laws as the price of their everlasting happiness sometimes was insufficiently presented. Also, a mistaken understanding of the supremacy of personal conscience, the subjective criterion for morality, was often conveyed, neglecting especially the possibility of a person possessing an erroneous conscience that could lead to damnation and the necessity for human beings to work humbly and constantly to form their consciences correctly in accordance with God's will as manifested through Christ's one true Church.

ESCHATOLOGY

A lack of precision in catechetics in the recent past has also occasionally led to an inadequate treatment of the ultimate realities of heaven and hell, death and judgment, and the truth of purgatory. The transcendent, transtemporal, and transhistorical nature of the kingdom of God "was not always present".[2] The good practice of teaching the Church's social justice doctrine can sometimes lead to a faulty overshadowing of Saint Paul's words, "If for this life only we have hoped in Christ, we are of all men most to be pitied" (1 Cor 15:19), and the teaching of the Epistle to the Hebrews, "For here we have no lasting city, but we seek the city which is to come" (Heb 13:14). Archbishop Buechlein observes that the "eschatological dimensions of the Beatitudes as well as of the moral and sacramental orders are not always adequately taught." Contemporary society tends to consider such teachings passé, hence not plausible to modern people.

SACRAMENTS

It is of great importance when instructing children and youth about the sacraments to make certain that those seven efficacious signs instituted by Christ are situated by our catechetical teaching in the Lord's paschal mystery and are presented as the unique means by which the Holy Spirit makes human beings capable of sharing a new heavenly life in Christ, as a result of His dying and rising. The sacraments are not merely important human events marking the milestones of one's life; rather, they are saving encounters with the risen Savior, bringing about, through divine action, a "graced transformation" of the recipient. Seeing the sacraments as sublime acts of worship and adoration is vital to understanding them correctly.

The essential character and role of the ordained minister in sacramental actions in the life of the Christian community and the absolute centrality of the Holy Eucharist as the summit and source of the whole sacramental system are occasionally distorted in the way they are explained. The historical right and duty of the Church's hierarchy to regulate and legislate about sacramental validity and legality and to determine when and if sacraments are valid and/or licit always should be presented with clarity and properly explained.

Finally, we should remember that how we pray and worship affects our beliefs, just as our beliefs affect how we pray and worship (*Lex orandi est lex credendi*). Successful and sound catechesis is not possible without being integrated into the official prayer life of the Church, that is, into the sacred liturgy and into the private prayer life of every student and teacher. It is only in that context that one never forgets that divine truth is not our property, that it belongs to God and is guarded by the Church Christ founded.

SEPTEMBER 20, 2002

2

CATHOLIC SCHOOLS

Our Schools

THE QUEST

The coming annual celebration of Catholic Schools Week in our country provides thoughtful Catholic people with an opportunity to reflect on our Catholic schools, to see better why so many of the Church's resources in our nation and in our own Diocese are devoted to those institutions, and to grasp a deeper understanding of what is behind their establishment and maintenance.

There is almost no place where the intersection and interaction between faith and reason, religion and science, the secular world and the Church, can be better seen or more successfully confronted than in genuine Catholic schools. They give a chance for conscientious Catholic parents to start out their children and adolescents on that path of life which can enable them to find the correct and vital answers to the great questions that normally abide deep in the heart of every human being: Who am I? Where have I come from? Where am I going? Why is there evil? What is there, if anything, after this life on earth? Does human existence have a purpose; can I know it for certain; and what is it? If such a purpose exists, what can or must I do to achieve it?

In his encyclical letter *Faith and Reason*, our Holy Father, Pope John Paul II, remarks that prominent among the different ways that the Catholic Church is commissioned to serve humanity by Jesus, her divine Founder, Who is the Way, the Truth, and the Life (Jn 14:6), is the "*diakonia* [service] of the truth".[3] He says, "Being responsible for that truth means loving it and seeking the most exact understanding of it, in order to bring it closer to ourselves and others in all its saving power, its splendor, and its profundity joined with simplicity."[4] In some ways, this describes a Catholic school.

COUNCIL

The Second Vatican Council proclaims,

> The influence of the Church in the field of education is shown in a special manner by the Catholic school. No less than other schools does the Catholic school pursue cultural goals and the human formation of youth. But its proper function is to create for

the school community a special atmosphere animated by the Gospel spirit of freedom and charity, to help youth grow according to the new creatures they were made through baptism as they develop their personalities, and finally to order the whole of human culture to the news of salvation so that the knowledge the students gradually acquire of the world, life and man is illumined by faith.[5]

The Council states that Catholic schools aim at preparing young people to serve "the good of the earthly city", while at the same time teaching and inspiring them to serve "the spread of the Kingdom of God", so that "by leading an exemplary apostolic life, [a Catholic graduate can] become, as it were, a saving leaven in the human community."[6]

OUR HISTORY

In various parts of the world there are a variety of reasons for the existence of Catholic schools. In our own United States, there were, in our early history, no public schools. In some places, especially in frontier communities, Catholic schools were established where otherwise there would have been no schools. However, the basic reason for our numerous American Catholic schools derives from the orientation of the earlier government schools. After the general establishment of tax-supported public schools, which coincided with a vast Catholic immigration wave, the Bishops of the United States noticed many newly arrived Catholics losing their faith or having it weakened because the public schools they were forced to attend were basically Protestant institutions, using non-Catholic and even anti-Catholic textbooks, prayers, Bible versions, and so on. Even those few that were not in that line were often permeated with false and dangerous philosophies, such as the teachings of John Dewey.

Under the impact of the powerful and pervasive secular humanist religion, of the growth, if not in percentage of population, then in the political influence of non-Christians, of many anti-religious judicial decisions, and of the increased spirit of religious indifference, agnosticism, and relativism (the erroneous view that one religion is as good as another or that religion is merely a matter of one's personal taste or opinion), our State-run schools, in their secularized eagerness to accommodate our pluralistic society, currently have become, no longer Protestant, but rather covertly or even overtly hostile to Christ and the truth of His gospel. Jesus, of course, and His Church and His grace must be central to the thoughts and hearts of all Catholic parents. This is why, more than ever before, concerned Catholic parents, who realize their responsibility for the eternal salvation of the souls of their offspring, choose to establish and support Catholic schools.

True Freedom

I believe it was Anatole France who said, "Behold the equality of the laws of France. They equally forbid both rich people and poor people from sleeping under the bridges of Paris at night." This comes to mind when facing the fact that while Catholic parents are theoretically free in our land to send their youngsters to Catholic schools, in practice this is for many of them an impossibility. Their heavy school taxes can be used only for the secular (and godless) government schools, and these parents simply do not have the economic means to build and maintain Catholic schools. Although such things as school vouchers and tuition tax credits have been found compatible with our American constitutional arrangements, their enactment is almost always vigorously opposed by teachers' unions and the public school establishment, which are terrified by any thought of competition and see anything less than total and absolute government control and monopoly in education as a threat. Even the fact that school vouchers would save tax payers huge amounts of money does not deter the emotional opposition.

The Second Vatican Council says, "The Church gives high praise to those civil authorities and civil societies that show regard for the pluralistic character of modern society and take into account the right of religious liberty, by helping families in such a way that in all schools the education of their children can be carried out according to the moral and religious convictions of each family."[7]

JANUARY 24, 2003

[1] Report given to the National Conference of Catholic Bishops in June 1997 by Archbishop Daniel Buechlein, Chairman of the Bishops' Ad Hoc Committee to Oversee the Use of the *Catechism of the Catholic Church*.
[2] Ibid.
[3] John Paul II, encyclical *Fides et ratio* (September 14, 1998), no. 2.
[4] Ibid., no. 1, quoting his encyclical *Redemptor hominis*, no. 17.
[5] *Gravissimum educationis*, no. 8.
[6] Ibid.
[7] Ibid., no. 7.

Part Six

COMMUNION OF SAINTS

1

Saints, Angels and Devotions

Sacramentals

Contrasts

Sacramentals are "little signs" as compared to the sacraments, which are "great signs" or sacred mysteries. Christ instituted the sacraments, whereas the sacramentals were and are instituted by the Church, which Christ founded. There are only seven sacraments, but there are countless sacramentals.

The sacraments always bestow grace if the sign is placed properly by one who has the correct intention and the authority to do so and if there is no impeding obstacle. The sacramentals, in contrast, are only efficacious in imparting grace through the prayer and blessing of the Church and through the fervor and devotion aroused in the one using or receiving them.

The Second Vatican Council teaches, "Holy Mother Church has ... instituted sacramentals. These are sacred signs which bear a resemblance to the sacraments. They signify effects, particularly of a spiritual nature, which are obtained through the intercession of the Church. By them men are disposed to receive the chief effect of the sacraments, and various occasions of life are rendered holy."[1]

Examples

The *Catechism of the Catholic Church* explains that sacramentals are intended to sanctify "certain ministries of the Church, certain states in life, a great variety of circumstances in Christian life, and the use of many things helpful to man" (CCC 1668). They can also be the means to respond to certain cultures, needs, and the history of certain regions and people.

Sacramentals can be objects, such as pictures, statues, crucifixes, rosaries, religious medals, vestments, religious garb, scapulars, holy water, chalk, and things used in the sacred liturgy, such as chalices, patens, other sacred vessels, liturgical books, altars, altar cloths, cruets, incense, holy oils, church furnishings, and the like.

Sacramentals can also be actions or gestures, such as blessings and the ceremonies of Mass and those that surround the celebration of the sacraments. They can include the blessing of abbots and abbesses, the institution in ministries, such as readers and acolytes, the consecration of virgins, the dedication of churches and the consecration of altars, the consecration of bells and the blessing and consecration of the holy oils.

SEASONS

Certain sacramentals are associated with particular days in the liturgical calendar. The blessing and distribution of ashes marks the annual beginning of Lent. Easter food is blessed on Holy Saturday. The palms on Palm Sunday and the newly blessed Easter Water we take home after the Easter Vigil each year mark the end of the yearly paschal celebration. The blessed wafers at Christmas and the Christmas nativity scenes we put up in our churches and houses each year as well as the blessed candles we take to our homes on Candlemas Day are further examples of sacramentals with which we are all familiar.

Many devout Catholic families arrange for a priest to bless their homes each year, especially on or near one of the great "water feasts" of Easter, Pentecost, or Epiphany. Most Catholics ask to have their new car or new home specially blessed, while fervent farmers usually ask for blessing for their seeds, machinery, and fields.

Milestones in life can also be marked by special blessings, such as the blessing of a mother before or after childbirth, the blessing for travelers, or the nuptial blessing at a wedding Mass. The celebration of the fifteenth birthday of children in some Hispanic cultures calls for a special celebration and blessing.

GREAT VARIETY

Sacramentals constitute a wide diversity of actions and objects. Almost every human activity and human artifact can be blessed. The Roman Ritual and Book of Blessings show that gradually all the universe can be touched by the Incarnation of God, reclaimed from the stain and soil of sin, and made holy. There are blessings for offices, factories, streets, roads, occupations, typewriters, airplanes, wine, beer, food of different kinds, and just about everything else that can be imagined.

It is enriching to learn something of the history and meaning of various sacramentals, such as the spirituality associated with wearing the scapular, the story of the miraculous medal, and the origin of the five-decade rosary and the other kinds of rosaries and chaplets in use. In addition to being a means of grace, sacramentals can also have an important didactic function, reminding not only children but also all who encounter and use them of the spiritual dimension involved in human life and destiny.

Holy water, for instance, when used devoutly and with appropriate contrition, can remit venial sins. The stoops at the entrance to a church help us recall that we must approach the Lord in worship with pure hearts and remind us as we enter a building called a "church" that we entered God's Family, called the Church, through the water of Baptism.

ATTITUDE

We should always treat sacramentals with great respect and make frequent use of them. Our use of sacramentals, of course, must avoid anything that even approaches superstition. It would be outrageous and sinful to suppose that some "thing" or "action" could manipulate God or effect, apart from His sovereign will, anything at all.

Catholic homes and families should possess and use sacramentals. While some blessings are reserved to the ordained ministry, even lay people can give certain blessings (for instance, parents can and should bless their children often). Holy water, palms, blessed candles, a crucifix, some sacred pictures and the like should be in every Catholic home. We should remember, however, that just because something is "religious", it is not necessarily beautiful. As much as possible we should avoid tawdry, cheap, and ugly religious artwork. Our esteem for sacramentals and that of others will be enhanced if the objects and actions are in good taste.

AUGUST 1, 1997

Angels

THEIR MONTH

October can be called the month of the holy rosary, since the Feast of Our Lady of the Rosary occurs during it. It is the month with many other special liturgical celebrations as well, such as the Feast of Saint Francis of Assisi and Saint Thérèse of Lisieux. It is also called the month of the Guardian Angels, since on October 2nd each year we have the Feast of the Guardian Angels. Jesus revealed that we each have a guardian angel (Mt 18:10). Pious belief also maintains that nations, institutions, families, schools, parishes, and the like, also each have a guardian angel.

It is a truth of our Catholic faith, a dogma that Catholics must believe, that God created not only the visible world, but also invisible and mighty spirits, called angels, and that He created them before He created the world. We also hold that the angels are personal beings, and not just powers or some type of energy. Three angels mentioned in the Bible have names that we know (the Archangels, Michael,

Raphael, and Gabriel). It is also a defined doctrine that God created Lucifer and the other fallen angels as good and that they became evil through the misuse of their own free will and, thus, are the devils and demons, led by Satan.

Saint Gregory the Great and Saint Augustine point out that the word "angel" (in Hebrew *Malak*) means, in Greek, messenger or ambassador. This indicates more the function of angels, while the word "spirit" denotes their nature. Angels are pure spirits, far above all visible creation. They are endowed with intellects enormously superior to those of humans and also with free will. Untouched by matter, angels are immortal by nature.

REVELATION

The *Catechism of the Catholic Church* tells us, "The existence of the spiritual, non-corporeal beings that Sacred Scripture usually calls 'angels' is a truth of faith. The witness of Scripture is as clear as the unanimity of Tradition" (CCC 328). The *Catechism* reminds us that the angels belong to Christ. They are His angels. This is clear from any reading of the New Testament (Mt 25:31; Col 1:16; Heb 1:14, and so on).

It is generally agreed among theologians that we would not know of the existence of angels if God had not revealed this. God sent them many times in the period of the Old Testament, as He prepared the world for His divine Son, to intervene in human history and in human affairs. Evidence of this can be found in most books of the Old Testament (including Genesis, Deuteronomy, Judges, Kings, Tobit, and so on).

It is in the New Testament that we see most clearly how the existence and function of angels are centered in Jesus. As the *Catechism* puts it, "From the Incarnation to the Ascension, the life of the Word incarnate is surrounded by the adoration and service of angels" (CCC 333).

CHURCH

From the very beginning of the Catholic Church angels played an important role (Acts 5:18–20; 8:2–29; 10:3–8; 12:6–11; and 27:23–25). They continue to give the Church the benefit of their mysterious and powerful help.

In the earthly liturgy (especially the Mass, Liturgy of the Hours, and sacraments), the myriads and myriads of angels in the heavenly court join the Church. While God is being worshipped in and through Christ by His Church on earth, at the same time the great and eternal liturgy of heaven is taking place, involving, along with us, the Church triumphant. This is one of the reasons why, for instance, in the strictest sense of the words, there can never be a "private Mass". Even if a priest is alone when He celebrates the sacred sacrifice or reads the Divine Office, the angels are there to adore with him.

In the course of her official prayers, in both the Latin and Eastern Rites, the Church invokes the intercession and assistance of the angels, begging them to join us in loving and worshipping the thrice-holy God. At the end of each September she celebrates the feast of the great Archangels, and in the funeral liturgy she asks that the angels lead the deceased person's soul into paradise.

APPEARANCES

In the course of the history of salvation, angels have appeared to men and women. They do this by the will of God (or in the case of the devils, by His permission). When they are described in Sacred Scripture, they usually are said to appear as young men, often dressed in white. Whether they actually assume a kind of material reality in their appearances or merely are cast on the human senses by some supernatural act of God is not known.

Artists' conceptions of angels, of course, are total fantasy. Since the Middle Ages they have often been depicted with wings, crowns, haloes, and so forth. Often they are made to look meek and feminine. Sometimes they are shown as plump little babies. Recently films and TV have contributed to various "angelic fantasies and nonsense". All of this sometimes makes modern people relegate angels to the realm of fairy tales, legends, and children's fancy. Sometimes even superstitions can gather around the use of angelic images or doctrine. Sometimes well-meaning people think that dead babies turn into angels. Obviously, care must be taken to use the prayers and friendship of angels in a doctrinally orthodox way.

Adult Catholics should never become so sophisticated that neglect to think about the "invisible" in which they profess to believe at the Creed at Sunday Mass. Perhaps every October we all should again pray as we did as children: "Angel of God, my guardian dear..."

OCTOBER 3, 1997

The Infant of Prague

TWO WAYS

Most of our modern depictions of the Nativity of Jesus (Lk 2:1–20) try to be faithful to the Gospel narrative. The practice of a realistic *presepio* or "creche", or "crib", specially constructed to recall all the obvious circumstances and events surrounding the birth of our Savior, probably can be traced back to the year 1223 at Greccio in Italy, where Saint Francis of Assisi set up such a representation, using hay and straw and a live ox and ass. Brother Thomas of Celano, the friar who wrote about this, says, "There simplicity was honored, poverty was exalted, humility was commended, and Greccio was made, as it were, Bethlehem. The night was lighted up like day and it delighted men and beasts."[2]

In addition to such a depiction of the divine Infant, which has many important aspects for our spiritual enrichment, there was and continues to be another way to depict the Christmas mystery. This second way, which is also quite legitimate and useful, is to look with the eyes of faith beyond external appearances, noting that the Child of Bethlehem, even at His birth, was and is the Lord of the world, the Judge of the living and the dead, the eternal Son of God, the second Person of the Most Blessed Trinity.

FROM SPAIN

In sixteenth-century Spain, the spirituality of the people, deriving in large measure from such great personalities as Saint Teresa of Avila (sometimes called "The Big Flower"), often emphasized this second way of depicting the Infant Redeemer. It was in Spain that the (miraculous) statue of the Infant of Prague originated. It is a wood carving lightly coated with wax. In 1556, Maria Manriquez de Lara, as part of her wedding trousseau, brought the statue from Spain to Bohemia, when she became the bride of the Czech nobleman Vratislav of Pernstyn. Through inheritance the statue passed into the possession of a Princess Polyxena Lobkowitz, who gave it, for safekeeping, to the Discalced Carmelite Fathers at the Church of Our Lady of Victory in Prague in the year 1628, giving them also the garments in which the statue was clothed when it arrived in the Czech lands.

AN APOSTLE

Shortly after the gift of the statue to the Carmelites, a Swedish Protestant army captured Prague and sacked the city, raping and killing the inhabitants. The Carmelites escaped, however, and fled to Munich, Germany. Showing special hatred for Prague's Catholic churches, the Protestants mutilated or destroyed the images and statues they were able to find, and this included the statue of the Infant of Prague. They knocked off its hands and threw it on a trash heap.

There it remained for many years until found and restored, through the heroic efforts of the Carmelite friar Father Cyril of the Mother of God, who returned from Munich when it was again safe for Catholics to live in Prague. He became "an apostle" of devotion to the statue. Praying before the statue one day, he claimed to have heard distinctly the voice of Jesus saying, "Give me My hands, and I will give you peace. The more you honor me, the more will I bless you." Not only did he arrange to have the hands replaced and the statue refurbished and placed in a silver and glass case in a most privileged place in Our Lady of Victory Church in Prague, but until he died in 1675, he promoted and fostered devotion to that image of the divine Infant.

HISTORY

Beginning with the Carmelite friars who have cared for the Church of Our Lady of Victory over the years and who once escaped death during a terrible plague by praying before the statue, devotion to Christ, as depicted in that statue, has given rise to many claims of miraculous cures and miracles of grace. Nobles and commoners, the rich and poor, Czechs and people of almost all other nationalities have attested and even today attest to the spiritual value of devotion to our Lord under His title of Infant of Prague. This devotion is especially appropriate and intense around the Solemnity of the Nativity of Jesus, December 25.

The original chapel that housed the statue was approved, blessed, and consecrated by Ernest Cardinal Harrach, the Archbishop of Prague, in 1648. Many popes down the centuries have fostered devotion to the Infant of Prague, including, in our century, Pope Leo XIII, who founded a Sodality of the Infant of Prague in 1896, and Pope Saint Pius X, who made the Sodality into a Confraternity a short time later.

TODAY

The statue can still be seen today in Prague in its original, restored form. The left hand holds a globe surmounted by a cross, signifying the universal kingship of the newborn "King of the Jews" (Mt 2:2). The right hand is raised in blessing, with the fingers in the traditional way in which the Supreme Pontiff blesses, that is, the two fingers upraised to symbolize the two natures in Christ and the thumb and other two fingers joined to represent the Holy Trinity. The rings on the forefinger are an *ex voto* from a nobleman, Count de la Haye, whose daughter was miraculously cured of a fatal illness before the statue. The jeweled crown is a gift from Prince Ignatius Martinic, who was the Burgrave of Bohemia. Religious sisters from Saint Joseph Church in Mala Strana, as they have done for centuries, still regularly change the vestments on the statue to conform in color to the liturgical seasons of the year.

Devotion to our Lord as the Infant of Prague will help us to remember the marvelous reality beneath the simplicity, the poverty, and the humility of the cave and stable in Bethlehem. It will help us to recall in the days before Christmas that He, Who came once as our Savior, will return one day as our Judge, but in the meanwhile, He remains with us to shelter and heal us with His grace and to fill our hearts with the love that will enable us to recognize Him and to welcome Him properly when He comes.

DECEMBER 19, 1997

2

LIFE OF BLESSEDNESS

Blessed Teresa of Calcutta
I

WHO IS SHE?

On Sunday, October 19, 2003, this year's Mission Sunday, our Holy Father, Pope John Paul II, beatified Mother Teresa, one of the most extraordinary women of the last century. Since the time of her death in 1997, many miracles have been attributed to her intercession, even including one here in our Diocese of Lincoln at the Carmelite Convent in Agnew. She was born in Skopje, Albania, on August 26, 1910, and was named Agnes Gonxha Bojaxhiu. She entered religious life in 1928, taking the religious name Teresa, and was sent to India for her novitiate. She then taught geography there and became the principal of Saint Mary's High School in Calcutta. But, moved by the wretched poverty she saw around her in the Subcontinent, she sought and obtained permission from the Holy See in 1948 to live outside her convent and help the "poorest of the poor".

She became an Indian citizen in 1949 and founded the Missionaries of Charity, opening her first home in India to take care of the homeless, the destitute sick, and the dying. Working for many years in obscurity, she suddenly became well known throughout the world when some rather famous journalists, writers, and celebrities "discovered her and her work". Vocations flocked in (and still do), and she subsequently founded an order of religious brothers in 1966 and an order of contemplative nuns in 1976. She was awarded the Pope John XXIII Peace Prize in 1971 and the Nobel Peace Prize in 1979.

AUTHENTIC

In the 1960s, a cynical media editor in the U.S., a liberal, doubting the things he heard about Mother Teresa, sent two of his fellow cynical liberals to "expose" her "hypocrisy". When they arrived in Calcutta and searched for her, they were surprised to find her helping to unload a group of dying human beings from a cart in which her sisters had collected them from the gutters. They saw her personally take care of the most disgusting of the group, a man from whom she was removing maggots and worms from his open sores and wounds. The stench was terrible, but the journalists were shocked that she was always smiling. They stayed with her for two weeks and were even more astonished that she personally always undertook the worst jobs, like emptying and cleaning bedpans. They were even more dumbfounded by her hours of prayer each day and her simple life-style, sleeping on a mat on the floor and dining only on rice and tea. Even the cynical liberals were convinced she was "real".

She opened houses for the poor in the slums of the entire world, including some in our own country and even in places where Catholic religious were usually not welcomed, such as China, Russia, Yemen, and so on. She and her sisters cared for AIDS patients, prostitutes, drug addicts, battered women, unwanted babies, the starving, the homeless, and the most destitute of humanity.

HER WORDS

Blessed Teresa said,

> We have all been created for greater things—to love and be loved...Works of love are works of peace and purity. Works of love are always a means of becoming closer to God, so the more we help each other, the more we really love God better by loving each other. Jesus very clearly said, "Love one another as I have loved you." Love in action is what gives us grace. We pray and, if we are able to love with a whole heart, then we will see the need. Those who are unwanted, unloved, and uncared for become just a throwaway of society. That is why we must really make everybody feel wanted.[3]
>
> The greatest disease in the West today is not TB or leprosy; it is being unwanted, unloved, and uncared for. We can cure physical diseases with medicine, but the only cure for loneliness, despair, and hopelessness is love. There are many in the world who are dying for a piece of bread, but there are many more dying for a little love. The poverty of the West is a different kind of poverty— it is not only a poverty of loneliness but also of spirituality. There is a hunger for love, as there is a hunger for God.[4]
>
> Unborn children are among the poorest of the poor. They are so close to God. I always ask doctors at hospitals in India never to kill an unborn child. If there is no one who wants it, I'll take it. I see God in the eyes of every child—every unwanted child is welcomed by us. We then find homes for these children through

adoption. You know, people worry all the time about innocent children being killed in wars, and they try to prevent this. But what hope is there in stopping it if mothers kill their own children? Every life is precious to God, whatever the circumstances.... We teach natural family planning to the poor in our many centers around the world. Women are given beads so that they can count the days in their cycle. A husband and wife should love and respect each other to be able to practice self-control during fertile days.[5]

PRAYER

Blessed Teresa remarked,

Prayer is needed for children and in families. Love begins at home and that is why it is important to pray together. If you pray together you will stay together and love each other as God loves each one of you.... Children need to learn to pray, and they need to have their parents pray with them. If we don't do this, it will be difficult to become holy, to carry on, to strengthen ourselves in faith.[6]

Start and end the day with prayer. Come to God as a child. If you find it hard to pray, you can say, "Come Holy Spirit, guide me, protect me, clear out my mind so that I can pray." Or if you pray to Mary, you can say, "Mary, Mother of Jesus, be a mother to me now, help me to pray." When you pray, give thanks to God for all His gifts, because everything is His and is a gift from Him... If you trust in the Lord and the power of prayer, you will overcome any feelings of doubt and fear and loneliness that people commonly feel.

If there is something that is worrying you, then you can go to Confession ... and become perfectly clean, because Jesus forgives everything through the priest. It is a beautiful gift of God that we may go to Confession full of sin and come out perfectly pure.... Just as we have acts of love, so must we have acts of contrition. Remember that God is merciful, He is the merciful Father to us all. We are His children and He will forgive and forget if we remember to do so. Examine your heart first, though, to see if there is any lack of forgiveness of others still inside, because how can we ask God for forgiveness if we cannot forgive others? Remember, if you truly repent, if you really mean it with a clean heart, you will be absolved in God's eyes. He will forgive you if you truly confess. So pray to be able to forgive those who have hurt you or whom you don't like, and forgive as you have been forgiven.[7]

OCTOBER 24, 2003

Blessed Teresa of Calcutta
II

FAMILY

Those who knew Mother Teresa well always recalled that her family strongly influenced her vocation. Her parents were very devout Catholics, but because her father died when she was nine years old, it was her mother who seemed to have had the greatest influence on her. When her father died, her mother refused to give way to discouragement but simply required that her four children pray more intensely to be able to face the grave family problems resulting from his early death.

From a young age on, Mother Teresa (then called Agnes) refused to waste time thinking about the past but learned to concentrate on the present moment. In helping her family as a child, she already indicated a disposition to assist others. She never seemed to ask what others might do to help; rather, she always asked herself, What can I do? She learned to pray much, but she always went from her prayers to helping others. An observer of her young years said that the simplicity, sincerity, and love that were so apparent in her later life could already be discerned in her youth.

Her only surviving niece recently remarked about her after her beatification in Rome on last October, "She was more than an aunt to me, but almost a sort of spiritual mother, but this was in a very simple way, without any flourishes, without any mysticism. Today I can truly say that she really influenced my life and the lives of my husband and children. But, at the time, we weren't thinking in those terms. We are a very quiet family, without a trace of religious extremism."

HER WORK

A sign that Mother Teresa posted outside the chapel of the motherhouse of her religious community indicates her point of view about her life and labors.

> We are not here for the work, we are here for Jesus. All we do is
> for Him. We are first of all religious, we are not social workers,

not teachers, not nurses or doctors, we are religious sisters. We serve Jesus in the poor. We nurse Him, feed Him, clothe Him, visit Him, comfort Him in the poor, the abandoned, the sick, the orphans, the dying. But all we do, our prayer, our work, our suffering is for Jesus. Our life has no other reason or motivation. This is a point many people do not understand.[8]

She said,

Do not worry about why problems exist in the world—just respond to people's needs. Some say to me that if we give charity to others, it'll diminish the responsibility of government towards the needy and the poor. I don't concern myself with this, because governments do not usually offer love. I just do what I can do: the rest is not my business. God has been so good to us: works of love are always a means of becoming closer to God. Look at what Jesus did in His life on earth! He spent it just doing good. I remind the sisters that three years of Jesus's life were spent healing the sick and the lepers, children and other people; and that's exactly what we're doing, preaching the Gospel through our actions...We feel what we are doing is just a drop in the ocean, but that ocean would be less without that drop. For instance, we started our schools to teach poor children to love learning and to be clean. If we hadn't, these children would be left on the street.[9]

ATTITUDES

Blessed Teresa said,

God is not separate from the Church, as He is everywhere and in everything and we are all His children...When we gather in His name, this gives us strength. The Church gives us our priests, the Mass, and the Sacraments, which we need in our daily lives to do our work. We need the Eucharist (Jesus in the Host and Holy Communion) because unless we are given Jesus, we cannot give to Him.

The Church is our family and like any family we need to be able to live together. Bishops invite the Missionaries of Charity to open new homes all the time and often help us find the houses. I do not see being a Catholic and belonging to the Catholic Church as a restriction: we just need to love and understand each other. I get asked about my opinions on the role of the Church today, on women's place within it, and what the future holds, and I say I don't have time to worry about all these issues—there are too many things to do in my everyday work. We are serving Christ. In our house, He is Head of our family and He makes all the decisions. For Christ, the Church is the same yesterday, today, and tomorrow. To God, everything is simple—God's love for us is greater than all the conflicts, which will pass.[10]

At another time she said, "Love is not patronizing and charity isn't about pity, it is about love. Charity and love are the same—with charity you give love, so don't just give money but reach out your hand instead. When I was in London, I went to see the homeless people where our sisters have a soup kitchen. One man, who was living in a cardboard box, held my hand and said, 'It's been a long time since I felt the warmth of a human hand.'"[11]

HAPPINESS

Mother Teresa said,

We have a right to be happy and peaceful. We have been created for this—we are born to be happy—and we can only find true happiness and peace when we are in love with God: there is joy in loving God, great happiness in loving Him. Many people think, especially in the West, that having money makes you happy. I think it must be harder to be happy if you are wealthy because you may find it difficult to see God: you'll have too many other things to think about. However, if God has given you this gift of wealth, then use it for His purposes—help others, help the poor, create jobs, give work to others. Don't waste your wealth. Having food, a home, dignity, freedom, health, and an education are all God's gifts too, which is why we must help those who are less fortunate than ourselves.[12]

Therefore, the only sadness I ever feel is if I do something wrong, if I hurt Our Lord in some way, through selfishness or uncharitableness, for instance. When we hurt the poor, and we hurt each other, we're hurting God. Everything is God's to give and to take away, so share what you've been given, and that includes yourself...Be happy now and if you show through your actions that you love others, including those who are poorer than you, you'll give them happiness, too. It doesn't take much—it can be just giving a smile. The world would be a much better place if everyone smiled more. So smile, be cheerful, be joyous that God loves you.[13]

OCTOBER 31, 2003

Blessed Teresa of Calcutta
III

CONVERTS

One of the persons who received Holy Communion from the hands of the Holy Father himself during the beatification Mass for Mother Teresa, which took place in Saint Peter's Square in Rome last October 19, was a thirty-eight-year-old Indian lady named Monica Besra. Although there had been many miracles attributed to the intercession of Mother Teresa that were reported to the Holy See, it was the healing of Monica Besra in 1998 that the authorities of the Holy See accepted as the "deciding miracle" having no possible natural explanation, thus allowing the beatification to go forward.

Monica Besra, a married mother of five living in West Bengal State, was a Hindu and was suffering terminally from a huge, inoperable cancerous tumor and from advanced tuberculosis. The Missionaries of Charity, who were caring for her, prayed for the intercession of Mother Teresa, and the woman was completely healed on the first anniversary of Mother's death. Monica has since become a Catholic, and she claims, although the Church authorities presently do not, that the healing also included her husband's recent recovery from alcoholism. She says that she had always loved Jesus even before she converted to Christianity and even as a Hindu had prayed to the Blessed Virgin Mary. For this reason, even while still a pagan, she gave all her children Christian names.

In another conversion story, some years ago a young woman who was about to receive her doctorate in physics from a university in France, although an atheist, decided to spend a month working with Mother Teresa in Calcutta. One day she surprised Mother Teresa by going to her, throwing her arms around her neck, and announcing, "I have found Jesus here!" Mother Teresa asked her what she meant, and she replied, "I just went to confession and received Holy Communion today for the first time in fifteen years! I am now a believer again."

PRAYER

Mother Teresa had already said in 1947, "The aim of the Missionaries of Charity is to quench the infinite thirst of Jesus on the cross for love and for souls", by "laboring for the salvation and sanctification of the poorest of the poor."[14] Father Brian Kolodiejchuk says of her, "Satiating the thirst of Jesus for souls was the ultimate motivation of all she did. This aim never left her heart and mind. All her energies were directed toward it. This thirst of Jesus permeated every aspect of her life, in her prayer as well as in [her] service. This was the charism she received and naturally all revolved around it."[15]

Mother Teresa insisted that the rule and constitutions of her Missionaries of Charity have a requirement for her Sisters to spend at least four hours in prayer each day. She herself never missed daily Mass and meditation and always tried, no matter how pressing other needs were, to spend at least one or more of her four hours of daily prayer in front of the Blessed Sacrament. Her Sisters noticed her profound dedication to Eucharistic adoration, even on occasions when she was involved in long and tiring journeys and even when she was in seriously failing health later in life. She often said, "Holiness is not a luxury of the few, but a simple duty for you and for me."[16] "Once you fall in love with Jesus, everything else follows and becomes easy in a way." She also frequently said, "By blood and origin I am all Albanian. My citizenship is Indian. I am a Catholic nun. As to my calling, I belong to the whole world. As to my heart, I belong entirely to the Heart of Jesus."[17]

POPE'S WORDS

When he beatified her, Pope John Paul II in his homily remarked, "Jesus' words to his disciples [Mk 10:44] ... show us the way to evangelical 'greatness'. It is the way walked by Christ himself that took him to the Cross: a journey of love and service that overturns all human logic. *To be the servant of all!* Mother Teresa of Calcutta ...allowed this logic to guide her. Mother Teresa, *an icon of the Good Samaritan*, went everywhere to serve Christ in the poorest of the poor. Not even conflict and war could stand in her way."[18]

The Supreme Pontiff observes,

> First and foremost [she] was a *missionary*: there is no doubt that the new Blessed was *one of the greatest missionaries of the 20th century*. The Lord made this simple woman who came from one of Europe's poorest regions a chosen instrument (cf. Acts 9:15) to proclaim the Gospel to the entire world, not by preaching but by daily acts of love towards the poorest of the poor [Mt 5:14; 25:40]. A missionary with the most universal language: the language of love that knows no bounds or exclusion and has no preferences other than for the most forsaken.[19]

The Bishop of Rome goes on to say,

> A missionary of charity, a missionary of peace, *a missionary of*

life, Mother Teresa was all these. She always spoke out in defense of human life, even when her message was unwelcome. Mother Teresa's whole existence was a *hymn to life*. Her daily encounters with death, leprosy, AIDS, and every kind of human suffering made her a forceful witness to the Gospel of life. Her very smile was a "yes" to life, a joyful "yes",… a "yes" purified in the crucible of suffering. She renewed that "yes" each morning, in union with Mary, at the foot of Christ's Cross. The "thirst" of the crucified Jesus became Mother Teresa's own thirst *and the inspiration of her path of holiness*.[20]

CARDINAL MARTINS

The prefect of the Vatican Dicastery that oversees and advises the Pope about beatifications and canonizations, Cardinal José Saraiva Martins, talked about an incident in the experience of Mother Teresa. She had brought to her Home for the Dying in Calcutta a miserable woman she had found in a gutter, whose pitiful body was covered with festering sores. Mother Teresa welcomed her warmly and spent hours washing her, cleaning her sores, and giving her medicine, salve, clean bandages, and other help. However, the woman never stopped cursing. Mother Teresa gently wiped away her feverish sweat and moistened her burning lips, but the obscene, profane, and terrible words still poured out of her mouth. But, just as she was close to death, she stopped and asked, "Sister, why are you doing this? Not everyone behaves like you. Who taught you?" Mother Teresa answered, "My God taught me." The woman said, "Introduce me to your God." Mother Teresa kissed her and said, "You already know my God. My God is called Love." The woman asked to be taught the Creed, consented to Baptism, and then died.[21]

Before Mother Teresa spoke to the United Nations' General Assembly, the Secretary General, introducing her, said, "This is the most powerful woman on earth. This is the woman who is welcomed everywhere with respect and admiration. She is truly the 'United Nations', for she has welcomed into her heart the poor from every corner of the earth!" Mother Teresa, blushing, began her speech, "I am only a poor woman who prays…"[22]

NOVEMBER 14, 2003

Jasna Gora
I

POLISH SHRINES

Beautiful religious shrines are characteristic of Poland. They are found in large numbers along the countryside highways and footpaths, in private gardens and yards, as well as in villages and cities. They are well cared for and inspiring. Also, in many Polish municipalities one finds numerous sanctuaries and churches with venerated images, especially of our Lady under one or the other of her heavenly titles. Those sanctuaries and churches, some ancient, some modern, are not only preserved clean and neat by the devout population, but are almost always filled with praying people, young and old, even outside of the times of liturgical services.

The most important of all the Polish sanctuaries dedicated to the Blessed Virgin Mary is that of Jasna Gora, which means "Bright Mountain", often called "Claremont". Located there in a fortress monastery in the gritty industrial city of Czestochowa on the Warta River is one of the world's most venerated icons of Mary, ranking in universal fame with those of Our Lady of Perpetual Help and of The Mother of God of Vladimir and Kazan. More than four million pilgrims from Poland and from all over the world visit Jasna Gora annually to honor, venerate, and pray before the famous icon of the Black Madonna, beseeching Mary's intercession.

THE ICON

The icon itself was painted on dark wood. Its exact origin is somewhat mysterious. It depicts Mary standing in a half-portrait and presenting the Child Jesus to the world by extending her right hand. She is gazing outward in a majestic yet humble look, matching that of the image of Christ next to her. The walls of the chapel that holds the icon are filled with *ex-voto* offerings, with braces and crutches by the thousands, and with centuries-old testimonies from countless people from every walk of life, giving witness to the fact that the icon and the shrine have been the scene of many spiritual conversions and innumerable physical, miraculous healings. In my trip last month to Poland, I had the privilege of offering Mass on the special and ancient altar directly in front of and beneath the holy icon, and thus I had a chance to study it closely. By the way, that was a most moving experience, especially to hear thousands of beautiful pilgrims' voices singing hymns such as "Czarna Madonna" and "Serdeczna Matko".

A pious legend says that the icon was painted by Saint Luke on the table of the Last Supper. However, recent scientific, microscopic, and chemical studies indicate that the icon was most likely painted in the sixth century and originated somewhere in the Byzantine-Balkan area of Europe in that era.

TRAVELS

How the icon of Our Lady of Czestochowa arrived at Jasna Gora is also the subject of legend. We know for sure that it was consigned to the monastery there by Prince Ladislaus Opolski during or near the year 1382. The Jasna Gora Monastery had been founded centuries before by Greek Rite Basilian monks, but by the fourteenth century it had already been for some years in the possession of the Latin Rite monks called the Pauline Fathers, a religious order founded by Saint Paul the Hermit, the friend of Saint Anthony the Abbot.

The icon at first was owned by the Imperial Family of Byzantium (Constantinople) and in the ninth century was given as part of a marriage dowry to one of the imperial princesses, who carried it with her to the Grand Duchy of Kiev. It was then placed by her in the Palace of Belz in present---day Hungary, where it was venerated by many thousands of Catholics for about five hundred years. However, in 1382 the Muslim Tartars, in their effort to conquer Europe for the Islamic religion, attacked Belz, and an arrow was shot into the icon striking the image of Mary's throat.

To protect the icon from further damage, Ladislaus, who was the ruler of Hungary at that time but was originally from Poland, decided to take it to Poland for safekeeping. We know for certain that he turned it over to the Pauline monks. However, a legend says that he did not originally intend to do this but was heading with it for Upper Silesia when the horses hitched to the wagon carrying the icon refused to go beyond the hillock where the monastery was. So he stayed there and consigned it to the Pauline monks at Czestochowa. From afar the monastic knoll gleamed in the sunlight, and hence the monastery acquired the name Jasna Gora.

ATTACKS

In the year 1430 an army of Hussites, a sect of Bohemian heretics, attacked the monastery, killing most of the monks there and, out of hatred for the Catholic faith, smashing the icon into three pieces. One of the heretics also slashed at the picture with his sword causing the slash marks still visible on Mary's cheek in the icon. He was lifting his sword to continue hitting the image when he dropped dead of a heart attack, causing the rest of the superstitious Hussites to flee in terror from the icon.

When the picture was restored, the Poles surrounded the sanctuary with a formidable fortress-like wall to protect in the future the chapel where the icon was enshrined and to guard the adjacent basilica and monastery of the Pauline monks. In subsequent centuries there were many attacks against the fortress-shrine, all in vain, attacks by Cossacks, Mongols, and the Russian Orthodox, culminating in an attack by King Gustavus Adolphus of Sweden in the seventeenth century. With only a tiny handful of soldiers to defend against twelve thousand Lutheran Swedes, all seemed lost. The monastery prior of the time, Kordecki, ordered a religious procession with the icon to be held along the outer walls of the monastery, and somehow this caused the Swedish army to pack up and go home, leaving the monastery and the icon unscathed. Later that year, 1656, the Polish king, Jan Kazimir, came to the monastery for a thanksgiving Mass and celebration, in the course of which he solemnly proclaimed Mary to be the Queen of Poland, a title that Poles bestow on her in the Litany of Loreto to this very day.

Although they did great damage to the city of Czestochowa, the scars of which can be seen even today, the liberals, socialists, Nazis, and Communists, who did so much harm to Poland in recent times, always avoided damaging the shrine itself. However, the Pauline monks on occasion did think it prudent to hide the icon in those times when they feared it might be damaged by invaders or by anti-Catholic ideologues.

AUGUST 22, 2003

Jasna Gora
II

IDENTITY

The sacred icon of Our Lady of Czestochowa, venerated for more than 1,500 years, is deeply identified by the Polish people with their Catholic faith, and that faith, in turn, has been always maintained by them as an essential part of their very ethnicity and nationhood. Our Holy Father, Pope John Paul II, says, "The image of Jasna Gora expresses a tradition and a language of faith still more ancient than our history…"[23] "If we want to know how this history [of Poland] is interpreted by the heart of the Poles, we must come here, we must listen to this shrine, we must hear the echo of the life of the whole nation in the heart of its Mother and Queen."[24] The Pope goes on to remark that only in Jasna Gora does any Polish person "truly feel free".[25]

Both as a college student, seminarian, priest, Bishop, and Cardinal, Karol Woytila often prayed before the icon of Our Lady of Czestochowa. Now, as the Pope, he has paid several visits to the Jasna Gora Monastery. He states on the first of his papal visits there, "Poles are accustomed to link with this place, this shrine, the many happenings of their lives, the various joyful or sad moments, especially the solemn, decisive moments, the occasions of responsibility, such as the choice of the direction of one's life, the choice of one's vocation, the birth of one's children, the final school examinations, and so many other occasions."[26]

PILGRIMS

The Supreme Pontiff notes,

> [The Poles] are accustomed to come with their problems to Jasna
> Gora, to speak of them with their heavenly Mother, who not only
> has her image here, one of the best known and most venerated
> pictures of her in the world, but is *specially present here*. She is
> present in the mystery of Christ and of the Church, as the [Second
> Vatican] Council teaches. She is present for each and every one
> of those who come on pilgrimage to her, even if only in spirit and
> heart when unable to do so physically.[27]

He also observes, "More and more people [from neighboring nations], from all
over Europe and outside Europe"[28] are coming to pray before the image of Our
Lady of Czestochowa.

In this year of the holy rosary, proclaimed for the entire Catholic world by Pope
John Paul II to extend from last October to this coming October, the Pauline Fathers
at Jasna Gora have placed a gigantic banner across the whole front of the fortress-
monastery, which says, quoting the Pope, "The Rosary Is the School of Mary".
Special rosary devotions are being held there daily from sunrise to sundown,
especially in the adjacent basilica. In addition to countless people from Poland, an
astonishing number of pilgrims from other countries can be seen there. When I
was in Czestochowa last July, I saw thousands of pilgrims from such places as
Hungary, Germany, England, Australia, and the United States.

POPES

Attached to the outside of the ancient icon are beautiful golden and bejeweled
crowns placed over the heads of the images of Jesus and Mary. There is a large
collection of such crowns in the treasury of the monastery, many given to the shrine
over centuries by royalty and important historical personages. The crowns currently
on the picture were sent to the shrine by Pope Saint Pius X. Pope Pius XI, when he
was Archbishop Achille Ratti, the Nuncio to Poland at the time of recovery of
Polish independence after the First World War, often visited and prayed at the
shrine. (Remember that Poland had lost its national existence for 120 years before
that, having been divided up between Austria, Russia, and Prussia.)

On the day he was elected Pope, Blessed John XXIII told the Primate of Poland
that he recalled his many visits to Jasna Gora when he was the Apostolic Delegate
in Bulgaria. He then asked that prayers to the Mother of God be constantly said at
the shrine for his intentions. Pope Paul VI, in his early years as a priest in the Holy

See's diplomatic service, worked at the Apostolic Nunciature in Warsaw and often prayed at the shrine. When Pope, he caused an image of Our Lady of Czestochowa to be placed in his private chapel and expressed a desire, never realized because of the Communist government then in power, to visit the shrine as Pope.

Among the Popes who prayed at Jasna Gora before being elevated to the See of Peter are: Pope Clement VIII, Pope Clement X, Pope Clement XI, Blessed Pope Innocent XI, and Pope Innocent XII.

OTHER VISITS

After he was elected the Bishop of Rome, our present Holy Father horrified the experts in heraldry by insisting that the letter "M" be on his coat of arms. (Evidently neither numbers nor letters are supposed to be on coats of arms.) It was a sign of his deep Marian spirituality, signaled by his episcopal and pontifical motto, addressed to the Blessed Virgin Mary: *"Totus Tuus"* (I am all yours). Visiting Jasna Gora, he said, "The call of a son of the Polish nation to the Chair of Peter involves an evident strong connection with this holy place, with this shrine of great hope. So many times I had whispered *Totus tuus* in prayer before this image."[29]

The Supreme Pontiff added, "Everything *through Mary*. This is the authentic interpretation of the presence of the Mother of God in the mystery of Christ, and of the Church, as is proclaimed by Chapter VIII of the Constitution *Lumen gentium* [of the Second Vatican Council]. This interpretation corresponds to the tradition of the saints, such as Bernard of Clairvaux, Grignion de Montfort, and Maximilian Kolbe."[30]

Not only Popes but many famous people have visited and enriched Jasna Gora. Lech Walesa left his Nobel Peace Prize and Medal there. The great novelist Henryk Sienkiewicz (*Quo Vadis, The Deluge, With Fire and Sword*, and so on) and the great musician and statesman Ignace Jan Paderewski visited and left precious gifts there. The Polish King Jan Sobieski III, who defeated the Muslim hordes besieging Vienna in 1683, ascribed his Christian victory to Mary's prayers and the prayers of the pilgrims at Jasna Gora, as did all the Christians of Europe who were praying the rosary the century before when Don Juan of Austria at the battle of Lepanto defeated the Muslims, who were bent on trying to destroy Christianity and exterminating all Christians.

SEPTEMBER 5, 2003

Mary and the Church
I

COUNCIL

May is the month that is traditionally given over by devout Catholics to special veneration of the Blessed Virgin Mary and to an annual period of reflection on her particular place in God's economy and His plan for the salvation for the human race. From the most ancient period of Christianity down through the centuries, the mystery of Mary always was joined in thought and meditation to the mystery of the Catholic Church. This was illustrated most vividly during the Second Vatican Council, when the Fathers of the Council on October 29, 1963, voted to incorporate the doctrine they intended to teach about the Blessed Virgin Mary into the principal document of that Council, which is the *Dogmatic Constitution on the Church*. The entire eighth chapter of that dogmatic constitution concerns Mary and her relationship with Christ and with His Church. It was in his closing allocution at the end of the third session of that Ecumenical Council, on November 29, 1964, that Pope Paul VI officially bestowed on Mary the title, "Mother of the Church".

Berengard, a Church Father, had noted that, while Mary belongs to the Church and, in a sense, is the Church's daughter, it is also true, at an even deeper level, that she can be called the Mother of the Church,[31] an idea echoed by Pope Leo XIII.[32] Quoting Bruno of Asti, Henri de Lubac remarks that, "Since she is the 'daughter of Jerusalem, who is our mother from on high', she is mother of the Church we constitute."[33] Bossuet calls Mary "the mother of the new people"[34], and Saint Ephrem says that Mary is "the earth in which the Church was sown".[35]

The *Catechism of the Catholic Church* states, "By her complete adherence to the Father's will, to his Son's redemptive work, and to every prompting of the Holy Spirit, the Virgin Mary is the Church's model of faith and charity. Thus she is [as the Second Vatican Council claims] a 'preeminent and ... wholly unique member of the Church'; indeed, she is the 'exemplary realization' (*typus*) [*Lumen gentium*, nos. 53 and 63] of the Church" (CCC 967).

ICON

The *Catechism* goes on to call Mary "the eschatological icon of the Church", saying, "After speaking of the Church, her origin, mission, and destiny, we can find no better way to conclude than by looking to Mary. In her we contemplate what the Church already is in her mystery on her own 'pilgrimage of faith', and what she will be in the homeland at the end of her journey. There, 'in the glory of the Most Holy and Undivided Trinity', 'in the communion of all the saints' [*Lumen gentium*, no. 69], the Church is awaited by the one she venerates as Mother of the Lord and as her own mother" (CCC 972). The Second Vatican Council remarks, "In the meantime the Mother of Jesus, in the glory which she possesses in body and soul in heaven, is the image and beginning of the Church as it is to be perfected in the world to come. Likewise she shines forth on earth, until the day of the Lord shall come, a sign of certain hope and comfort to the People of God."[36]

Father Olier says, "The holy religion of Jesus Christ has its beginning in the secrecy of the heart of the most holy Virgin." The Sequence for the Assumption in the Rodez Missal, notes that Mary conceived Christ in her heart before she conceived Him in her womb.[37] Henri de Lubac remarks, "When, as the 'silent Mother of the silent Word', [Mary] held blindly to the mysteries of God, watching all things and keeping them and pondering them in her heart [Lk 1:29, 51], she prefigured that long train of memory and intense meditation which is the very soul of the tradition of the Church."[38]

VIRGIN AND MOTHER

Saint Mary, who was present by God's providence with the apostles when the Holy Spirit came down upon the incipient Church that Christ founded (Acts 1:14), is the model and image of the Catholic Church both in her unsullied virginity and in her divine maternity. Honorius of Autun writes, "The glorious Virgin Mary stands for the Church, who is also both virgin and mother. [The Catholic Church] is mother because every day she presents God with new sons in baptism, being made fruitful by the Holy Spirit. At the same time she is virgin because she does not allow herself to be in any way corrupted by the defilement of heresy, preserving inviolate the integrity of the faith."[39]

Carl Feckes states,

> As Mary bore the earthly Christ, so the Church bears the eucharistic Christ. As the whole life of Mary is centered upon the bringing up and protecting of Christ, so again the deep life and solicitude of the Church are centered on the Eucharist. As Mary gives the earthly Christ to the world ... and from this gift are born the children of God, so also the eucharistic flesh and blood produced by the Church should form living children of God. As Mary offered up Christ together with him at the foot of the Cross, so the whole Church, at each Mass, offers the sacrifice with him.[40]

Isaac of Stella writes that our Lady and the Church "both give to God the Father a posterity; Mary, sinless, gave the body its Head; the Church, in the remission of sins [Jn 20:23], gives the Head its body [Eph 1:22–23]. Both are thus Mother of Christ, but neither of the two bears Him wholly, without the other."[41]

REDEEMED

In speaking about the Blessed Virgin Mary, it is good to stress, in order to avoid any undue exaggerations, that, although she is the most eminent and important member of the Church and greatest of all creatures that have come from the hand of God, she is still "one of the vast family of the redeemed".[42] As for each of us, God is also her Savior (Lk 1:47), and all her greatness comes only "through the redemption which is in Christ Jesus" (Rom 3:24). Our Redeemer is her Savior. Like all of us, she was in need of grace and mercy which could only come from God. "She was included, together with the whole race, in Adam's sentence; ...she incurred his debt, as we do; but ... for the sake of Him who was to redeem her and us upon the Cross, to her the debt was remitted by anticipation."[43]

As Blessed Pope Pius IX observes, she is redeemed like ourselves, but in a manner altogether different, a manner "more sublime".[44] Preserved free from sin from the instant of her conception in the womb of Saint Ann, her mother, God filled her with grace (Lk 1:28) "so that his only Son might be born of her, and with him, the Church in her wholeness...[For it was in her ... womb] that the whole Church was betrothed to the Word and united to God by an eternal alliance."[45] As Pope John Paul II notes, "It can clearly be seen how the relationship between Mary and the Church is a fascinating comparison between two mothers."[46] Because the Catholic Church "does the will of God" and "hears the word of God and does it", she, like Mary, is called by Christ Himself His Mother (see Lk 8:21; Mt 12:50; Mk 3:35).

APRIL 30, 2004

Mary and the Church
II

FROM THE PONTIFF

At the beginning of his pontificate more than a quarter of a century ago, Pope John Paul II wrote,

> Since Pope Paul VI, inspired by that teaching [of the Second Vatican Council], proclaimed the Mother of Christ "Mother of the Church", and that title has become known far and wide, may it be

permitted to his unworthy Successor to turn to Mary as Mother of the Church...Mary is Mother of the Church because, on account of the Eternal Father's ineffable choice and due to the Spirit of Love's special action, she gave life to the Son of God, "for whom and by whom all things exist" [Heb 2:10] and from whom the whole of the People of God receives the grace and the dignity of election. Her Son explicitly extended his Mother's maternity in a way that could easily be understood by every soul and every heart, by designating, when he was raised on the Cross, his beloved disciple as her son [Jn 19:26–27]. The Holy Spirit inspired her to remain in the Upper Room after our Lord's Ascension, recollected in prayer and expectation, together with the Apostles, until the day of Pentecost, when the Church was to be born in visible form, coming forth from darkness [Acts 1:14]. Later, all the generations of disciples, of those who confess and love Christ, like the Apostle John, spiritually took this Mother to their own homes, and she was thus included in the history of salvation and in the Church's mission from the very beginning.[47]

IDIOMS

Serlo of Savigny notes, "Mary is figured in the Church, and the Church is figured in Mary."[48] "There is, in fact, a constant exchange of attributes and mutual interpenetration between the two, which provides the basis for a certain 'communication of idioms'."[49] Cardinal Henri de Lubac researched how, from the early years of the Church through the High Middle Ages, the same biblical symbols in the Church's Tradition are applied to both Mary and the Catholic Church with "ever increasing profusion".[50] Both the Catholic Church and our Lady are called the New Eve, the Mother of all the spiritually living, the tree of Paradise whose fruit is Christ, the Ark of the Covenant, Jacob's Ladder, the Gate of Heaven, the fleece of Gideon, the Tabernacle of the most High, the throne of Solomon, the valiant woman of the Book of Proverbs, and the sign in heaven and the Crusher of the serpent from the Book of Revelation and the Book of Genesis.[51]

Other titles bestowed equally on Mary and on the Catholic Church are: the Garden enclosed, the sealed Fountain, the Tower of David, the immaculate Virgin and City surrounded by angels, the Mystical Vine, the Scepter of orthodoxy, the new Earth, the Dawn heralding the Day of Salvation, the Bush that burns but is not consumed, and so on. In Mary the whole Church is outlined, since she "comprises in an eminent degree all the graces and perfections" of the Church.[52] Paul Claudel remarks that "it is from [Mary], forever in place before his gaze, that the Eternal takes the measure of all things."[53]

Remarks

Saint Ambrose says, "How beautiful are those things which have been prophesied of Mary under the figure of the Church."[54] Some more modern writers have called the Blessed Virgin Mary "the ideal figure of the Church"[55] and "the mirror in which the whole Church is reflected".[56] She is the "type and model [of the Church], her point of origin and perfection".[57] The "form of our Mother the Catholic Church is according to the form of the Mother of Jesus".[58] The Congregation for the Doctrine of the Faith writes, "Mary is totally dependent upon God and completely directed towards him, and at the side of her Son, she is the most perfect image of freedom and of the liberation of humanity and of the universe. It is to her as Mother and Model that the Church must look in order to understand in its completeness the meaning of her own mission."[59]

The Bishop of Rome says,

> Built by Christ upon the Apostles, the Church became fully aware of these mighty works of God on the day of Pentecost, when those gathered together in the Upper Room "were all filled with the Holy Spirit and began to speak in other tongues, as the Spirit gave them utterance" (Acts 2:4). From that moment there also begins that journey of faith, the Church's pilgrimage through the history of individuals and peoples. We know that at the beginning of this journey Mary is present. We see her in the midst of the Apostles in that Upper Room, "prayerfully imploring the gift of the Holy Spirit."[60]

Quoting Charles Péguy, Henri de Lubac says, "In her 'youthful splendor' [Mary] is already the new universe which the Church is to be; the long panorama of the People of God climbs slowly and painfully to the peak that our Lady already occupies at a stroke."[61] He also says that we must remember that at the end of time the Church will be ultimately "all fair", in accordance with her destiny as Christ's Spouse, as Mary was by the work of the Holy Spirit from the first moment she sprang into existence.[62]

Magnificat

Pope John Paul II says,

> The Virgin Mother is constantly present on this journey of faith of the People of God towards the light. This is shown in a special

way by the canticle of the "Magnificat" [Lk 1:46–55], which, having welled up from the depths of Mary's faith at the Visitation, ceaselessly re-echoes in the heart of the Church down through the centuries. This is proved by its daily recitation in the liturgy of Vespers [Evening Prayer] and at many other moments of both personal and communal devotion...

The Church, which from the beginning has modeled her earthly journey on that of the Mother of God, constantly repeats after her the words of the Magnificat. From the depths of the Virgin's faith at the Annunciation and the Visitation, the Church derives the truth about the God of the Covenant: the God who is Almighty and does "great things" for man: "holy is his name"...In contrast with the "suspicion" which the "father of lies" sowed in the heart of Eve the first woman, Mary, whom tradition is wont to call the new Eve and the true "Mother of all the living", boldly proclaims the undimmed truth about God, the holy and almighty God, who from the beginning is the source of all gifts.... The Church, which even "amid trials and tribulations" does not cease repeating with Mary the words of the Magnificat, is sustained by the power of God's truth, proclaimed on that occasion with such extraordinary simplicity. At the same time, by means of this truth about God, the Church desires to shed light upon the difficult and sometimes tangled paths of man's earthly existence.[63]

MAY 7, 2004

Mary and the Church
III

MARIAN TONE

One of the lesser known but still very important characteristics of the Second Vatican Council is what our present Holy Father, Pope John Paul II, calls its "Marian tone". This tone "marked the Council from its beginning". The year after he announced his intention to call the twenty-first Ecumenical Council in the Church's history, Blessed Pope John XXIII recommended that the entire Church have "recourse to the powerful intercession of Mary, Mother of grace, to pray for the Council", and he called the Blessed Virgin Mary "the heavenly patroness of the Council". It was on the Feast of the Purification of Mary in 1962 that Blessed John

XXIII issued a command that the Council should begin on October 11 of that year, explaining that he had chosen that date because it was the anniversary of what the Ecumenical Council of Ephesus had done on that date in A.D. 431, which was to declare and proclaim that Mary was validly and legitimately to be called *Theotokos,* or "Mother of God".[64] In his opening address to the Second Vatican Council, Blessed John XXIII said that he entrusted the Council itself to Mary, the "Help of Christians, the Help of Bishops", imploring her motherly assistance for the successful outcome of the Council's work.

Pope John Paul II notes that "the Council Fathers also turned their thoughts expressly to Mary in their message to the world at the opening of the Council's sessions, saying: 'We successors of the Apostles, joined together in prayer with Mary, the Mother of Jesus, form one apostolic body', thus, linking themselves, in communion with Mary, to the early Church awaiting the Holy Spirit (cf. Acts 1:14)."[65] The Holy Father then goes on to say, "The entire exposition [about Mary] in the eighth chapter of the *Dogmatic Constitution on the Church* clearly shows that terminological precautions did not prevent a very rich and positive presentation of basic doctrine, and expression of faith and love [for Mary], whom the Church acknowledges as Mother and Model."[66]

Canticle of Canticles

The Book of the Bible called the "Canticle of Canticles" or the "Song of Songs" (which is a Hebrew expression meaning the greatest of all songs) is a poem about ideal human love, describing the depth and sacredness of the married union of a man and woman. However, in the light of the New Testament, Catholic Tradition has always interpreted the message of that book to be mainly the nuptial union between Christ and the Catholic Church, having within it a symbol as well of the union of Jesus and the individual Christian soul and of the Holy Spirit placing the Blessed Virgin Mary in the history of salvation (Mt 9:15; Jn 3:29; 2 Cor 11:2; Eph 5:23–32; Rev 19:7).

Father Louis-Françóis d'Argenten writes,

> Since it is true that the Holy Church is the well-beloved Spouse of Jesus Christ, Who speaks to her in the sacred Song, and similarly that all the souls who make up a part of this Church may speak to him as the whole does of which they are a part, it is most certain that the most holy Virgin, who is first and noblest among the souls that make up the Church, and she who has the highest worth in herself alone, and who is more beloved by God and more favored with his graces than all the rest of the Church together, is truly that dear Spouse, that dove, that unique and incomparable one to whom

the whole holy Song is addressed: and that is why the commentators usually give three senses to all its words; the one concerning the Church in general, the other concerning each soul in particular, and the third—which is apparently the principal one—concerning the most holy Virgin.[67]

Godefridus of Admont writes, "although all the mysteries of this book fit perfectly either the universal Church or each faithful soul in the bosom of the Church, conveying in a spiritual manner ... the mutual love of the Bridegroom and the Bride, they nevertheless seem to fit more 'specially' the Blessed Virgin Mary, who, above all souls, was singularly full of 'special' dilection and deserved above all to be 'specially' loved by the divine Bridegroom."[68]

LINKAGE

Pope Paul VI, who presided over the Second Vatican Council after the death of Blessed John XXIII, linked the thought of the Council with the Canticle of Canticles, joining the image of the Blessed Virgin Mary with the reality of the Church in his great apostolic exhortation entitled *Marialis Cultus*. There he calls Mary the perfect model of the Catholic Church at worship and prayer. Pope John Paul II remarks that this assertion of his predecessor,

> is a corollary...to the truth that points to Mary as a paradigm for the People of God on the way to holiness. That the Blessed Virgin is an exemplar in this field derives from the fact that she is recognized as a most excellent exemplar of the Church in the order of faith, charity, and perfect union with Christ, that is, of that interior disposition with which the Church, the beloved spouse, closely associated with her Lord, invokes Christ, and through him worships the eternal Father.[69]

Quoting Saint Ephrem, Henri de Lubac says that the "whole Church 'rejoices in the Blessed Virgin' and ... participates in her privilege. Together with her the whole Church hears the call of the Bridegroom in the Song: 'Come from Libanus, come', and with her replies: 'Come, ... let us go forth' ...across the centuries toward the consummation."[70]

THE COUNCIL

Pope John Paul II writes, "After proclaiming Mary a 'pre-eminent member', the 'type' and 'model' of the Church, the Second Vatican Council says: 'The Catholic

Church, taught by the Holy Spirit, honors her with filial affection and devotion as a most beloved mother'".[71] The Council goes on to say that devotion to the Blessed Virgin, "as it always existed, although it is altogether singular, differs essentially from the cult of adoration which is offered to the Incarnate Word, as well as to the Father and the Holy Spirit, and it is most favorable"[72] to that cult, adoring God alone. The Holy Father says, "There is a continuity between Marian devotion and the worship given to God: indeed, the honor paid to Mary is ordered to and leads to adoration of the most Blessed Trinity."[73] The Council teaches,

> The various forms of piety toward the Mother of God, which the Church within the limits of sound and orthodox doctrine, according to the conditions of time and place, and the nature and ingenuity of the faithful, has approved, bring it about that while the Mother is honored, the Son, through whom all things have their being [Col 1:15–19] …is rightly known, loved, and glorified and … all His commands are observed.[74]

MAY 14, 2004

---

[1] *Sacrosanctum concilium*, no. 60; cf. CIC, can. 1166; CCEO, can. 867; quoted by CCC 1667.

[2] Thomas of Celano, *First Life of Saint Francis* 85.

[3] Mother Teresa, *A Simple Path*, comp. Lucinda Vardey (New York: Ballantine Books, 1995), back cover.

[4] Ibid., p. 79.

[5] Ibid., pp. 55–56.

[6] Ibid., p. 19.

[7] Ibid., pp. 13–15.

[8] Mother Teresa, *Simple Path*, pp. 93–94.

[9] Ibid., pp. 114–15.

[10] Ibid., pp. 59–60.

[11] Ibid., p. 85.

[12] Ibid., p. 179.

[13] Ibid., pp. 180–81.

[14] Kolodiejchuk, Interview, pt. 3; www.yourcatholicvoice.org/print_news.php?ID=417.

[15] Ibid.

[16] Ibid., pt. 2.

[17] Mother Teresa, Simple Path, pp. xxvi–vii.

[18] John Paul II, "Mother Teresa Towers", p. 6, no. 1.

[19] John Paul II, "The Profound Lesson of Mother Teresa's Life: 'Being Christian Means Being Witnesses of Charity'", Audience for Pilgrims, October 20, 2003, *L'Osservatore*

Romano, no. 43 (October 22, 2003): 7, no. 2.

[20] Ibid., no. 4.

[21] Cardinal José Saraiva Martins, Homily at Thanksgiving Mass for the beatification of Mother Teresa of Calcutta, October 20, 2003.

[22] Ibid.

[23] John Paul II, "Presence of the Mother of God in Life of Church and Country", homily at Jasna Gora, June 4, 1979, *L'Osservatore Romano*, no. 24 (June 11, 1979): 10.

[24] Ibid., p. 11.

[25] Ibid.

[26] Ibid., p. 10.

[27] Ibid.

[28] Ibid.

[29] Ibid.

[30] Ibid., p. 11.

[31] Berengard, *In Apoc.* (PL 17, 875–76); quoted by Henri de Lubac, The Splendor of the Church, trans. Michael Mason (San Francisco: Ignatius Press, 1999), p. 333 (hereafter abbreviated LSC).

[32] Leo XIII, encyclical *Adiutricem* (September 5, 1895), no. 7.

[33] LSC 333, quoting Bruno of Geni, *De laudibus B.M.V.* (PL 165, 1021b).

[34] Bossuet, *Quatrième Sermon pour l'Annonciation* (*Oeuvres oratories* 2:6), quoted by ibid.

[35] Saint Ephrem the Syrian, quoted in A. Muller, *Ecclesia-Maria*, p. 148, and in turn quoted by LSC 333.

[36] *Lumen gentium*, no. 68; cf. 2 Pet 3:10; quoted by CCC 972.

[37] Quoted by LSC 322.

[38] LSC 343–44, quoting Santeuil, *Hymn for the Purification*.

[39] Honorius of Autun, *Sigillum beatae Maria* (PL 172, 499d); quoted by LSC 322.

[40] Carl Feckes, "Maria als Vorbild, Mutter und Herz der Kirche", in *Das Mysterium des hl. Kirche*, 2d ed. (Paderborn, 1935), pp. 270–71; quoted by LSC 329.

[41] Isaac of Stella, *Sermo* 61 (PL 194, 1683); quoted by LSC 327.

[42] LSC 334.

[43] John Henry Newman, *Mary, the Mother of Jesus* (New York: Catholic Book Exchange, 1894), p. 55; quoted by LSC 335.

[44] Pius IX, bull *Ineffabilis Deus*; quoted by LSC 335.

[45] Pseudo-Ildephonsus, *Sermo 2 de Assumptione B.M.V.* (PL 96, 252); quoted by LSC 335.

[46] "John Paul II, "Mary Is Pattern of Church's Holiness", *L'Osservatore Romano*, September 13, 1995, p. 7, no. 6.

[47] John Paul II, encyclical *Redemptoris hominis* (March 4, 1979), no. 22.

[48] Serlo of Savigny, *In navitate B.M.* (p. 117 in Tissier's edition); quoted by LSC 328.

[49] LSC 328.

[50] LSC 317.

[51] See LSC 317–19.

[52] *Vie intérieure de la très Sainte Vierge* 2:75; quoted by LSC 341.

[53] *Paul Claudel interroge le Cantique des Cantiques*, p. 23; quoted by LSC 342.

[54] Saint Ambrose, *De institutione virginis*, chap. 14, no. 89 (PL 16, 326); quoted by

LSC 321.

[55] Dillenschneider, *Le Mystère de la corédemption mariale* (1951), p. 79; quoted by LSC 320.

[56] Pierre Ganne, S. J., "La Vierge Marie dans la vie de l'Église", in *Diologue sur la Vierge* (1950) p. 152; quoted by LSC 320.

[57] LSC 320.

[58] Pseudo Ildephonous (PL 96, 269d); quoted by ibid.

[59] Congregation for the Doctrine of the Faith, *Instruction on Christian Freedom and Liberation* (March 22, 1986), no. 97.

[60] John Paul II, encyclical *Redemptoris Mater* (March 25, 1987), no. 26, quoting *Lumen gentium*, no. 59.

[61] LSC 342.

[62] Ibid.

[63] John Paul II, *Redemptoris Mater*, nos. 35, 37.

[64] Motu propio *Concilium* (February 2, 1962).

[65] John Paul II, "Council's Teaching on Mary Is Rich and Positive", General Audience, December 13, 1995, *L'Osservatore Romano*, December 20–27, 1995, p. 13.

[66] Ibid.

[67] Louis-Fraçóis d'Argentan, *Conférences sur les grandeurs de la très sainte Vierge* 2:337–38; quoted by LSC 370.

[68] Godefridus of Admont, PL 174, 972; quoted by LSC 370.

[69] John Paul II, "Mary: Model of the Church at Prayer", General Audience of September 10, 1997, *L'Osservatore Romano*, no. 38 (September 17, 1997): 7, no. 1, quoting *Marialis cultis*, no. 16.

[70] LSC 373, quoting a hymn to our Lady by Saint Ephrem the Syrian.

[71] John Paul II, "Blessed Virgin Is Mother of the Church", General Audience of September 17, 1997, *L'Osservatore Romano*, no. 39 (September 24, 1997): 11, no. 1, quoting *Lumen gentium*, no. 53.

[72] *Lumen gentium*, no. 66.

[73] John Paul II, "Faithful Have Filial Devotion to Mary", General Audience of October 22, 1997, *L'Osservatore Romano*, no. 44 (October 29, 1997): 7, no. 2.

[74] *Lumen gentium*, no. 66.

Part Seven

CONTEMPORARY ISSUES

1

THE SACREDNESS OF LIFE

Clever Apes

GRADUAL POISON

One of my weaknesses is a certain disposition to enjoy fishing. I have been known to quote approvingly from God's inspired word in that regard (Jn 21:3). Recently I have not found much time to indulge that weakness of mine, but several years ago I had the joy of participating in a salmon expedition to try to outwit the fish in Lake Michigan. You can imagine my surprise, however, when our guide on that occasion emphatically warned us not to eat any fish we caught more than once a week and, indeed, to avoid eating the larger fish altogether.

It seems that air pollutants from far off steel mills and chemical factories gradually fall, molecule by molecule, into the Great Lakes and then are assimilated into the fatty tissue of the fish. These pollutants are deadly for human beings to ingest and eventually are fatal even for the unfortunate fish.

This gradual poisoning process could be an apt parable for what may be spiritually and intellectually happening to all of us in the culture in which we find ourselves immersed. We may be taking into our hearts and minds and attitudes various kinds of dangerous poisons, but because this is happening so gradually, we may never notice their lethal effects until it is too late and we find our eternal destiny in jeopardy or in ruins.

MANIPULATION

In the June 1999 issue of his fascinating magazine *Culture Wars*, Doctor E. Michael Jones tells the story of a woman named Bertha Hunt. Evidently, in the 1920s it was not customary for women to smoke, at least in public. Bertha and some women friends on March 31, 1929, lit up some Lucky Strike cigarettes while walking on Fifth Avenue in New York. The press was alerted ahead of time about what was to happen and "played it big". Bertha announced that her

313

cigarette was a "torch of freedom" and that she was trying to smash taboos and discrimination against women, that she was promoting equality with men, and so on. What the public never learned, however, was that Bertha was in the employ of a certain Eddie Bernays, a public relations expert, who received a substantial retainer of more than $25,000 from the American Tobacco Company to persuade women to smoke. As Doctor Jones observes, "What billed itself as a feminist promotion of emancipation of women was in reality a public relations ploy to open a new market for tobacco by getting women addicted to cigarettes." The women's market for cigarettes helped increase the revenues of the American Tobacco Company by more than $32,000,000 in one year alone by this kind of effort.

Even now, gentle reader, you are probably being manipulated far more than you may suspect by politicians and their agents as well as by "psychological experts" hired by commercial interests, to say nothing of vast numbers of sinister people dedicated to making you adhere to any number of false ideological views. The silent and imperceptible poison perhaps continues to seep, molecule by molecule, into your system of values and beliefs.

Logic

Teachers of elementary logic often play the game of asking their students what they would do if they were washed up on a remote island and the first man they met told them that everyone on the island always lied and never told the truth. It is the intrinsic contradiction of our culture, which proclaims as a dogma that there are no dogmas and encourages us to judge as bad those who are considered judgmental. The liberal media and those who control it continually tell us absolutely that there are no absolutes and that we "ought" not ever to say "ought". Many people are too dull or distracted even to imagine they are being controlled by such "outside forces", being lured into illogical traps, or to catch the problem or care about it.

Modern Sadducees drum into our brains, usually through lewd or semi-rational entertainment, that human beings have no spiritual dimension, no immortal souls, and certainly no supernatural destiny. To them we are nothing more than a species of clever apes, who are expected by the liberal elite to control our ape-like inclinations to some types of violence and to smoking, but not to sexual promiscuity. Like brute beasts in the grip of passions, hormones, non-thinking instincts, and external stimuli, many of our fellow human beings are currently manipulated into accepting or at least not caring about abortion, contraception, homosexuality, divorce, feminism, priestesses, inclusive language, and, in the words of Peter Kreeft in *Crisis*, about breaking "the iron chain that binds our sexual activity to our God." And, so the poison seeps in.

CONTRAST

C. S. Lewis points out quite eloquently the difference between a Christian and an unbeliever.

> The one believes that men are going to live for ever, that they were created by God and so built that they can find their true and lasting happiness only by being united to God, that they have gone badly off the rails, and that obedient faith in Christ is the only way back. The other believes that men are an accidental result of the blind workings of matter, that they started as mere animals and have more or less steadily improved, that they are going to live for about seventy years, that their happiness is fully attainable by good social services and political organisations, and that everything else … is to be judged to be "good" or "bad" simply in so far as it helps or hinders that kind of "happiness".[1]

He notes that while believers and unbelievers may be able to agree on mutual approval of some things such as "efficient sewers and hospitals and a healthy diet"[2], sooner or later their differences will surface. "The Christian and the Materialist hold different beliefs about the universe. They can't both be right. The one who is wrong will act in a way which simply doesn't fit the real universe. Consequently, with the best will in the world, he will be helping his fellow creatures to their destruction."[3]

Be careful, dear friends, that the poison has not imbedded itself deeper into the tissue of your being and personality than you really know. These are some of the thoughts I gather up when I go fishing.

JULY 16, 1999

Suicide

MORTAL SIN

The current pro-death culture in our country and, indeed, in many parts of the world has allowed the desire for "freedom" and "autonomy" so to distort our value system that suicide is actually looked upon by some people as a "right". The denial of God as the Lord of all human life allows such persons as the evil "suicide doctor", Jack Kevorkian, to proclaim at the National Press Club that "all religion is irrational."

Self-destruction is growing in various areas of our society, especially among the teenage population and among the elderly and chronically ill. Persuaded by a fear of pain or by impatient relatives or by the heathen media, suicide is becoming "socially acceptable" in some sectors of our declining "civilization". Lack of belief in the immortality of the human soul as well as lack of belief in eternal reward and punishment make it impossible for some people to "see anything wrong" in suicide. Obviously, a nonbeliever would not find it possible as well to see any redemptive value in human sorrow or suffering. Some modern existentialist philosophers, such as Camus and Sartre, actually extol and praise suicide as a "rational option".

For us Catholic Christians, however, suicide always is objectively a mortal sin. It is particularly horrible since, if it is successfully carried out, it makes repentance impossible and damns the perpetrator to eternal torment in hell. Of course, to have a mortal sin imputed to a person, it is necessary that there be full deliberation and full consent of free will. Nowadays, it is supposed that people who commit suicide often are mentally ill in some way, which makes their full and free consent or their deliberation less than that required for a serious sin. This is why, in contrast to past practice, people who commit suicide frequently can be given Christian burial.

CHESTERTON

Gilbert Keith Chesterton writes about suicide in his classic work entitled *Orthodoxy*: "Under the lengthening shadow of Ibsen, an argument arose whether it was not a very nice thing to murder one's self... Not only is suicide a sin, it is *the* sin. It is the ultimate and absolute evil, the refusal to take an interest in existence; the refusal to take the oath of loyalty to life. The man who kills a man, kills a man. The man who kills himself kills all men; as far as he is concerned he wipes out the world. His act is worse (symbolically considered) than any rape or dynamite outrage. For it destroys all buildings: it insults all women."[4]

Chesterton goes on, "[The suicide] cannot be bribed, even by the blazing stones of the Celestial City. The thief compliments the things he steals, if not the owner of them. But the suicide insults everything on earth by not stealing it. He defiles every flower by refusing to live for its sake. There is not a tiny creature in the cosmos at whom his death is not a sneer."[5]

STEWARDS

Human life is a gift from God. This gift, however, is not given to us to own absolutely. Rather it is confided to us in stewardship. Someday, each human being must give an account of his stewardship to the Lord and Master of the universe. The beginning and end of human life are and remain in the hands of our Almighty Creator and Redeemer. The solemn injunction "You shall not kill" (Ex 20:13) was not only written by God in stone on Mount Sinai, but it is written by Him on every human heart. This applies not only to the lives of our fellow human beings, but to our own life as well.

The perpetrators of the horrible and wicked acts of suicide, murder, and abortion are succumbing to the first and most ancient of temptations: "Your eyes will be opened, and you will be like God, knowing good and evil" (Gen 3:5). Blasphemously attempting to usurp what God has assigned to Himself, the suicide (who knows what he is doing and deliberately wills it) outrageously and foolishly attempts to manipulate God Himself. The consequences of such folly are eternally lethal.

Human lives, even those involved in continuous suffering, those in a permanent vegetative state (PVS), those of the mentally challenged and disabled, those of the handicapped, are precious and valuable for every follower of Christ.

Our Holy Father, Pope John Paul II, writes, "A source of joy is found in the *overcoming of the sense of the uselessness of suffering*, a feeling that is sometimes very strongly rooted in human suffering (Col 1:24). This feeling not only consumes the person interiorly, but seems to make him a burden to others. The person feels condemned to receive help and assistance from others, and at the same time seems useless to himself. The discovery of the salvific meaning of suffering in union with Christ *transforms* this depressing *feeling*".[6] In his great encyclical *The Gospel of Life*, the Pope writes, "The sacredness of human life gives rise to its inviolability, written from the beginning in man's heart, in his conscience".[7]

PROPAGANDA

A powerful propaganda machine is already in motion in our country to manipulate public opinion toward the acceptance of "doctor-assisted suicide". You can be sure that the media, especially television, will focus on a false notion of liberty and freedom in order to persuade people that they have the "right" to kill themselves. In Oregon recently a referendum was passed (accompanied by unbelievable amounts of anti-Catholic hatred) favoring suicide. This is currently tied up in court battles, but it provides an ominous portent for our future.

Assisted by cowardly politicians and immoral lawyers, the media have already succeeded in promoting in our country the sexual morality of a hamster cage and the merciless slaughter of millions of innocent babies in abortion. Suicide appears to be next on their agenda. Will you do something about that?

SEPTEMBER 6, 1996

Professional Killers

HOLLAND

There are in the Netherlands, I am told, a growing number of secret societies of the elderly and the handicapped. These secret societies have various recognition signs, such as certain kinds of winks and handshakes. The elderly and the handicapped have formed these societies to save their own lives and to help each other avoid some of the doctors and hospitals intent on killing them.

Euthanasia laws in Holland permit doctors and medical personnel to murder people. Technically, the law requires the consent of the person to be murdered or his family. However, it appears that that aspect of the law is not enforced at all. Consequently, doctors decide whom to kill, with or without consent, and after they do their murders they are not sanctioned. Although the Dutch doctors who admit they engage in murder say they usually kill the elderly and the handicapped, they also admit to killing occasionally the feebleminded, the poor, and people suffering from depression, any person they feel suffers from an impoverished "quality of life". Like Jack Kevorkian in our own country, they often "do in" even people with no trace of serious, much less terminal illness.

THE GROUP

As a group, the professionals involved in the healing and health-providing professions are probably among the most compassionate and considerate people one can encounter. In addition to abiding by the highest standards involving the technical application of the science and art of medicine and surgery, they are, most frequently, people of moral and ethical integrity.

However, just as some of these people have allowed themselves to become involved in the abominable act of abortion, we can expect that some will also be involved in the horror of mercy killing or euthanasia, changing from healers to killers. The culture of death continues to grow in our country. Several decades ago, in Nazi Germany, the medical profession, in the person of numerous physicians and researchers, was in the forefront of the hideous torture of Jews and Gypsies and others and of the widespread killing of those whom the Nazis called "useless eaters".

No one is morally bound to use extraordinary means to prolong life, either his own or that of another for whom he has responsibility. Withholding or withdrawing "extraordinary means", of course, is not the same as direct euthanasia, which is always immoral. Also pain-control therapy is permitted, even if this should incidentally hasten death, so long as that death is not intended and so long as the means used to end the pain is not death. A good end does not justify the use of an evil means.

TEACHING

The teaching of the Catholic Church about these matters is most clear:

> Nothing and no one can in any way permit the killing of an innocent human being, whether a fetus or an embryo, an infant or an adult, an old person, or one suffering from an incurable disease, or a person who is dying. Furthermore, no one is permitted to ask for this act of killing, either for himself or herself or for another person entrusted to his or her care, nor can he or she consent to it, either explicitly or implicitly. Nor can any authority legitimately recommend or permit such an action. For it amounts to the violation of the divine law, an offense against the dignity of the human person, a crime against life, and an attack on humanity.[8]

Painkillers are permitted, of course, but a dying person should not be deprived of consciousness unless he is first able to satisfy his moral duties (such as sacramental confession) and family obligations and is able to prepare himself for meeting Christ, the Judge of the living and the dead.

The "right to die" does not mean the right to procure death either by one's own hand or through someone else. Rather it means the right to die peacefully, with human and Christian dignity, refusing, if so desired, the application of extraordinary means to prolong life.

EXPERIENCE

Those who work with the dying in hospice care and in pastoral ministry assert that once effective pain control is in place, even those in terminal conditions will not seek euthanasia. People of faith, who understand not only the spiritual and eternal dimension of human existence, but also see in the mystery of the Cross something of the meaning and significance of human suffering, will flee from any suggestion of euthanasia.

Occasionally relatives and sometimes even close family members, however, will try to persuade a sick or elderly person to seek to be murdered. Sometimes they do this for reasons of misguided compassion. (I could not stand to see her suffer so much! What they really mean is that this is annoying to my personal comfort and pleasure.) Sometimes the selfishness is blatant. (Grandmother is going to spend the money we are supposed to inherit for nursing home and hospital expenses.)

Sometimes this persuasion comes from a pagan outlook. (We shoot horses with broken legs and "put to sleep" crippled pets. Why not humans, too?) Sometimes the chronically or terminally ill can be made to feel guilty or useless by the attitudes, actions, or words of relatives and friends and on that score or because of psychological depression can be persuaded to ask to be put to death. Sometimes under the influence of pain or painkillers, people will make a decision to be put to death that is far from free or deliberate.

SLOPE

Once society puts its foot on the slippery slope of euthanasia, the consequences can be more manifold and deadly than may be anticipated. Recently a local newspaper published the results of an anonymous survey among doctors in Nebraska. Several doctors admit that they have engaged in euthanasia. The excuses are innumerable and the anecdotes endless: abnormal babies, miserable life, too heavy a burden on family and society, extreme suffering, and so on. It may be time in America to start forming secret societies such as they have in Holland unless we can convert our fellow citizens to a Christian attitude toward human life and toward human destiny.

SEPTEMBER 20, 1996

2

ABORTION

Sad Anniversary

EACH JANUARY

For almost two hundred years no one ever thought that the United States Constitution permitted, indeed gave a right to, legalized homicide. Then suddenly, one January day, the Supreme Court, unelected judges, declared that they found that killing babies was a right bestowed by the Constitution and that mothers and doctors have a right to kill tiny, helpless, innocent babies before they are born. In little more than twenty years, the practice of baby killing has claimed millions of victims in the United States. More recently, cowardly and evil politicians have condoned and promoted the practice of partial birth abortion, puncturing the skull of partially born infants and then cruelly sucking out their brains with a machine, while the infants writhe in horrible pain.

Every Friday morning, in the City of Lincoln, some mothers bring their babies to the city's Planned Parenthood Clinic to be killed. This is very sad to behold and surely is a revolting spectacle for anyone who cherishes the value of human life, knowing that every human being is an image of God (Gen 1:27) and has been redeemed by the blood of Christ. Each January, decent people in our country remember with sorrow the vile act of the Supreme Court in the case entitled *Roe v. Wade*, which opened the doors to the killing of the innocent. The disregard for human life, represented by widespread abortion, is probably a prelude to the fostering of suicide and the further legalized killing of the handicapped, the incurably ill, and others whom society and the media can persuade the public and the victims themselves to consider worthless.

CONTRACEPTION

The immoral practice of artificial contraception, statistically, does not diminish the practice of abortion, because the promotion of this practice encourages sexual promiscuity. Also, it is important to know that many types of contraceptives are actually abortifacient. The "pill", for instance, sometimes inhibits ovulation, but it also sometimes inhibits nidation, or the implantation of the baby in the wall of the uterus. The human child is then expelled and discarded. The IUD as well as the so-called "morning after" pill definitely cause abortions. People who use such devices as well as the doctors who would prescribe them are, of course, guilty of more than the mortal sins of impurity involved in artificial birth prevention. Their hands, as well as the hands of their political supporters, drip with the blood of the innocent.

Doctor Janet Smith, from the University of Dallas, says, "It is foolish for pro-lifers to think that they can avoid the issues of contraception and sexual irresponsibility and be successful in the fight against abortion. For, as the Supreme Court stated, abortion is 'necessary' for those whose intimate relationships are based upon contraceptive sex".[9] For people who practice the immorality of artificial contraception, abortion easily becomes a thinkable alternative to an unwanted pregnancy.

LINK

Even those who are on the side of Planned Parenthood and its works admit that there is a link between artificial birth prevention and abortion. Alfred Kinsey says, "At the risk of being repetitious, I would remind the group that we have found the highest frequency of induced abortion in the group which, in general, most frequently uses contraceptives."[10] Population Action International states, "Experts estimate that even with highly effective and virtually universal contraceptive use, at least two out of ten women would need an abortion to terminate an unwanted pregnancy over the course of their reproductive lives."[11] The same group also insists, "In the absence of perfectly reliable contraception, women often rely on abortion" as a necessary back-up to contraception, even in countries with a good contraceptive availability.[12]

Dr. Alan Guttmacher and Dr. John Rock signed a statement that says, "It was recognized by conference participants that no scientific evidence has been developed to support the claim that increased availability of contraceptive services will clearly result in a decreased illegal abortion rate."[13]   Just a few years ago, a detailed article in the *Atlantic Monthly*, largely ignored by the pro-abortion and pro-contraception media, demonstrated, beyond any question, that the recent sex-education program and contraceptive experiments in New Jersey were a total failure in reducing the number of teenage pregnancies.[14]

WHAT TO DO?

It is necessary for all Americans who are devoted to the cause of the natural law and the cause of preventing the killing of innocent human beings to rededicate themselves to their convictions as the sad January anniversary comes around each year. Prayer, too, for the conversion of the wicked promoters of abortion as well as for their pusillanimous and evil political allies is vital. God's grace can effect what is beyond human reach.

Attitudes toward human life and its antechamber, sexual activity, must be regulated by human consciences that are properly formed by divine law, as interpreted by the Church. The evil of abortion often is subsequent to the evils of fornication, adultery, and artificial birth prevention. Therefore, purity and chastity and proper family life, within licit marriage, are causes that also deserve attention and care, especially from parents and others charged with the responsibility of educating and forming the young.

Careful study of such important documents as the great encyclical of Pope John Paul II *The Gospel of Life*, as well as *Humanae vitae* of Pope Paul VI, will assist a conscientious Catholic to articulate better the moral truths involved in these issues.

Lay Catholics especially have a duty to bring the good news of Jesus into their political, social, and family undertakings. This certainly includes matters concerning the morality of life and the morality of sexual activity. How one votes in elections should also be influenced by a faith that is alive and vibrant and by a moral outlook guided by the Gospel. In God's good time, provided His children cooperate with His grace, perhaps the sad anniversary of the monstrous Supreme Court decision each January will be changed into another kind of celebration.

January 17, 1997

Humanae Vitae

JOY AND DISTRESS

At the beginning of his great 1968 encyclical letter *Humanae vitae*, Pope Paul VI writes, "The transmission of human life is a most serious role in which married people collaborate freely and responsibly with God the Creator. It has always been a source of great joy to them, even though it sometimes entails many difficulties and hardships." Standing in the line of an unbroken doctrinal and moral position, from Christ to the present time, our present Holy Father, Pope John Paul II, has recently stated that "the [Catholic] Church is aware of the various difficulties married people can encounter, especially in the present social context, not only in following but also in the very understanding of the moral norm that concerns them."[15]

However, the Pope goes on to say that the Church also reminds them "that the way to finding a solution to their problems must come through full respect for the truth of their love".[16]

This month of March marks the anniversary of the issuance by my predecessor of happy memory, Bishop Glennon Flavin, of his pastoral letter directed to Catholic spouses and Catholic physicians concerning the moral evil of artificial birth prevention, a letter written in careful and full conformity with what the Catholic Church has always taught in this matter. Apart from the fact that many forms of birth control are actually abortifacient (for example, the IUD, the "patch", often the "pill", and so on), the practice of contraception in itself is, in the words of the Pope, "intrinsically illicit", introducing a substantial limitation in the reciprocal gift of themselves that spouses are to give to each other in love.

AUTHORITY

Pope John XXIII says: "Needless to say, when the Hierarchy has made a decision on any point, Catholics are bound to obey their directives. The Church has the right and obligation not merely to guard ethical and religious principles, but also to declare its authoritative judgment in the matter of putting these principles into practice."[17] Pope Paul VI writes, "No member of the faithful could possibly deny that the Church is competent in her magisterium to interpret the natural moral law."[18]

Pope Pius XII teaches:

> Nor must it be thought that what is expounded in Encyclical Letters does not of itself demand consent, since in writing such Letters the Popes do not exercise the supreme power of the Teaching Authority. For these matters are taught with the ordinary teaching authority, of which it is true to say, "He who heareth you, heareth me" [Lk 10:16]; and generally what is expounded and inculcated in Encyclical Letters already for other reasons appertains to Catholic doctrine. But if the Supreme Pontiffs in their official documents purposely pass judgment on a matter up to that time under dispute, it is obvious that that matter, according to the mind and will of the Pontiffs, cannot be any longer considered a question open to discussion among theologians.[19]

THE TEACHING

Although the ancient world was short of correct biological and physiological information, there were many types and attempts at artificial birth control known to exist from the first years of the Church's life down through the ages. The earliest Fathers of the Church clearly taught the wickedness of these attempts and practices. The traditional teaching of the Catholic Church on this issue has never varied. Until the 1930s all of Christianity was in accord about the immorality of artificial contraception. It was only about sixty-five years ago that various Protestant churches and denominations began to teach practices hitherto considered immoral as moral.

Humanae vitae says, "The Church, ...in urging men to the observance of the precepts of the natural law, which it interprets by its constant doctrine, teaches that each and every marital act must of necessity retain its intrinsic relationship to the procreation of human life. This particular doctrine, often expounded by the magisterium, is based on the inseparable connection, established by God, and which man on his own initiative may not break, between the unitive significance and the procreative significance which are both inherent in the marriage act."[20] Pope Pius XI states: "Any use whatsoever of matrimony exercised in such a way that the act is deliberately frustrated in its natural power to generate life is an offense against the law of God and of nature, and those who indulge in such are branded with the guilt of a grave sin."[21]

NFP

Sometimes there are grave reasons why a couple might try to limit the number of their children. Such things as serious health concerns, provision for the children already begotten, the possibility of transmitting serious congenital defects, and so on, could be licit reasons for using Natural Family Planning. Of course, selfishness is never a valid reason for this or any human behavior, nor is the simple desire for a mother to have a career outside the home, the wish for greater material prosperity, and so forth. Natural Family Planning is something totally different from artificial birth prevention, although both can have similar practical results.

The old "calendar rhythm method" is no longer used in NFP. Our diocesan program can assist couples in the most modern and yet fully moral techniques as well as help them to a better and more complete understanding of the richness and beauty of their marriage vocation. Married couples should be careful to obtain their information about NFP from competent and well-trained personnel, because many people who say, "It does not work for us" either are doing something in error or have obtained incorrect information from someone.

The vocation of married life and parenting is, by God's will, sublime. However, especially during Lent, it is appropriate for married couples and for all adult Catholics to reflect seriously on the responsibilities and moral duties that accompany that vocation.

MARCH 13, 1998

Day of Infamy

Each Year

When I was a little boy in Milwaukee, our family lived across the street from the family of a man who was an officer in the United States Navy. He had been in the naval reserve and had been activated in the autumn of 1941, just in time to be present for the attack on Pearl Harbor on December 7, 1941. We old-timers remember the speech of President Franklin Roosevelt the next day, asking Congress to declare war on the Japanese Empire. He called December 7, 1941, "a day which will live in infamy". After the war, Commander Watson (our neighbor across the street) said he would never forget the terrible date of December 7, 1941, since it irrevocably altered his life and destroyed the lives of million of human beings.

Unfortunately, there is another "day which will live in infamy" in our country's history. It is January 22, 1973. On that date, the United States Supreme Court claimed to find in the Constitution a right to kill little babies before they are born. It is a date that is seared into the collective memory of our nation's history. Since that terrible decision, more than one million three hundred thousand innocent children have been cruelly put to death every year in the U.S., and the slaughter goes on unabated.

Humane

My grandfather and my great-grandfather were in the meat business. They hauled cattle and swine, and they also had holding lots and a small meat-packing plant, with an adjoining butcher shop. Their own human feelings of sensitivity caused them, many years ago, to dispatch their cattle and swine in the most painless and quick way. Today, humane societies and societies for the prevention of cruelty to animals seek to insure that there is no unnecessary cruelty in the meat-packing operations in our land.

These days, however, when mothers bring their little babies to the abortion clinics to have them killed (such as those that show up at the Planned Parenthood facility in Lincoln on Friday mornings), there are no representatives of any "society for the prevention of cruelty to children" to oversee how the death penalty is carried out. Cattle and swine are treated more humanely than our fellow human beings. The innocent little ones are slaughtered often in the most gruesome and horrible ways with unspeakable pain and suffering inflicted upon them. There are several hundred of these vile and evil killings every month in our State of Nebraska.

Hypocrisy

It seems logically and tragically inconsistent for people to claim that they are against the death penalty when they are not against abortion. Convicted murderers often have years of appeal after a fair trial. They are few in number (in Nebraska, four in the last several years compared to more than 100,000 abortions in Nebraska in the same time period). They are found guilty by a court, whereas the little victims of abortion do not even have a trial. Convicted felons have witnesses at their execution and are put to death in a way short of prolonged torture. (Incidentally, my views on the death penalty are the same as those of the *Catechism of the Catholic Church* and the encyclical *The Gospel of Life*.)

The ultimate in hypocrisy, of course, is found in those people who make noises against the death penalty for murderers, while they actually belong to and even serve on the board of Planned Parenthood, the largest abortion business in the country and perhaps the world, if you do not count the human butchers in China. To those who say you cannot be credible on the abortion issue unless you oppose the death penalty for murderers, I always reply it is really the other way around, that is, you have no credibility on the death penalty issue unless you equally or even more vigorously oppose what the Second Vatican Council calls the heinous sin and abominable crime of abortion.

TEACHING

Pope John Paul II says,

> Abortion and euthanasia are crimes which no human law can claim to legitimize. There is no obligation in conscience to obey such laws; instead there is a grave and clear obligation to oppose them by conscientious objection. From the very beginning of the Church, the apostolic preaching reminded Christians of their duty to obey legitimately constituted public authorities (cf. Rom 13:17; 1 Pet 2:13–14), but at the same time it firmly warned that "we must obey God rather than men" (Acts 5:29).[22]

The Holy Father goes on to say,

> It is precisely from obedience to God—to whom alone is due that fear which is acknowledgement of his absolute sovereignty [Ex 1:17]—that the strength and the courage to resist unjust human laws are born. It is the strength and courage of those prepared even to be imprisoned or put to the sword, in the certainty that this is what makes for "the endurance and faith of the saints" (Rev 13:10). In the case of an intrinsically unjust law, such as a law permitting abortion or euthanasia, it is

therefore never licit to obey it, or to "take part in a propaganda campaign in favor of such a law, or to vote for it."[23]

Multiple Facets

Abortion has multiple victims. In addition to the innocent child who is brutally killed, the perpetrators and their supporters are also victimized by the practice. Above all, the women who undergo the procedure are victims. Not only are there many more deaths and injuries to them even from so-called legal and sanitary abortions than the liberal propaganda machine would allow you to know, but post-abortion syndrome psychologically haunts many if not most of them for the rest of their lives. Project Rachel is available to assist them, but we all must help them, remembering that, like Christ, we must hate the sin, but love the sinner. "Problem pregnancies" must also be the object of our compassion and concern. If you know someone who does not want a child who is on the way, please tell me. I will find a good home for the child and will find a way to give help to the mother. Please do not allow another child to be killed unjustly here in Southern Nebraska. Do not let the "day of infamy" to continue to besmirch our part of the world if you can do something to alleviate it.

JANUARY 22, 1999

Pilate's Mouthful

Autonomy

"You will be like God" (Gen 3:5). This ancient demonic temptation still resonates through the human race, and, like the mother of all humanity called Eve, there are many even now who succumb regularly to this blandishment of the serpent. This becomes exceptionally clear in one of the more recent rulings of the Supreme Court of the United States, fostering the killing of innocent babies before they are fully born (*Planned Parenthood v. Casey*, decided June 29, 1992).

Not only does the court itself pretend to usurp divine prerogatives, but also, in its fanatic dedication to abortion, it absurdly attempts to bestow these attributes of God upon the common citizenry of the country. It says, "At the heart of liberty is the right to define one's own concept of existence, of meaning, of the universe, and of the mystery of human life." Totally unhinged from God and utterly disconnected from truth, this idea about the "heart of liberty" enshrines secularism and godlessness as the "national religion". It implies that there is no truth, or least no attainable truth, about the basic questions that arise in every human soul and certainly no obligation to follow the truth.

WHY NOT?

When one reduces God and truth to mere opinion, when one makes Church and religion into simply human preferences, when all morality is determined by what the Congress, the President, or the Supreme Court decides is right or wrong—or what any individual decides is right or wrong—and when money, prosperity, and good feelings are supreme in human estimation, it is quite understandable that relativism and its inevitable companion, nihilism, should be stalking our culture. The trench-coated killers of Littleton, Colorado, appear to be the logical and consistent consequence of practicing the "national godless religion". After all, it is unconstitutional to talk about Jesus or openly to pray to Him in public schools, although one can mention and even teach there the doctrines of Marx and Hitler.

Who is to say that the Littleton killers' definition and concept of existence, based on hate, racism, murder, and suicide, were wrong, given the views of the Supreme Court? Maybe the killers were only exercising their "right to define their own concept of existence" as "the heart of liberty", and it varied from the current "concept" of society about these things. So why were they wrong? Anyway, given the prevalence of the false philosophy of relativism (what is wrong or evil today could very well be considered good and salutary tomorrow, and vice-versa), who is to say that, following the dogmas and doctrines of the "national godless religion", the wicked values that the killers espoused and practiced might not be called virtues in the future? In this past century, racism was considered good in Germany and class hatred was a virtue in the Soviet Union. The majority of high-school students in the United States currently feel that lying and cheating in examinations are not bad, "if you can get away with it". Just a few decades ago abortion was a crime in all the states of the Union and universally condemned as an abominable act by all Christians. Now it is vigorously supported and promoted by the President of the United States, his wife, the Supreme Court, many politicians, and, overwhelmingly, by the media.

MORE COMING

Justice Scalia recently wrote, "Day by day, case by case, [the Supreme Court] is busy designing a Constitution for a country I do not recognize."[24] The Court, following the lead of a debauched presidency and the degenerate media, is moving toward making homosexual conduct and marriage a constitutional right, claiming to find in the Constitution an understanding that men and women are not only equal but also identical, to the great satisfaction of radical feminists. Even people who find homosexual activity to be repulsive, immoral, and contrary to their religious beliefs will be forced to act against their consciences and rent to homosexual couples, hire them as teachers, and so on. It will not be long, according to present trends, before suicide and medical murder for the old, sick, handicapped, and crippled will be found to be "rights" in the Constitution.

Recently, I received a letter from a lady in the state of Maine. She is a social worker who was employed in a state-run home for delinquent boys. Because the home permitted and promoted sexual misconduct and the use of pornography by these children, she quit her job and started a private institution for delinquents without these aberrations. Now, however, she is going to be closed down by the government unless she introduces sexual activity and pornographic smut to those in her institution. Evidently, the "national godless religion" that uses your tax dollars for such things as paying an "artist" to display a crucifix in a jar of urine finds limits when "one's own concept of existence, of meaning", and so on, differs from the current *zeitgeist*.

NUMB

The great question of Pontius Pilate (Jn 18:38), although originally asked with sarcasm and irony, continues to be decisive in human affairs, and the answer given by our Lord (Jn 14:6) continues to be the only possible solution to the cultural crisis and the hopeless corruption in which we presently are immersed. "What is truth?" It is what is taught by Jesus Christ and, even more, by His Divine Person. He is, in His human and divine nature, in His very being, the Truth. Contradicting the false teaching of the Supreme Court, Pope John Paul II, in his encyclical letter *Faith and Reason*, tells us that truth is knowable and attainable. He says further, "Truth and freedom either go together hand in hand or together they perish in misery."[25]

Like the pagan Romans of another time, we are in danger of having our minds numbed by *panes et circenses* (bread and circuses) and of passing from personal slavery to our errors, to our passions, to modern fashions, to commercial and political manipulation, and to obscene and mindless entertainment, over into the passive acceptance of tyranny and despotism. Not only "back then", but even now, we can say, "Pilate asked a mouthful!" We, as Christians and Catholics, must answer his question with our lives and our work.

JUNE 18, 1999

3

STEWARDSHIP OF CREATION

Disciple's Response

A MITE

Many years ago a pastor of a parish remarked one Sunday evening, as he finished counting the weekly collection, "The widow's mite (Lk 21:1–4) was only a penny. From the looks of the collection today we have a parish full of widows." In reflecting on this remark in later years, another priest said, "It would not be bad to have a parish full of such widows as the one Jesus noticed and commented on, because she gave a huge proportion of her income back to the Lord. If our people would only give a fraction of what she gave to God, they and we would be deeply blessed."

In a parish in another state where I was the pastor, I especially noticed, when I arrived there, a couple who seemed to donate more time to work in the parish than most others. There was not a parish undertaking for which they did not volunteer. The husband, who had a very modest factory job, even went out of his way to help maintain the landscape around the parish buildings. The mother was a homemaker. I was astounded to learn that they were the parents of fourteen children. The children were neat and clean, well cared for, well behaved, and obviously well instructed by them. All of the children were attending or had attended Catholics schools, and the rather high tuition was always paid on time. The older children were already successfully launched in life, and the whole family was most cheerful and pleasant. I was amazed to learn that this family also donated several thousand dollars a year to the parish. When asked by me "how they did it", they would only smile and say, "When you are generous to God, God is generous to you."

TITHE

In the Old Testament, God's Chosen People were required to give back to Him, from Whom all things come, a tenth of their income. For every ten cattle or sheep, one belonged by right to God. One of every ten sheaves of grain had to be returned to God.

In the New Testament, although technically the tithe is no long morally binding, it remains a good measurement for what is expected of us. Many devout Christians still tithe their income, seeking in this way to satisfy their obligation in Church law to contribute to the support of their parish and to help themselves understand how they are only stewards of the good gifts of the Almighty. If they work forty hours a week, the first four hours of their profits, salary, or wages belong to God. The system that many Catholic families use is to give 5 percent to their parish, and the other 5 percent to other demands and appeals and requests for their charity.

Obviously, requirements of justice, such as decent family support, may not permit each household to tithe, although that should remain the ideal. However, 3 percent of gross income to one's parish might satisfy Church law and moral obligations in such cases. If a family sits down and sets out its priorities from a perspective of faith, it can be surprising how many luxuries and unnecessary items can be purged from a family budget, making room for a proper support for their parish. A look at entertainment expenditures and the costs of cosmetics alone might yield an adjustment in how a family spends its money. A good starting point for each individual might be the question: "What do I own, and what owns me?"

STEWARDSHIP

In 1992 the Bishops of the United States issued an important pastoral document entitled *Stewardship: A Disciple's Response*. They said, "Being a disciple of Jesus Christ leads naturally to the practice of stewardship. These linked realities, discipleship and stewardship, then make up the fabric of a Christian life in which each day is lived in an intimate, personal relationship with the Lord."

Looming in the consciousness of every Christian should be the stern words that each of us is going to hear one day from our divine Judge, "Turn in the account of your stewardship, for you can no longer be steward" (Lk 16:2). Everything we are and have, all that we might accumulate and own throughout our lifetime, comes from God. To Him we must surrender it all on the day of our death. But, that is not all. We must tell Him how we have used each thought, each word, each breath, and every one of our least possessions. In a certain sense these were simply given to us "on loan" from our Creator and Redeemer. At the end we must return them in full along with the "interest".

The Bishops conclude their statement with, "Central to our human and Christian vocations, as well as to the unique vocation each one of us receives from God, is that we be good stewards of the gifts we possess. God gives us this divine and human workshop, this world and Church of ours. The Spirit shows us the way. Stewardship is part of the journey."

BLESSINGS

When a Catholic contributes time, talent, and treasure to the Church, he not only blesses others, but he also is deeply and richly blessed himself. Saint Francis of Assisi says, "It is in giving that we receive", and our divine Savior says, "It is more blessed to give than to receive." The Bible also remarks that "God loves a cheerful giver." Echoing such thoughts, the American Bishops write, "Giving means receiving more."

From the testimony of countless people, it can be safely asserted that those who practice genuine stewardship, generously giving back to God a substantial portion of what they have received from Him, are never wanting for themselves and their loved ones. Being a true disciple of Jesus has its cost, but the reward is joy beyond our imagination, in time and in eternity. A husband and father who tithes his income to the Church says, "Most of all it brings a sense of happiness and peace of mind as I continue my journey through life." May this peace and happiness come to us all.

OCTOBER 4, 1996

Betting, Lotteries, and Gambling

RECREATION

It is clear that betting, playing a lottery, and gambling can be legitimate and moral ways of relaxing and recreating. These activities are not inherently immoral, but certain moral principles and norms must govern them. Deliberately violating such norms could make these activities wrong and sinful.

Certainly, it would be wrong, for instance, for a family breadwinner to gamble and unnecessarily risk money that is needed for the support and well-being of a wife and children. People who have a gambling addiction are bound not to indulge in such activities at all. Their friends and family members, too, are morally bound to avoid being enablers.

BETTING

Betting is a contract in which the parties agree to give a reward to whichever of them correctly guesses a certain fact or future event (such as which horse will win a race). A bet can be licit under certain conditions. First, it cannot be an inducement to a sinful act. (I'll bet you cannot drink a quart of whiskey in an hour!) Second, all the betters must be equally uncertain about the point in dispute. Third, all the betters must understand the terms of the bet in the same way. Fourth, all intend to pay and are able to pay if they lose.

If one of the bettors is certain beforehand about the outcome of the bet, he cannot keep his winnings but must return them to the others, unless he has previously informed the other bettors about his certainty and they doubted him and bet anyway.

LOTTERY

A lottery or raffle is a contract by which prizes are distributed by lot or chance. Participating in or running a lottery or raffle is licit provided that, first of all, there is no fraud. Also, all the participants must understand the terms of the lottery. Important, too, is the proportion in the lottery, which is to say that the individuals who participate must have a hope of winning that is in proportion to the price of each ticket sold. It would be immoral, for example, to charge five dollars a "chance" to a thousand people to obtain a thirty-dollar prize. Those who sponsor a lottery are allowed, in social justice, only to make a reasonable profit.

Sometimes, however, for a "good cause" those who purchase tickets waive their rights in a lottery and are satisfied to view their purchase of a ticket as simply a donation.

It is legitimate for Catholics to agree or disagree politically about the desirability of raising government funds through lotteries or gambling.

GAMBLING

Gambling is a contract in which the participants in a game of chance (poker, dice, bingo, and so on) agree to give the winner a prize (money or something of value). Betting on a game of billiards or other game of skill is not, strictly speaking, the same as gambling.

Gambling is moral provided the stakes are legitimately accessible to the persons in the game. For instance, a lawyer cannot gamble his client's money, or a priest his parish funds, or a debtor the money he owes to settle just debts. There must be no fraud or deceit (stacked decks, loaded dice, and so on). Certain facial expressions or deceitful tones of voice and the like are only permitted if such tricks are accepted by the players as part of the game. Finally, there must be equality of risk for all the participants, with an equal hope of winning and equal risk of losing. An expert poker player, for example, would commit a sin if he played with an inexperienced player unless he first warned the inexperienced person about his skill.

CIVIL LAW

It is generally conceded that the civil laws that regulate betting, gambling, and lotteries usually are purely penal laws, that is, to disobey them is not a sin, but if one is convicted of their violation, he is morally bound to pay the civil penalty, which may include fines, prison sentences, and so on. Disobeying civil laws about gambling, moreover, may involve sins against prudence and also foster in oneself or others a sinful disregard for just laws.

In states or countries where gambling debts or activities are invalid in civil law, a loser may, in conscience, refuse to pay, and the winner may not collect.

To play the stock market is not immoral, provided that the general moral principles governing gambling and betting are observed. Social justice would probably make violations of civil laws in the area of stock-market activity sinfully immoral acts.

GAMBLING HOUSES

Professional gambling houses obviously make their livelihood from the profits of their operation. Thus, they can only stay in business if "the house" wins regularly. It is difficult to imagine that they observe the moral norms that must govern gambling. Also, organized crime and other elements of social decay are frequently involved in the gambling business. One is morally obliged to avoid places known to be operated by criminals or operated immorally.

While poor people as well as wealthy people have a right to any legitimate recreation and paternalism should be avoided, it is proper to oppose certain types of advertising for gambling that target the young and the disingenuous with promises of wealth without informing them of the nature of the risks or that induce people to laziness, materialism, and consumerism. Gambling, like alcoholic beverages or fire, is a good servant but a bad master.

JANUARY 10, 1997

4

Sexuality

Fornication

Euphemisms

Current political correctness as well as a normal human tendency to use nice words to cover up uncomfortable realities has led to some interesting modern expressions. Someone facetiously once told me that the "correct" way now is to speak of Snow White and the seven vertically challenged.

The grave sin of fornication is likewise covered up in our current language by various euphemistic expressions, such as living together, cohabitation, shacking up, being sexually active, and so on. The entertainment and communications media frequently promote and foster this kind of sin. Sneers and scoffing generally confront young people striving to be pure. The perennial temptations toward this sin, which come from the world, the flesh, and the devil, are enhanced in modern times by such filthy organizations as Planned Parenthood, which promotes sexual promiscuity by passing out contraceptives even to the very young and by the advertising and music industries, which sometimes match and surpass television programs and films in depravity. Decent and chaste young people today have to contend with a constant drumbeat of peer pressure and ridicule, while many tell them in all sorts of verbal and non-verbal ways that "everybody does it."

Revelation

It is a beautiful tribute to the courage and convictions of many young Catholics that, notwithstanding the pressures and temptations, they keep themselves pure and are edifying examples of self-mastery. Sacred Scripture is very clear about the evil of fornication, which the *Catechism of the Catholic Church* calls "carnal union between an unmarried man and an unmarried woman. It is gravely contrary to the dignity of persons and of human sexuality which is naturally ordered to the good of spouses and the generation and education of children" (CCC 2353).

The Bible says, "Be sure of this, that no immoral or impure man ... has any inheritance in the kingdom of Christ and of God" (Eph 5:5). Saint Paul also states in the Bible, "Neither the immoral, nor idolaters ... will inherit the kingdom of God" (1 Cor 6:9–10).

The ancient city of Corinth was noted for its pornography, prostitution, and fornication. This is why Saint Paul was so emphatic to the Christian converts who lived there: "Do you not know that your bodies are members of Christ? Shall I therefore take the members of Christ and make them members of a prostitute? Never! Do you not know that he who joins himself to a prostitute becomes one body with her?...Shun immorality.... Do you not know that your body is a temple of the Holy Spirit within you, which you have from God? You are not your own; you were bought with a price. So, glorify God in your body" (1 Cor 6:15–20).

CHURCH TEACHING

The recent declaration of the Holy See regarding sexual ethics states the consistent and unchangeable doctrine of the Church; namely, that those who try to vindicate a right to sexual union before marriage are teaching what is totally "contrary to Christian doctrine".[26] This is true even when there is a clear intention about a future marriage or where marriage is impeded by circumstances or when it seems necessary in order for love to be preserved.

The declaration states,

> Through marriage, in fact, the love of married people is taken up into that love which Christ irrevocably has for the Church, while dissolute sexual union defiles the temple of the Holy Spirit which the Christian has become. Sexual union therefore is only legitimate if a definitive community of life has been established [by a valid marriage] between the man and the woman.... As far as the faithful are concerned, their consent to the setting up of a community of conjugal life must be expressed according to the laws of the Church. It is a consent which makes their marriage a Sacrament of Christ.[27]

Experience and sociological research have established a clear correlation between premarital sex and future married unhappiness. The rate of divorce is many times higher for couples who have engaged in premarital sex, either with each other or with others. Also, marriages of fornicators are more stormy, filled with more suspicion, jealously, quarrels, and so on, than marriages of those who have striven and strive to obey God's law about sexual activity.

The care and concern that the Church has for unwed mothers and their offspring and the Church's devotion to the pro-life cause sometimes can convey a false impression that the Church does not consider fornication to be a mortal sin and does not unequivocally condemn it as evil. Fornicators who die unrepentant, of course, are damned to hell for eternity.

KEEPING PURE

Prayer, especially in time of temptation, and the regular reception of the sacraments, especially confession, are indispensable helps to keeping oneself chaste. Control over thoughts and imagination and avoiding unnecessary occasions of sin are also vital for this purpose. Custody of the senses, particularly the eyes, and filling one's mind and time with wholesome activity are extremely important. Resisting temptation can be a source of merit when done under God's grace and without vanity. Humility, that is, recognizing one's weakness and the concupiscence that is in everyone as a result of original sin, is absolutely necessary for the practice of chastity.

Dating and company keeping, especially for engaged couples, always requires a measure of prudence and caution. People who truly love each other do not deliberately cause harm to each other, especially spiritual harm, which might jeopardize the other's eternal salvation. Genuine love involves self-control in order to avoid becoming a false love, which is merely a type of selfishness and self-aggrandizement. Such false love is the enemy of married joy.

AUGUST 29, 1997

Youthful Purity

MARTYRDOM

In preparation for our celebration of the Holy Year of the Great Jubilee and in the actual celebration itself, our Holy Father, the Bishop of Rome, has asked that we preserve vividly the precious memory of the martyrs. The acts of our martyrs, says the *Catechism of the Catholic Church*, "form the archives of truth written in letters of blood" (CCC 2474). As the *Catechism* puts it, "*Martyrdom* is the supreme witness given to the truth of the faith: it means bearing witness even unto death" (CCC 2473).

Many of the martyrs for the Catholic faith were put to death because of their refusal to worship and adore false gods. While the heathen gods of the ancient world are no longer generally worshipped in contemporary society, we should not suppose that false gods no longer exist. They are all about us, and frequently to refuse to worship them can result in painful consequences for modern Christians, even death. One very prominent false god in our times, of course, is illicit sexual activity, which joins irresponsible hedonism to the desecration of the sacredness of marriage and married love.

VIRGINS

In the long catalogue of her saints, which is the true history of the Catholic Church, the Church has always reserved a special place for those who were not only martyrs, but also virgins. The Church always respects the high vocation of marriage and parenting. It is not out of any puritanical or Manichean disdain for God's gift of chaste married love that the Church holds virginity for the sake of God's kingdom to be an even higher calling (Mt 19:10–12; 1 Cor 7:25–35); rather it is out of loyal obedience to the instructions and attitude of her divine Founder (Mt 22:30).

From her earliest days the names of great virgin-martyrs were enshrined in the Church's memory, names such as Agnes, Barbara, Lucy, Agatha, Anastasia, and, certainly, the Queen of the Martyrs, the Blessed Virgin Mary, who, at the foot of the Cross, shared intimately in the saving death of Jesus.

OUR TIMES

It is not necessary to go far back into history, however, to discover the memory of virgin-martyrs. One hundred and nine years ago in Corinaldo, Italy, a girl was born to a very poor family. She was one of five children. Her father died when she was still in infancy. Her mother struggled to support the family as a tenant farmer near Nettuno in some marshy and unproductive land. The girl's name was Maria Goretti. She was a cheerful and beautiful child, always willing to help and never downcast despite great poverty and even hunger. Her family shared a house with another tenant family, a member of which was an eighteen-year-old boy, who had twice tried to become physically close to her. She always refused his advances.

As was the custom in those days, Maria received her first Holy Communion at the age of twelve. She told her mother then that "I would rather die a thousand deaths than commit one mortal sin." She only received Holy Communion twice more before the young man tried to rape her. She resisted and told him, "It is a sin. God does not want this. You will go to hell." In his passion he struck her with a knife from the kitchen in the little house were they were alone at the time. He left her dying, bleeding from numerous stab wounds.

Taken to the hospital, the twelve-year-old spontaneously forgave her murderer before her painful death, prayed for his conversion, and then said, "Now it is Jesus I am going to see." Her murderer was sentenced to life in prison, where he was converted by grace into a saintly person and, after being paroled, spent the rest of his life in a most austere monastery doing severe penance. Pope Pius XII canonized Saint Maria Goretti in 1950 and proposed her as a model for modern teenagers.

HOMOSEXUAL

In 1885 King Mwanga ascended the throne of Uganda in Africa. He was a homosexual with an eye for handsome young men. He immediately appointed such men to his court, including some relatives and friends of his family. These were Charles Lwanga and Matthias Murumba (Kalemba) and twenty others who were Catholics. The King then tried to persuade these men to engage in deviant sex acts with him. They indignantly refused, citing their Catholic faith.

Furious at these youths, the King ordered them to be killed unless they complied with his perverted wishes. One by one they were asked, and, upon their refusal to commit what they openly said were mortal sins, they were put to death. Some were run through with a sword either by the King himself or by his agents. Others were tied up, wrapped in straw mats, and set afire. They all died with prayers on their lips, forgiving their evil killer. Canonized by Pope Paul VI in 1964, the lives of the Uganda martyrs were held up by the Holy Father as an example for young people in today's world.

NOWADAYS

In our present culture, indecency is often given free reign. The media, especially in their commercial and entertainment segments, shamelessly try to prey upon adolescent youngsters at a vulnerable time in their lives, when they are struggling with personal problems of self-mastery and self-control. Pornographic words and images are spewed out upon them. Chastity, virginity, and purity are mocked, scoffed at, and mercilessly ridiculed. The martyrdom of the Uganda youths and Maria Goretti is incomprehensible to most of our modern world. It seems that groups such as Planned Parenthood "expect" youths to be "sexually active", and in their simplicity some young people attempt to "live up to such expectations", to their present and eternal unhappiness.

In such an atmosphere it is remarkable that so many of our fine Catholic youths continue to live heroic lives of decency and noble chastity, an example to their elders. May the holy martyrs of olden days and more recent history always be for these young people the promise of the new millennium and the new century, examples and intercessors so that they might ever appreciate and love the beauty of holy purity.

OCTOBER 8, 1999

Cohabitation

FRIVILOUS

It is a sad commentary on contemporary society that so many people have very little regard for their eternal salvation. Guided only by the base instincts of their fallen human condition, such people are devoted to selfish pleasure seeking, with almost no sense of responsibility or commitment. This is especially the case of those couples who "cohabit" before marriage. Cohabitation is a more or less permanent form of the lethal sin of fornication. Sometimes euphemistic expressions are used to say a couple is "sexually active", living together, "shacking up", and so on, but it all means the same thing.

The constant teaching of the Catholic Church, which is God's law found clearly in Sacred Scripture (Eph 5:5; 1 Cor 6:9–10), is that people who live that way are committing continuous mortal sins, and, if they die unrepentant and therefore unforgiven in such a state, they are damned forever. That a person frivolously would place his eternal happiness in unnecessary jeopardy is heinous enough, but possibly to doom another, under the pretext of "love", to an eternity of torture, hate, and terror in hell seems to be the height of egoism and self-indulgent folly. Of course, it is precisely because the use of sex in marriage is holy and sacred that its use outside of marriage is a type of desecration, making it obscene and impure.

STATISTICS

Even prescinding from the divine law that forbids fornication and adultery, and leaving aside consideration of the disastrous spiritual and supernatural consequences of these sins of the flesh, there are other, natural, measurable, and perceptible consequences of cohabitation that can and should be known to all. Last August the Committee on Marriage and the Family of the National Conference of Catholic Bishops (of the U.S.) published an interesting information report containing some discussion of these consequences.

Those who cohabit in the United States, when they marry, have a 50 percent higher chance of divorce than do those who do not live together before marriage. In some parts of Europe the rate is 80 percent. In the U.S. 76 percent of those who cohabit say they plan to marry their partner, but only half of them ultimately do so. It is the women, in these circumstances, who are usually deceived and abandoned.

OTHER MATTERS

Surveys and statistics conclusively show that couples who cohabit before marriage have more conflicts over money after they marry than couples who are pure before marriage. Also, during their cohabitation as well as after they marry (if they do), cohabiting couples have a much higher incidence of domestic violence. It seems that jealousy and suspicion about faithfulness are present in much heavier doses in such couples. Dysfunctional patterns derive also from the lack of a sense of permanence in those relationships. If there are children involved either from the cohabitants themselves or from some previous relationships of either of them, the stress level is almost always unusually high in their relationship, and, of course, the innocent children normally suffer very much. Children are often used by such couples as pawns to obtain leverage in facing contentious issues with each other. Researchers have found that those cohabiting couples who eventually marry are much less effective at conflict resolution than couples who followed God's law.

Studies also show that women are more likely to cohabit only once, while men are more likely to cohabit with a series of partners. Persons who experience disruption in their parents' marriage are more likely than their opposites to be candidates for cohabitation.

TEACHING

The *Catechism of the Catholic Church* teaches, "By its very nature conjugal love requires the inviolable fidelity of the spouses. This is the consequence of the gift of themselves which they make to each other. Love seeks to be definitive; it cannot be an arrangement 'until further notice.' The 'intimate union of marriage, as a mutual giving of two persons, and the good of the children, demand total fidelity from the spouses and require an unbreakable union between them.'"[28]

The *Catechism* also says, "*Fornication* is carnal union between an unmarried man and an unmarried woman. It is gravely contrary to the dignity of persons and of human sexuality which is naturally ordered to the good of spouses and the generation and education of children. Moreover, it is a grave scandal when there is corruption of the young" (CCC 2353).

Pope John Paul II states,

> The Church, for her part, cannot admit such a kind of union, for ... reasons which derive from faith. For, in the first place, the gift of the body in the sexual relationship is a real symbol of the giving of the whole person: such a giving, moreover, in the present state of things cannot take place with full truth without the concourse of the love of charity, given by Christ. In the second place, marriage between two baptized persons is a real symbol of the union of Christ and the Church, which is not a temporary or "trial" union but one which is eternally faithful.[29]

Quoting the Catholic Bishops of Kansas, the USCCB Secretariat for Family, Laity, Women, and Youth recently noted, "'As society no longer adheres to traditional moral values and norms, scandal becomes less and less a concern to many people' (*A Better Way*, p. 9). The burden of scandal (in these matters) falls not just on the cohabiting couple, but on our sexually permissive society. The cohabiting couple is living contrary to the Church's teaching about marriage and sexual love. By acting as if they are married when in fact they are not, they risk scandalizing the believing community."[30] Sinful scandal, of course, does not mean merely causing amazement or shock, but it means inducing others to sin by example. Our Holy Father exhorts us all to correct cohabiting couples charitably, enlighten them patiently, and show them the example of Christian family life. Also, he tells us to teach young people morality and religious principles to help them avoid the pitfall of cohabitation.

NOVEMBER 5, 1999

Evil Human Cloning
I

WHAT IT IS

Last April President Bush was kind enough to invite me to the White House to attend his conference on the issue of human cloning. He undoubtedly knows about my pro-life views, which coincide with his on the cloning issue. At that time the president stated his unequivocal opposition to human cloning. He congratulated the House of Representatives on their passage of a bill to outlaw all human cloning in our country and urged the United States Senate to follow suit, which, unfortunately, it did not do, partially because, so it appears, of heavy lobbying (and campaign contributions?) from various parts of the pharmaceutical industry, anxious to be able to use cloned human beings for experimental and research purposes, thus, perhaps, being able to meet possible foreign competition from places where cloning still would be allowed.

Human cloning is a biological procedure in which, to put it in oversimplified terms, genetic material (usually a cell nucleus) is taken from a body cell of a person and injected into a human egg, which is then stimulated to begin human embryonic development. The cloned human being is genetically identical to the person whose body cell was used. It is an attempt to create human beings who are more or less "copies" of already existing human beings.

Recent News

Experiments involving the cloning of diverse biological organisms has been going on in laboratories in different parts of the world for many years. However, when the announcement was made about the successful creation of Dolly, a sheep, by means of cloning, it quickly became apparent that, since higher mammals could successfully be cloned, the procedure could apply with relative ease also to human beings. Thoughtful people, even among many who reject Christian moral principles and Catholic teaching concerning the divine law regulating matters about human reproduction, immediately began to take a few steps back from this procedure to question some of the social, economic, and political consequences of human cloning. This included people who might possess few or no philosophical or ethical values on which to make their judgment. Discussion became more acute when it was learned that, although Dolly appeared normal, she had in fact many physical weaknesses and defects. Also, before she was arrived at, the cloning experiments had produced hundreds of grotesque monsters, many of which soon died, but others that had to be killed.

In recent weeks, a bizarre religious sect called the Raelians, claiming about 55,000 members worldwide, has been making announcements about cloned human beings being born to their adherents. There is reasonable doubt about the truthfulness of those announcements, but the real possibilities represented by the sect's claims cannot be disregarded.

Two Kinds

Basically all human cloning is the same thing. It is the purpose or destination for the human clones that gives a different common name to two "types" of cloning. One is usually called "reproductive cloning", which means that the clone is intended to become a fully developed human being and, therefore, is taken out of a laboratory test tube or dish in which it was made and then implanted either in a human uterus or in some kind of artificial womb. This kind of cloning, of course, is clearly and profoundly immoral. The other kind, which is even more evil and immoral, is given a variety of names, usually euphemisms to disguise the real purpose and goal of the procedure. It is sometimes referred to as "therapeutic cloning", "DNA regenerative medicine", "research and scientific cloning", "nuclear transplantation", or "somatic cell transfer", and so on.

The idea is to use at least one human gamete to produce in a laboratory a human zygote, later becoming a human embryo that can be chopped up for scientific research or for such purposes as forming stem-cell lines that are alleged (with almost no evidence to support the claims) to be able to cure all sorts of diseases in the future.

CONSENSUS

Strangely enough, there is a general political consensus about outlawing "reproductive cloning" in the United States because of the possible monsters it would create and because of the unknown social calamities it might visit on the country. The basic political dispute presently centers on the second "type" of cloning. However, it has been pointed out that once you permit any kind of human cloning, it would be nearly impossible to monitor or police the "type" used and thus restrict the goal of anyone using the procedure. Furthermore, by outlawing only "reproductive cloning", the law in effect would be compelling the killing of all cloned human beings at whatever stage of development they might be.

Also, it should be known that among the monsters that some modern researchers are thinking about bringing into existence through cloning are various kinds of chimaeric (animal-human) embryos. The future of *homo sapiens*, our whole human species itself, could be placed in jeopardy sooner than we suspect by "mad scientists".

HOLY SEE

It is good to remember that being involved in making human clones is a heinous and grave sin, but it is certainly not immoral to be a human clone. Therefore, as Richard Doerflinger observes, the innocent victim of human cloning should not receive a government sanctioned death penalty merely for the "crime of existing".[31]

Last March at the United Nations, the Holy See's representative stated: "The Holy See firmly supports a world-wide and comprehensive ban on human cloning, no matter what techniques are used and what aims are pursued. Its position is based on (1) biological analysis of the cloning process and (2) anthropological, social, ethical, and legal reflection on the negative implications that human cloning has on the life, the dignity, and the rights of the human being."[32]

In his great encyclical *Faith and Reason* (*Fides et ratio*), our Holy Father, Pope John Paul II, condemns as one of the grave philosophical errors of our age what he called "scientism". Since scientism, the Pope says, "leaves ... no space for the critique offered by ethical judgment, the scientistic mentality has succeeded in leading many to think that if something is technically possible, it is therefore morally admissible".[33]

JANUARY 10, 2003

Evil Human Cloning
II

NO ANCHORS

In a speech before the House of Commons on November 12, 1936, Winston Churchill said that his country was "decided only to be undecided, resolved to be irresolute, adamant for drift, solid for fluidity". Although he was writing about another matter, his words could easily describe the erroneous philosophical relativism that has been guiding much of Western civilization in recent times in so many areas of human thought and activity. Without any objective benchmark principles, much less any moral absolutes or clear ethical standards, people today are often told simply to "follow their consciences", which is defined as "doing whatever you please", that is, pure subjectivism. Those "consciences", of course, are personal opinions that usually are manipulated and formed, not by the natural law or by divine revelation or by the teaching of Christ's Church, but rather by such things as fashion, the media, hormones, concupiscence, sociologists, psychologists, votes of a majority, public opinion polls, and various "opinion makers", whose views on morality, if they have any at all, are highly questionable.

It is not surprising, then, that the technological possibilities regarding human cloning that have been opened by modern research should throw some political leaders into consternation and anchor-less moral confusion. This is especially true of those persons in whose minds the Galileo myth persists, depicting the Church as anti-scientific and obscurantist, and who have constructed for themselves a system of sexual and life-issue immorality, based on selfishness, hedonism, and irresponsible pleasure, in contradiction to traditional Catholic teaching.

MORAL MESS

In 1999, according to the Center for Disease Control, 21,501 children were born in the United States who were conceived in test tubes or lab dishes. According to Doctor James Turner, in that same year, more than 170,000 children so conceived were killed because they were considered abnormal or superfluous, usually by flushing them into the sewers. At the present time, it is thought that there are more than 100,000 frozen human embryos preserved in various hospitals, clinics, and other places in our country. Speaking of this matter, our Holy Father, Pope John Paul II, says, "The tendency to use morally unacceptable reproductive practices betrays the absurd mentality of a 'right *to* a child', which has replaced the due recognition of the 'right *of* a child' to be born and later to grow in a fully human way."[34]

It is generally supposed that, no matter what laws are enacted about human cloning, sooner or later some rogue scientist will (if it has not already been done) clone a human being. Abortion centers, fertility clinics, sperm banks, and the like provide abundant material for this so-called "scientific research". In many college towns in our country, university coeds even advertise in newspapers and magazines that their human ova are for sale.

CONSEQUENCES

In our world today, however, it is pleasantly surprising to see that some nonbelieving scientists, though uninfluenced by Christian morality, are now unexpectedly joining us in questioning human cloning. Although they usually do this from a false consequentialist premise, their testimony could be helpful in persuading some lawmakers and public opinion to address the matter correctly.

For example, Vyacheslav Tarantul, the head of Russia's Molecular Genetics Institute, recently wrote that all human cloning efforts in Russia have led to horrific biological deformations. He said, "It is theoretically possible to clone a human being, but who will take the responsibility if a monster is born? This risk exists in 99 percent of the cases."[35] He noted that in almost every case of cloned higher animals abnormalities and anomalies have been found, cancer in particular. Gina Kolata has claimed that human cloning efforts by Communist Chinese scientists have met with similar results.[36]

The European Parliament recently voted (271–154) to "repeat its insistence that there should be a universal and specific ban at the level of the United Nations on the cloning of human beings at all stages of formation and development".[37] This was done in the face of German opposition because of a desire by the present German government to remove all legal protection for human embryos in order to strengthen the German biotechnology industry. As in many parts of the United States, there are some people abroad who want to be permitted to make cloned human beings so they can use them in medical and scientific experiments and then destroy them.

HOLY SEE

The Father of lies continues to try to deceive the human race, whispering down through the centuries to those who will listen to his appeal to their pride and disobedience: "You will be like God" (Gen 3:5). Confronting this perennial and diabolical deception, the Church proclaims, in the words of Pope Paul VI, "Unless we are willing that the responsibility of procreating life should be left to the arbitrary decision of men, we must accept that there are certain limits beyond which it is wrong to go, to the power of man over his own body and its natural functions—

limits, let it be said, which no one, whether as a private individual or as a public authority, can lawfully exceed."[38]

In the United Nations, the Holy See asserted: "Regardless of the objective for which it is done, human cloning conflicts with international legal norms that protect human dignity."[39] It is also said: "Even if cloning is pursued with the aim of making a human baby that will mature into adulthood so that there is no destruction of the human embryo, this activity is still an affront to the dignity of the human person....Cloning objectifies human sexuality and commodifies the bodies of women. Moreover, women are deprived of their innate dignity by becoming suppliers of eggs and wombs."[40] Particularly evil is that cloning which "masks the reality of the creation of a human being for the purpose of destroying him or her or to produce embryonic stem cell lines or to conduct other experimentation."[41] "In the cloning process the basic relationships of the human person are perverted: filiation, consanguinity, kinship, parenthood. A woman can be the twin sister of her mother, lack a biological father, and be the daughter of her grandfather. *In vitro* fertilization has already led to the confusion of parentage, but cloning will mean the radical rupture of these bonds."[42] "From the dehumanizing nature of this technique would flow many disturbing consequences."[43]

JANUARY 17, 2003

[1] C. S. Lewis, "Man or Rabbit?" *God in the Dock: Essays on Theology and Ethics* (Grand Rapids, Gerdmans, 1994), p. 109.

[2] Ibid.

[3] Ibid., p. 110.

[4] G. K. Chesterton, *Orthodoxy*, in *The Collected Works of G. K. Chesterton*, vol. 1 (San Francisco: Ignatius Press, 1986), pp. 275–76.

[5] Ibid., p. 276.

[6] John Paul II, apostolic letter *Salvifici doloris* (February 11, 1984), no. 27.

[7] John Paul II, encyclical *Evangelium vitae* (March 25, 1995), no. 40.

[8] Congregation for the Doctrine of the Faith, Declaration on Euthanasia, *Iura et bona* (May 5, 1980), chap. 2.

[9] Janet Smith, "The Connection between Contraception and Abortion", http:/www.goodmorals.org/smith4.htm.

[10] Alfred Kinsey, presentation at 1955 conference sponsored by Planned Parenthood, quoted by Mary Claderone, *Abortion in the United States* (New York: Hoeber, 1956), p. 157.

[11] Quoted by Dr. Kenneth D. Whitehead, "Do Sex Education and Access to Contraception Cut Down on Abortions?" Culture of Life Foundation and Institute, http://www.christianity.com/cc/articleO,,PTID4211%7CCHID102755%7CCID235513,00.html.

[12] Ibid.

[13] Ibid.

[14] Ibid.

[15] John Paul II, "Marital Act Must Be Total Gift of Person" (February 27, 1998), *L'Osservatore Romano*, no. 10 (March 11, 1998): 2, no. 3.

[16] Ibid.

[17] John XXIII, encyclical *Mater et magistra* (May 15, 1961), no. 239.

[18] Paul VI, *Humane vitae*, no. 4.

[19] Pius XII, encyclical *Humani generis* (August 12, 1950), no. 20.

[20] Paul VI, *Humanae vitae*, nos. 11–12.

[21] Pius XI, encyclical *Casti connubii* (December 31, 1930), no. 56.

[22] John Paul II, *Evangelium vitae*, no. 73.

[23] Ibid.

[24] 116 S.Ct. at 2373.

[25] John Paul II, encyclical *Fides et ratio* (September 14, 1998), no. 90.

[26] Sacred Congregation for the Doctrine of the Faith, declaration *Persona humana* (December 29, 1975), no. 7.

[27] Ibid.

[28] CCC 1646, quoting *Gaudium et spes*, no. 48, § 1.

[29] John Paul II, apostolic exhortation *Familiaris consortio* (November 22, 1981), no. 80.

[30] *Marriage Preparation and Cohabitating Couples* (1999), no. 7.

[31] Testimony of Richard M. Doerflinger before the Senate Commerce Subcommittee on Science, Technology and Space, May 2, 2001.

[32] "The Views of the Holy See on Human Cloning", text released by Holy See's mission at the United Nations, *Zenit*, March 3, 2002, no. 1.

[33] John Paul II, encyclical *Fides et ratio* (September 14, 1998), no. 88.

[34] Pope John Paul II, "Children: A Message of Life and Hope", address to Third World Meeting with Families, October 14, 2000, *L'Osservatore Romano*, no. 42 (October 18, 2000): 3.

[35] Statement made to the ITAR-TASS News Agency, reported January 6, 2003.

[36] Gina Kolata, "The Promise of Therapeutic Cloning", *New York Times*, January 5, 2003, sec. 4, p. 7.

[37] Report on the Commission Communication "Life Sciences and Biotechnology—A Strategy for Europe", amended November 21, 2002.

[38] Paul VI, *Humanae vitae*, no. 17.

[39] "Views of the Holy See on Human Cloning", no. 5.

[40] Ibid., no. 4.

[41] Ibid., no. 6.

[42] Pontifical Academy for Life, *Reflections on Cloning* (1997), no. 3.

[43] Testimony of Richard M. Doerflinger before the Senate Commerce Subcommittee.